Gesture: Visible Action as Utterance

Gesture, or visible bodily action that is seen as intimately involved in the activity of speaking, has long fascinated scholars and laymen alike. Written by a leading authority on the subject, this long-awaited study provides a comprehensive treatment of gesture and its use in interaction, drawing on the analysis of everyday conversations to demonstrate its varied role in the construction of utterances. Adam Kendon accompanies his analyses with an extended discussion of the history of the study of gesture – a topic little dealt with in previous publications – as well as exploring the relationship between gesture and sign language, and how the use of gesture varies according to cultural and language differences. Set to become the definitive account of the topic, *Gesture* will be invaluable to all those interested in human communication. Its publication marks a major development, both in semiotics and in the emerging field of gesture studies.

ADAM KENDON, internationally known for his work on gesture and communication conduct, has been a guest at the Institute for Research in Cognitive Science, University of Pennsylvania since 2000 and has been associated with the University of Naples 'Orientale' and the University of Calabria since 1996. His previous books include *Sign Languages of Aboriginal Australia* (Cambridge University Press 1988), *Conducting Interaction* (Cambridge University Press 1990), and *Gesture in Naples and Gesture in Classical Antiquity* (2000), a translation of a nineteenth-century treatise on Neapolitan gesture. He has published over ninety papers in journals and scholarly collections and is an editor of the journal *Gesture*.

Gesture: Visible Action as Utterance

Adam Kendon

CAMBRIDGE
UNIVERSITY PRESS

PUBLISHED BY THE PRESS SYNDICATE OF THE UNIVERSITY OF CAMBRIDGE
The Pitt Building, Trumpington Street, Cambridge CB2 1RP, United Kingdom

CAMBRIDGE UNIVERSITY PRESS
The Edinburgh Building, Cambridge, CB2 2RU, UK
40 West 20th Street, New York, NY 10011-4211, USA
477 Williamstown Road, Port Melbourne, VIC 3207, Australia
Ruiz de Alarcón 13, 28014 Madrid, Spain
Dock House, The Waterfront, Cape Town 8001, South Africa
http://www.cambridge.org

First published 2004

Printed in the United Kingdom at the University Press, Cambridge

Typeface Times 10/12 pt

A catalogue record for this book is available from the British Library

ISBN 0 521 83525 9   hardback
ISBN 0 521 54293 6   paperback

Contents

Acknowledgements

This book has been 'in progress' for a number of years. The encouragement, help, and critical comments on its earlier drafts or on selected chapters from it by many different people over these years have been of great importance and value to me. Mandana Seyfeddinipur convinced me, at an early stage, that I really must write this book, and she has never ceased in her insistence on this and in her support and encouragement. I am very grateful to Mark Liberman at the University of Pennsylvania Linguistics Department for making it possible for me to teach a seminar on gesture in that Department. This provided me with an important incentive to actually put some of the chapters down on paper and I am grateful to the participants in that seminar who read these chapters and commented on them. I am also indebted to Daniele Gambarara who was instrumental in making it possible for me to be a Visiting Professor at the University of Calabria, as well as at the 'Orientale' in Naples, where I have been able to teach courses drawn from this book and the examples it contains. The presentation of much of the material found in this book in these seminars and lectures, as well as in seminars in San Marino, Odense, Berlin, and elsewhere, has helped to clarify my thinking. The critical comments of those who participated in these occasions have been most valuable.

Cornelia Müller of the Free University of Berlin has given me constant support and encouragement and read with great care a number of chapters in their earlier versions and I have benefited much from her comments and criticisms. Early drafts of some of these chapters were read by students in her courses at the Free University and their comments have also been helpful. Jurgen Streeck, of the University of Texas at Austin, also made use of many chapters in their earlier versions in one of his courses, and the comments of his students, as well as his own comments, especially in relation to Chapters 12 and 13, have been most useful. Federico Rossano of Bologna also read several chapters at an early stage and made comments of value and interest. Ulrike Bohle of the Free University of Berlin read with great care an earlier draft of the entire book and drew my attention to numerous inconsistencies of expression and presentation. Eve Sweetser of the University of California read most of the manuscript and offered useful suggestions and much encouragement. Marianne Gullberg of the Max Planck Institute for Psycholinguistics in Nijmegen also read an earlier draft of the entire book and she provided me with many very valuable criticisms and suggestions. I am grateful to Sherman Wilcox for his comments on Chapters 14 and 15. Nevertheless, thankful though I am to all of these people, I have not always followed their excellent suggestions, and I alone am responsible for what appears in this book.

All the line drawings used in Chapters 7–13 and Chapter 15 have been drawn directly from images extracted from the video recordings used as sources for the examples described and analysed in this book. It seems to me that such drawings are generally preferable to 'frame grabs'. Not only can one show, in the drawing, just the details that are pertinent for the exposition, but the problem of publishing photographs of people who might wish to remain anonymous is completely avoided. Karin Becker of Berlin kindly undertook to do the drawings used in Figures 8.11, 9.2, 9.3, 9.4, 9.5, 10.2, 10.3, 10.4, 10.11, 10.12, 10.15, 10.17, 10.18, 12.3 and 13.2. All the other drawings are by myself.

A few illustrations have been borrowed from other publications. Figure 3.1 is from a copy of John Bulwer's *Chirologia . . . Chironomia* (1644) in Princeton University Library, Figure 3.2 is taken from a copy of *The Art of Painting* by Gerard De Lairesse (1768) owned by Bryn Mawr College, Figure 3.3 is from a copy of Charles Lebrun's *A Method to learn to Design the Passions* owned by the Library of the University of Michigan. I am grateful to each of these institutions for making reproductions of these pictures available and for permitting me to use them here. Figure 4.1, and Figures 10.1 and 12.1 are reproduced from a copy of a first edition of Andrea de Jorio's *La mimica degli antichi investigata nel gestire napoletano* (1832) that is in my own library. Figure 14.1 is reproduced from *The International Dictionary of Gestures* by Tom Brun. Every effort has been made to contact the copyright holder of this publication, but without success. The picture is used here with apologies and we hope that in a future edition we will be able to officially thank the copyright holder for permission to use this image. Figure 15.1 is used with the kind permission of Marianne Gullberg, Figure 15.2 is used with permission from MIT Press, Figure 15.4 is used with the permission of Walter De Gruyter of Berlin and Figure 15.5 is used with permission from Lawrence Erlbaum and Karen Emmorey. Figure 16.2 is used with the permission of Heather Brookes and of John Benjamins of Amsterdam. Figures 13.1 and 16.1 are taken from David Efron's *Gesture, Race and Culture* published in 1972 by Mouton of The Hague. According to Walter De Gruyter, the owner of Mouton's publications, the status of the copyright for this material cannot be verified. These pictures are used here with apologies and it is hoped that we can give proper thanks to the copyright holder when this has been found. Chapter 11 is partly based upon material previously published in Kendon and Versante (2003), and many of the drawings in this chapter have also appeared previously in that publication. I thank Lawrence Erlbaum for permission to re-use this material here.

The video recordings from which I have drawn the examples described in Chapters 7-13 and Chapter 15 have been gathered in many different ways over a period of many years. A detailed account of this material is provided in Appendix II. Much of it, however, has been drawn from recordings that have been made since 1991 in Campania, Italy, where I have had the good fortune to teach and study at the University of Salerno, at the Istituto Universitario Orientale in Naples (now the Università degli Studi di Napoli "Orientale") and at the University of Calabria I, the campus situated near Cosenza in Calabria. At these institutions I have had the indispensable assistance of students and others in the processes of collecting and gathering material on which so many of the studies reported here have been based.

I remain indebted to professoressa Pina Boggi Cavallo for her willingness to accept me as a visiting faculty member in her department in the University of Salerno and the assistance she gave me in putting me in situations where I was able to make video recordings. Maria de Simone, also of Salerno, was of great assistance in the transcription and analysis of the material I gathered while I was there. In 1996 I began my association with the Istituto Universitario Orientale in Naples and here I am deeply grateful to the professional support and friendship over many years of Jocelyne Vincent Marrelli, Massimo Marrelli, Carla Cristilli, Bruno Genito and Arturo Martone. In Naples, where much of this book was written, I should also like to mention a special thanks to Bruno Genito for letting me use his studio apartment, whenever possible, for my stays in Naples.

Laura Versante collaborated with me closely on the study of pointing presented in Chapter 11 and I am indebted to her for many observations and clarifying discussions. Teresa Stanzione was important for the work reported in Chapter 10 and Carmen Pacifico helped with the work on the Open Hand Prone gesture family presented in Chapter 13. Maria Graziano collaborated on the study of the Open Hand Supine ('palm up open hand') family of gestures that is also reported in Chapter 13. I thank her for many useful discussions. She also very kindly checked all the transcriptions of the Neapolitan and Italian examples (any faults that remain are mine, however). I would also like to acknowledge the help of Chiara Alfetra, Rosaria D'Alisa, Ornella D'Auria, Cinzia Capone, Antonella Caprarelli, Rafaella Sollo, Gigliola Stizzo, Angela Vallo and Silvana Verde, who provided recordings or helped in their realization and who helped with their transcription and interpretation.

Financial assistance for some of the work reported in this book has been provided by grants from the Wenner-Gren Foundation for Anthropological Research of New York, from funds provided by Fondi Europei FSE (from the European Union in Brussels) as a part of a contract with the Centro Interdipartimentale dei Servizi Linguistici e Audiovisivi at the Istituto

Universitario Orientale, in Naples, coordinated by professoressa Jocelyne Vincent. I have also been supported by a grant from the Istituto Italiano per gli Studi Filosofici of Naples.

Through the years and despite my frequent and (at times) prolonged absences, my wife has always supported my endeavours. For this, and for much else besides, it is impossible to thank her enough.

Philadelphia
December 31, 2003
Naples
June 24, 2004

1   The domain of gesture

Willingly or not, humans, when in co-presence, continuously inform one another about their intentions, interests, feelings and ideas by means of visible bodily action. For example, it is through the orientation of the body and, especially, through the orientation of the eyes, that information is provided about the direction and nature of a person's attention. How people arrange their bodies and how they orient them and place them in relation to each other or to features in the environment, provides important information about how they are engaged with one another and about the nature of their intentions and attitudes. Activities in which objects in the environment are being manipulated, modified or rearranged, are indispensable for grasping a person's aims and goals and interests. Of equal importance, however, are actions that are seen to be purely expressive. Here we find those configurations of action in the face and body that appear as displays of feeling and emotion, as well as actions that often play a central role in the accomplishment of important moments in social interaction. Greeting, showing gratitude or affection, challenge, threat, submission, compliance, all are accomplished through a range of different expressive actions.

Beyond this, however, are those actions that are employed as a part of the process of discourse, as a part of uttering something to another in an explicit manner. Thus, people may refer to something by pointing at it, they may employ the hands in complex actions organized to show what something looks like, to indicate its size or its shape, to suggest a form, object or process by which an abstract idea is illustrated, or they may show, through visible bodily actions, that they are asking a question, making a plea, proposing an hypothesis, doubting the word of another, denying something or indicating agreement about it, and many other things. There are also visible actions that can serve as alternatives to spoken words and socially shared vocabularies of such actions are commonly established. In some circumstances, indeed, entire languages that function as autonomous systems in their own right have been fashioned from visible action. In other words, there is a wide range of ways in which visible bodily actions are employed in the accomplishment of expressions that, from a functional point of view, are similar to, or even the same as expressions in spoken language. At times they are used in conjunction with spoken expressions, at other times as complements, supplements, substitutes or as alternatives to them. These are the *utterance uses* of visible action and it is these uses that constitute the domain of 'gesture', the domain to be explored in this book.

In the Western tradition an interest in visible action as utterance, or gesture, is of very long standing. There are systematic discussions of it from Classical Antiquity and scholarly attention of a recognizably modern kind becomes evident toward the end of the sixteenth century. In the seventeenth century interest in the possibility that gesture could form the basis for a universal language was discussed and, in the eighteenth century, when the possibility for a natural, rather than a divine explanation for the origins of language first came under serious consideration, the idea that gesture might have been the medium in which language first was formed was often suggested. Partly as a consequence of this, gesture languages, and especially sign languages in use among the deaf, were seriously studied for the first time in this period. These interests continued into the nineteenth century, and several important figures in what was to become anthropology and psychology made valuable contributions to the study of gesture. From the end of the nineteenth century, however, interest in gesture declined rather markedly and it did not begin to revive until about the seventh decade of the next century. From then on there has been a steady multiplication in studies of gesture and certain developments suggest that 'gesture studies' is emerging as a recognized field of study. In 1996 the first international conference devoted entirely to gesture studies was held in Albuquerque, New Mexico. Annually, from 1998 onwards, there have been further conferences on gesture studies in Germany, France and Portugal, and in 2002 the first meeting was held of the International Society for Gesture Studies in Austin, Texas. Papers from these meetings have been published in Santi et al. (1998), McNeill (2000a), Cavé et al. (2001), Posner and Müller (2004), and Rector, Poggi and Trigo (2003). *Gesture*, a journal devoted to gesture studies, was launched in 2001.

There are several reasons for this recent growth of interest in gesture. First, detailed studies of how gesture and speech are interrelated (which take advantage of audio-visual recording technology) have shown that these two activities are so intimately connected that they appear to be governed by a single process. Yet, as a little reflection shows, the way in which gesture and speech serve as modes of expression is quite different. Speech uses an established vocabulary of lexical forms organized in structures that unfold as a temporal succession, according to rules of syntax. Gesture, on the other hand, especially when used in conjunction with speech, tends not to have these features and is often regarded as expressive because it is depictive or pantomimic. Yet, how can a person, in creating an utterance, *at one and the same time,* use both a language system and depictive and pantomimic actions? As a close examination of the coordination of gesture with speech suggests, these two forms of expression are integrated, produced together under the guidance of a single aim. Is this because they are expressions of two different forms of thought that originate jointly in a single, 'deeper' process? Or are they integrated as a consequence of how a person, engaged in producing an utterance, adapts two separate modes of expression and conjoins them in a single rhetorical aim? Do the gestural expressions that so often are integrated with spoken expressions provide insight into the processes of thought that lead up to the organization and pronunciation of sequences of words? Or do they, rather, contribute in their own right to what is being said, and so enrich an expression that would otherwise be poorer if constructed out of words alone? Taking gesture into consideration has raised anew some important issues regarding the relationship between verbal language, imagery and thought and has challenged theorists who would try to build a model of the speech production process. It now seems clear that such models cannot be derived from a consideration of speech alone, but how gesture is to be incorporated still remains a matter to be resolved.

Second, micro-analyses of communication conduct in face-to-face interaction (also taking advantage of audio-visual recording technology) have shown that visible bodily action, including gesture, can play a crucial role in the processes of interaction and communication. It has become clear that visible bodily action is often integrated with speech in such a way as to appear as if it is its partner and cannot be disregarded, if we are to have a full understanding of how utterances within the context of an interaction are intelligible for the participants. Close study of communication conduct in interaction has also shown that gesture is often used, from moment to moment in everyday encounters, as a form of expression in alternation with speech, as well as in conjunction with it. What governs the choice of its use? When do speakers bring in the use of gesture and when do they not employ it? What does this imply about speaker understanding of the contrasting properties of speech and gesture as modalities of expression? How do we incorporate such observations into accounts of 'recipient design' – how speakers adjust their utterances for the benefit of their interlocutors?

Gesture has long attracted interest because it seems to be a 'universal' and 'natural' form of expression. Although it seems to be something that is spontaneous and created through the whim of the individual, at the same time it can be shown to be regulated and subject to social convention. In some circumstances, indeed, when speech is unavailable whether for environmental, ritual or physiological reasons, gesture can become a form of language all by itself. The study of gesture, thus, seems to promise us special insights into the way in which individual forms of expression are transformed by social processes into socially shared communicative codes. These questions have become especially acute in recent years with the growth of interest in sign languages, and this is a third reason why gesture has attracted interest in recent years. What is the relationship between 'sign' and 'gesture'? Are sign languages an extreme form of specialization of gesture or is there a radical difference between gesturing in everyday life among speakers and the signing of sign-language users?

Yet a fourth development has rekindled interest in gesture. This is the mid-twentieth-century revival of interest in the question of the evolutionary origins of language. This question, much debated in the eighteenth century, was largely dropped as a matter for serious discussion by the end of the nineteenth century, in part because of the paucity of evidence in terms of which the various theories about language origins could be evaluated. Mainly as a result of the enormous expansion of knowledge in palaeoanthropology, archaeology, neurology, and primate communication, a discussion of the question of language origins again seems possible and the relevance of gesture to this issue has again been raised. The idea that gestures might have constituted the first form of language was first seriously put forward in the eighteenth century, but by the beginning of the twentieth century it had become just one among a number of different speculative ideas on language origins. In the light of recent work on gesture and sign languages, and some rather spectacular studies that suggest that apes have a capacity to learn language if it is presented to them in the gesture modality, the gesture theory of language origins has been refurbished and has once again become attractive to many.

In this book we take up several of these issues, but not all of them. After a discussion, in Chapter 2, of the question as to how visible actions are recognized as 'gesture', the history of the study of gesture is surveyed. In Chapter 3 we begin in Roman Antiquity, with a discussion of the work of Quintilian, whose treatment of gesture in his treatise on rhetoric (published about AD 100) acquired great influence by the end of the sixteenth century, when an interest in gesture in something like a modern sense began. We discuss some of the contributions of this century and the one that followed, and continue with a consideration of the philosophical importance that came to be attributed to gesture in the eighteenth century. Chapter 4 is devoted to four nineteenth-century figures who are very important for the study of gesture: Andrea de Jorio of Naples, Edward Tylor of Oxford, Garrick Mallery in the USA and Wilhelm Wundt of Leipzig. Chapter 5 tells of how interest in gesture declined at the beginning of the twentieth century, how it re-grew, and how it has developed from the 1950s until the year 2000. In Chapter 6 we survey some of the classification schemes that have been proposed for gestures. This serves as an introduction to the different functions attributed to them from the eighteenth century until the present.

These historical chapters give background for what follows. Chapters 7 to 13 present series of studies of gesture use in everyday interaction. Notwithstanding the long history of reflection on gesture, it is only within recent decades that a technology has been available that permits detailed examination of just how participants in interaction employ gesture in relation to speech. Although we still lack an adequate conceptual apparatus, transcription system and terminology for dealing with the phenomena of gesture, sound-synchronized visual recordings make it possible to turn moments of gesture use into *objects of inspection*. We can gather together, classify and compare as specimens utterances in all their multi-modal complexity, we can dissect them and show how they are constructed.

In the studies presented we explore some of the ways in which gesture is organized in relation to speech, as this may be observed in a wide variety of discourse settings. A large number of examples are described, all taken from video recordings of naturally occasioned interactions. We show, through these descriptions, how gesture is organized as an activity, how it is organized in relation to speaking and how it contributes to the total meaning of the utterance of which it is a part. We discuss representational gesture, gestures of pointing, and a number of different kinds of so-called pragmatic gestures which serve in a variety of ways as markers of the illocutionary force of an utterance, as grammatical and semantic operators or as punctuators or parsers of the spoken discourse.

From the examples presented we argue that when speakers use gesture they do so as an integral part of the act of producing an utterance. An utterance is looked upon as an 'object' constructed for others from components fashioned from both spoken language and gesture. It is maintained that the gestures used by speakers as they speak are partnered with speech as a part of the speaker's *final product* and are as much a part of the utterance's design as the speaker's words. Since, semiotically, gestures are often quite different from words, the question of how they collaborate with words in producing the meaning-complex of the utterance of which they are a part seems to be particularly interesting. We hope that our descriptions and discussions in these chapters will illuminate this.

In Chapters 14 and 15 we discuss gesture when it is used without speech. Chapter 14 describes various *kinesic codes*, including sign languages, both as these have developed among the deaf and also as they have developed in speaking communities, as in factories, monasteries or certain tribal societies. In Chapter 15 strategies of expression common among speakers when using gesture are compared to some of those found in sign languages. The two chapters together argue that there is a continuity between 'gesture' and 'sign'. This implies that there is a continuity between all kinds of systems of symbolic expression, from the simplest to the most complex. 'Language' when thought of in the narrowest 'linguistic' terms, whether spoken, written or signed, is thus an end point on a continuum of systems of symbolic expression.

In Chapter 16 we return to a consideration of gesture use in conjunction with speech and discuss the impact of culture. We look at studies of historical change in gestural expression, examine codified gestures and their geographical distribution, consider their origins and functions, and review recent studies that consider how the relation between gesture and speech may be affected by the grammatical and semantic structure of the language spoken. The chapter closes with a discussion of the idea of the 'communication economy' (or 'communicative economy' as Hymes 1974 called it) and suggests that the place of gesture in such an economy may vary according to how the whole range of expressive modalities is adapted to the ecological requirements for interaction within a given culture. The city of Naples is used as an example for exploring these ideas.

In a final chapter we briefly assess the status of gesture, both in history and as it appears in the light of the investigations of it presented in this book, and conclude with a suggestion about what it may teach us about the character of human language.

There are a number of important topics not treated in this book. Nothing is said about the neurological foundations of gesture, notwithstanding recent exciting developments. Gesture from a developmental point of view is not discussed and we do not review what has been done on gesture in infants and very small children. Also excluded is a discussion of gesture from a biologically comparative point of view. There is now much available on communicative behaviour among non-human primates and other animals which could usefully be considered in relation to human gesture, but this is beyond our scope. The emphasis in this book is semiotic, linguistic and cultural. Issues in neurology, psychology, human development and biological comparisons must be left for others to deal with.

2   Visible action as gesture

'Gesture', we have suggested, is a name for visible action when it is used as an utterance or as a part of an utterance. But what is 'utterance', and how are actions in this domain recognized as playing a part in it?

In this book we shall use the term 'utterance' to refer to any ensemble of action that counts for others as an attempt by the actor to 'give' information of some sort. We draw here upon a formulation of Goffman (1963, pp. 13-14) in which he pointed out that although, whenever people are co-present to one another they cannot avoid providing information to one another about their intentions and involvements, about their status as social beings and about their own individual character, and so may be said to 'give off' information, people also engage in action that is regarded as explicitly designed for the provision of information and for which they are normally held responsible. Through these kinds of actions, to use Goffman's expression, people are said to 'give' information. Here 'utterance' will refer to any action or complex of actions that is treated by the participants within the interactional occasion, whatever this might be, as 'giving information' in this sense. That is, an 'utterance' is any unit of activity that is treated by those co-present as a communicative 'move', 'turn' or 'contribution'. Such units of activity may be constructed from speech or from visible bodily action or from combinations of these two modalities (see also Goffman 1981). 'Gesture' is the visible bodily action that has a role in such units of action.

Speech is a highly specialized activity and it seems always to be recognized, whether or not the language employed is understood. The features that determine whether or not visible bodily action is recognized as a part of 'utterance', on the other hand, deserve some examination. When, as a student of 'gesture', one sets about the task of observing and analysing this domain of action one does not observe and analyse *all* kinds of visible bodily action, or at least one does not deal with all kinds of visible bodily action in the same way. Some aspects of visible bodily action are singled out and treated as 'gesture' while other aspects are left on one side or are treated differently. What are the criteria that are followed in making these differentiations? Can the characteristics of actions that come to be dealt with as 'gesture' be described? These are the questions investigated in this chapter.

'Gesture' as the word is currently used is defined in the *Oxford English Dictionary* (2nd edition, 1989) as "a movement of the body, or any part of it, that is expressive of thought or feeling". In earlier uses the word also referred to deportment or to how a person carried the body. However, throughout the evolution of its meaning it is the manner of action and the expressive significance of this that is referred to. Furthermore, there is always the implication that the actor is deemed to exercise at least some degree of voluntary control over any movement regarded as 'gesture' and what it expresses. Usually 'gesture' is not used to refer to those visible bodily expressions of thoughts or feelings that are deemed inadvertent or are regarded as something a person cannot 'help'.

Thus, actions such as waving goodbye, the pointings and pantomimes that people sometimes engage in when communication by talk is impossible or the head waggings and arm wavings that accompany talk are usually referred to as 'gesture'. Laughter, smiling or weeping, on the other hand are not usually referred to in this way. When, occasionally, they are, this tends to imply that the expression was 'put on' or that it was a show or a performance, and not 'genuine' as an expression of emotion (Ekman and Friesen 1982). The word 'gesture' is also not usually employed to refer to the movements that people make when they are nervous, such as hair-pattings, self-groomings, clothing adjustments and the repetitive manipulation of rings or necklaces or other personal accoutrements. In ordinary interaction such movements tend to be disregarded, or they are treated as habitual or involuntary, and although they are often revealing and may sometimes be read by others as symptoms of the individual's moods or feelings, they are not, as a rule, referred to as 'gestures'.

Further, there are many actions that a person must engage in if they are to participate in interaction with others, which, again, though they may be revealing of the person's attitudes and feelings, are not usually regarded as 'gestures' because they are treated as being done for the practical necessities of interaction rather than for the sake of conveying meaning. Thus, although the distance a person may establish in relation to an interlocutor in interaction may be taken as an indication of their attitude toward the other or of their understanding of the nature of the interaction that is taking place (Mehrabian 1969), the movements that are involved in setting up or establishing the spatial orientational organization of an encounter are not usually considered 'gestures', perhaps because they are treated as being done, not for their own sake, but for the sake of creating a convenient and appropriate setting for the interaction. As a rule, participants tend not to notice them, unless they somehow violate the expectations that, within a given culture, people maintain about how occasions of interaction are structured spatially (Hall 1966). For example, when someone seems to edge closer to another than the other expects, or when they sit far off and do not move up, such actions may be taken as expressing interpersonal attitudes, feelings or intentions, but are not generally regarded as 'gestures' if, as is usually the case, they are done in a way that subordinates them to actions that must be done merely to maintain whatever spatial and orientational arrangement the participants of a given conversation may be using (Kendon, 1973, 1990a: Chapters 7 and 8).

Likewise, practical actions carried out within the context of face-to-face interaction, such as eating or smoking or knitting, though sometimes integrated within the organization of interaction so as to serve expressive purposes, are nevertheless not usually considered gestures. The actions required in eating, drinking or smoking may sometimes be used as devices to regulate the interaction. People who meet to talk over coffee, for instance, may vary the rate at which they drink up their coffee and, as a result, can regulate the amount of time spent in the interaction. Lighting a cigarette or relighting a pipe can often be elaborated as a way of 'buying time', as when a person needs to think a little before replying. Yet, despite the communicative significance such activities undoubtedly have, participants do not usually treat such activity as if it is intended to communicate anything. To spend time getting one's pipe ready to light up may be a way of taking 'time out' of a conversation; it is not to engage in a conversational move or turn, even though it may play a part in structuring the moves or turns of which the conversation is composed.

The movements necessary for any practical action may, however, in their performance, be embellished in such a way as to render them more than 'merely practical'. In pouring a wine at table, for example, it is possible for the person pouring the wine to 'merely' pour the wine. But it is also possible that all the actions involved - raising the bottle to display it, adjusting the angle for the pour, twisting the bottle at the end of the pour to stop a drop of wine from running down the side of the bottle, moving on to the next guest - may be performed so that they are so elaborated with flourishes that they come to be openly recognized as having an expressive aspect. As this happens, they may come to take on the qualities of gesture.

On the other hand, gestures may sometimes be disguised so that they no longer appear as such. For example, Morris, Collett, Marsh and O'Shaughnessy (1979) have reported that in Germany there is a gesture in which the forefinger touches the side of the head and is rotated back and forth. It is used to mean 'he's crazy' and it is regarded as a grave insult. Its use has been the cause of fights and one may be prosecuted for performing it in public. A surreptitious version of it has appeared, however, in which the forefinger is pressed against the cheek. In this version the gesture can be performed in such a way that it could be mistaken for scratching the cheek or for pressing a tooth that was giving discomfort. Likewise, Morris and colleagues also report that in Malta the gesture known as the Italian Salute or *bras d'honneur* is regarded as so offensive that one can be prosecuted for performing it in public. According to

Morris the Maltese have evolved a way of performing this gesture so that it could be mistaken for a mere rubbing of the arm, and not a gesture at all. In this version the left arm is held straight with the hand clenched in a fist, while the right hand gently rubs the inside of the left elbow.[1]

Such examples are of interest because they show that participants in interaction are able to recognize, simply from the way in which an action is performed, whether it is intended as communicative or not. For an action to be treated as 'gesture' it must have features that make it stand out as such. Such features may be grafted on to other actions, turning practical actions or emotional displays into gestures as we have just described. Such features may also be suppressed, turning movements from gestures into incidental mannerisms or passing comfort movements.

Characteristics of gestural action

What are the features that an action must have for it to be treated as a gesture? In a study designed to pursue this question (partially reported in Kendon 1978) twenty people were each shown, individually, a film of a man giving a speech to a fairly large gathering. The film had been made at a *Te*, or pig prestation ceremony among the Enga, who live in the Western Highlands of Papua New Guinea.[2] The people who watched the film were all English-speaking Australians of European background. Furthermore, none of them were students of psychology or any other behavioural science and were therefore free of any preconceptions such studies might have provided. The film shown was about four minutes long and it was shown without sound. Each person was asked to describe, in their own words, what movements they had seen the man make. Each subject was allowed to see the film as many times as they liked. The account of the movements observed was given in a 'non-directive' interview with the experimenter in which care was taken to use only the descriptive vocabulary that the subject employed. The aim was to find out what movements the subjects picked out in their descriptions and to find out what different sorts of movements they identified.

In the course of the film the man who was speaking engaged in elaborate movements of his arms and head, he walked forward, he manipulated the handle of an axe he was holding, he tugged at his jacket, he touched his face

[1] De Jorio (2000) describes many examples that illustrate how people can disguise a gesture as a mere action. See, for example, pp. 179–180, p.185, p.188, pp. 260–261.

[2] 16 mm film made by the author in the Enga Province, Papua New Guinea, 1976. Human Ethology Laboratory, Department of Anthropology, Research School of Pacific Studies, Australian National University, Canberra, Australia.

and nose. All subjects, without exception, first said that they saw movements which they described as deliberate, conscious, and part of what the man was trying to say. All subjects also said that they saw some other movements that they described as 'natural' or 'ordinary' with no significance. Thus not only was a distinction drawn by all twenty people between significant movements and other movements, all twenty mentioned these significant movements first, and only later, and sometimes only after some probing, did they mention other movements.

A stop-action projector was used so it was possible for the subject to point out precisely where the different movements identified as significant occurred. All subjects were able to do this without any hesitation, and there was very considerable agreement as to which movements were considered as a significant part of what the man was trying to say and those which were 'natural' or 'ordinary' or of no significance. Thirty-seven movement segments were commented on. In all cases a majority of subjects assigned them either to the significant or to the natural category, and there were only four segments in respect to which more than five out of the twenty subjects differed from the majority in how these movements were to be assigned.

From the way the subjects reported the movements they noticed and the order in which they reported them, we may infer the following classification:

(1) Movements seen as deliberate, conscious, governed by an intention to say something or to communicate. These were the movements that were considered to be, in one observer's words, "part of what the man was trying to say".

(2) Movements seen as having to do with sustaining or changing a given bodily position or orientation. These included movements of the whole body, as when the man walks forward to take up a new position in space. Also included were movements of the head and eyes when these were interpreted as movements entailed by changes in the direction of attention.

(3) Movements seen as involved in the manipulation of objects or clothing. These were also regarded as deliberate, however they were not regarded as being governed by any sort of communicative intention. The movements assigned to this category were those that had to do with holding the axe, changing the axe handle from one hand to the other, and adjusting the coat.

(4) Movements seen as 'nervous' or 'incidental'. These were usually mentioned last, often only after the interviewer had insisted that they mention all the movements that they had seen. They were usually regarded as being of no significance, although a few observers used them as evidence for the speaker's mood or emotional state. They were not seen as intentional.

A consideration of the characteristics of the movement segments selected by these observers as part of the orator's deliberate expression as compared to those selected as 'natural' or 'ordinary' or of no significance allows us to arrive at some understanding of the features of deliberately expressive movement as compared to other kinds of movement.

Deliberately expressive movement was found to be movement that had a sharp boundary of onset and offset and that was an *excursion*, rather than resulting in any sustained change of position. For limb movements, deliberately expressive movements were those in which the limb was lifted away from the body and later returned to the same or a similar position from which it started. In the head, rotations or up–down movements were seen as deliberately expressive if the movement was repeated, or if they did not lead to the head being held in a new position, and if the movements were not done in coordination with eye movements. If they were, then the observers would say that the man was changing where he was looking or attending, and this was considered different from the movements regarded as part of what he was saying. A movement of the whole body was regarded as part of the man's deliberate expression if it was seen as *returning* to the position from which it began, and did not result in a sustained change in spatial location or bodily orientation or posture.

Movements that involved manipulations of an object, such as changing the position of an object (as changing the axe handle from one hand to the other), were never seen as part of the man's deliberate expression. They were usually referred to, if mentioned at all, as 'practical'. Movements in which the man touched himself or his clothing were also never regarded as parts of deliberate expression. These movements were, by almost all subjects, completely overlooked at the outset. They were dismissed as 'natural' or 'nervous' or 'of no importance' when the subject's attention was drawn to them.

Although, in this study, we have only the observations offered by detached observers, the consistency of the discriminations made and the very readiness with which these observers made them, suggest that they reflect a practice commonly followed by ordinary participants in everyday interaction. It seems that participants single out and treat differentially some aspects of each other's behaviour as somehow more salient to the immediate communication than other aspects. Goffman (1974, Chapter 7) has drawn attention to this differentiation in the treatment participants in interaction accord various aspects of each other's behaviour by his concept of *attentional tracks*. He suggests that in any social encounter there is always an aspect of the activity going forward that is treated as being within a *main-line* or *story-line* track. A domain of action is delineated as being relevant to the main business of the encounter, and it is oriented to as such and dealt with accordingly. Other aspects of activity are not included, but this does not mean that they have no part to play. Goffman suggested a *directional* track in which there is "a stream of signs which is itself excluded from the content of activity but which serves as a means of regulating it, bounding, articulating and qualifying its various components and phrases" (p. 210). He also distinguished a *disattend track*, to which are assigned a whole variety of actions that are not counted as being part of the interaction at all, such as what he calls "creature comfort releases" - scratching, postural adjustments, smoking, and so forth - that are, so to speak, allowable deviations from the behavioural discipline to which all participants in a focused encounter are expected to conform.

This kind of differential attention to behaviour in interaction can readily be demonstrated in the children's game of Timmy. In this game, one player, the Challenger, gets another, the Responder, to agree to imitate his actions. The Challenger says: "do as I do" and then holds up the left hand, fingers straight and fully spread, and, with the right hand, touches each fingertip of the left hand with the right index finger in succession, and says "timmy" each time this is done, in this way going from little finger to thumb and back again. The hands are then lowered and clasped together in a relaxed manner in a resting position. The Responder is then expected to follow the Challenger's instruction to "do as I do." While all Responders imitate the timmy performance just described, they almost never imitate the resting position of the Challenger's hands.

This game shows that people are highly consistent in what they decide to treat as background action and foreground action. The game works because the Challenger can be secure in assuming what it is that the Responder will include as relevant aspects of the behaviour to be imitated. The Challenger can rest secure in this assumption, in part, because it appears that some actions are almost invariably assigned main-track status, simply by virtue of what sort of actions they are. Vocalization and speech are specially oriented to and take a kind of first place in the attentional hierarchy. However, certain patterns of bodily movement are also given main-track status simply because of the character they have as movements.

It is suggested that the twenty observers in the experiment just described were operating much as they would if they were in interaction with another or if they were attending to the speech maker as members of his audience. They were attending to him in a highly differentiated fashion and what stood out for them as salient and worth reporting were those movements that share certain features which identify them for the observer as deliberate and, in this case, intended as communicative. Just as a hearer perceives speech, whether comprehended or not, as 'figure' no matter what the 'ground' may be, and just as speech is always regarded as fully intentional and intentionally communicative, so it is suggested that if movements are made so that they have certain dynamic characteristics they will be perceived as 'figure' against the 'ground' of other movement, and such movements will be regarded as fully intentional and intentionally communicative.

It is proposed that movements may vary in the extent to which they can be said to have those features which we shall here refer to as the *features of manifest deliberate expressiveness.* The more a movement shares these features, the more likely it is to be given privileged status in the attention of another and to be seen as part of the individual's effort to convey meaning. What is normally called 'gesture' are those movements that partake of these features of manifest deliberate expressiveness to an obvious degree. Movements that have these characteristics are treated as if they are performed by the actor under the guidance of an openly acknowledged communicative intent and the actor will be regarded as being fully responsible for them. The word 'gesture' tends to be used for such actions.

In other words, movements made under the guidance of an openly acknowledged intention to convey meaning are directly perceived as such as a consequence of characteristics of the movement's dynamic features which 'compel' the observer to see them in this way. If an action is an excursion, if it has well defined boundaries of onset and offset, and if it has features which show that the movement is not made solely under the influence of gravity, then it is likely to be perceived as gestural. So far as I know, this proposal has not yet been experimentally tested directly, although this would certainly be possible. One could construct animated figures whose movements could be varied according to specifiable parameters. In this way, one could see within what range of such parameters observers would see movement as gestural.

Experiments in movement perception, such as those of Heider and Simmel (1944) and Michotte (1950, 1962), have demonstrated that under certain conditions objects such as squares, circles or triangles, observed moving in relation to one another, are seen as animate beings involved in various kinds of interaction. Michotte (1950) showed that what sort of interaction the rectangles he used in his displays are seen to be involved in, and even what feelings are attributed to them, is precisely dependent upon the way in which they are made to move in relation to one another. Lethbridge and Ware (1990) have taken this work further, using computer generated animations, and have been able to make precise specifications as to what kinds of movement are seen as movement of a living organism and what kinds of dynamic relations between abstract objects are seen in terms of social interactions.

Work by Johansson (1973) on the perception of biological motion is also relevant here. In Johansson's experiments actors had small lights placed on various well separated parts of their bodies and they were filmed in a dark room. Observers then viewed the films. When a static image was seen, observers saw only a random scatter of light points. When the film of the actor walking or running or dancing was seen, observers immediately saw this motion for what it was. Subsequent work using this technique has shown that such perception of biological motion is also present in human infants (Fox and McDaniel 1982) and cats (Blake 1993), suggesting that the discrimination of animated movement is a basic feature of the processes of movement perception. Bassili (1978), showing observers films of actors enacting facial expressions in which all that could be seen were white spots placed at different points of the face so that only movement features were revealed, found that this was sufficient for the discrimination of several different emotions. Dittrich et al. (1996) showed that human observers can also discriminate different patterns of emotion on the basis of different movement configurations of point light displays derived from whole body expressions of emotion (as described by Roth 1990), rather than just the face.

These studies lend strength to the idea that deliberate expressiveness is *manifest*, it is perceived *directly*, and requires no deductive processes leading to an *inference* of an intention. The intentionality of an action is something that is directly perceived. That is, it is the quality of the action as intentional (not the specific intention, necessarily) that is directly perceived. In other words, an action that is gestural has an immediate appearance of gesturalness. This means that a movement having this appearance will be discriminated and recognized as such directly. A detailed specification of what forms and movement patterns are required for a gesture to be discriminated remains, however, a matter for further work.

Defining 'gesture'

'Gesture' we suggest, then, is a label for actions that have the features of manifest deliberate expressiveness. They are those actions or those aspects of another's actions that, having these features, tend to be directly perceived as being under the guidance of the observed person's voluntary control and being done for the purposes of expression rather than in the service of some practical aim. Participants in interaction readily recognize such actions and they tend to be accorded the status of actions for which the participants are held responsible.

Whether an action is deemed to be intended or not is something that is dependent entirely upon how that action appears to others. As the examples of how the performance of the illegal German and Maltese gestures may be camouflaged reminded us, people can manage their actions so that they can appear fully intentional or not, as it suits them. Actions can be varied so that they have more of the properties that will lead them to be treated as intentionally expressive, or fewer of them. This fact in itself is evidence that the judgement of an action's intentionality is a matter of how it appears to others and not a matter of some mysterious process by which the intention or intentions themselves that may guide an action may be known.

How actions that vary in terms of the features of manifest deliberate expressiveness are interpreted, however, will depend upon context. On the military parade ground, even very slight deviations from correct posture or attire may be interpreted as and treated as deliberate insults. In Malta, presumably, though I may perform the *bras d'honneur* in such a way as to permit me to claim, to a policeman, that I had an ache in my arm, to the person for whom the gesture was intended I may not wish to make such a claim. I may wish him to recognize the insult for what it was. What may be 'gesture' in one circumstance may be 'incidental movement' in another. 'Gesture', thus, cannot be given a definition that is independent of how the participants in any situation are treating each other's flow of actions. What will be counted as intentionally expressive and treated as such may vary from one situation to another.

Nevertheless, it remains that there is a core of visible bodily movement phenomena that is usually referred to as gesture. Various attempts have been made to classify what is found in this core into its different varieties. As we see in Chapter 6, where we review these classifications, we find that, although there is much variation in the terminology employed, there is underlying agreement. Furthermore, in very broad terms these classifications are really quite similar to the classifications that were offered, either implicitly or, in some cases, explicitly, by the subjects in the gesture-perception experiment I have described. Though different names may be used, it seems evident that people treat each other's behaviour differentially in a highly similar fashion.

3   Western interest in gesture from Classical Antiquity to the eighteenth century

Discussion of gesture in Classical Antiquity

In the Western tradition, among the Greeks and, later, the Romans, gesture was recognized as a feature of human expression that, being powerful, must be shaped and regulated in accordance with the aims of creating persuasive or effective discourse. Aristotle saw it as part of the technique used by public orators to sway the feelings of the crowd, but he rather disparaged it, regarding gesture, tone of voice, and other theatrical techniques, as detracting from the ideal of just and proper discourse which, he believed, should require only facts and the principles of reason. Later, in the Roman tradition, these aspects of oratorical technique came to be valued somewhat differently. For example, Cicero discusses gesture and facial expression in his discourses on oratory but, unlike Aristotle, he regarded them as worthy of cultivation. Nevertheless, in his discussion, he emphasizes how gesture and, especially, the face, were to be used to express the feelings that lie behind a discourse. They should be employed in a measured and dignified fashion, not at all in the manner of gesture as used by mimes and actors, whose techniques were regarded as quite different from those of the public orator (Lamedica 1984).

The most complete discussion of gesture from the Roman era is in the eleventh Book of *Institutio oratoria* ('Education of the Orator') by Marcus Fabius Quintilianus, written in the first century AD (Maier-Eichorn 1989, Graf 1993, Aldrete 1999, Dutsch 2003 are recent discussions). Quintilian was a rhetorician from Spain who taught in Rome and had received an imperial grant for his work. His book is a comprehensive treatise on all aspects of rhetoric. It lays out a complete programme for the education of a young orator and is the fullest account that has come down to us of Roman rhetorical doctrine. Quintilian's discussion of gesture is found in the treatment of Delivery in Section III, the final Section of Book XI of the *Institutio*. At the beginning of this Section, following Cicero, he divides Action or Delivery (*actio* or *pronuntiatio*) into two components: Voice (*vox*) and Movement (*motum*) which he later also refers to as *gestus*. Quintilian declares that both aspects of Delivery are of great importance, although he says that "the voice has our first claim on our attention, since even our gesture is adapted to suit it" (XI, III.14).[1]

For Quintilian, as for other early writers, *gestus*, which is usually translated as 'gesture', refers not only to actions of the hands and arms but also to the carriage of the body, the postures it can assume, the actions of the head and face, and the glance. Thus, the section that includes a discussion of how the hands and arms are to be used begins with a discussion of the head, how it should be held and moved. It continues with an account of the glance, which is seen as being of the greatest importance for the creation of the overall emotional effect of the discourse. There are comments on the eyebrows, on the use of the nostrils in expression, and also a discussion of the neck. However, the section that deals with the hands and their uses in speaking is by far the lengthiest and most detailed. It is clear from how the hands are dealt with that Quintilian sees their actions as being most closely involved with speaking. In subsequent treatments of Delivery in treatises on rhetoric, especially from the seventeenth century onwards, the hands receive the most extensive discussion and what is said about them in these later treatments is largely based on Quintilian. This is how Quintilian begins his discussion of the hands:

> As for the hands, without which all action [i.e. Delivery] would be crippled and enfeebled, it is scarcely possible to describe the variety of their motions, since they are almost as expressive as words. For other portions of the body merely help the speaker, whereas the hands may be almost said to speak. Do we not use them to demand, promise, summon, dismiss, threaten, supplicate, express aversion or fear, question or deny? Do we not employ them to indicate joy, sorrow, hesitation, confession, penitence, measure, quantity, number and time? Have they not power to excite and prohibit, to express approval, wonder or shame? Do they not take the place of adverbs and pronouns when we point at places and things? In fact, though the peoples and nations of the earth speak a multitude of tongues, they share in common the universal language of the hands. (Book XI, III.85-87)

It is to be noted that the actions of the hands that Quintilian lists are almost all gestures which either mark a kind of discourse action or speech act (such as 'demand', 'promise', 'summon', 'dismiss') or are a vehicle for showing a feeling ('joy', 'sorrow', 'hesitation'). He mentions only 'measure', 'quantity', 'number' and 'time' as gestures that could perhaps be regarded as gestures that serve to convey some aspect of referential content.

Quintilian draws a distinction between gestures which "naturally proceed from us simultaneously with our words" and those by which one indicates

---

[1] All quotations from Quintilian are by Book, section and line number from the Loeb edition, English translation by H. E. Butler (Quintilianus 1922).

things by means of mimicry. These are gestures that describe objects through descriptive action or pantomime. They should be avoided by the orator. Quintilian says that the orator's "gesture should be adapted rather to his thought than to his actual words" (XI, III.89). Pointing to the self or to another to whom one is making reference is acceptable, for this indicates the object of thought, but it is not correct to use gestures to illustrate the content of what is being said. According to Quintilian, and here he follows Cicero, the orator uses gestures to convey the force of what is being said and to indicate the objects of his thought, but not as a substitute for what he says in words. To do this is to follow the practices of the popular stage and it would not be fitting for the dignity of the law courts (in Quintilian's time the only remaining locus of oratory, since oratory had long since disappeared from Roman political life). Quintilian then describes some eighteen specific gestures which he recommends for use. These gestures are described as being suited to the various parts of the oration, to marking out the different points the speaker is making, to show attitudes such as admiration, wonder or rejection, or to indicate what today we might refer to as speech acts such as interrogation, certainty in assertion, pleading and the like.

Quintilian follows his account of specific gestures with some remarks on how gestures should be placed in relation to spoken discourse. He agrees with "earlier instructors" that the "movement of the hand should begin and end with the thought that is expressed. Otherwise the gesture will anticipate or lag behind the voice, both of which produce an unpleasing effect" (XI, III.106-107). He opposes any rigid rule governing the relationship of speech and gesture. Some teachers of gesture, he observes, have recommended that there should be an interval of three words between every movement. While this will make sure that the hands are not idle for too long and will also ensure that they will not engage in too much activity, Quintilian nevertheless believes that the organization of gesture should be adapted to the rhythmical organization of the discourse. He regards it as an error to mark up, in advance, just at which points in a speech a gesture should fall. He says (XI, III.110), "[i]t is therefore better, in view of the fact that all speech falls into a number of brief clauses, at the end of which we can take breath, if necessary, to arrange our gesture to suit these sections". He then follows with some observations on how gesturing should be adapted to the liveliness or emotional intensity of the delivery. He closes his discussion with several paragraphs on what he regards as errors or faults in the use of gesture.

Quintilian's discussion of gesture occupies a rather small section of his work, relative to his entire treatise. We do not know what use was made of this part when it was written. It becomes important, however, once an interest in gesture revived at the beginning of the seventeenth century, for the treatises on Delivery that then began to appear, which paid much attention to gesture, drew very largely on what Quintilian had to say.

From the Renaissance to the seventeenth century

Although Quintilian's book was known throughout the Middle Ages, it was known only imperfectly and the study of rhetoric during this period, insofar as it drew upon Latin authors, was mainly shaped by certain surviving works of Cicero and the *Rhetorica ad Herennium*.[2] During this period, in teaching rhetoric, it was the intellectual aspects of the subject that received emphasis. This included *inventio*, or Invention (how to develop topics for a discourse), *dispositio* or Disposition (how the discourse was to be structured) and *elocutio* or Style (the various kinds of tropes and how these were to be used). The other divisions, *memoria* or Memory (techniques for committing speeches to memory) and *pronuntiatio* or Delivery (how to perform a speech), received but little attention.

Despite this, as Schmitt (1990) has shown, during the Middle Ages considerable attention was paid to bodily comportment and gesture for formalized gestural actions were of great importance in legal ritual.[3] Also, there were treatises devoted to body management serving as instructional manuals for the religious and there were discussions of the bodily attitudes and gestures to be employed in conducting prayer and other religious ceremonies. Gesture was developed formally as a mode of communication to replace speech in certain monastic orders (see Chapter 13). However, it is not until the end of the sixteenth century that gesture is first seen to become a focus of philosophical or scientific concern. Several factors played a role in this.

To begin with, the full text of Quintilian's treatise did not become known to early modern Europe until the beginning of the fifteenth century (a complete manuscript was found in 1416). Also found in the same period were some previously lost treatises of Cicero. The discovery of these texts caused great excitement in humanist circles and it led to the revival of the idea, championed by both Cicero and Quintilian, that the orator should be at once a philosopher and a man of action of high moral integrity and fully involved in public affairs. Of special importance was the discovery of the complete text of Cicero's *De oratore* which made possible a much better understanding of how Roman orators actually practised their art. This, together with a full appreciation of the work of Quintilian, made possible a much more complete view of Roman rhetoric which could now be better appreciated in a practical, as well as in a theoretical way. As a result, rhetoric came to be seen as a matter of practical import as well as of intellectual training (Conley 1990).

[2] A treatise on rhetoric written c. 86-82 BC by an unknown author, at one time often thought to be the work of Cicero.

[3] This is documented in Germany in the thirteenth century in the illustrated versions of the *Sachsenspiegel* or 'Saxon Mirror', an exposition of Saxon customary law originally written by Eike von Repgow of Dessau. For a study of the gestures depicted in the *Sachsenspiegel* see Amira (1905). See also Dobozy (1999).

Other developments in the sixteenth century, both religious and political, further contributed to the trend towards recognizing Delivery as important. These included certain changes in the organization of religious services, with an increased prominence being given to the sermon. First among Protestants, then among Catholics, the priest's role as a teacher and preacher was enhanced. This was in response to competing divisions within the church. The priest became a persuader as well as a manager of ritual. Delivery, thus, was of renewed relevance and it began to be taught systematically in universities and schools, especially those run by Jesuits (the Society of Jesus was founded in 1540). As a part of this training the Jesuits, in particular, recognized the importance of skill in acting and so they incorporated it as a regular feature of the curriculum. We may suppose that this led to an increased interest in the role of gesture and probably contributed to attempts to formulate general principles for teaching it. Furthermore, it seems likely that the widening diffusion of the complete text of Quintilian's book contributed to the idea that gesture could be taught. Once gesture is seen as something interesting, Quintilian's descriptions of gestures would have received much more attention. They are sufficiently detailed to make it possible to imitate them and they could be used as a basis for teaching. Earlier, gesture had been thought of as something natural, that could not be taught, but the principles laid down by Quintilian suggested that, after all, the teaching of gesture according to some general rules was possible.

Also of consequence was that, during the first half of the sixteenth century, certain philosophical developments gave rise to a change in how the various branches of knowledge were to be organized. Peter Ramus of Paris (Pierre de la Ramée 1515-1572), whose work had a far reaching influence throughout Protestant Europe, attempted a simplified classification of the various branches of learning based upon an understanding of the various methods followed. He proposed that rhetoric be divided into two parts only: *elocutio* or Style and *pronuntiatio* or Delivery. Invention and Disposition were to become part of logic, while Memory was to be left out altogether. As a result, treatises on rhetoric came to concentrate on those aspects of it that were most closely connected with the techniques of performing a speech (see Knox 1990).

Other developments, beyond the field of rhetoric itself, also contributed to an expanded interest in gesture and, without doubt, contributed to the writing of treatises on this topic from a scholarly point of view. The development of the ideal of the finished gentleman or courtier through the circulation of books such as Castiglione's *Il libro del cortegiano* ('The Book of the Courtier') (1527) and Della Casa's *Il Galateo* (1558), which described the mode of conduct an aspiring courtier should follow, spread the idea that there were universal standards of civil behaviour appropriate for those who belonged to the classes of power or who were associated with such people. This led to the development of a greater awareness that there are different modes of behaviour, some more suited to 'courtliness' than others. Conduct, thus, and not just social position given by birth, could influence a person's status. This, too, contributed to the idea that it would be interesting and useful to study the ways in which people expressed themselves.

Also important was the expansion of contacts between Europeans and peoples of other lands, especially the encounters with the natives of the New World. This led to the realization that, although spoken languages were diverse and unintelligible, communication was yet possible through gesture and greatly reinforced the idea that universal principles of expression and communication could be found in gesture. This, in turn, contributed to the idea that a general theory of gesture was possible (see Knox 1990 and Burke 1993).

As a result of all these developments, gesture came to be seen as something important and interesting in its own right and, as scholars began to be more specialized in the topics they dealt with, there were some who took it up. Thus in 1571 Arias Montanus included in his biblical commentaries an extensive study of gestures, claiming that this was the first time that this neglected field had received systematic attention.[4] In 1616, in Vicenza, Giovanni Bonifacio published his *L'Arte de' Cenni*, which, among other things, is a comprehensive survey of all the signs it is possible to make with bodily action. In 1627, in Milan, Francesco Bartolomeo Ferrari published his *De veterum acclamationibus et plausu libri septem* which is an exceedingly detailed study of the gestures of acclamation. The same writer also undertook a treatise entitled *Syntagmata de artificiosa manuum loquela*, unfortunately lost, but which appears to have been an attempt at a description of gestures used in speaking. In England John Bulwer published his *Chirologia or the Naturall Language of the Hand and Chironomia or the Art of Manual Rhetoricke* in 1644.

Of the various works just mentioned, those of Bonifacio and Bulwer are the most often recalled today. Bonifacio's book is broad in scope. It deals both with the signs or gestures that can be performed by bodily actions and also with clothing and ornamentation. Bulwer's book deals only with actions of the hands. However, both were written with the aim of providing a prominence and importance for the role of gesture in human life which the authors believed it to have.

---

[4] Arias Montanus, *Liber Ieremiae, sive de actione* (1571), referred to in Knox (1990, 1996).

L'Arte de' Cenni ... of Giovanni Bonifacio (1547-1645)

Bonifacio's book is one of the earliest to be published in Europe that is devoted exclusively to gesture. It was published in Vicenza in 1616 under the following title which, as will be seen, provides a good summary of the aims and contents of the work*:*

> *L'Arte de' Cenni con la quale formandosi favella visibile, si tratta della muta eloquenza che non è altro che un facondo silentio. Divisa in due parti. Nella prima si tratta dei cenni, che da noi con le membra del nostro corpo sono fatti, scoprendo la loro significatione, e quella con l'autorità di famosi Autori confirmando. Nella seconda si dimostra come di questa cognitione tutte l'arti liberali, e meccaniche si prevagliano. Materia nuova à tutti gli huomini pertinente, e massimamente à Prencipi, che, per loro dignità, più con cenni, che con parole si fanno intendere.*

> The Art of Signs with which a visible language is formed, deals with the mute expressiveness that is none other than an eloquent silence. It is divided into two parts. The first part deals with the signs that are made by us by the parts of our body, revealing their meanings which are confirmed by famous authors. In the second part it is shown how all the liberal and mechanical arts make use of this knowledge. New material pertinent for all men and particularly for Princes who, because of their dignity, make themselves understood more with signs than with words. (Translation by AK)

Giovanni Bonifacio was born to a noble family in Rovigo. He studied jurisprudence in Padova and had practised as a lawyer and magistrate in several cities, including Venice. He wrote plays, some poetry, and a history of the city of Treviso, several legal treatises, a short book on the "Republic of the Bees..." (1627) and a book on the "Liberal and Mechanical Arts as they have been Demonstrated by Irrational Animals to Humans" (1628). *L'Arte de' Cenni...* , aside from his history of Treviso, remains his most original (and curious) book and perhaps his most well known today (see Benzoni 1970).

L'Arte de' Cenni. . . is an attempt to describe all the signs that it is possible to make with the body, and it also considers significations made through clothing. Bonifacio believed that "as one knows the will of the master through the activities of his servants, so from bodily actions one can comprehend the inclinations of the soul, and from the acts, gestures, and bearing of bodily members our internal feelings can be conjectured" (p. 17, trans. AK). He believed that bodily signs reveal more clearly and truthfully than words a person's feelings and intentions. At the same time, however, he believed that if one can master the art of using the body to make signs one can control the impression that one makes on other people.

As the title explains, the book is divided into two parts. All of the signs that can be made by the various parts of the body are described in the first part, while the second part deals with gestures and signs used in the various professions. In describing the gestures of the body, Bonifacio begins with the head - because the head stands as master over all the other parts of the body. He follows with a discussion of the face. Here, although he shows himself to be very well aware of the claims of physiognomy, quoting, for example, from the work of Della Porta,[5] he maintains that it is only through the dynamic changes in the face that one can gain truths about inner feelings. From the face he proceeds to discuss the gestures of the arms, the hands, the fingers, even the nails, and he then moves downwards from the chest, to the abdomen, to the genitals, to the knees and to the feet. In many cases, in support of his interpretations, he brings in quotations from the most authoritative authors - Virgil, Ovid, Dante, Petrarch, Ariosto. He notes that we can understand many gestures as having a natural origin, but at the same time, recognizes that there are many which, though they seem natural, are yet governed by convention and can be done erroneously.

Bonifacio's book was written with the hope that it might help restore to use what he regarded as the more natural and common mode of expression that is found in gesture. He laments that man has almost given up the natural language of gesture but has, instead, devised an almost infinite number of words and has sought to formulate rules by which he can express things for the ear which would be much more naturally and easily expressed for the eye. He complains that just as man, in his restlessness and depravity, has not stood firm in the true faith that God had bestowed upon him, but has madly created all manner of different doctrines, to the point that there is no agreement any more, so he has created such a great diversity of languages that, from one region to the next, men cannot understand one another. The mute eloquence of gesture, on the other hand, were it restored to use, would make possible a greater understanding among men (paraphrased from a passage on pp. 172–173).

As Knox (1996) points out, previous authors had written of gesture as an important supplement and auxiliary to effective oratory. Bonifacio's idea that gesture could be a universal language that could replace the confusion of spoken languages was new. It was soon to be put forward by others, however, and it was the idea that gesture was the universal and natural language of mankind that was also the guiding theme of the next work we discuss, that of John Bulwer.

---

[5] Giovan Battista Della Porta *De humana physiognomia* (Naples 1586), Italian version titled *Della fisonomia dell'huomo* (Naples 1598). See Magli (1995, Chapter 6) for a discussion.

The *Chirologia* and *Chironomia* of John Bulwer (1606-1656)

Chirologia: or the Naturall Language of the Hand of 1644, bound together
with a second volume, the *Chironomia: or the Art of Manual Rhetoricke,*
appear to be the first books dedicated entirely to gesture to be published in
English. Bulwer, who was a London physician, also wrote three other books
about the body in communication. In 1648 he published a book on methods
for teaching the deaf, *Philocophus: or the Deafe and Dumb Man's Friend,*
which includes the device of a finger-spelling alphabet, possibly the first to
have been invented. In 1649 he published *Pathomyotomia: Or a Dissection
of the Significative Muscles of the Affections of the Minde*, an analysis of
the facial expressions of emotion and the muscle movements that produce
them, which includes some account of the gestures of the head. His last book,
published in 1653, was an attack on the practices of changing the natural form
of the body for reasons of custom. Its title was *Anthropometamorphosis, Man
Transform'd: Or the Artificial Changeling*. He also promised two other books
which would have accompanied the *Chirologia...Chironomia* to be entitled
Cephalelogia and *Cephalenomia* which would have dealt with the natural
gestures of the head and the art of gesture of the head, respectively. These
books appear never to have been written.[6]

In the Preface to the *Chirologia* Bulwer states that he was inspired to embark
upon the work by a passage in Francis Bacon's *Advancement of Learning* in
which Bacon notes that whereas Aristotle had discussed physical appearance
he had said nothing about gesture. He resolves, accordingly, to write a treatise
on gesture which he regarded as "the only speech which is natural to man, it
may well be called the tongue and general language of human nature which,
without teaching, men in all regions of the habitable world do at the first sight
most easily understand" (p. 16).

Bulwer's account of the "natural language of the hand" is divided into two
parts, the "Chirologia or the Natural Language of the Hand" and the "Dactylogia,
or the Dialects of the Fingers". To the first part is added "A Corollary of the
Speaking Motions, Discoursing Gestures or Habits of the Hand" in which
sixty-four gestures are described which use the whole hand. To the second part
"A Corollary of the Discoursing Gesture of the Fingers" is added, in which we
find described twenty-five gestures in which specific fingers are involved. For
each gesture, in each part, after a brief description, an account of its meaning
and use is given, illustrated by examples drawn occasionally from his own

---

[6] On Bulwer see Cleary (1959 and Cleary in Bulwer 1974). Wollock (1996) is a detailed study of
Bulwer's interest in the education of the deaf. It includes a discussion of *Philocophus* as well as
details of his life not found elsewhere. Wollock (2002) examines Bulwer's views on language and
cognition in relation to those of Francis Bacon.

Fig. 3.1 Chirogrammatic Plate B from *Chirologia: or the Natural Language of the Hand* by John Bulwer (1644). From a copy in the library at Princeton University. Reproduced with permission.

observations, but mainly from sources such as the Old and New Testaments, classical authors including Plutarch, Tacitus, Xenophon, Ovid and Virgil, and a few contemporary authors including Valeriano and Erasmus.

Bulwer regarded these natural motions of the hands and fingers as showing a high degree of eloquence. However, he maintained that if they are to attain their full power they must be shaped by art. In the Preface to the *Chironomia* he disputes those rhetoricians who believed that nature alone was sufficient and argues there that to attain true power of discourse one must consult the "oracle of Quintilian" and thereby learn "decency of expression" which so depends upon the art of gestures that "decency is properly spoken of gesture and motions of the hand and body" (p. 153). He notes that the "defects of extemporary and jejune orations have been covered by the elegancies of this artifice [i.e. the art of gesture]; and that those that have come off unhandsomely with their expressions for want of these comely and palliating graces of elocution were ever laughed at and justly derided" (p. 154).

Bulwer notes that the Romans were especially aware of the importance of using gestures artfully and he justifies his *Chironomia* in part as an effort to place before the public the Roman art of gesture in a more accessible fashion. He draws heavily on Cicero and Quintilian, but he also makes much use of the work of Ludovico Cresollius, a French Jesuit whose *Vacationes autumnales sive perfecta oratoris actione et pronunciatione*, published in Paris in 1620, is among the earliest treatises for orators, after Quintilian, that includes more than a passing discussion of how to use the hands when making speeches.

Bulwer is concerned to show that the artistic use of gesture must be founded upon the natural. The meanings of the gestures employed have their justification in their natural origins, but their employment must be carefully regulated by the requirements of appropriateness, grace and decorum. He adds to the *Chironomia* a section called the *Apocrypha of Action*, in which he outlines the several ways in which the rules of good gestural usage may be broken and here we find that a number of the gestures that he has described in the *Chirologia* as natural are nevertheless not to be used by orators because they are considered vulgar or inappropriate.

Bulwer's two treatises on gesture are notable for the plates that are included which depict the hand shapes and positions of the gestures that he describes, both for the 'natural speaking motions' and for gestures guided by the art of chironomia (Fig. 3.1). Apparently his was the first publication in which this was done. In each Chirogrammatic Plate twenty-four gestures are depicted, each one labelled with a letter of the alphabet. These letters are used to identify each picture in the explanations that accompany them. It is curious to note, however, that with each Plate Bulwer suggests that the gestures "besides their typical significations are so ordered to serve for privy cyphers for any secret intimation" (ibid., p. 116).

Besides the detailed description of manual gestures that Bulwer provides in the *Chirologia...Chironomia* (as well as some account of gestures of the face and head that are given in his *Pathomyotomia*), his general theoretical attitude is of considerable interest. Bulwer believed that the "language of the hand" was natural, and that gestures, like hieroglyphs, showed a direct relationship between form and meaning. In this he was a follower of Bacon. However, as Wollock (2002) shows, Bulwer's view of language was different from that of Bacon who maintained that languages were artificial constructions. Bulwer, being a physician in his orientation, saw gesture as if it is a kind of symptom of the state of the soul. His view of language was that it is something that resides within us and is thus something that is to be discovered. This idea is in sharp contrast to the idea that it would be possible to create a universal language that was being pursued by his contemporaries, for example by Bishop Wilkins (1614-1672), who, in his *Essay toward a Real Character* (1668), sought to construct a universal language as an invention, similar to mathematics. As Wollock remarks, Bulwer's view that language resides within us as a part of our nature is a view of language that seems akin to some modern views now emerging in cognitive linguistics (e.g. Johnson 1987, Lakoff 1987). Such views are in opposition to the view of language as an arbitrary and logical construction which has tended to dominate Western thinking on language since at least the seventeenth century.

The influence of Bulwer's book is a matter of dispute. Copies of it have always been scarce. It was printed but twice, in 1644 and in 1648. Probably many copies were lost in the great fire of London in 1666. It is not cited by the authors of works on rhetorical delivery that were subsequently published, and yet several of these works show remarkable parallels to Bulwer and it is presumed that they were influenced by him, nevertheless.

Gesture in art

During the latter part of the sixteenth and early seventeenth centuries, the new awareness of and interest in bodily comportment and gesture and its communicative significance extended beyond the domain of manuals of rhetoric and social conduct. We find it in the pictorial arts as well. Already, in 1440, Leon Battista Alberti, in his treatise on painting, had discussed how the emotions should be represented through the depiction of appropriate bodily movements and facial expressions. This is also dealt with by Leonardo Da Vinci in the posthumous compilation of 1507 known as the *Trattato della Pittura*. He recommended that artists keep notebooks in which to note

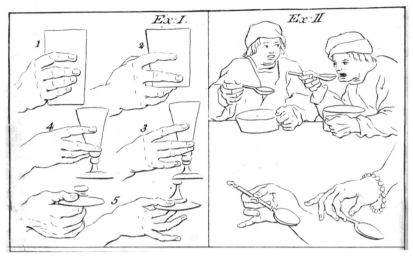

Fig. 3.2A Two pictures from *The Art of Painting* (1738) by Gerard de Lairesse which illustrate how people of different social backgrounds may handle drinking vessels or a spoon.

Fig. 3.2B From Plate XIV (Ex. 3 and 4) and Plate XV (Ex. 5 and 6) of *The Art of Painting* illustrating different modes of giving and receiving. All figures reproduced with permission from a copy in the Bryn Mawr College Library.

observations of human behaviour in streets and market places (see Baxandall 1988). In Holland, during the latter part of the seventeenth century Gerard de Lairesse became increasingly well known to younger artists and others who frequented his studio where he gave weekly lessons on painting. The advices he offered were so highly regarded that he was induced, in his later years, (and despite his blindness) to set them down and the result was his *Groot Schilderboek* ('Great Painting Book'), first published in Dutch in 1707. This rapidly gained a reputation for the thoroughness with which it covered every branch of painting, and it was soon translated into French, German and English (see Lairesse 1738). Lairesse shared the widely held view that a person's inner emotions and personality are revealed through observable bodily movements. Painters must know, therefore, how to render these movements in a way that is as understandable as possible. He provides detailed instructions accompanied by drawings on how bodily motion should be represented, but he also includes observations on how education, background and social class can affect behaviour. These observations should be included in any painting, for people reveal their identity and background not only through their clothes but also through their postures and the way in which they handle objects. He provides detailed drawings which illustrate, for instance, the different ways in which a cup or a spoon may be held at table (Fig. 3.2A), and how these differences reveal differences in cultivation, upbringing or social class. He likewise provides drawings that illustrate the different ways in which the act of giving can be depicted and how these differences can depict the different attitudes on the part of the giver and the receiver, such as love, affection, pride, cowardice, respect, benevolence, generosity or gratefulness (Fig. 3.2B). Like Leonardo, he recommends that the aspiring artist should go about in public and observe and make notes on the ways in which people of different backgrounds and stations in life comport themselves.

Lairesse's book was very influential, making an important contribution to the development of what Alastair Smart (1965) has referred to as a "formal language of gesture" that was widely employed by painters in the eighteenth century. During this period an elaborate set of conventions developed as to how the various passions and emotions should be depicted and painters, who saw themselves as the exponents of an art that was a sister to literature (content was as important as form, and paintings told stories and depicted historical events), were urged to make their paintings "legible". Jonathan Richardson (cited by Smart), whose writings played an important role in moulding the taste of the period, at least in England, wrote that "painting is a sort of writing".

Besides Lairesse, the writings of Charles Lebrun were of great importance. Lebrun was active in Paris in the late seventeenth century, where he taught at the Royal Academy, and he became very well known for his treatise on

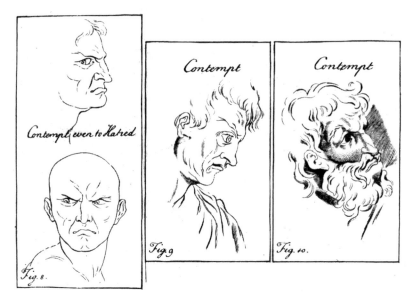

Fig. 3.3 'Contempt' from *A Method to learn to Design the Passions* by Charles Lebrun. From the London edition translated and engraved by John Williams, 1734

the representation of the passions. This book, published first in 1698 and translated into English in 1702, provides a series of descriptions of how the face comes to be organized for each of twenty-two passions, including Admiration, Veneration, Pure Love, Ecstasy, Contempt, Jealousy, Anger, Fear, and so on. His descriptions are detailed and accompanied by diagrams. Contempt, for example, "is expressed by the Eye brows knit and lowering towards the Nose, and at the other end very much elevated; the Eye very open, and the Pupil in the middle; the Nostrils drawing upwards; the Mouth shut, with the corners somewhat down, and the Under-Lip thrust out further than the Upper one" (Lebrun 1980, p. 29)[7] (Fig. 3.3). As Smart (1965) points out, while a skilled painter could arrive at convincing facial and bodily expressions on his own, if he had handbooks such as Lairesse and Lebrun to refer to he could much more readily make use of a shared set of conventions and thus his painting would be much more legible. Smart provides an interesting set of illustrations to show how quite different artists followed the same conventions in depicting veneration, all of them following the precepts of Lebrun and Lairesse.

[7] Taken from the translation of 1734 of Lebrun's book by John Williams, reprinted by the Augustan Reprint Society (Lebrun 1734 [1980]). Lebrun's attempt to establish descriptions for how the face is disposed for each of the different passions may be compared with the much later work of scientists, beginning with Darwin (1872) and extending to our own times in the work of Ekman (e.g. Ekman 1982), which has sought to establish the precise muscular bases for the facial expression of the emotions.

Especially interesting, also, is the relationship between the behaviour of actors on the stage and painting in this period. The famous London actor, David Garrick, came to be regarded as the greatest actor of his day in England for his performance of *Richard the Third* in 1741. Hogarth has portrayed him as he appears in a scene in which the king awakens from a horrifying dream, and in doing so appears to have followed lebrunian and lairessian conventions. Evidently, however, Hogarth's painting actually represents Garrick's performance. Garrick himself, thus, developed his performances according to conventions of expression that were also being followed in painting. That actors did learn from painting (and perhaps painters learned from actors) is evident from such books as Wilkes' *General View of the Stage* (1759) in which it is recommended that actors learn from "Poetry, Painting, Music and Oratory ... for there is an affinity between all the arts and they are mutually assistant to each other". [8]

Further developments in the art of gesture

Actors, thus, may have drawn from the language of painting to fashion their language of expression on the stage, but the language of expression used in painting was but a codification of good systematic observation. As we have seen, writers such as Lairesse recommended field observation. However, acting had its own traditions and it was not, of course, dictated by conventions in painting alone. Indeed, a painter such as Hogarth, especially in his famous moral series (such as *Marriage à la mode* or *The Rake's Progress*), also adopted conventions from the theatre. In the eighteenth century, however, a great interest in the development of a realistic and natural acting style developed, especially in France, but also elsewhere. What the actors did, and how, through their actions, they represented their feelings and relationships, became as important as the words they uttered, if not more so.

There developed in relation to acting a considerable body of doctrine concerning gesture which can be seen as constituting a highly articulated art of gesture. This was based on a well-established vocabulary of gestures which were well known to the educated public throughout Europe. This vocabulary of gestures included both small and subtle movements as well as grandly expressive forms. Whether used by orators or by actors on the stage, as well as in painting, they were regarded as playing a vital role in bringing the substance of what was being conveyed before the eyes of the spectators or audience

---

[8] Cited in Smart (1965). For a useful essay on the eighteenth-century idea of a language of the passions and the way in which this language, in different forms, is employed in poetry, painting, acting and music see Rogerson (1953).

in a concrete and visual form. Although, in this art of gesture, pantomime and descriptive gestures were not included, there was a very extensive set of gestures that were used to express in a detailed way a wide range of mental attitudes, social situations and also, in the case of orators, aspects of the structure of the discourse. In addition, extensive use was made of space. Explicit rules were formulated about where and how the actor or orator should direct his gestures so that their deictic effect could be exploited. The gestures and bodily postures employed in this art of gesture, although founded on natural expressions (or what were believed to be natural expressions), were consciously shaped by techniques designed to make them conform to aesthetic rules so that they would always be pictorially apt and pleasing, even when moments of great passion and pain, and even death, were being presented. A work of great importance for this is Johann Jakob Engel's *Ideen zu einer Mimik* (Berlin 1785-1786) which will be discussed in Chapter 6.

There was a close relationship between the gestural forms taught as part of oratory and those taught in acting. Indeed, as part of the training in rhetoric which had been a central component of education since the fifteenth century, the acting of plays - often the Latin comedies of Terence and Plautus - was considered an essential part of a basic education. Through this the pupils were to learn good pronunciation and good gestures, all a part of civility and manners. This ensured that these gestural techniques, at least among the educated classes, were carried into daily life. It made it possible for the techniques of acting and oratory to draw upon the shared understanding of gesture - an understanding shared across all of Europe, it should be added, so that, to a considerable degree, language differences were transcended. Furthermore, these techniques were used not only on the stage, in the pulpit, the courtroom and on ceremonial occasions of all kinds, but they also were used in the salons and thus became incorporated into the actions of everyday conversation (see Barnett 1987).

However, in this period, also, it was increasingly recognized that how one conducted oneself in conversation and in oratory was of great importance if one aspired to a position of influence in society. As Lord Chesterfield wrote (in 1729) in one of his famous Letters to his son: "A man can make no figure without it [i.e. eloquence], in Parliament or in the Church, or in the law; and even in common conversation, a man that has acquired an easy and habitual eloquence, who speaks properly and accurately, will have a great advantage over those who speak incorrectly or inelegantly...." (Chesterfield, Letter 45, November 1729; cited in Conley 1990, p. 212). This attitude, widespread in France as well as in England, led to a great demand for books that would teach eloquence or the art of speaking well, and this did indeed include much on gesture. Among the many books published in France was the *Traité de l'action de l'orateur*, a book attributed to Michel Le Faucheur and published in 1657, and which formed the basis of another important French book on oratory which concentrated mainly on gesture, Abbé Dinouart's *L'eloquence du corps dans le ministère de la chaire* of 1754. The book attributed to Le Faucheur was published in an English edition in 1727 as *The Art of Speaking in Publick: or an Essay on the Action of an Orator; as to his Pronunciation and Gesture.* It had great success there and its publication is seen as one of the key events that began what came to be known as the Elocutionary Movement, that inspired a number of works in English on how to speak well in public and which had considerable influence on English education in the latter half of the eighteenth century.[9]

Although Le Faucheur's book included much about gesture, the books that form part of the Elocutionary Movement in England that followed contained much less. At least, they evidently did not include as much about gesture as some teachers thought desirable. Thus it was that Gilbert Austin (1791-1813) was led to write his *Chironomia* in which he sought to provide rules for the use of gesture in delivery for clergymen, members of parliament and actors (Austin 1806 [1966]). His book is one of the clearest and most systematic treatises on gesture in the tradition we have been considering. Although it was published in 1806 it is very much an eighteenth century work. It is a systematic compendium of much that the Art of Gesture tradition embodied and is an excellent source for understanding the doctrines on gesture that had been developed within this. It contains some interesting insights into the way gesture and speech may be organized in relation to one another (these will be noted in Chapter 5). It also includes (and this is its most original aspect) what is possibly the first attempt to develop a formal notation for gesture - an attempt which is still well worth considering today and which has influenced the work of some contemporary scholars (for example La Mont West 1960, who developed a notation system in connection with his work on North American Indian sign languages, and also David McNeill 1992). Austin's book was very successful and proved highly influential in subsequent developments in the teaching of rhetoric, especially in the United States, where formal teaching of Delivery or Elocution persisted even into the beginning of the twentieth century. (See, for example, Bacon 1875, Adams 1891, Ott 1902, Mosher 1916, all works which are indebted to Austin.)

---

[9] See Angenot (1973) for French literature on rhetorical gesture of this period. For the English Elocutionary Movement see Conley (1990: 213-216) and references therein.

Gesture and the philosophy of language

As we saw above, Quintilian expressed the view that gesture forms a universal language. This idea does not appear to have been much discussed or questioned, indeed it appears to have been widely accepted, and when, in the fifteenth century, rhetoric began to be restored in its importance, as far as gesture was concerned, at first it was assumed that it could not be, indeed ought not to be, explicitly taught. It was supposed that it was best learnt by imitating those who were most skilled in its use. Such a view would be quite compatible with the idea that gesture is a universal language. Quintilian, however, (not surprisingly) did not agree. He writes (XI, III.11): "Those, however, who think it sufficient for men to be born to enable them to become orators are welcome to their opinion, and I must ask them to be indulgent to the efforts to which I am committed by my belief that we cannot hope to attain perfection unless nature is assisted by study." The treatises on gesture of the seventeenth and eighteenth centuries generally follow Quintilian on this point (as they do on most others). We noted Bulwer's view above, which is similar to that of Abbé Dinouart (1754) who distinguished "action of instinct" and "regulated action". He compared the one to an uncut diamond, the other to one that has been cut: nature and technique are conjoined, thus, to produce perfection (Angenot 1973). The gestures employed by orators, in other words, originate as natural expressions. What the teacher of gesture has to do is to discern those forms that are best suited to oratorical purpose and shape the natural to conform to this.

The idea that gesture is somehow more closely connected to 'nature' than spoken language and that it is a form of communication common to all mankind, widely believed as it was, recommended gesture to those philosophers of the eighteenth century who opened up the discussion on the question as to whether language could have a natural, rather than a divine origin. To many thinkers of the period it seemed that, in gesture, it might be possible to see how a form of symbolic communication might have begun and how the transition could have been made from 'natural' signs to the shared or 'instituted' signs that make up a language. If this could be understood then an understanding might be gained of how language itself came about, whose signs were recognized as arbitrary to such a large extent. Furthermore, it seemed that gesture, being natural, might offer a form of expression not yet distorted by the conventions of language. And because gesture was deemed to be natural, something that men did not really have to learn to do (they only had to learn to refine it), it was believed that its forms of expression must be common to all mankind and therefore it could form the basis for a universal form of language.

These themes came to dominate thinking about gesture in the eighteenth century and explain the interest that was taken in it. It should be added, however, that this interest focused very much upon the possibility that gesture could serve as a mode of expression independently of speech. With the exception of Bonifacio, noted above, notwithstanding the fact that treatises on the eloquence of the body dealt with how gesture should be used in relationship with spoken discourse, in the philosophical discussions of the time the contemporaneous relationship between gesture and speech was not what was focused upon (contrast this to the preoccupations in gesture studies today!). It was gesture as an autonomous medium of expression that was of interest. It was the possibility that, because it was 'natural' and so was somehow 'primitive' and could, in consequence, throw light on issues such as language origins and the nature of thought, that made gesture so attractive as an object of study and discussion.[10]

One of the first thinkers of importance in the eighteenth century to suggest that gesture might have been the earliest form of language was Giambattista Vico (1688-1744) of Naples. In his *Scienza nuova* ('New Science'), first published in 1725 and revised and brought out in a third and final edition in 1744 (see Vico 1984), he formulated a highly original view of the origin of language in which he saw gesture serving as the first form of linguistic expression. For him language had its origins, first of all, in the human capacity for imagination or *fantasia*. Through the *fantasia*, images were created which, at first, were transformed into actions that represented them - these mimetic actions were either gestural or they were inscribed in sand or on rock or on some other surface - and it was only later that a connection was established between visual signs and aural forms, which then could become the beginnings of words. The further process, by which visual representations of the images created by the *fantasia* came to serve also as signs for more general concepts or for other things than just themselves, came about through metaphor. Vico saw the linguistic sign as being derived by processes of metaphorical extension from representations of images created by the imagination that were primarily visual. These representations were either gestures or inscriptions. In the beginning, on his view, humans were mute, and communicated by gesture, not by speech.

Vico's book did not, at the time it was written, attain much recognition, and indeed his views on language and its origins have received more than passing attention only quite recently (see Danesi 1996). Of greater importance for the debates about language origins in the eighteenth century and, because of the role of gesture in this, in consequence of greater importance for the subsequent development of gesture studies, was the work of Etienne Bonnot de Condillac

---

[10] For a history of theories of language origins, especially of the gesture theory, see Hewes (1978).

(1715-1780), who put forward a detailed model for understanding the origin of language in his *Essai sur l'origine des conaissances humaines* ('Essay on the Origin of Human Knowledge') which was first published in 1746 (Condillac 1971 is the Thomas Nugent translation relied on here, and see Wells 1987).

In this book, Condillac stated that the origin of language could be understood if we could understand the way in which instituted signs came to be established. To account for this, Condillac invited his readers to engage in a thought-experiment: "Suppose that some time after the deluge two children, one male the other female, wandered about in the deserts, before they understood the use of any sign" (p. 169). He suggests that these two, once they came to live together, would by instinct, at first, recognize each other's natural expressions and, as a result, assist one another. However, each would come to recognize each other's cries and actions, first as accidental signs of need but then, once they could learn to produce them voluntarily, and thus call out in the other some desired response, they would gradually come to serve as shared signs and therefore as instituted signs.

Condillac thus suggested that language first began to emerge as a kind of institutionalization of cries prompted by emotions combined with the bodily actions that are executed in times of need in attempts to satisfy those needs. He supposed that once natural gestures could be produced voluntarily and so become transformed into instituted signs, it would come to be realized that vocal sounds could serve as instituted signs just as well as conventionalized bodily gestures. Indeed, they would be more convenient. In this way the use of vocalization in language would develop and thus the development of speech would come about. However, Condillac recognized that the transition from the language of action to spoken language was never abrupt and that for a long time the two modes of expression were intermixed. Gesture, for him, thus, is of great interest because it is related to the first form of linguistic expression. It is also easier, more direct, and more arousing than speech. It deserves study because of what it may teach us about forms of expression before spoken language.

A somewhat different way in which gesture could be seen as being interesting for philosophers was raised by Denis Diderot (1713-1784). Diderot, who was a member of the same circle of philosophers as Condillac, was the leading figure behind the famous *Encyclopédie* of which he was also general director, a publication which played a crucial role in the dissemination of the philosophical ideas of the French Enlightenment. He wrote plays, novels and literary criticism, but he also wrote two famous philosophical *Lettres* in which, very much in the spirit of the sensationalist philosophy of the time, he examined the question of what possible knowledge a person could have, were he deprived of one or other of his major senses. Thus, in 1749 he published his

Lettre sur les aveugles ('Letter on the Blind') and his *Lettre sur les sourds et muets* ('Letter on the Deaf and Dumb') in 1751 (see Diderot 1916 [1751]). This last is the publication of interest here. In it he explored the issue of what kind of thinking would be possible and whether any sort of language would be possible in someone deprived of the ability to hear. In this *Lettre* he expressed the view that, by the study of the expressions of those born deaf, we might come to apprehend the original nature of language. Diderot supposed that the linear nature of spoken language imposed constraints on expression and he argued that the structure that thought appeared to have, as this might be inferred from its verbally expressed forms, as much reflected the structure of the particular language employed as it did that of thought itself. He recognized that languages differed in the way in which words were ordered in sentences and that this was a matter of convention or tradition and did not necessarily reflect the way in which ideas occur to someone. If we were to analyse the gestural expressions of one who was born deaf, however, we would be able to find out what the natural or original order of expression might be. Thus he says: "a man born deaf and dumb has no prejudices with regard to the manner of communicating his thoughts. Consider that inversions [i.e. word order conventions] have not passed into his language from another, and that if he uses them it is nature alone which suggests their use" (Diderot 1916 [1751], pp. 166-167).

Diderot took a great deal of interest in the differences between the expressive capabilities of spoken language and gesture. He recognized that there may be considerable difficulties in the way of a complete translation between the two media. He maintains that "there are gestures so sublime that the noblest eloquence can never translate them" (p. 167). He appears to suggest that gesture may provide a more direct, less artificial means for the expression of thought. These ideas were closely connected with contemporary developments in theatre, in which an altogether more natural style of acting was coming into fashion in which the idea that a play should be visually interesting rather than a mere recitation of elegant verse was being developed. This, inevitably, meant that much greater interest was being taken in the expressive power of gesture.

Gesture, the deaf and the basis for a universal language

These philosophical concerns provided a climate in which the sign language of the deaf came to be seen to be of very great interest. The gestures employed by the deaf could be viewed legitimately as *signs*, that is, as vehicles conveying concepts directly. This meant that the deaf could be appreciated as having at least the potential of normal human intelligence, that communication would be possible if one learnt their language and that, once this communication was established, they could be educated (see Siegel 1969).

This was the approach taken by Abbé Charles-Michel de l'Epée (1712-1789) in his pioneering work with the use of sign language in the education of the deaf. In this work (first published in 1776)[11] he developed a method of teaching the deaf French, but he taught them French through the medium of manual signs, not by trying to get them to speak. His interest, in the first place, was to be able to teach the deaf to reason clearly and to bring order to their ideas. He set no store on teaching them to speak for he realized that their natural mode of expression, that of gesture, constituted a system of linguistic signs for them. What he set out to do was to help the deaf develop their own system of signs so that they could think and reason and entertain abstract ideas.

He took as his starting point the gestural system of communication the deaf in his charge had already developed and his first step was to learn it himself. He then set about teaching them French by developing manual signs for French words and grammatical forms from signs already in use by the deaf, following procedures of semiotic extension and systematization.

For example, he noticed that the deaf he was working with tended to toss the hand backwards over the shoulder several times, if they wanted to indicate something was in the past. So a backward movement of the hand became established as a marker for the past tense - two backward movements for the perfect tense, three for the pluperfect. Likewise, to establish signs for the French articles *un* and *une* he used signs the deaf already used to stand for 'man' and 'woman'. Sometimes it was not possible to find a sign in the existing deaf vocabulary that could correspond to a French word, however. In this case de l'Epée attempted to analyse the idea behind the word in question into what appeared to him to be its components for which signs could be found. Thus he analysed 'believe' into the ideas of 'know' plus 'feel' plus 'say' plus 'not see'. The combination of signs so produced could then be correlated with the written version of the French word.

As de l'Epée himself made clear, in this approach complex and abstract ideas were to be analysed into their concrete parts. They were to be anchored, that is, in bodily and sensory experience and expressed through signs that gained their meaning through a natural connection with these actions and

---

[11] Abbé C.-M. de l'Epée (1776). *Institutions des sourds-et-muets par la voie des signes méthodiques. Ouvrage qui contient le Projet d'une Langue Universelle, par l'entremise des Signes naturelles, assujettis à une Méthode* (Education of the Deaf and Dumb by means of Methodical Signs; Work here includes the project for a Universal Language through the medium of Natural Signs, organized by a Method), Paris: Nyon.

sensations. He believed that, in this way, through various combinations of these simpler signs, all manner of complex ideas could be conveyed. He claimed this approach would both simplify the language and lead to much greater clarity and precision in the representation of ideas. He argued, further, that the gesture language so created would be superior to any spoken language and could serve as a systematic universal language.

De l'Epée's successor, the Abbé Roch-Ambroise Cucurron de Sicard (1742-1822), also was an enthusiastic proponent of the idea that the system of gesture signs developed for teaching the deaf could form the basis for a universal language. For example, he wrote in his *Cours d'instruction d'un sourd-muet de naissance* (1799) that the system of signs he proposed "can fulfil the hopes of those who, for so long, had desired a general means of communication, independent of all articulated languages".[12]

The idea that the language of gesture signs, as developed by de l'Epée and Sicard, could form the basis of a universal language was critically examined by Joseph Marie de Gérando (or Degérando) (1772-1842) in his *Des signes et de l'art de penser* (1800). He pointed out that the complex sequences of elementary signs that were needed to express abstract ideas were much too cumbersome. They were abbreviated for everyday use and as this happened they lost whatever tie they might have had to natural expressions and became, in fact, signs whose meanings were established by convention. He further pointed out that even signs that had an apparently natural tie to what they expressed when used in France might well be interpreted and used quite differently somewhere else. They could not, thus, be used everywhere and be universally understood (for a full discussion see Knowlson 1965).

This criticism of the idea that a *methodical* sign language, such as developed by de l'Epée and Sicard, could serve as a basis for a universal language did not deter the idea that gestural expression was more natural than spoken expression. It continued to be believed that the study of gesture could throw light on universal features of human expression and this certainly inspired travellers, missionaries and explorers with an ethnographic interest to describe the use of gestures among the 'uncivilized' races whose lands and customs were being documented ever more thoroughly. De Gérando himself, in his *Considerations of the Methods to follow in the Observations of Savage Peoples* of 1799, published as a contribution to the Society for the Observers of Man (the first ethnographic society), urged the necessity of learning the language of the savage peoples that were to be observed. To do this, he said, one should begin with the 'language of action' and one should make careful observations on the gestures used, for it would be through this that one could progress to an acquisition of the spoken language (see Stocking 1982).

---

[12] Translation (by AK) of a quotation from p. 496 of Sicard's *Cours*, given on p. 506 in Knowlson (1965).

Conclusion

Gesture first becomes a topic of discussion in relation to how it is to be used as a part of Delivery, that is as a part of the performance of a public speaker. The importance of gesture as a component of acting was, of course, well known in Ancient Greece and Rome, but little in the way of any account of this survives. Since oratory was an essential part of the studies of any well-educated Roman, however, perhaps it is not so surprising that doctrines concerning it should have been developed which could be used by teachers in formal instruction. It is in this context that the first systematic discussions of gesture are to be found. While, in Quintilian, a good deal of space is devoted to Delivery with an accordingly quite lengthy discussion of gesture, throughout the Middle Ages this aspect of rhetoric was given little attention. It was only following the discovery of the complete text of Quintilian's work and the discovery of further rhetorical works by Cicero that a new view of rhetoric began to develop. This gave rise to a renewed interest in the idea that the educated person should enter more fully into the political arena so, in consequence, skill in Delivery came to have a greater importance. The development of the role of the priest as a teacher and preacher over and above his role as master of ceremonies in religious rituals also promoted a new interest in the skills of Delivery. Gesture, as a part of Delivery, thus became an object of interest. In addition, perhaps as a consequence of the spread of mercantilism, with the development of the possibility of people from outside the aristocracy coming to play a role in the court, there developed toward the end of the sixteenth century an interest in the idea that one could control and manage one's comportment to achieve social and political ends. This also contributed to a new consciousness of the nature of everyday behaviour and its communicative significance.

The beginning of the seventeenth century saw the publication of a number of books which dealt extensively with gesture. In this chapter we have described two from this period. Then, after noting the interest in gesture that was also developing among painters and actors, we discussed the further development of the treatment of gesture as a part of rhetoric that continued into the eighteenth century and how the idea of acquiring good style in public speaking and in conversation came to be widely diffused on the continent of Europe as well as in England. This was a further stimulus to the production of books on eloquence which included treatments of gesture.

Other themes were also present, however, such as the idea of gesture as a universal form of human expression which could form the basis of a universal language. By the eighteenth century, one of the central issues of debate came to be the possibility that language could be accounted for in natural terms, without divine intervention. This led to a profound exploration of the nature of language, of signs and of the nature of thought and understanding (see Stam 1976). Because gesture was seen as a means by which thoughts could be expressed but which, at the same time, appeared to be natural and universal, it offered itself as a starting point for the development of a model for understanding how a system of signs could have been established and come to form a language.

Condillac, as we saw, was the first to try to develop these ideas in detail and his *Essai*, which had great influence over the whole debate, made his notion of 'language of action' central to the process by which a language could arise. Because of this, gesture came to be seen as an object of high philosophical interest. Diderot raised the question of how thought would be possible through a language of gestural signs alone and this, somewhat later, made possible the work of de l'Epée and his successor Sicard on the nature of the sign languages used by the deaf and the possibility that these languages could form the basis of a universal language. This also showed how important it would be to collect information on the gestural expressions of non-European peoples, especially the 'savages' of the New World. Accordingly, observations on gesture had an important place in the programme of anthropological observation formulated by de Gérando and others at the very end of the century.

These themes - the universal and primitive nature of gesture, the possibility that it can form a sort of bridge to the arbitrary forms of spoken language and so play a crucial role in theories about language origins, and the significance of sign languages for the understanding of the relationship between thought and language - continued to inform the study of gesture in the nineteenth century. However, the expansion of anthropological and archaeological knowledge, the development of historical linguistic science, and the rise of evolutionism, led to some changes in emphasis in the study of gesture, as we shall see in the next chapter.

4 Four contributions from the nineteenth century: Andrea de Jorio, Edward Tylor, Garrick Mallery and Wilhelm Wundt

In the course of the nineteenth century several important works on gesture were published. In this chapter we look at four of these: Andrea de Jorio's treatise on Neapolitan gesture, published in 1832; the treatment of gesture in the work of Edward Tylor, published in 1865; Garrick Mallery's work on gesture inspired by what he had learned of sign languages in use among the Plains Indians of North America, published in 1880; and Wilhelm Wundt's analysis of gesture in relation to the emergence of spoken language, which first appeared in 1901. De Jorio's book is notable both because it is probably the first ethnographic study ever to be published which describes the forms and functions of gesture within a particular community - that of Naples - and also because it is one of the earliest books in which ethnography is used in relation to archaeology. Tylor shows how the study of gesture can throw light on the processes that underlie the development of symbolic communication, whether in gesture, picture-writing or spoken language. Tylor, Mallery and Wundt each make significant advances in the understanding of sign languages, in some respects anticipating discoveries that were not to be made until the second half of the twentieth century. In Mallery's work we not only have detailed observations on sign language as used among the Plains Indians of North America, we also have a wide ranging survey of what was then known of the phenomena of gestural expression in general. Wundt, likewise, makes theoretical advances in the study of gesture, in particular in respect to the development of a semiotic classification of gestures.

As will be clear, especially in the work of Tylor, in these nineteenth century contributions there are continuities with the interests of the previous century, such as the question of the possible universal character of gesture as a form of expression, questions about the relationship between gesture and spoken language and whether gesture, as a form of language, could have preceded speech in the course of human history. There are also new perspectives, however, due to developments in archaeology, geology and prehistory. First of all, the archaeological discoveries at the buried Vesuvian cities of Herculaneum and Pompeii, that began to be widely known in the last decades of the eighteenth century, had a profound impact on how the ancient Romans were perceived (Pucci 1993). Because daily life in Pompeii was shown, through these archaeological discoveries, to have much in common with the daily life of modern common people living in the same area, there developed the idea that the practices and customs of the people of the popular classes preserved those of antiquity. This played an important role in the development of the study of folklore in Europe. In the work of Andrea de Jorio, so far as the study of gesture was concerned, it led to the development of an ethnographic approach to the subject. Developments in geology and prehistory, from the middle of the century onwards, led to a revision in the way human history was thought of - it became apparent that the human race was of much greater antiquity than had hitherto been imagined. While the revision in thinking that this led to had no direct consequences for gesture studies it did, nevertheless, alter the general framework in terms of which human culture was understood and it made possible the idea of cultural evolution with the concomitant view that the various 'savage' societies that were becoming increasingly known, represented earlier stages in human cultural evolution. This, in turn, altered the framework within which observations on gesture use in 'savage' societies were interpreted.

From 1859 onwards, following the publication of Darwin's *Origin of Species*, the way humans were thought of in relation to other species changed radically. This did not have any immediate consequences for the study of gesture, however. Darwin's work and influence are not to be found in Tylor's work (published in 1865) in which, in any case, he was not concerned with human origins but with the development of human cultures and the implications of this for the idea of human psychic unity. Mallery makes no explicit reference to Darwin, although he does devote a brief part of his discussion to the relation of human gestures to animal gestures and shows, in other ways, that Darwinian thinking had an influence on him. Wundt sought to establish continuities between language and basic expressive movements, as mediated by gesture. He relied upon the idea of continuities between humans and animals but he did not adopt explicitly Darwinian concepts regarding the mechanisms of the evolutionary process.

Darwin himself had little to say about gesture. In his discussions of language, (in *The Descent of Man* of 1871, Vol. I, pp. 53-62), although he mentions the auxiliary role of gesture in the early development of language, he concentrates mostly on the vocal character of language and argues that man used his voice for speaking since to use his hands would have been inconvenient. His publication *On the Expression of the Emotions in Man and Animals* of 1872, though of immense importance for the later study of communicative behaviour in both humans and animals, was not directly pertinent to the study of gesture. In the nineteenth century, thus, Darwin had little direct bearing on the development of gesture studies. With the possible exception of Wundt, we cannot find much in the way of a Darwinian presence in this field until, in the latter half of the twentieth century, the question of language origins was re-opened.

Andrea de Jorio (1769-1851)

Andrea de Jorio's *La mimica degli antichi investigata nel gestire napoletano* ('Gestural expression of the ancients in the light of Neapolitan gesturing') was published in Naples in October 1832. As its title suggests, the aim of the book was to show that an understanding of modern Neapolitan gesturing could be useful in interpreting the representations found in the ancient mosaics, frescoes, vases and statues of classical times, especially those that had been excavated from Herculaneum and Pompeii, the cities adjacent to Naples that had been buried by an eruption of Vesuvius in AD 79. Because de Jorio believed that the everyday gestural expressions of the common Neapolitans had been maintained through cultural inheritance from the gestural practices of the ancient Greco-Roman inhabitants of that city, he thought that an understanding of them would be of value for the work of archaeologists in that area. Accordingly, the book contains extensive descriptions of the gestures in use in Naples in de Jorio's day, together with much information about the contexts in which they were used and their significance. Such a descriptive study of the gestural practices of a particular people had not been undertaken before and this ethnographic character of the book is one of its most original features. Although the value of the work as a handbook for the interpretation of ancient monuments is not now generally accepted, as an ethnography of gesture and as a commentary on various methodological and semiotic issues in the study of gesture the book still has much to offer.

De Jorio's book attracted attention when it was published, and went on to become quite widely known, retaining, to this day, its reputation as a classic in the field. Modern discussions include Gadeau (1986), Magli (1986), Haskell (1993), Kendon (1995), Carabelli (1996) and Schnapp (2000). The English edition prepared by Kendon (de Jorio 2000) includes a lengthy Introduction with details of de Jorio's life and archaeological work, as well as a close study of *La mimica*.

Andrea Vincenzo de Jorio was born in 1769 on the island of Procida, in the Bay of Naples, into a family distinguished in both jurisprudence and the Church. He died in Naples in 1851. Early in his youth he decided to dedicate himself to the Church. He was ordained as a priest and went on to be appointed as a Canon of the Cathedral of Naples in 1805. However, he also took up archaeology at quite an early age. He became well known in antiquarian circles and established a noteworthy private collection. His first archaeological work, a study of a Greco-Cumaean tomb, was published in 1810 and in 1811 he was appointed Curator of Fictile Vases at what was then known as the *Real Museo* or Royal Museum (subsequently the *Real Museo Borbonico* and, since

1861, the *Museo Archeologico Nazionale di Napoli*). Thereafter, de Jorio was quite active as an archaeologist and by 1839 he had published fifteen books, including works on archaeological method, detailed surveys of the finds at Herculaneum and Pompeii, studies of the so-called Temple of Serapis at Pozzuoli, the system of aqueducts at Pompeii, and several guides to the Museum and to sites of archaeological interest in Naples and Pozzuoli.

Through these archaeological works, de Jorio established himself as a meticulously observant scholar. He insisted on the importance of examining original finds directly and of undertaking archaeological studies in the field, an approach new at the time, when scientific archaeology had not yet fully emerged. He also took a great interest in the customs and practices of his contemporary Neapolitans. He believed that the common people of Naples preserved in their beliefs and practices and their modes of expression many of the characteristics of their ancient ancestors and that an understanding of them could provide a key to the understanding of much that was being revealed through excavation. As he is reported to have said: "We must not ever forget that the ancients prayed, loved, played, drank and danced as we do. Therefore, in order to know well the customs of antiquity I have visited the workshops of our artisans, I have followed our washerwomen to the banks of the streams, our grape-gatherers in the vineyards, our fishermen on the sea, and so forth" (quoted by Doria in Dumas 1999, p. 174, trans. AK). Although folkloric studies in Naples and elsewhere in Italy were to become quite well known, these did not develop until after the middle of the nineteenth century (Cocchiara 1981). With his attention to contemporary popular custom and the ethnographic character of *La mimica* de Jorio was at least thirty years ahead of his time.

La mimica is organized in a series of sections of varying length. After an Introduction and a long section on method called the 'ABC of Gestures' one hundred and eight sections follow, each one of which discusses a different meaning or group of meanings and their gestural rendering. In an appendix, sixteen pictorial tableaux are presented (engraved from specially commissioned paintings by Gaetano Gigante), representing scenes from everyday life in Naples which show how many of the gestures described are used. Each picture has a commentary which describes the scene and discusses the uses of the gestures illustrated (see Fig. 4.1 for an example).

De Jorio insisted that gestures should always be studied in their contexts of use, for it is only in this way that we can understand what their meanings might be. He says that the meaning of a gesture can only be understood if it is taken in conjunction with the way the body as a whole is posed, the expression of the face, and how the glance is directed, and he adds that we must also be careful to observe how it fits within the conversation and with how people are reacting

Fig.4.1. Plate II from de Jorio's *La mimica* (1832). De Jorio's commentary on this plate may be summarized as follows: A young married woman is asking a public letter writer to write a letter for her to her absent husband. Her left hand is extended with the palm open, facing upwards, in a gesture of request, her right hand is placed over her heart, thus declaring the letter must be about love. The forward position of her head, the intensity of her gaze and facial expression, show the intensity of her feelings and that she demands the letter contain a request that these feelings be reciprocated. The letter-writer has turned to her and is asking, with some impatience, "What precisely should I write?" and as he does so he lifts his left hand up holding it with thumb and forefinger in contact using a gestural expression that, as de Jorio describes (see de Jorio 2000, p. 129, No. 4), serves in asking a precise question. To the left of the picture, meanwhile, we see another woman approaching the letter-writer's table. Perhaps she is the woman's sister. She lifts her left hand upwards above her shoulder, hand held with palm facing upwards and open, in a gesture that declares that what the young woman is asking the letter-writer to write is nonsense. Rather, as she indicates with the gesture for 'money' seen performed by her right hand, the young woman should be writing to her absent husband for money. De Jorio uses this tableau, as he uses the others he also commissioned, to illustrate some of the ways in which Neapolitans used gestures in the little dramas of everyday life. His commentaries often contain interesting information about contemporary Neapolitan customs and culture and serve to demonstrate his belief that a comprehension of the contexts of use of gestures is essential for their understanding.

to one another. It is only by studying them as they appear within situations of interaction that we can understand how they serve in communication. The pictorial tableaux and their accompanying commentaries were his attempt to show how this was to be done.

De Jorio is very careful in how he describes gestures. He repeatedly draws attention to how different gestures that share some features of movement or hand shape in common, nevertheless are in contrast with one another. He gives many examples to show how an alteration in hand orientation or a change in the manner or amplitude of movement can radically change meaning. For example, a gesture in which the index finger and middle finger are extended, then repeatedly separated and brought together, can be used to mean that two people are very close, for example that they are lovers. It is important, however, to perform this gesture with the palm of the hand facing downwards, for if oriented so as to face sideways, it means cutting something with scissors or, as a metaphor, 'gossip' (de Jorio 2000, p. 90, p. 392).

De Jorio explicitly mentions many such contrasts in orientation, movement, or other aspects of performance. Although he never expresses the more general notion, familiar to us today, that gestures may be described in terms of sets of contrasting features of hand shape, hand orientation, movement pattern and movement dynamics, it is clear that he does not think of each gesture as an isolated action, but sees that it is produced as an action always in contrast with other possible actions and can only be interpreted in the light of an understanding of this. He insists that all gestures have what he calls a "double aspect", that is, that they are at once both physical actions and meaningful acts (ibid., p. 31). Meaning and form are inseparable and for this reason one must pay the closest attention to the details of the physical execution of a gesture. However, such descriptions must be done to make clear how gestures contrast with one another as meaningful actions. Merely to give an account of how the body parts move would be insufficient.

De Jorio notes that, in gesture, in contrast to spoken language, there is a relationship between form and meaning. Gestures, he says, are the "imitation or similitude of an internal sentiment expressed with external action" (ibid., p. 374). Notwithstanding this, he recognizes that gestures are shaped by culture. He says: "The foreigner perhaps hearing the expression *Neapolitan Gesturing* will believe it is the same for all of the [Kingdom of] the Two Sicilies. How wrong he would be! Go, let us not say to Sicily, but simply to Puglia and one will see what other source of rich gesturing is to be met there in the particular dialect of those provinces" (ibid., p. 17, italics in the original). Seeking to limit the scope of his work, he states that he will be concerned "only with Neapolitan gesturing" (ibid.).

De Jorio says that gestural expression "is not a language" in the strict sense (ibid., p. 8), yet he recognizes that there are so many similarities that it is appropriate, in analysing it, to apply concepts derived from the study of spoken language. He shows the ways in which such grammatical features as person, number, comparison, tense and aspect may be expressed in gesture, and he discusses the ways in which gestures may be combined to form compounds and how they may be organized into syntactic relationships. He also discusses gesture in terms of the devices of rhetoric, such as metaphor, metonymy, synecdoche or irony, and thus shows how it may come to be part of a true discourse.

Although de Jorio says that he intends to concentrate mainly on what he calls "natural gestures", he recognizes, nevertheless, that natural and conventional forms overlap. He includes accounts of conventional forms as long as they are, in his judgement, widely shared in the population (ibid., p. 17). He includes many expressions that are, as he says, the natural consequences of some activity or attitude but many others which are highly conventionalized. He has been criticized for this (e.g. Cocchiara 1959, p. 262), but from a consideration of the way in which de Jorio orders his material and from many of his comments it seems clear that he was not confusing different classes of expression but was aware, rather, that between the natural and the conventional there can be no clear division.

This may be illustrated by considering the forms of expression provided in the section on *Attenzione* ('Attention'). De Jorio includes here an account of how a person shows attention by fixing his eyes on something, perhaps combining this with putting his head a little on one side, or holding the hands behind the back as he leans forward to inspect an object of interest. These expressions are best understood as overt manifestations of the process by which the eyes or ears are maintained in a constant and selective orientation to a particular source of stimulation. However, in the same section, he also describes actions that are stylized exaggerations of what a person does when he attends to something. For example, when something looked at is of particular interest, one opens one's eyes wide, pulling back the eyelids as far as one can. If one uses one's thumb and forefinger to do this, however, as de Jorio describes it, "one wishes to show that the eyes are too small to take in the supposed grandeur or elegance of something and hence the gesture becomes a burlesque" (de Jorio 2000, p. 103). Likewise, cupping the hand behind the ear is an action performed naturally by the hard of hearing, or by someone in circumstances where ambient noise makes it difficult to hear what another is saying. However, this same action can be used as a way of showing exaggerated or feigned attention to someone's speech. In this way it becomes a comment or a deliberate expression of an attitude rather than just an action that is instrumental in facilitating the reception of auditory signals. As de Jorio says, with this action one pretends "to give maximum attention to something that does not merit it" (ibid., pp. 102-103).

De Jorio not only recognized that conventionalized forms are related to natural forms of expression. He also explains how natural forms of expression of feeling could, in the right circumstances, come to be used as enactments which thereby do not so much express feelings, as *represent* them. He describes how such natural expressions of rage as biting one's finger or tearing the hair can also be used as a way of imitating another's rage, or in pretending to be angry, or in expressing anger in irony. Again, in his discussion of tiredness de Jorio says that one of the most important consequences of fatigue is that the body becomes immobile with the arms left hanging down. He says (ibid., p. 123): "so if one wishes to show that one is tired out, one inclines one's head a little and allows one's arms to drop down". Here what might be said to be the natural consequences of fatigue are shown to be used as a way of demonstrating one's exhaustion to another. This display is not used only when a person is *actually* fatigued, however. It is also used as a way of showing tiredness in a metaphorical sense. Elements from these symptoms may be used to show that one considers something boring or tiresome and, by extension, it may become a gesture by which one shows one's opinion of someone. By dropping the arms, letting the head fall to one side, and letting out a brief sigh "one can as well say 'Oh! What tedium! What a bore!' Or 'Oh that bore!'" (ibid., p. 123).

De Jorio remains to this day a rich source of information about different kinds of gestural expression. We can use his descriptions in drawing comparisons with gestures in use in Naples today and thus we can say something about the history of gestures in this part of the world. His book is also valuable as a source of ideas about the kinds of communicative and interactive circumstances that can lead to the development of gestural communication. We can glean much that is relevant for this from his commentaries and from the various anecdotes that he gives to illustrate gesture use elsewhere in the book. We shall return to this in a later chapter.

Edward Tylor (1832–1917)

Edward Tylor is regarded as one of the founders of what later came to be called cultural anthropology. In his first anthropological work, *Researches into the Early History of Mankind* (1865), he set out to explore, through various avenues, the underlying question of whether cultural similarities found in different parts of the world were to be accounted for by diffusion or by parallel processes arising because of the fundamental unity of the human mind. He concludes that it is through parallel invention that cultural similarities often arise and thus he maintained that, from the point of view of evolution, all the human races were of the same species. However, he believed that there was evidence for cultural evolution. He thought that there was evidence that there had been progress from simple to more complex technologies, however this progress had not been uniform - so that some cultures represented earlier stages in this evolutionary process than others.

His work was positioned, thus, in an evolutionary tradition and was informed by the idea of human progress. It was written against the immediate background of a conservative reaction to evolutionism that was current at the time, a rearguard action against Darwinian theory, that maintained that the rude and savage state of many peoples was a result of a degeneration, a falling away from the higher state in which man had been originally created by God (Stocking 1982 and Bohannan in Tylor 1964).

Tylor begins his book with a consideration of language. He states (p. 14) that "the power which man possesses of uttering his thoughts is one of the most essential elements of his civilization". He points out, however, that the word 'utterance' means to 'put outside' and that the power of uttering thoughts is the power to put thoughts outside by any means. He urges that we do not restrict utterance to speech but that we recognize that there are many different ways in which utterance, in this sense, can be achieved. He suggests that the "principal means" by which humans can express their thoughts, besides that of speech, are gesture-language, picture-writing and word-writing.

Gesture-language and picture-writing should have a special claim on our attention, however, because, though we can almost never understand how particular words have come to be used for the meanings they have, we can often see how a sign in gesture-language or an expression in picture-writing serves to represent its meaning. This being so, Tylor proposes that a study of gesture-language and picture-writing can provide us with an understanding of the processes that are fundamental to language formation. Tylor does not maintain that gesture-language was the first form of language. He says that this idea "has no support from facts" (*Researches,* p. 15). He does add that "it may be plausibly maintained, that in early stages of the development of language, while as yet the vocabulary was very rude and scanty, gesture had an importance as an element of expression, which in conditions of highly organized language it has lost" (ibid.). However, what he suggests is that the study of gesture-language will throw light upon the fundamental nature of language and so, indirectly, contribute to an illumination of the question of language origins.

Tylor then proceeds to give a detailed and sophisticated account of deaf signing, based partly on various published accounts, but also including information collected by himself from a German deaf signer who had been educated at the Berlin Institute for the Deaf and Dumb. Following this, he provides a brief survey of some other uses of sign, including sign language as used among the North American Indians, the Cistercian monks (who observed a vow of silence but used a sign language in situations where communication was unavoidable), oratorical gesture, gestures in acting and gestures of submission and greeting as these had been reported from various parts of the world. He considers in some detail the question of how the study of gestures can throw light upon the way in which the meanings of seemingly arbitrary signs comes to be established. In the last of his four language chapters he deals with picture-writing and its development into alphabetic writing, showing that there may be parallels here with the development from pictorial gesturing to arbitrary language forms.

In these four chapters Tylor seeks to establish five points. First, he argues that the detailed observations provided on sign language as used by the deaf (including personal testimonies from deaf people) is proof that linguistic communication is possible without speech. Second, from his review of American Indian sign language, deaf sign language, and the gesture systems used in everyday life, he concludes that not only do all humans make use of gesture as a mode of utterance, but that they do so in highly similar ways. The gestures of greeting and submission are highly similar from one part of the world to another; while in sign languages, whether those of the deaf or of the American Indians, the same classes of pantomimic and pointing signs are made use of; and there are examples of deaf persons who, using signs, were able to communicate with 'savages' from other nations, without any difficulty. For Tylor this means that, although gesture signs for specific things may differ from one group to another, the basic principles employed in the creation and use of such signs are the same. In this sense he claims that gesture-language is universal.

Tylor's third point is that the processes by which gesture signs come to be established as meaningful are the same as the processes by which words are established as meaningful. The arbitrary relationship between words and their meaning, which is so striking a feature of spoken language, can be understood as an outcome of a process that can also be seen at work in the development of signs in gesture-languages and picture-writing systems. He compares the derivation of signs, as described in the autobiography of Otto Freiderich Kruse, a deaf teacher of the deaf, with etymologies of words "in the Aryan languages" (p. 63). According to Kruse, to sign 'bird' one makes a gesture to show something that flies or to sign 'plant' you make a sign that refers to something that sprouts from the ground. In the same way, the roots of many Aryan words (so Tylor states) suggest that words for objects often originated as words that described actions. "Thus, the horse is the *neigher*; stone is what *stands,* is *stable*; water is that which *waves, undulates*; the mouse is the *stealer*, and age is what *goes on*; the oar is what *makes to go*; the serpent is *the creeper*, and so on. That is to say, the etymologies of these words lead us back to the actions of neighing, standing, waving, stealing, etc." (*Researches,* p. 63). Regardless of the medium in terms of which linguistic signs are being fashioned, thus, the principles that govern their formation remain the same.

The fourth point Tylor argues is that gesture-language and speech-language are less independent of one another than is often believed. He points out that the so-called uneducated deaf and dumb are reared in an environment of speakers. "And on the other hand, no child attains to speech independently of the gesture language, for it is in great measure by means of such gestures as pointing, nodding, and so forth, that language is first taught" (ibid., p. 64). He reviews the autobiographies of the deaf to show that, although they lacked speech, they yet had a means of expression that enabled them to think. He argues that observations made by Samuel Heinicke (a pioneer in teaching the deaf in Germany) and observations made of Laura Bridgman[1] show that the deaf invent regular mouth articulations which they use as if they were words. He also points out that the fact that deaf children can be taught to articulate, to use these taught articulations as words and also to use written language, shows that there is a bridge between the two modes of expression. He concludes (ibid., p. 74): "These two kinds of utterance are capable of being translated with more or less exactness into one another; and it seems more likely than not that there may be a similarity between the process by which the human mind first uttered itself in speech, and that by which the same mind utters itself in gestures." Thus he is arguing that gesture-language and spoken language are different expressions of the same underlying capacity.

Finally, in the chapter on picture-writing, Tylor is concerned to show that there are similarities between gesture-language and picture-writing, in the first place. In the second place, by pointing out what was then known about the evolution of Chinese writing, on the one hand, and the development from hieroglyphics to alphabetic writing on the other, we see another instance of the way in which arbitrary linguistic forms can evolve out of expressions that were originally pictorial. He suggests, thus, that the principles that govern picture-writing are like those that govern gesture-language, and so also the evolution of spoken language.

Tylor thus, through his study of gesture-language, demonstrated a number of important points. He found in the evidence of gesture-language a powerful argument for the existence of general psychological principles ruling the development of varying communicative signs. By showing that gestural

---

[1] Laura Dewey Bridgman (1829-1889) became deaf and blind at the age of two. She became famous as a result of the efforts of Samuel Howe, among others, who taught her to communicate by a tactile system of finger-spelling. See Freeberg (2001) for a recent account.

expression could indeed be linguistic and that it could be a vehicle of thought he was able to suggest how its study might throw light upon the nature of the capacity for language and to reveal something of the general principles by which languages have come about. In this way he is able to show the relevance of the study of gesture for a number of fundamental questions about human nature in general and language in particular.

Garrick Mallery (1831-1894)

Garrick Mallery was a colonel in the US army and Chief of the Signalling Division, involved in campaigns against the Indians in the West and, subsequently, in the administration of the Indian territories. The contact he had with Indians aroused his interest in them and he was eventually assigned to the US Bureau of Ethnology where, under the general direction of its Chief, J. C. Powell, he undertook to gather and organize as much information as he could on Plains Indian sign language and Indian picture-writing. The publication of interest here is his progress report on this project which was published by the Smithsonian Institute in Washington DC in 1881 under the title *Sign Language Among North American Indians Compared with that Among Other Peoples and Deaf Mutes*. This book, reprinted in 1972, remains one of the most thorough and comprehensive books on gesture ever written (Mallery 1972).

Mallery begins his report by reviewing the arguments that suggest that gesture preceded speech as the first form of language. He refers to the view, widely held in previous centuries and based on biblical arguments, that man must have had a spoken language from the first, since otherwise he could not be man, for he could not reason and entertain abstract thought without speech. This view gave rise to the search for the one primordial spoken language. However, as our knowledge of the vast range of different languages throughout the world expanded this became ever harder to sustain as a viable project. Mallery suggests, rather, that we may imagine that humans existed as such *before* they were capable of speech for, as he says, "some writers" have now conceded that "mental images or representations can be formed without any connection with sound, and may serve for thought, though not for expression" (Mallery 1972, p. 274). "It is certain", Mallery continues, "that concepts, however formed, can be expressed by other means than sound. One mode of this expression is by gesture..." (ibid.). He shows that gestures in what he calls the lower animals are more discriminating than their vocalizations; he says that gestures in babies are also more diverse and expressive than their vocalizations; and he cites the evidence of deaf mutes, referring in particular to the Abbé de l'Epée's success in teaching spoken languages such as French or Latin to the deaf by means of signs. He points out that these foreign languages were "obtained through the medium of signs" and argues that this is "conclusive proof that signs constitute a real language and one which admits of thought, for no one can learn a foreign language unless he had some language of his own, whether by descent or acquisition, by which it could be translated, and such translation into the new language could not even be commenced unless the mind had already been in action and intelligently using the original language for that purpose" (ibid., p. 277).

Mallery concludes that both voice and gesture must have been used from the beginning, but he appears to believe that gesture at first was probably more important. Whether gesture had an absolute priority or not, however, need not be decided. "It is enough to admit that the connection between [gesture and speech] was so early and intimate that gestures, in the wide sense... had a direct formative influence on many words; that they exhibit the earliest condition of the human mind; are traced from the remotest antiquity among all peoples possessing records; are generally present in the savage stage of evolution; survive agreeably in the scenic pantomime, and still adhere to the ordinary speech of civilized man by motions of the face, hands, head, and body, often involuntary, often purposely in illustration or for emphasis" (ibid., p. 285).

He adds, and it is important to note this, that "none of the signs to be described, even those of present world-wide prevalence, are presented as those of primitive man. Signs, as well as words, animals and plants have had their growth, development and change, their births and deaths, and their struggle for existence with survival of the fittest" (ibid., p. 285). Thus he does not regard the gestures of the Indians that he describes as being in any sense 'primitive'. Further, he rejects the idea that gesture and signing are necessarily elaborated as a kind of replacement for speech or that their greater use is an indication of a more primitive condition. He says, rather, "that a common use of gesture depends more upon the sociologic conditions of the speakers than upon the degree of copiousness of their oral speech" (ibid., p. 293).

The remainder of the report consists of a quite thorough and systematic survey of much that was then known about gesture. Mallery reviews the use of gesture among the Romans, both by their orators and in pantomime; he provides a useful summary of the work of Andrea de Jorio (until de Jorio 2000, his was the fullest account available in English), and briefly discusses the use of gesture by modern actors and orators. Then he turns to a lengthy discussion of what had been learned about the sign language of the Plains Indians. The report has appended to it as "Extracts from Dictionary" a partial list of the signs Mallery had collected. There then follows examples of dialogues and discourses, with some of these examples analysed for their syntax and compared with similar analyses of discourses by deaf signers.

The final part of the main report is entitled "Results sought in the study of sign language." Here Mallery summarizes what he sees as the main values of his research. First of all, a thorough understanding of the nature of gesture and sign language will improve the ease by which people may communicate with one another, as, for instance, Europeans with Indians. More important, however, is the light the study of Indian sign language will throw on our understanding of the nature of language generally. Like Tylor, Mallery believes that the processes that underlie the formation of signs are paralleled in the development of verbal meanings. He also thinks that an understanding of gesture may help us understand the beginnings of writing. For him, gesturing is just like picture-writing, except, of course, that the gestures are done in the air, and so fade, whereas gestures done in a graphic medium do not.

Mallery also summarizes the findings of several observers on the syntax of sign languages and provides a series of illustrations from his own observations of Plains Indian sign language. He describes how, in these languages, such operations as comparison, opposition, conjunction, preposition and interrogation are accomplished and how gender and tense are marked. These are compared with what has been observed in other sign languages and similarities are pointed out. He admits that his collection of examples of narratives, speeches and dialogues in Indian sign language "has not yet been sufficiently complete and exact" to allow firm conclusions to be drawn about syntax but, he says, "so far as studied it seems to be similar to that of deaf-mutes and to retain the characteristic of pantomimes in figuring first the principal idea and adding accessories successively in the order of importance, the ideographic expressions being in the ideologic order" (ibid., p. 363). He summarizes the views of Rémi Valade (1854), who had written a book on the grammar of sign language in which the 'sign talker' is compared to an artist, "grouping persons and things so as to show the relations between them, and the effect is that which is seen in a picture" (ibid., p. 360). He adds, however, that the artist can only present something as it appears in a single moment, whereas the signer "has the succession of time at his disposal, and his scenes move and act, are localized and animated, and their arrangement is therefore more varied and significant" (ibid.). He takes the view that this "pictorial" mode of expression was perhaps characteristic of spoken language in its "early infancy" and believes, thus, that the study of signing, whether of "deaf-mutes" or Plains Indians, can throw light on the "early mental processes in which the phrase or sentence originated" (ibid., p. 359).

He also thinks that the study of Plains Indian sign language will be a help in archaeological research, especially because, as he attempts to show, there is a relationship between the signs in this system and the pictographs the Indians use. However, he says that "[t]heir signs, as well as their myths and customs, form a part of the palaeontology of humanity to be studied in the history of the latter as the geologist, with similar object, studies the strata of the physical world" (ibid., p. 368). Thus, although he recognizes the sign language of the Plains Indians, like the other sign languages he refers to, as being fully languages, as we have seen, he yet does look upon them as being somehow closer to earlier forms of linguistic expression and thus as providing insights into the processes by which language came about.

Wilhelm Wundt (1832-1920)

Wilhelm Wundt is generally regarded as the founder of modern experimental psychology. Although there were others before him who undertook psychological experiments, in 1879, in Leipzig, Wundt opened the first laboratory officially designated for experimental psychology (Boring 1957). Wundt believed that psychological phenomena were to be studied in their own right but since he espoused a doctrine of psycho-physical parallelism, regarding psychological phenomena as autonomous and parallel to physiological phenomena and not caused by them, he could rely not just on introspection but also on observation and measurement of behaviour and physiological reactions as correlates of inner experience. He sought to describe the contents of experience in terms of the basic elements of sensation and feeling and in terms of an active, attentional process he termed *apperception*. He thought that it would be possible to explain the organization of mental experience in terms of certain basic laws which specified the regularities with which experience develops in time.

He worked in a highly systematic fashion, beginning with the study of sensation and feeling and proceeding with studies of apperception (or attention as we might call it today), and then undertaking the study of language which, he believed, would provide the best way to explore the more complex operations of the mind. After this, he undertook to study the realm of social phenomena, including magic and religion. His output is legendary. His bibliography runs to nearly 500 entries which, on the average, are upwards of 100 pages long. The last twenty years of his life were occupied by writing an immense treatise on *Völkerpsychologie* - really a kind of psychological anthropology - which covered a full range of topics, including magic, myth and religion. This treatise, which eventually extended to twenty volumes, begins with a discussion of language - this occupies the first volume of the book - and Wundt's discussion of gesture occupies the second chapter of this volume (see Wundt 1973).

Wundt sought to show how human language was an elaborate development from basic expressive movements. These are organized in a variety of patterns which are distinctive for the various affective states the individual experiences. Observed by others, these expressive patterns induce similar feelings, which themselves are similarly expressed. This is how feelings come to be shared and it is the basis for communication. However, such sharing of feeling through the commonality of expressive action is only the beginning. Because humans can conceptualize their experiences, their movements can become indicative of such conceptualizations. This is the basis for the development of bodily movements which have *conceptual* reference rather than simply affective import. Furthermore, by association, expressive movements can come to express not just conceptualized feelings but additional conceptions associated with them. One person's imitative responses to another's expressive movements become *answering* movements, not just imitations. For Wundt, thus, the movements of the body that are characteristic of emotional expression form the basis for bodily movements that can have conceptual expressive import as well. Thus gesture is the first form of language.

Wundt examined deaf sign language in considerable detail, as he encountered it in Leipzig (at Heinicke's institute for deaf-mutes) and elsewhere. He also reviewed the available material on American Indian sign language (drawing on Mallery), on Neapolitan gesture (from de Jorio's work) and Cistercian sign language. He suggested that the study of these gesture-languages could provide insight into the psychological processes which make language possible. He recognized that if one is to try to investigate the origins of words, one can never find their ultimate origin, for all words in contemporary languages are but descendants from words in earlier languages. The origins of gestures, on the other hand, can be fully grasped when their relationships with general principles of expressive movement can be understood. He suggests that, in gesture, we can see how the forms employed are derived from forms that had an immediate relationship to its meaning, and in this sense they can reveal to us the original nature of language. This view is very similar to the views of Tylor and Mallery discussed above.

Wundt offers a classification of the various forms of gesture based on principles that today we would call semiotic (see Chapter 6) and he discusses the various ways in which gestures in the gesture-languages he studied can serve as sign equivalents of parts of speech. There are signs for objects, signs for properties, signs for processes and signs for actions. Such classes of gesture are not always to be distinguished by the form they take. It often depends on how they are performed. For example, to express the verb 'lift' the palm may be repeatedly raised. Raising the palm slowly and with a strained expression, on the other hand, expresses the notion of weight or heaviness. 'Light' and 'lightness' can be expressed by a rapid upward lift done with quickness and ease. Likewise, to indicate 'tooth' one merely touches a tooth. To indicate whiteness one exposes all the teeth and sweeps the finger across them. To indicate the concept of hard, one taps one's tooth twice.[2]

Wundt then discusses the various ways in which the meanings of gestures can evolve. He suggests that whereas gestures that are indicative or descriptively mimetic retain their specific concrete meanings, gestures which have acquired symbolic meanings can develop many different meanings and thus show a high degree of ambiguity. For example, the Neapolitan gesture in which the index and little finger are extended with all other fingers bent inwards may originally have been derived from a representation of a bull's head with horns. However, it has acquired numerous different meanings. If it began as a representation of the bull as a symbol of dangerous power, it can from there come to represent a threat or a request to be protected from threat, and it may have come to be used as a gesture to indicate marital infidelity insofar as a man who has been cuckolded is said to grow horns. On the other hand, since there is nothing like a literary tradition in respect to gestures we cannot observe semantic change in gestures as we can in words. Further, because even a fully symbolic gesture is derived from a form that once was a concrete representation of some object or action, its concrete meaning tends not to disappear altogether when it is used, whereas the concrete meanings of words very often do.

Wundt then deals with the question of syntax, or the ordering of signs in signed sentences, both in deaf sign language and in the sign language of the North American Indians. He observes that there is no fixed order to the signs in signed sentences; nevertheless he argues that there is a *lawfulness* to the way in which signed sentences are constructed. To this extent sign language sentences are just as truly syntactical as spoken language sentences, although the principles may appear to be rather different. Wundt believed that in the development of a signed sentence the starting point is the sentence as a whole, the total configuration of the ideas to be expressed. The ordering of the gestures in the sentence as it is expressed is determined by those aspects that are most prominent or most determinate in the idea-configuration: these are placed first. Thus, if the idea to be conveyed is that it was an *apple* that the boy gave to his father, then *apple* would be signed first, followed by the agent, goal and action. On the other hand, if it was the *action of giving* that was most prominent, it might be this that would be placed first, and so on.

---

[2] These observations anticipate those of recent investigators (e.g. Supalla and Newport 1978) on the basis of which it is claimed that sign languages can have a highly complex inflected morphology.

His discussion concludes with a long section in which he argues that gestural communication, though a natural product of the development of expressive movements, is nevertheless subject to developmental processes that also are found in spoken language and it is, thus, a specifically human development and different from the gestural expressions found in animals.

Wundt thus sees gesture to be important as a phenomenon to be studied for the light it can throw on how language arose. For him, not only does he see gesture as having a direct derivation from expressive movements but he also believed (as did Tylor) that, in gesture, the process by which symbolic forms come to be established is 'transparent' in the way that it is not if we study the origins and development of words. Thus he writes: "If the etymology of speech must content itself with the investigation of original forms, it has to accept them as historically given and not as derived. For just this reason, then, they remain inexplicable. The etymology of a gesture, on the other hand, is indicated when its psychological meaning and its connection with the general principles of expressive movement is recognized" (Wundt 1973, p. 72). Later on he concludes that "gestural communication supplies a model example for the development of language, distinguished by the simplicity and clarity of its phenomena" (ibid., p. 149).

Conclusion

Taken together, the four works described in this chapter show that, by the end of the nineteenth century, a high level of understanding of the nature and significance of gesture had been reached. De Jorio's book is rich in its detail of description, its insights into the character of gesture as a medium of expression and in its suggestions regarding the role of gesture in everyday interaction. Tylor shows the value of the study of gesture for our understanding of the processes involved in the development of symbolic communication. Mallery's comprehensive review sets the stage for a sophisticated general view of gesture in its several different aspects. Wundt's work, as well as that of Tylor and Mallery, made significant advances in the understanding of the nature of sign language. Wundt also provided for a well articulated semiotic classification of the different kinds of gesture.

The theoretical outlook of each of the four works we have considered is different. Tylor, although he did not think of gestural expression as more primitive than spoken expression, believed that through its study one could more readily perceive the nature of the processes of symbol formation than one could by studying spoken language. Mallery seems to have had a similar view. However, he thought the Indians he studied represented an earlier form of human life. He states that "the North American Indians may be considered to be living representatives of prehistoric man" (Mallery 1972, p. 359). Accordingly, he is inclined to think expression in gesture reveals mental processes that are characteristic of an earlier stage of human mental evolution. Wundt clearly takes this point of view, for he saw gesture as a step along the way from elementary physiological reactions to fully evolved language.

De Jorio stands apart from these themes. He nowhere expresses the view that gesture is a more primitive form of expression than speech nor does he regard its study as worth undertaking for the light it might throw on general problems such as language origins or processes of symbol formation. Rather, he sees gestural expression simply as a component of Neapolitan culture and seeks to understand it just from this point of view. He seeks to demonstrate that the expressive practices of the Neapolitans are inherited directly from those of their ancestors. As Schnapp (2000, p. 165) has put it, for de Jorio the "Neapolitans are neither pagan nor savage but, quite simply, a people who enjoy a clear family relationship with the ancients". To this we might add that, for de Jorio, the ancients are like the moderns, they are ordinary human beings who lived as humans do today. Notions such as savagery versus civilization, ideas of degeneration or of progress seem absent from de Jorio's point of view. As Schnapp (p.166) also says, "de Jorio's austere work brought into being a new discipline: the anthropology of everyday life". This was something for which the nineteenth century, especially the post-Darwinian nineteenth century, was not yet ready. To this extent de Jorio was ahead of his time and this, in part, explains why his book did not have any real influence. To the extent that it was quoted, it was usually as a source of curious examples rather than anything else.

As the nineteenth century drew to a close there was a marked decline in the interest in gesture. Particularly striking was the turn against sign language, in spite of the respect and insights concerning this that Tylor, Mallery and Wundt displayed. Questions about the origin of language also fell into disrepute, at least among linguists, and this also led to a lack of interest in gesture. The kind of detailed ethnography of the communicative practices of everyday life that de Jorio's work suggested simply was not followed up. This decline in interest, and the reasons for it, as well as what brought about the eventual revival of interest in gesture which came about in the last decades of the twentieth century, will be the topics of the next chapter.

5   Gesture studies in the twentieth century: recession and return[1]

Recession and its causes

Tylor, Mallery and Wundt well represent the interest that was taken in gesture in the latter half of the nineteenth century and the kind of significance that was attached to its study. Following in their wake we find that many scholars in the period extending into the second decade of the twentieth century included gesture as part of their interests. H. Ling Roth (1889) published a long study of the gestures of greeting. Several of the pioneers of Australian anthropology, including Howitt (1890, 1904), W. E. Roth (1897), Spencer and Gillen (1899, 1904) and Carl Strehlow (see Strehlow 1978), paid considerable attention to the sign languages of the Australian Aborigines. Gestures and the use of sign language were among the topics studied by A. C. Haddon and his team on their expedition to the islands of the Torres Straits (Haddon 1907). There were also a number of publications on American Indian sign languages subsequent to Mallery's work, although it is notable that few of these are very substantial and few were written by professional linguists or anthropologists. Among linguists, following Wundt, gesture was, for a time, included as an important topic for discussion. For example, Leonard Bloomfield, in his first general book on language, published in 1914, in which he declares his devotion to Wundtian psychology, begins with a chapter on the origin of language. He devotes several pages to the exposition of Wundtian theory and includes, accordingly, a consideration of gesture which, like Wundt, he regards as especially instructive from the point of view of understanding how symbolic expression came about (Bloomfield 1983).

However, towards the end of this period, interest in gesture and sign languages receded markedly, at least in the English-speaking world. For example, in English, after 1900, apart from a few textbooks on rhetoric that appeared before 1915 and which included treatments of gesture, books that deal with gesture extensively include only *The Language of Gesture* by MacDonald Critchley (1939), David Efron's *Gesture and Environment* (1941) and Charlotte Wolff's *Psychology of Gesture* (1945). More than thirty years

---

[1] Some of the material in this chapter is based on Kendon (1982).

were to elapse before books on the subject again began to be published. A revised version of Critchley's book appeared in 1975 and Desmond Morris published *Manwatching* in 1977. This was a book that included a good deal about gesture. Then, in 1979, with three colleagues, Morris published *Gestures: Their Origins and Distribution.* Publications on this topic in scholarly journals are likewise very few in this period. Of the 2,342 references on "body movement and non-verbal communication" listed by Martha Davis in her two bibliographies, which span the years 1900 to 1981, there are only 62 entries listed that deal with gesture (Davis 1972, Davis and Skupien 1982). With regard to sign languages used among the deaf, although William Stokoe published his pioneering linguistic analysis of American Sign Language in 1960, further serious work on this topic was rather slow in following. As we see below, nearly ten years were to elapse before interest in his work spread beyond a small handful of people. The study of sign language did not begin its major expansion until after 1975.

Anthropological studies of gesture and tribal sign languages were likewise sparse. Thus there have been but two original scholarly publications on American Indian sign language since 1930, and until Farnell (1990), only one Ph.D. dissertation on the subject had been completed (West 1960). So far as Australian Aboriginal sign languages are concerned, between 1914 and 1954 there seems to have been only one publication, whereas before 1914 there had been several. It is remarkable that the author of this lone paper, Mervyn Meggitt, who wrote on Warlpiri sign language, felt himself compelled to defend his decision to write on the topic against charges that it might be of "dilettante rather than of scientific interest" (1954, p. 2). From then until 1988 (see Kendon 1988b) there were but three more publications on this topic.

What caused this decline in interest? The main reason seems to be that the theoretical issues for which the study of gesture and sign language had been relevant had ceased to be of importance. Gesture, as we have seen, was regarded by many thinkers as more 'natural' than speech and its study was thus linked to the question of the origin of language. However, a concern with this question, hotly discussed as it was through the eighteenth and much of the nineteenth centuries, had been dropped as a respectable topic by the beginning of the twentieth century. Indeed, it had even been officially prohibited by linguists by the latter half of the nineteenth century. In 1865 the Linguistic Society of Paris ruled all papers on language origins out of order. In 1872 the president of the Philological Society of London gave an address which likewise condemned all speculation on language origins as futile (Stam 1976). A move away from a concern with origins also occurred in anthropology. During the nineteenth century, under the influence of Darwin, it was considered entirely appropriate to interpret the new knowledge of primitive cultures then becoming available in evolutionary terms. However, by the beginning of the twentieth century, when structural-functional analyses of societies began to predominate and the doctrine of cultural relativism became established, the history of culture and society was given much less consideration and the idea that primitive cultures, so-called, might be representatives of an earlier stage in human evolution, was no longer accepted. Interest in gesture, therefore, could no longer be justified from an evolutionary or historical standpoint. It could still be considered from the standpoint of psychology or linguistics. However, these disciplines, also, did not develop in a way that was to be hospitable to the study of gesture, as will be explained below.

It is also important to note certain changes that occurred in the ideology of deaf education at the end of the nineteenth century, which led to the widespread abandonment of sign language as a medium of instruction and often to its complete prohibition in the classroom, and even the playground. Sign language came to be viewed as something less than a language and thus not worthy of serious attention. At the second International Congress of Instructors of the Deaf and Dumb, held in Milan in 1880 (Facchini 1983), it was argued very strongly that if the deaf could be taught to speak they could much more easily fit in with everyday life than they could if they could only use signs. This argument, combined with new methods based on a detailed analysis of processes of speech articulation which bore the prestige of high German science, was enough to ensure the passage of a resolution which declared "the incontestable superiority of speech over sign" and that, accordingly, "the method of articulation should have preference over that of signs" in the instruction and education of the deaf (Lane 1980, p. 155). Furthermore, the pure oral method was to be preferred because the use of signs simultaneously with speech was thought to distract the pupil's attention from the task of learning speech and lip-reading and it was also deemed injurious to the precision of ideas. Subsequently, national organizations in various European countries and the United States followed the Milan Congress and, except for a few centres, the use of signs in deaf education was abandoned and even prohibited.

Psychology, linguistics and the study of gesture to 1950

The developments in psychology that were unfavourable to the study of gesture were the emergence of behaviourism and the rise to prominence of psychoanalysis. Both developments emphasized the study of those aspects of behaviour that were beyond the conscious control of the individual. Behaviourism led to the investigation of processes that could be accommodated in terms of such apparently simple principles as the conditioned reflex, the law of effect, and reinforcement. The phenomena of higher mental processes, which could be accommodated only with difficulty in these terms, and this included language, were largely ignored (Edward Tolman was a notable exception, see Tolman 1948). Psychoanalysis emphasized the 'irrational' and the 'unconscious' and maintained that human behaviour is determined to an important degree by forces beyond the reach of conscious control. The psychoanalytic orientation encouraged an approach in which irrational unconscious processes were emphasized at the expense of a concern with processes of a seemingly more rational, conscious character. If gesture received attention, as it did occasionally (Krout 1935 and Wolff 1945 are examples), it did so for what it could indicate about underlying motivations or about the character or personality of individuals. More broadly, in psychology, although there was interest in the expressive aspects of behaviour (notable works during the period we are considering here include Allport and Vernon 1933 and the long series of studies on the expression of emotion in the face reviewed in Bruner and Tagiuri 1954), despite the work of Wundt, this interest rarely included an interest in gesture.

If gesture is too much a part of deliberate expression and too much governed by social convention for it to be of interest to psychologists, it might be considered a suitable object of study for linguists. Indeed, in view of the semiotic orientation to gesture, as we might describe it today, that informs so much of the work of de Jorio, Tylor, Mallery and Wundt, we might have expected some linguists to have developed an interest. A few in fact did so.

Linguistics as an autonomous discipline emerged in the first two decades of the twentieth century, separately in Europe and the United States (Robins 1967; Sampson 1980). For our present concern with the history of the study of gesture, it is the growth of linguistics in the United States that seems most relevant. Here what was known as 'structural linguistics' or 'descriptive linguistics' came to be dominant. This was developed in the first place largely through the work of Franz Boas and his pupil Edward Sapir, both of whom were cultural anthropologists as much as linguists. They sought to establish rigorous procedures by which the unknown and unwritten languages of the American Indians could be written down. The procedures that were developed provided a method for analysing spoken languages from the point of view of the speakers themselves. It is particularly to be noted that since, in undertaking these analyses, work had to be done with living speakers, rather than with texts, it became important to establish principles by which behaviour that was significant for the linguistic system was to be distinguished from other behaviour. This meant that the relationship between spoken language and other aspects of behaviour, whether vocal or gestural, which appeared to play a part in communication, had to be given some attention. Both Franz Boas and Edward Sapir accepted that gesture should be considered part of a broad patterning of communicative behaviour of which spoken language is another part, and they pointed out the role it may play in the process by which spoken utterances achieve their meaning.

Boas, at Columbia University, in the late 1930s encouraged one of his students, David Efron, to undertake a systematic comparative study of gesture. This was motivated in part by a desire to demonstrate the worthless nature of theories of racial inheritance that were, at that time, emanating from Nazi Germany and gesture was selected as a phenomenon to be studied because of its high visibility and because it had been claimed, by Nazi theorists and others, to be an inherited trait and a mark of racial character. Efron compared the gesturing styles of East European Jewish and Southern Italian immigrants in Manhattan. His study, published in 1941, remains one of the most important ethnographic studies of gesture (it is discussed further in Chapter 6 and Chapter 16). Efron made extensive observations in the field, including field recordings using sixteen millimetre film, which he subjected to intensive analysis. He showed beyond question that there are marked and striking differences between the gesturing styles of the two groups. However, he went on to compare the gesturing styles of the Americanized descendants of these two groups and showed that the more completely assimilated they were the less different were their gesturing styles. This was taken as a conclusive demonstration that the use of gesture is a matter of cultural tradition, and not a matter of racial inheritance.

Edward Sapir (1951[1927]), for his part, had written of how "The unwritten code of gestured messages and responses, is the anonymous work of an elaborate social tradition" (p. 556). He said of this code that "it is by no means referable to simple organic responses. On the contrary, it is as finely certain and artificial, as definitely a creation of social tradition, as language or religion or industrial technology" (ibid.). Although Sapir did not himself do any studies of gesture, and although he had no students who did so, his approach left open the possibility that its study could be included as part of a broader linguistic-like analysis of culture.

On the whole, however, as the techniques of linguistic analysis developed, the interest of linguists tended to become more specialized and more abstract. In particular there was a sustained effort to free linguistics from any dependence on psychology. It was to be firmly established as a discipline in its own right. This was given particular emphasis by Leonard Bloomfield. Whereas, as we noted above, in his first book he had sought to ground linguistics in Wundtian psychology, when he came to publish his second (and more famous) book, in 1933, he declared that "we can pursue the study of language without reference to any one psychological doctrine, and that to do so safeguards our results and makes them more significant to workers in related fields" (Bloomfield 1933, p. vii). Although, in his 1933 book, he refers to gesture, he writes of it almost dismissively, as if it held little of interest. He pointed out that gesture accompanies all speech and that "to a large extent it is governed by social convention", but he adds that "most gestures scarcely go beyond an obvious pointing and picturing" and that "even where gestures are symbolic, they go little beyond the obvious". In regard to gesture-languages, he remarks that "these are merely developments of ordinary gestures and that any and all complicated or not immediately intelligible gestures are based on the conventions of ordinary speech". (All quotations from p. 39.) These comments probably had a dampening effect and most writers on linguistics appear to have followed him in not regarding gesture as worth serious study. As Dwight Bolinger (1946) has put it, gesture has seemed unattractive as a branch of inquiry essential to linguistics, above all because it seems that gesture is only partly governed by convention. Linguists, Bolinger suggests, have, on the whole, been devoted to the notion that phenomena are linguistic only if they are "precisely analogous to the ordinary morphemes, long since freed of their instinctive ties" (p. 95). They have sought to divest themselves of any responsibility for investigating anything that does not fit such a narrow mould.

Bolinger himself, however, maintained that the notion of 'language' as an object of study by linguists is an arbitrary, although convenient abstraction. He said that we should not insist upon what this abstraction excludes before the full implications of phenomena that accompany language, such as gesture, are fully understood. Likewise, Kenneth Pike (1967) has insisted that "language ... must not be treated in essence as structurally divorced from the structure of nonverbal human activity .... Verbal and nonverbal activity is a unified whole, and theory and methodology should be organized or created to treat it as such" (p. 26). Similarly, Zellig Harris (1951) has suggested that the boundaries between the linguistic and the non-linguistic are to be drawn only at the point where it is no longer possible to apply the methods of contrastive analysis. Until gestures have been systematically studied by these methods, therefore, it must remain an open question as to just what their relationship to spoken language may be.

Edward Trager, at one time associated with Edward Sapir, in developing his work on what he called 'paralanguage' (Trager 1958) is one of the linguists of this period who actually attempted to extend the boundaries of the linguist's concern beyond the study of the purely segmental aspects of speech (another was Norman McQuown, see McQuown 1957). In this work he sought to show how the methods of structural linguistics could be applied to such things as intonation, voice quality, and the non-articulate sounds which speakers sometimes employ in spoken utterance (so-called 'vocal segregates'). This was part of a much more ambitious programme, however. In collaboration with the anthropologist Edward Hall, Trager sought to develop the idea that communication comprised a complex of structured codes in the modalities of voice, body motion, spatial patterning and even the use of physical objects and the physical environment (see Hall and Trager 1953; Hall, 1959).

Trager's work provided much of the inspiration for Ray Birdwhistell, whose project for 'kinesics' constituted the most ambitious and explicit attempt to extend the methods of structural linguistics beyond the boundaries of spoken utterance. Birdwhistell (1952, 1970) coined the term 'kinesics' to suggest a discipline to parallel linguistics, which would be concerned with the analysis of visible bodily motion and which would include, it may be presumed, the phenomena of gesture. His work has been widely quoted and there is no doubt that, in drawing attention to the possibility of a systematic study of body motion as an organized language-like code, he encouraged a number of people to take up the study of gesture (Kendon and Sigman 1996). Birdwhistell himself appears to have felt, however, that the more complex kinds of gesture and gesticulation could not be dealt with by the methods of analysis he was proposing. Thus he wrote of these: "At the moment I am inclined to regard such behavior as examples of derived communication systems. As such, they are not the primary subject matter of kinesics at the present" (1970, p. 126).

It is possible that the programme that Trager, Birdwhistell and others were proposing might have got under way, and so might have brought about a body of systematic work that would have provided a place in linguistics for the study of gesture, had it not been for the redirection of interest of many in linguistics and related disciplines brought about by the work of Noam Chomsky (from 1957 onwards). Chomsky's work in linguistics emphasized the analysis of linguistic competence over the study of language as observable through acts of speaking. He directed attention to the inner mental apparatus that was proposed as responsible for the existence of any language whatsoever and gesture, in any case not being integrated into the concerns of most linguists, was consigned, along with much else, to the waste-basket of 'performance'– at the height of Chomsky's influence this meant that it was definitely not worthy of attention.

Nonverbal communication and the study of gesture

At the same time as these developments were underway, there emerged a new interest in what came to be known as 'nonverbal communication' (sometimes 'nonverbal behaviour'). It might be supposed that this would have provided the setting for an expansion of studies of gesture. Paradoxically, however, during the years when the study of nonverbal communication was in the ascendance in psychology and psychiatry rather little work on gesture was undertaken. Gesture returned as a focus of interest following certain developments in linguistics, the study of cognition, and the study of language acquisition by apes, all of them topics which developed apart from the development of the study of nonverbal communication.

The concept of nonverbal communication appears to have first become current toward the end of the fourth decade of the twentieth century. It was at about this time that audio-recording and sound synchronous audio-visual recording technology began to be available cheaply enough for it to be possible for students of human behaviour to make use of it. Already, in the years immediately preceding World War II, film and photography had begun to be used in anthropological work. Gregory Bateson, together with Margaret Mead, made extensive use of film and photography in their studies of everyday behaviour among the Balinese and their publication, *Balinese Character* (Bateson and Mead 1942), had an important influence in showing the possibilities opened up by the use of such technology. Immediately after the Second World War Gregory Bateson, working as an ethnographic consultant with psychiatrists at a Veterans Administration hospital in Palo Alto, California, sought to bring to bear on an analysis of the dynamics of family life his insights from his work in New Guinea (see Bateson 1936) and Bali. As he had done in Bali, so in Palo Alto, he turned to the use of film as a method for analysing the details of interaction between members of families. Here the interest was in families in which one member was disturbed and the project involved the exploration of the idea that a disturbed family member was the product of the dynamics of the interactions within the family (see Bateson, Jackson, Haley and Weakland 1956). The psychiatrists with whom Bateson worked included Jurgen Ruesch, Frieda Fromm-Reichman, Jay Haley, Paul Watzlawick and Don Jackson. These were psychiatrists who had become interested in the idea that the process of psychotherapy was a consequence of the social interaction between patient and therapist and that this should become an object of study. Both Jurgen Ruesch and Frieda Fromm-Reichman had earlier turned to the idea of making recordings of therapy sessions for later analysis and Bateson brought in the idea of using film for this process as well.

The results of these early studies made it apparent that, in the interactions that transpired in psychotherapy as well as in the interactions among family members that Bateson's films made it possible to observe, far more than words are involved in communication. It was soon realized that tones of voice, modes of hesitation, styles of talking, patterns of intonation, vocal quality, bodily posture, bodily movements of all sorts, glances, facial expressions, were all playing a very important role in how the interactions proceeded and how the participants came to react to and to understand one another. Early publications reflecting this realization include works such as Ruesch and Bateson (1951), Bateson (1955) and Pittinger, Hockett and Danehy (1960). Of considerable historical importance was the extended seminar initiated in 1955 at the Institute for the Advanced Study of Behavioral Sciences in Stanford, California by Frieda Fromm-Reichmann which came to be known as Natural History of the Interview project (see Bateson 1958). Besides Fromm-Reichman (who died very soon after the beginning of this project) the linguists Charles Hockett and Norman McQuown were involved, as well as Gregory Bateson and Ray Birdwhistell. This seminar produced one of the first attempts ever to undertake a multi-modal analysis of films of occasions of social interaction in which all aspects of spoken and kinesic activity were examined and analysed in relation to one another. The outcome of this seminar, although never published in full (see McQuown 1971), was of considerable importance for the further development of the greatly enriched view of human communication that was emerging at this time. (See Leeds-Hurwitz 1987 and Kendon 1990a, Ch. 2 for historical accounts of this.)

The concept of nonverbal communication that came to be explicitly formulated during this period arose largely as a result of attempts to apply ideas from information theory and cybernetics to human interaction. This had its origin in a series of conferences held at the Josiah Macy Jr. Foundation in the years 1944-1956 in which engineers and mathematicians involved in the development of information theory and cybernetics met in discussion with social scientists, including Gregory Bateson, Margaret Mead and others (Heims 1975, 1977. See also von Foerster, Mead and Teuber 1949-1953, Schaffner 1956). Bateson, with Jurgen Ruesch, soon sought to apply ideas from information theory to human communication (see Ruesch and Bateson 1951; Ruesch 1953, 1955). Information theory and cybernetics provided new and highly general models for the analysis of communication processes and seemed to offer hope that human communication could be provided with powerful new tools for analysis. Once human action was conceived of as if it were a code in an information transmission system, the question of the nature of the coding system came under scrutiny. Much was made of the distinction between analogical codes and digital codes. Aspects of behaviour such as facial expression and bodily movement which appeared to vary in a continuous fashion were said to encode information analogically. This included gesture, insofar as it was thought to be 'pictorial', and the indexical character of much gesturing also seemed clearly to be analogical in nature.

It was this apparently clear dichotomy between 'analogical' and 'digital' encoding in human communication that gave rise to the concept of 'nonverbal communication'. Such communication was seen as employing devices quite different from those of spoken language and it was regarded as having sharply different functions. Nonverbal communication was seen as having to do with the processes by which interpersonal relations are established and maintained, whereas the digital codes of spoken language were concerned with conveying propositional information. This was given a succinct formulation by Gregory Bateson (1968). In remarking that "human kinesic communication, facial expression and vocal intonation far exceed anything that any other animal is known to produce", Bateson continues by suggesting that "our iconic (i.e. analogical) communication serves functions totally different from those of language and, indeed, perform functions which verbal language is unsuited to perform". He goes on: "It seems that the discourse of nonverbal communication is precisely concerned with matters of relationship ... From an adaptive point of view, it is therefore important that this discourse be carried on by techniques which are relatively unconscious and only imperfectly subject to voluntary control" (Bateson 1968, pp. 614-615).

Such a statement typifies well the notion of nonverbal communication that has informed so much of the research that has been done under that rubric. Guided by such a notion, it is clear that gesture is not likely to occupy the centre of attention. Ruesch himself is unclear as to exactly how gesture should be dealt with. In some places in his writings he assigns it to the same position in his classificatory scheme as language. Elsewhere, gesture is placed with all other forms of nonverbal codification. He speaks of how "words and gestures stand primarily for other events, they have little intrinsic value of their own and therefore are readily regarded as symbols. In contrast, silent actions (exclusive of gesture) always have a potentially two-fold function: they are an implementation in their own right, or they may stand for something else, or both" (Ruesch 1953, pp. 232-233). On the other hand, in another paper, gestures are not distinguished in this way. Although he recognizes gestures as part of a category of 'sign language', and so to be distinguished from 'action language' and 'object language' (see also the classification in Ruesch and Kees 1956), he later states that "although these various forms of nonverbal codification differ somewhat from each other, they can nevertheless be considered together for comparison with verbal codifications" (Ruesch 1955, p. 323). Consequently, gestures become grouped with all other aspects of behaviour that are more usually dealt with in studies of nonverbal communication as this came to be conceived.

Since the formulation of nonverbal communication that came to prevail was the one so clearly articulated by Bateson in the passage just quoted, in the expansion of research that followed, attention was directed, in the main, to aspects of behaviour that did not have the functions of spoken language.

Gesture, though often referred to, was little investigated in this tradition because, as Ruesch himself seemed to be aware, it was less clearly involved in the functions that had been postulated for nonverbal communication and it seemed to have a close association with verbal expression.

Despite this, some attempts to deal with gesture did appear. Ekman and Friesen (1969), for example, presented a systematic framework for the study of nonverbal behaviour and included in their classification scheme categories of action which they derived largely from the previous work of David Efron, and thus included 'gesture' in their scheme, even though they did not use the term (see Chapter 6). Morton Wiener and colleagues (Wiener et al. 1972) also attempted a conceptual organization of the field of nonverbal communication and they proposed the study of gesture as the centrepiece of what they took nonverbal communication to be.

Of these two papers, while the one by Morton Wiener and colleagues appears to have had little influence (just a few papers following their approach were published from Wiener's own laboratory - see Jancovic, Devoe and Wiener 1975), the one by Ekman and Friesen has been very widely cited. Nevertheless, it does not appear to have opened up new approaches to the study of gesture. Indeed, the typology Ekman and Friesen presented has often been taken by others as definitive and the paper might almost be said to have had the effect of closing off further investigation. Ekman himself, although he wrote several papers on the topic (e.g., Ekman 1976; Ekman and Friesen 1972; Friesen, Ekman and Walbott, 1979), directed most of his research energies to facial expression and the problems of its description (see Ekman 1982), and somewhat later to the study of deception and the behavioural manifestations thereof (e.g. Ekman 1985).

We may see, then, that despite the growth of linguistics, on the one hand, and a greatly increased concern with communication, especially nonverbal communication, on the other, gesture remained largely unstudied because it was left without a theoretical framework into which it could readily be fitted. So long as the focus of linguistics was purely on spoken utterance, and especially as this focus was upon idealized utterances abstracted from the vagaries of actual usage, the relationship between gesture and speech would remain obscure. So long as nonverbal communication was considered sharply separate from verbal communication, attention in this field would be directed mainly to those aspects of behaviour that contributed to the maintenance or change of interactions or relationships, or which were thought to reveal attitudes and characteristics of persons that are not revealed through a study of what is spoken. Gesture did not seem to fit here, either. It thus fell between two stools.

The return of gesture studies

Gesture began to be re-established as a topic of study in anthropology, linguistics and psychology, from the middle of the 1970s. Three changes in the intellectual climate can be noted as having brought this about. First, the issue of language origins once again began to be discussed and the idea that language had its origin as a form of gesture again played an important role in this discussion. This idea was further bolstered by the apparent success in teaching chimpanzees to use a form of sign language. This was also partly responsible for the development of the second change that contributed to the return of gesture studies. This was the revival of a serious interest in sign languages, which were soon found to be highly interesting systems, and which offered a strong challenge to the idea that language must, necessarily, be spoken. The third change was twofold: psychologists began once again to take an interest in mental processes and linguists modified their insistence on the separation of linguistics from psychology. Psychologists and some linguists became especially interested in language and its relation to thought ('psycholinguistics' was named and gained recognition as a field about 1950), an area of concern that had been studiously avoided, ever since the revolution of behaviourism in the 1920s. The growth of what came to be known as cognitive science, of which this was an early part, eventually provided a theoretically interesting context within which the relationship between gesture and speech could be studied. Thus it was that the issues that were of great interest to Edward Tylor and Wilhelm Wundt in the late nineteenth century returned to occupy the anthropologists, linguists and psychologists of the late twentieth century. And just as, then, it had seemed important to consider gesture, so it now again seemed important to do so, and for very much the same reasons.

Language origins and the status of sign language

Speculation on the question of language origins first revived in anthropology in 1964 with the publication in *Current Anthropology* of a paper by Charles Hockett and Robert Ascher called "The human revolution". This paper brought together the then relatively new information from human palaeontology, primate studies and studies on the history of the climate in Africa and offered a re-formulation of some of the main problems of human evolution. Prominent among these was the question of language and Hockett and Ascher, taking into consideration the new work then available on communication in various species of primates, bees and birds, proposed placing human language in a perspective in which it was compared, feature by feature, with communication systems in other animals. The authors did not consider the idea that language could be anything other than vocal, and gesture was not discussed. However, as we have noted, their paper created a climate in which the discussion of language in relation to ethology and evolutionary anthropology could be carried forward in a new way. Further articles on these themes soon began to appear. Among these was an important paper by Gordon Hewes (Hewes 1973) in which he marshalled arguments to support the hypothesis that the first form of language must have been gestural. His paper showed convincingly how wide a range of material relevant to the topic of language origins was now available. By emphasizing the role of gesture he brought it once again to the attention of a large number of people as a phenomenon that could have central theoretical importance.

One of the main pillars on which Hewes rested his argument was built from the findings of the Gardners who had reported what struck many as the quite surprising success in teaching a version of American Sign Language to a young chimpanzee (Gardner and Gardner 1969; 1971). For their findings to be properly evaluated, however, it became necessary to evaluate the status of sign language itself: was it *really* a language? How did the way in which Washoe (as the Gardners called their chimpanzee) came to learn it, and the progress she made with it, compare with how a human child learns a language?

Ursula Bellugi, who had studied problems of child language acquisition at Harvard University with Roger Brown, visited Washoe and was impressed by her accomplishments. One consequence of this visit was a joint paper with Jacob Bronowski of the Salk Institute on the issues that the work with Washoe raised for the understanding of the nature of language and what might be involved in its acquisition. In this paper (Bronowski and Bellugi 1970) the authors were only able to compare Washoe's acquisition of sign language with the acquisition of spoken language by humans, however, so when Bellugi was offered the possibility of starting her own unit at the Salk Institute to investigate the biological roots of language, it seemed that an investigation of how humans acquired sign language would be the best place to start. A true comparison with Washoe might then be possible. However, Bellugi and her colleagues soon realized that almost nothing was known about sign language itself. And so it was that a major project on the study of sign language was initiated, which was soon to trigger the extraordinary expansion in sign language studies that then followed (Bellugi 1981).[2]

It is remarkable that this only took place from 1970 onwards, fully ten years after William Stokoe had published a structural analysis of American Sign Language in which he had shown quite clearly that it was a linguistic system in its own right with its own properties (Stokoe 1960). At the time of

---

[2] Publications that sparked this expansion include Friedman (1977), Siple (1978), and Klima and Bellugi (1979).

Stokoe's work, the wider theoretical implications had not been appreciated. It seems that it required the realization that the question of the linguistic status of sign language was linked to fundamental questions about human origins and the biological roots of language for its serious study to gain wide support and attention.

Since that time, studies of sign languages have proceeded at an ever increasing pace. Sign language came to be understood by many as providing an important challenge to linguistic theory because it is seen that any general theory of language must now be formulated to include it, even though it is, in many ways, different from spoken language because it employs such a different medium of expression. Others, on the other hand, have sought to emphasize that sign languages are languages like any other. For many who took up research on sign language it was of great importance to demonstrate that, in every respect, it can be analysed in the same way as any spoken language. Only in this way, it was felt, would it be possible for it to gain acceptance as the principal medium of communication in deaf education. As we saw above, from the end of the nineteenth century a great prejudice against the use of signing in deaf education had developed and much had to be done to overcome this. One consequence of this concentration on what appear as the 'core' linguistic properties of sign was that certain issues of great theoretical interest, such as the apparently pictorial character of signs in deaf sign languages and its connections with gesturing in hearing people, were often avoided. More recently, now that the linguistic status of sign language is much more widely accepted these issues are receiving rather more attention (see Chapters 14 and 15).

Noam Chomsky, language acquisition and gesture studies

As we have noted, what appears to have initiated the modern tradition in research on sign language was, in the first place, the question of comparing language acquisition in children with its apparent acquisition in a chimpanzee. This question bore on very deep issues concerning the biological roots of language, and these issues were, at that time, being hotly debated. A key factor in this debate was the argument by Chomsky that the grammatical structures of language are not something that could have been learned by children through exposure to adult speech. According to Chomsky (Chomsky 1967), the child was obliged to "acquire a generative grammar of his own language on the basis of a fairly restricted amount of evidence" (p. 437), evidence that, furthermore, was of a "highly degraded sort" (p. 441). Chomsky says that "the child's conclusions about the rules of sentence formation must be based on evidence that consists, to a large extent, of utterances that break rules..." (ibid.). Accordingly, he argued, in order to account for the child's ability to use appropriate grammatical structures "we must postulate a sufficiently rich internal structure" (p. 437). This was formulated as the Language Acquisition Device, with which all children were said to be endowed. As a consequence of this Device the problem for the child "is not the apparently insuperable inductive feat of arriving at a transformational generative grammar from restricted data, but rather that of discovering which of the possible languages he is being exposed to" (p. 438).

A consequence of this proposal was a great rush of new research in which the first utterances of very young children were examined to see what kinds of grammatical structures might be found there (see, for example, Brown 1973). Much of this work took advantage of the technological capabilities of recording children in natural circumstances, and it was not long before video recording was added to this. It soon became apparent that it was necessary to examine children even younger than those who had begun to use words and, increasingly, the investigation of language acquisition in children shifted more and more toward the investigation of the acquisition of the ability to engage in actions of semantic significance of any sort. Gestures in very young children thus came to be a focus of interest. Many investigators came to maintain that language abilities emerge in the context of interactional exchanges between mother and infant. It was argued that action becomes significant in a socially communicative way because of the way it is embedded within the structures of the interactional exchanges that the mother creates with the infant (Bruner 1975; Trevarthen 1977; Bullowa 1979; Lock 1978; 1980). This viewpoint has made it possible to see that gesture and spoken utterance often have an equivalence of function. The emergence of the ability to engage in gesture is seen as an integral part of the process by which the capacity to use language comes about. Work such as that of Elizabeth Bates (1979) provided support for the view that both gesture and spoken language develop together and that they both develop in relation to the same combination of cognitive capacities. This reinforced the position that gesture and spoken utterance are differentiated manifestations of a more general process (see especially Volterra and Erting 1990).

Gesture and speech as two aspects of a single process

The view that gesture and speech are but two aspects of a single process that underlies the production of utterances had also been proposed on the basis of micro-analyses of the coordination of body movements and the phrasing of speech in adults. These micro-analyses (by Condon and Ogston 1966, 1967 and by Kendon 1972) had been undertaken at the prompting of observations and claims put forward by Birdwhistell, based on his work with the Natural

History of the Interview project already mentioned. As a consequence of close kinesic analyses that Birdwhistell had begun, using the films from that project, and of other analyses that he undertook in collaboration with Albert Scheflen at the Eastern Pennsylvania Psychiatric Institute in Philadelphia, Birdwhistell observed that the movements that speakers make when they speak are highly patterned and show structural features that are analogous to features of speech. He suggested that speakers make use of systems of kinesic markers. For example, he distinguished kinesic stress markers in patterns of movement in the head and eyelids and eyebrows of speakers that were associated with patterns of stress in speech. He described patterned differences in the direction of the movement of the head, eyes and hands, that were associated with stressed pronominals. These suggested that the speaker was providing, in movement, spatialized markers for self-referenced and other-referenced personal pronouns, as well as for stressed pronominals such as 'this', 'that', 'here', 'there', and the like. Birdwhistell first began to report these observations in the early 1960s. Publications summarizing them include Scheflen (1965) and Birdwhistell (1966, 1970).

Condon and Ogston (1966, 1967) demonstrated the patterned synchronization of body movement with speech at multiple levels of organization, showing how bodily movements of all kinds are patterned even with syllabic and phonological changes in speech. Kendon (1972) analysed the phrasal structure of the flow of movement in the hands and head of a speaker and showed how phrases of gesticulation could be seen as organized as a nested hierarchy of phrases that matched the nested hierarchy of speech phrases into which a discourse may be analysed. He stated (p. 204): "Just as the flow of speech may be regarded as an hierarchically organized set of units, so we see the patterns of body motion that are associated with it as organized in a similar fashion, as if each unit of speech has its 'equivalent' in body motion." He also said that "speech-accompanying movement is produced along with speech, as if the speech-production process is manifested in two forms of activity simultaneously: in the vocal organs and also in bodily movement, particularly in the movements of the hands and arms" (ibid.). In discussing the implications of these observations Kendon suggests (p. 206) that because the elaborate flow of movement was coordinated with highly fluent speech, "speech and movement that directly accompanies it, at least, are under the guidance of the same controlling mechanism" as if, that is, the speech output and the kinesic output are two aspects of the same process (see also Kendon 1980a).

Neither Condon and Ogston nor Kendon went on to develop the implications of their observations for theories of utterance production. This was to be undertaken in the first place by McNeill who, independently of the work of Birdwhistell, Condon and Ogston and Kendon, had also observed the integration of gesture with speaking and had been impressed by it (McNeill 1979, 1985). What impressed McNeill, in particular, was the fact that, in co-speech gesturing, the speaker appeared to be using various kinds of descriptive and pantomimic gestures to express content that was coordinate with the content of the associated speech, either in parallel with it or complementary to it. McNeill observed that the mode of expression in gesture is, as he puts it, holistic, global, imagistic, whereas in speech a categorial system of representation by arbitrary symbols is employed. For McNeill the challenge of the observation that speech and gesture are integrated in a unified way is to understand how two seemingly different modes of representation can be organized and presented simultaneously. In his subsequent work he has aimed "to provide a conceptual framework [that] at a minimum should explain how speech, which is linear through time, is related to the type of thinking that we see exhibited in the simultaneous gesture, thinking that is instantaneous, imagistic and global - analog rather than digital" (McNeill 1992, p. 11). He has argued that when co-speech gesturing can be deemed, in his terms, "idiosyncratic" and shaped by the speaker's own meanings rather than by social conventions, it can reveal dimensions of thought and conceptualization in the speaker that are not accessible through a study of verbal expression alone. He has written (ibid.) that with these kinds of gestures "people unwittingly display their inner thoughts and ways of understanding events of the world". He adds (McNeill and Duncan 2000, p. 143) "By virtue of idiosyncrasy, co-expressive speech-synchronized gestures open a 'window' onto thinking that is otherwise curtained. Such a gesture displays mental content, and does so instantaneously, in real time..."

To account for the integration with verbal language of the imagistic thinking such gesturing reveals McNeill has proposed a theory of the 'growth-point' according to which a given utterance is the product of a process of 'unpacking' that proceeds from an ideational complex in which global, synthetic, imagistic thought and thought in terms of categories that can be expressed in spoken language are inseparably intertwined. The growth point is the 'idea unit' from which an utterance arises and which the utterance, when fully fledged, still contains. The central idea of the growth point concept counters the idea that an utterance is built up, piece by piece, in a linear fashion, as has been proposed in information processing models such as that of Levelt (1989). Rather, what is to be expressed in the utterance is present all at once at its beginning. Its final form, its form as we can observe it in a speaker, is the product of a micro-genetic process in which imagistic thinking and thinking that uses linguistic categories engage together in a kind of dialectic process which leads, in the end, to the particular gesture–speech combination that is created by the speaker.

Others who have attempted to tackle the problem posed by the integration of gesture with speaking from a theoretical point of view include Kita (2000) and De Ruiter (2000). Kita's view is similar to that of McNeill in many respects, although he does not regard imagery as the basis of gesture. He thinks, rather, that gestures arise as virtual actions that a speaker makes as if acting within an imagined, virtual spatial environment. They are the product of what he refers to as "spatio-motoric thinking". Furthermore, Kita does not think that gestures are coordinated with speech because the two modes of expression derive from a common source. Rather, he suggests, "[g]estures and speech are produced by two independent (but often tightly coupled) processes, which collaborate toward the common goal of organizing information to be conveyed into a more readily verbalizeable shape" (Kita 2000, p. 171). For Kita, it appears, spatio-motoric thinking and its gestural productions can proceed independently of speech, which is the production of what he calls "analytic thinking". These two forms of thinking and the forms of expression that manifest them are brought into collaboration with one another as a result of the speaker's efforts to combine spatio-motoric thinking and analytic thinking together in a single utterance, efforts that are often necessary since what a speaker needs to express so often cannot adequately be achieved by means of one modality alone.

De Ruiter (2000) has attempted to devise a modification of Levelt's (1989) linear information processing model of the speaking process so that it can incorporate gesture. In this model the process by which an utterance is produced involves a succession of stages, each accomplished by a separate module, connected one to another in a fixed sequence. In De Ruiter's modification, a series of stages for the processing of gestures has been added that parallel those proposed for speech. Thus there is a Gesture Planner which gets things ready for the processor involved in the creation of motor programs for the execution of gestures. This parallels the Formulator responsible for speech output. However, plans for using both gestural and spoken modes of expression start at the same point in the De Ruiter model, at the stage represented by the Conceptualizer. According to De Ruiter, aspects of the idea unit that cannot be prepared for linguistic expression are prepared for gestural expression through a process called 'sketching'. A 'gesturary' of an already existing lexicon of gestures can be called upon, but it also involves formulations that will lead to the organization of motor programmes for original depictions and pantomimes. The temporal integration of gesturing and speaking is accounted for by saying that the formulation of output for the Gesture Planner occurs at the same time as the formulation of output for the Formulator (responsible for spoken output), however De Ruiter supposes that in subsequent processing, speech processes and gesture processes proceed independently. This is unlike the views of McNeill and Kita, both of whom believe that gestural expression and spoken expression shape each other in a reciprocal dialectic.

Functions of gesture

The models proposed by McNeill, Kita and De Ruiter, though differing in many respects, share in common the view that the gestures produced by a speaker while speaking are regarded as integral to the speaker's total expression. Others studying the relationship between gesture and speech do not look upon gestures in this way. Rather, they see them as somehow involved in the processes *leading up to* verbal formulation, but they do not regard them as making a contribution to the utterance's final expression. Thus, Freedman and his colleagues (Freedman 1972; Freedman 1977; Bucci and Freedman 1978; Freedman, Van Meel et al. 1986) have proposed that gestures made simultaneously with speaking mainly serve to facilitate *verbal* expression. They suggest they do so because they serve as a way of representing a concept that is to be expressed in such a way that the speaker can hold it present while a verbal expression is being worked out. They also suggest that gesturing may encode aspects of the discourse structure, and this may help the speaker to organize the syntactic and discourse patterns that are needed. Rimé (see Rimé and Schiaratura 1991) likewise sees gesture playing a role that facilitates the organization of conceptual structures for speaking. Other workers have supposed that gesture plays a role in processes by which a speaker finds the words that are needed for the sentences to be produced. Butterworth and Beattie (1978), noting an association between the occurrence of gestures with what they identified as speech planning pauses (but see Nobe 2000), hinted at this idea which has subsequently been elaborated by Butterworth and Hadar (1989) and Hadar and Butterworth (1997). The idea that gestures may help in lexical retrieval has also been strongly advocated by Robert Krauss and his colleagues (Krauss, Chen and Chawla 1996, Krauss and Hadar 1999, Krauss, Chen and Gottesman 2000). This view has been critically examined experimentally by Beattie and Coughlan (1998, 1999).

Some of those who emphasize the idea that gestures serve mainly to facilitate the process of speaking or the thought processes required for speaking, have played down the idea that they have any role of importance in communication. A controversy on this point has developed. Experiments have been published with results that have been interpreted as showing that gestures make no contribution to the understanding by another of the substance of what a person is saying (Krauss, Morrel-Samuels and Colasante 1991). However, other experimental work has been published that suggests, to the contrary, gestures do contribute to another's understanding of what someone is saying. Many of the studies from both sides of this controversy are reviewed in Kendon (1994). Later experimental studies bearing on this issue include those of Beattie and Shovelton (1999a, 1999b, 2001) in which it has been demonstrated that recipients may derive from the descriptive gestures speakers make when re-telling a cartoon story, information about the size and shape of objects, and the direction and manner of movement, which may not be explicitly referred to in speech. Other studies, such as those of Goldin-Meadow and her colleagues (summarized in Goldin-Meadow 2003b) have shown that in instructional settings both children and teachers derive information from each other's gestures and that this information can play a crucial role in the communication that takes place in instructional interaction. Both the child's own gestures and those of the teacher may be important for the outcome of the child's understanding of something.

In the Goldin-Meadow studies just referred to, some children were found who explained their solution to a problem that they had tried unsuccessfully to solve (such as a Piagetian conservation problem or a mathematical equivalence problem), but who displayed, in the gesturing that accompanied their explanations, evidence that they entertained more than one approach to the problem. That is, the information the children offered in words about their understanding differed from the information they offered in their gestures. These "mismatch" children (to use Goldin-Meadow's term) were the children who profited most from subsequent instruction by teachers. This was in part a result of the fact that the teachers perceived the children's gestures and responded with an understanding of them (evidence of their communicative significance, that is), but Goldin-Meadow and her colleagues also raised the question as to whether the children's gesturing in these circumstances also played a direct part in the child's thinking processes and they have provided some evidence that suggests this may well be so.

This work, together with a variety of observations made by others, leads to the idea (fairly close to the idea offered by Freedman two decades before, mentioned above) that, in gesturing, the speaker not only may provide information for recipients about his ideas about something, he may also provide information for himself about his ideas. For example, when describing a scene or an object from memory it was found in one study (De Ruiter 1998) that speakers often employed gestures as if they were being used as descriptive devices which aided in preserving for the speaker aspects of the appearance of the object in a quasi-graphical form, present for the speaker's own observation. This could assist him as he developed his verbal explanations. A line of research has developed, thus, that is seeking to explore the role of gesture in thinking processes (see, for example, Kita 2000, Alibali, Kita and Young 2000, Crowder 1996, Emmorey and Casey 2001).

It should be clear that any role that gesture may have in thought processes is not incompatible with its communicative functions (some have sometimes appeared to suppose that it is). Indeed, if we regard descriptive gestures, along with speech, as components of how people formulate their thoughts and if we recognize that further and more refined formulations are typically built upon previous ones, a speaker's own formulations may serve as steps toward better ones. This is the way in which thought develops. Once gestures are seen as a part of a speaker's formulation, and if it is recognized that speakers respond to their own formulations as if they are in dialogue with themselves, just as they may be with others, we can easily see how certain uses of gesture may play an important role in processes of cognitive change in individuals.[3]

A further point of debate concerns the question of what it is that gestures manifest or express. McNeill, as we have seen, claims that what he distinguishes as spontaneous, idiosyncratic, imagistic gestures are representations of the mental images of the speaker. Kita, on the other hand, regards such gestures as arising from the manipulatory actions that a person takes in acting within the framework of a virtual world. Streeck (see Le Baron and Streeck 2000 and Streeck 2002) has described how many gestures appear to derive from the patterns of action that a person employs when dealing with the objects being talked about. He has suggested that many gestures may draw upon the same patterns of action and motor skills that are used in dealing with real objects and supposes, thus, they are direct manifestations of bodily or manipulatory knowledge rather than imagistic encodings of mental concepts. Similar views have also been put forward by Young (2002).

The view that gestures derive their significance in the first place as manipulatory actions rather than as visual depictions perhaps can help us to understand why it is that even congenitally blind speakers may use gestures in ways that are not unlike their sighted counterparts (see Iverson 1998). It can also help us to understand the process by which gestures are understood by others in a new way (see also Chapter 9 for further discussion of this problem). Work on so-called 'mirror neurons' (Rizzolatti and Arbib 1998) suggests that recipients may understand the gestures of others not because they grasp visually the visual images gesturings may portray but because they grasp in a direct manner the pattern of action the gesturer is making and, as a result, can understand directly the purpose of the actions and the virtual objects they are being performed to create.

Conclusion

The themes we have mentioned in these paragraphs are among those that dominate gesture studies today. We may conclude by noting how, with the revival of gesture studies, interest in it has once again been linked to the study of questions involving cognitive processes connected to the nature of language and speech. That the study of gesture should again have pertinence for these

---

[3] Compare the view of Bakhtin (or Voloshinov) that any utterance is always addressed to another, even if that other is within the same person as the one who originates the utterance. See Clark and Holquist (1984) and Voloshinov (1976).

questions is due to the 'cognitive turn' taken by both psychology and linguistics somewhere about 1960. It is to be noted that this 'turn' was brought about in no small measure by the impact of the work of Noam Chomsky. As we mentioned above, his work had the consequence of changing the primary enterprise of linguistics away from describing languages towards that of describing the mental apparatus that enables language. And this restored to respectability the study of complex mental processes that had for so long been shunned. His work played a very important role in the development of what came to be variously known as cognitive psychology, cognitive studies or cognitive science. It was this orientation that created the context which, eventually, made it possible for the theoretical implications of the study of gesture in relation to speech to be developed, so allowing gesture, once again, to be seen as a phenomenon of significance in relation to certain preoccupations that have always been of concern: the nature of thought and its relationship to language. There is, perhaps, a certain irony in the fact that while it was the 'Chomskyan revolution' that turned the attention of linguists and others away from the study of what came to be called 'performance' (in contrast to 'competence' the understanding of which came to be the main goal of linguistics), it yet created the very conditions in which something messy like gesture, disdained as far too 'performative' by most (Chomsky himself has never shown any interest in it), could then become an object of respectable study and analysis, linked to such very ancient and abiding themes.

6   Classifying gestures

This chapter continues our examination of the history of the study of gesture by offering a comparative review of how gestures have been classified, from Quintilian to the twentieth century. The different classification schemes offered reflect the different ways in which gesture has been viewed as a form of expression or communication. As we shall see, gestures have been classified according to many different criteria, such as whether they are voluntary or involuntary; natural or conventional; whether their meanings are established indexically, iconically, or symbolically; whether they have literal or metaphorical significance; how they are linked to speech; their semantic domain - for example, gestures have been divided into those that are 'objective', serving to refer to something in the external world, and those that are 'subjective', serving to express the gesturer's state of mind. Gestures have also been classed according to whether they contribute to the propositional content of discourse, whether they serve in some way to punctuate, structure or organize the discourse, or indicate the type of discourse that is being engaged in; and whether they play a primary role in the interactional process, as in salutation, as a regulator in the process of turn-taking in conversation, and the like. All of these have been used as criteria for dividing the phenomena of gesture into types or classes. Not surprisingly, there is great diversity in terminology and authors differ in the emphasis they place on the various criteria they have used. Nevertheless, there seem to be some fundamental agreements about what gestures do which appear to be of very long standing. We conclude, however, that no attempt should be made to develop a single, unified classification scheme, since so many different dimensions of comparison are possible. Any given gesture, once understood in the context of its use, may be located on several of these dimensions simultaneously. Which aspect or dimension is given emphasis must depend upon the particular objectives of the inquiry being undertaken.

This conclusion, we suggest, is dictated by the nature of gesture itself. Gesture is a medium of expression that humans have at their disposal which they can use for a wide range of different expressive purposes. What forms of gesture are created and used depends upon the circumstances of use, the person's specific communicative purposes and what other modes of expression are also available. Gesture cannot be pinned down into a typology in any fixed way. The distinctions and classifications that are unavoidably created whenever it is discussed reflect the different understandings that students of gesture have had of how it functions. The particular classification systems developed are useful working instruments for a given investigation, but they should not be thought of as more than this.

Early classifications

Quintilian, in his *Institutio Oratoria*, as we saw in Chapter 3, organizes his discussion of gesture and bodily action in the first place according to the topology of the body. He begins with the head (XI, III. 68-71), continues with the glance, including various eye and eyebrow movements and postures (72-79), the nostrils and lips (80-81), the neck (82), the shoulders, torso and arms (83-84), the hands (85-124), and ends with the feet, and how the orator should and should not walk about when pleading (124-136). For the hands we may infer a further, functional classification. First he distinguishes mimic gestures from gestures that "naturally proceed from us simultaneously with our words" (88). Mimic gestures, which the orator should avoid, are those that indicate things by depicting some aspect of them or by suggesting an action associated with them, as in suggesting "a harpist by a movement of the hands as though they were plucking the strings" (88). Gestures that are naturally associated with words, which are acceptable in oratory, are described in some detail.

Although Quintilian does not offer a classification of them as such, it is possible to infer from his exposition four classes of gestures. These are (1) gestures which indicate states of mind or mental activities, (2) pointing gestures, (3) gestures which indicate swearing, accusing, pleading, and the like and (4) gestures that mark in various ways the structure of the discourse as in gestures that "deliver words to an audience" (97), mark different points in the discourse (99), round off steps in a rhetorical syllogism (102), or that are suited to different structural parts of the speech, such as the *exordium* or the statement of facts (92).

The distinctions drawn by Quintilian, or which may be inferred from his writing, influenced writers on gesture in the seventeenth century, some of whom presented classifications of a more systematic sort. Angenot (1973) has examined some of these. According to him, although several expositions follow the corporeal divisions that Quintilian used, several also follow functional taxonomies which show Quintilian's influence. These recognize divisions between types of cognitive activity, affective attitude, deictic gestures and certain syntactic gestures, such as those that mark the conclusion of a piece of discourse or the beginning of a new segment. Of particular interest seems to be the classification offered by Bary, in his *Méthode pour bien prononcer un discours et pour le bien animer* of 1679 (for bibliographic details see Angenot 1973). He established twenty fundamental types which serve, Angenot suggests, as emotional schemata (*abstraits émotionnels*), a basic vocabulary of bodily posturing and arm and hand action that provides the elements of expression. They include Interrogation, Frankness, Tenderness, Dominance, Rejection, Consternation, Triumph, Astonishment, Irony, Confusion (*pêle-mêle*), Showing something as essential or fundamental, Resolution, Showing what is notable, Narration, Teaching, Complaining, Exaggeration, Horror, Anger, Reproach.

The idea that vocabularies of expressive action could be established in this manner was further developed in the eighteenth century. As we mentioned in Chapter 3, such a vocabulary was widely shared and understood. It was taught in schools and so became common knowledge in the eighteenth century. As Dene Barnett has said, the "18th century art of gesture used a vocabulary of basic gestures, each with an individual meaning known to all in advance, and all performed in accordance with given techniques and precepts of style" (Barnett 1987, p. 7).

We may find such vocabularies in many treatises of the period. Here we will discuss two that were of special importance: the *Ideen zu einer Mimik* of Johann Jakob Engel (1785) and the *Chironomia* of Gilbert Austin (1802). Engel's treatise is important because it became well known throughout Europe and has been influential in both theatrical and philosophical circles (Wundt made use of Engel's work, for example). Austin's *Chironomia*, as we have already stated (Chapter 3), may be regarded as a summation of the post-Renaissance rhetorical tradition of gesture study. Austin's system of gesture classification, which is indebted, in part, to Engel, is one of the most complete and the most systematically presented of all that had been offered, up to this time, and it continued to be influential even into the twentieth century.

Johann Jakob Engel (1741-1802) was a leading figure in the German enlightenment. He was an editor of a well-known philosophical review, he taught philosophy at the Berlin Academy. He published novels and plays and wrote several philosophical essays on the nature of perception, gesture and dialogue, and was director of the National Theatre of Berlin. His book *Ideen zu einer Mimik*, which remains his best-known work, is a comprehensive discussion of all aspects of bodily expression written mainly for the benefit of actors. Here we give a brief account of the classification system he proposed.

Engel begins his classification with a distinction between movements that "originate from the mechanism of the body, as panting when out of breath after running, or closing the eyes from sleepiness" and movements that "depend on the activity of the soul, and are caused by its thoughts, sensations and purposes"

(Vol. I, Letter V, p. 32).[1] This latter class is then divided into *depictive* actions, *expressive* actions, and *physiological* actions (see Vol. I, Letter VI, pp. 41-42; Letter IX, pp. 67 ff). *Depictive* actions are those that depict or imitate some aspect of something. They are movements by which some object or action may be displayed. *Expressive* actions are those that are external signs of the internal passions and mental activities (and it is for these that Engel would prefer to reserve the term 'gesture'). These are further divided into *intentional* expressions and *imitative* expressions, which Engel also refers to as *analogous* or *figurative* expressions. *Intentional* expressions include such actions as bending toward something that we desire, posing ourselves as if to hit another when angry, extending the arms toward another when we feel love for them, putting up our hands in fear, and the like (that is, they are actions which are preparatory to carrying out some intended action and which can be understood as a precursor of that action). *Imitative expressions,* also referred to as *analogous* or *figurative* expressions, are those in which the actions engaged in are *analogous in structure* to the internal strivings or actions of the soul. Thus, moving the back of the hand away from us is analogous to the rejection of an idea; the manner of walking - whether quick and direct or slow and hesitant - can be analogous to the way in which our thoughts are progressing. In this way overt bodily actions can be used to signify internal mental activity. Finally, *physiological* actions are "involuntary phenomena, physical effects of the internal movement of the soul" (I, IX, 68). Such actions, or rather symptoms (as we might call them), include the tears of despair, the laughter of joy, the reddening of the face in shame, the pallor of fear.

Engel's classification proposes to encompass all kinds of movements. As Magli (1979) points out, in the theatre everything the actor does becomes a sign in the sense that, on stage, all is simulation. Perhaps because he is writing for the actor and not for the orator, however, he does not deal with those aspects of gesture that have to do with the structuring or the punctuation of discourse. In his classification, like the one we have inferred from Quintilian, gestures that depict objects or imitate actions are set aside as a separate class, and distinctions are also drawn between gestures that express concepts and those that express states of mind. The distinctions he draws are partly in terms of causes (mechanical, voluntary, involuntary) and partly in terms of semiotic status: whether the expression is a symptom, a gesture of depiction, a gesture which, in its action, directly displays the actor's intention (in modern terminology one might say that these gestures are intention movements), or a gesture as a *signifier* of mental activity.

We now turn to Gilbert Austin (1753-1837), who is indebted to Engel for parts of his classification scheme. Unlike Engel, however, he also deals

---

[1] All citations are from the Italian edition of Engel (Engel 1820). Translations by AK.

extensively with aspects of manual gesture that are involved in the structuring or punctuating of verbal discourse. This, of course, is because he was writing for orators as well as for actors, where this aspect of gesturing is very important.

Austin suggests that gestures of the hand may be considered from four points of view:

(1) The *instrument* that performs the gesture. This refers to whether the gesture is done by the dominant hand, that is, the one that is more advanced or elevated; or whether it is done by the subordinate hand, the one that is more retired and lower down.

(2) The *signification* of the gesture. This refers to the kinds of meanings gestures may have, and also whether these meanings are 'natural' or 'instituted'.

(3) The *quality* that a gesture may have. The qualities listed are Magnificence, Boldness, Variety, Energy, Simplicity, Grace, Propriety and Precision.

(4) *Style of delivery.* According to the style in which the discourse is being delivered, the proportion of the qualities (Magnificence, Boldness, etc.) present in gesture will vary.

The Styles of Speaking, according to Austin, are: Epic (as one sees on the stage in the acting of tragedies), Rhetorical (as one sees in public speakers in the pulpit, in courts of law, and so forth), or Colloquial (that is, in conversation in relatively informal situations, such as the salon). Speakers should adjust the balance of qualities that inform the gestures they use according to the type of discourse engaged in.

Of the points of view enumerated above, the one which deals with what Austin called the *signification* of gesture is of the greatest interest here, for it is here that he offers distinctions that can be compared with those of modern writers. The other points of view, as Austin discusses them, are more closely linked to the specific requirements of the art of delivery as they were relevant in Austin's time. Nevertheless, they should not be overlooked. Modern studies of gesture have paid insufficient attention to the 'instruments' employed in gesturing, and the issue of style in gesture has been little investigated. In particular, the way in which speakers adjust their use of gesture according to the speech register involved has hardly been studied, although it is well known that gesturing varies in both quality and quantity to a considerable degree, according to circumstance and situational proprieties (for one rare study see Lamedica 1987).

In classifying gesture according to its *signification* Austin divides gestures into those that are 'significant' and those that are, in his terms, 'not significant'. The 'significant' gestures are all those that serve in the expression of substantive meaning, or which have content. This class of gesture "is derived from the established usage of certain gestures for indicating certain persons, feelings or expressions..." (Austin 1966, p. 389). It includes (ibid.) "the index finger...points out persons or things, the hand laid on the breast refers to the feelings of the speaker, the finger laid on the lips signifies an injunction to silence, and many others". Those that are 'not significant' are gestures that "do not mark any particular sentiment; but are rather used to denote a sort of general relation in the expressions, and derive their significancy from the time and manner of their application, from the place in which they are used, and from their various combinations" (ibid., p. 390). With this class Austin recognizes how gesture can be used to mark certain discourse structures or to indicate relationships between them. There is a discussion of how such gestures are organized in relation to speech and he explains how they play a role in indicating the commencement or termination of discourse, in "explaining, extending or limiting...[or] enforcing ... the predominant idea" or in "suspending the attention previous to the more decided gestures" (ibid., p. 390).

Significant gestures are divided into 'natural' and 'instituted'. Instituted gestures, since these belong more to circumstances in which gestures are used in the absence of speech, either by the deaf or in comic acting and pantomime, are not part of Austin's concern. Natural gestures, are those which express "in universal language, threatening or invitation, pity or contempt, shame and triumph, submission or command, and many other sentiments, passions and desires" (ibid., p. 469). Following Engel, Austin recognizes *descriptive* gestures, which serve to describe the forms of objects or actions referred to, *expressive* gestures which relate to "feelings of the mind", and *indicative* gestures, "when an object is merely pointed out but not described" (ibid., pp. 478-480). *Expressive* gestures are further divided into *gestures of motive* (those referred to above as *intentional* gestures), *analogous* or *figurative* gestures, and *physiological* gestures.

Austin lists a number of significant gestures divided according to the parts of the body they make use of (ibid., pp. 482-484). Thus, for the head and face he lists nodding forward in assent, tossing the head back in dissent, aversion of the head in horror, leaning forward in attention. For the eyes he mentions "eyes ... raised in prayer", eyes that weep in sorrow, burn in anger and eyes that "are thrown in different directions in doubt and anxiety". For the arms we have gestures such as "The arm is projected forwards in authority" or "Both arms are extended in admiration". For the hands he lists: hand "on the head indicates pain or distress"; on the eyes "shame"; on the lips "injunction of silence"; "they are clasped or wrung in affliction"; they are "held forward and received in friendship". The body when "held erect indicates steadiness and courage", it is "thrown back" in pride, it stoops forward in condescension or compassion. And for the Lower Limbs we have "Their firm position signifies courage or obstinacy, [b]ended knees, timidity or weakness" or stamping with the feet indicates "authority or anger". In all he lists thirty-nine gestures of this type. He says, however, that these are but "a few" and that the catalogue "may be enlarged at pleasure" (ibid., p. 485). He then goes on to show how these simple significant gestures may be combined in various ways to create complex gestures, of which, in exemplification, he describes seventeen.

It will be seen, thus, that, so far as the so-called *significant* gestures are concerned, Austin entertained the idea of a vocabulary of expressive forms which can be assembled in various ways to create a large repertoire. In this he reminds us, for example, of Bary (see Angenot 1973), as already mentioned. As regards the *non-significant* gestures, Austin distinguishes five classes. *Commencing* gestures "begin the discourse or division, by simply raising the hand from rest..." (ibid., p. 390). *Discriminating* gestures include gestures which indicate "persons or object; or which are used for explaining, extending, limiting or modifying the predominant idea; or in question and answer, when made without vehemence" (ibid., pp. 390-391). *Auxiliary* or *alternate* gestures "serve to aid or enforce the gesture of the advanced hand" (ibid., p. 391). *Suspended* or *preparatory* gestures are gestures which create a suspension in attention, prior to a "descending stroke" which falls on some word which is to be given emphasis. *Emphatical* gestures "mark with force words opposed to or compared with each other, and more particularly the word which expresses the predominant idea" (ibid., p. 392).

It will be seen that, in contrast to the significant gestures, these gestures are defined in terms of how they relate to the structure of spoken discourse, serving to announce its onset, to prepare the hearers for some forthcoming action, to add emphasis or, so it would seem, to provide, with the discriminating gestures, a sort of spatial representation of the topical structure of the discourse. These gestures, according to Austin, are of great importance for the orator, who uses significant gestures much less often. As he says (ibid., p. 497): "The significant gestures however numerous and correct which a great actor makes in the representation of an entire dramatic character, bear no proportion to the greater number of his gestures which are not significant, and which are no less necessary, though not so splendid nor imposing."

Twentieth-Century Classifications

The classification schemes discussed so far have all been developed in relation to particular aspects of the art of gesture, whether this be on the stage or on the rostrum. Treatments of gesture developed more recently have been developed for scientific purposes rather than for the artist or actor. We begin with the scheme offered by Wilhelm Wundt (1973) at the beginning of the twentieth century, which shows the influence of Engel, whose work he consulted, although, in his own discussion, he does not deal with gesture in the context of the theatre. Then we discuss schemes developed by North American writers which currently have great influence in the field of gesture studies. These are the systems of Efron (first put forward in 1941), Ekman and Friesen (from 1969, which owes a great deal to Efron), and David McNeill (1992). Classification schemes have also been offered by Kaulfers (1931), Barakat (1969), Norbert Freedman (e.g. Freedman 1972), Wiener et al. (1972), Rimé and Schiaratura (1991), and Bavelas et al. (1992). The ones chosen here, however, are representative and perhaps have had the most influence.

Wilhelm Wundt

Wundt's classification is mainly semiotic, for it divides gestures according to how the form of the gestural action is related to what the gesture means. His first division is between *demonstrative* and *descriptive* gestures. Demonstrative gestures serve to draw attention to objects present, to indicate spatial relations, to refer to parties to the conversation, and to indicate body parts. The action of a demonstrative gesture is a pointing action. Descriptive gestures, which are subdivided into *mimic gestures, connotative gestures* and *symbolic gestures,* are gestures that stand for some object.

Mimic gestures are those which directly imitate some object or action. *Connotative gestures* are those in which some feature of something is taken as standing for the whole as when, for example, in a deaf sign language, the sign for 'man' is derived from an imitation of lifting the hat. These are not sharply distinguished from mimic gestures, however. If several characteristics or a total pattern of action is shown in the gesture, then it is mimic. If but one feature, it is connotative.

A *symbolic gesture* has a more complex relation with its referent. For example, in Plains Indian sign language a cupped hand may serve as a sign for a drinking gourd. In this case it imitates the shape of the gourd and is, thus, descriptive. However, when this same sign is used to refer to water, it is then symbolic. In such cases some concrete object or action which the gesture depicts is itself taken as standing for some more abstract concept.

Several features of Wundt's classification scheme are worthy of comment. First of all, his scheme is narrower in its application than the earlier schemes we have reviewed, for it really applies only to gestures made with the hands. Second, his classification suggests a progression in which seemingly arbitrary signs which function like words are derived from basic expressive movements (this is one of Wundt's most fundamental insights). Third, his classification applies only to referential gestures, that is, to gestures that designate, indicate, depict or in some other way make reference to some object or concept. Unlike Austin, he makes no reference to gestures that function as performatives or which have discourse structure marking, interactive or other pragmatic functions. Within the domain of referential gestures, as we may call them, however, like others he draws a main distinction between pointing gestures (demonstratives) and gestures that in some way have a characterizing relation with their object of reference.

Fourth, Wundt's classification uses a mixture of criteria. It is based partly on the semiotic status of the gesture, but partly on the techniques that are used in representation. Thus, among descriptive gestures, he not only makes semiotic distinctions between 'imitative', 'connotative' and 'symbolic' gestures. He also distinguishes between gestures in terms of their techniques of realization, distinguishing gestures that 'sketch' their object and those that are 'plastic', in which the hands themselves model the shape of the object referred to.

Finally, Wundt does not deal with gesture in its relation to speech. He concentrates entirely on gestures that operate in their own right and that form, in his terms, "gesture language" - whether this be the gestures described for the Neapolitans, the Plains Indians or the deaf. In this he differs from Quintilian and Austin, as well as from those later writers whose work we discuss.

David Efron

Probably the first twentieth-century attempt to deal with the relationship between gesture and speech was made by David Efron. In his investigation, which, as we mentioned in Chapter 5, was the first ever to undertake a systematic culturally comparative examination of gesture, he compared among inhabitants of Manhattan the gesture behaviour in conversation of first generation immigrant Southern Italians with first generation Yiddish speaking East European Jews, and also assimilated descendants of these two groups. As already noted, his investigation demonstrated that style of gesture use is cultural and not a matter of biological inheritance.

Efron's specific findings and methods are discussed in Chapter 16. Here we discuss his scheme of analysis. It was not developed as a typology of gesture, so much as a summary of the different ways in which gesture may be looked at and the different ways in which it may be used. His work has been used as the basis for later classifications or typologies of gesture, however, in particular by Ekman and Friesen (to be discussed next). In consequence, at least indirectly, it has been very influential.

Efron is concerned mainly with gesture as it is manifested in hand and arm movements. He deals with it in three perspectives: a *spatio-temporal* perspective in which gestures are described in terms of their movement characteristics; an *inter-locutional* perspective, which deals with the interactional functions of gestures; and a *linguistic* perspective, which deals with the various ways in which gestures may convey meaning, especially with how they do so in relation to speech.

Within the spatio-temporal perspective gestures are analysed in terms of

(a) the size of the radius of movement and from which part of the arm the movement originates;

(b) the form of the movement, whether it is sinuous, elliptical, angular or straight;

(c) the plane of the movement, whether sideways or transverse, towards or away from the auditor;

(d) the body parts involved in the gesticulation, distinguishing head gestures, digital gestures (considering several different types of finger positions), the laterality of the gestures (whether both hands are employed or only one, whether there is sequential transfer of motion from one arm to another or whether the arms operate in unison).

(e) the tempo of the gesture - whether it has abrupt transitions from one speed of movement to another (Efron calls these "dischronic transitions"), or flowing transitions.

Within the *interlocutional perspective*, gesturing is considered from the point of view of whether it involves the other person or not. Thus it is noted whether, in gesturing, the speaker catches hold of the body of the other person, whether gesturing among the interactants is simultaneous, the degree of space used in conversational groupings, and whether or not an object was used as a kind of extension of the arm in gesturing.

Within the *linguistic* perspective, two main types of gesture are distinguished: those which, in Efron's words, have a 'logical' or 'discursive' meaning, and those which are 'objective' in their meaning. The first are gestures which appear to portray, not any object of reference, but "the course of the ideational process itself". Such gestures may be *baton-like*, timing out with the hand the successive stages of what is referred to in speech, or they may be *ideographic*, in which they sketch in the air "the 'path' and 'direction' of the thought patterns." (Efron 1972, p. 96). These gestures do not convey meaning independently of speech, and the meaning they do convey is of an abstract kind, either like punctuation or as a kind of diagram of the ideational structure of the discourse.

'Objective' gestures, on the other hand, convey meaning independently of speech with which they may, or may not, co-occur. Efron distinguishes *deictic* or pointing gestures and *physiographic* gestures, which depict or characterize their referent. These are further divided into *iconographic* gestures which may depict either the form of an object or spatial relationships - as when one sketches the shape of something, shows the relative size of something, or indicates the spatial relationship of objects; and *kinetographic* gestures which depict a bodily action (as when one pantomimes typing to indicate one has been busy typing; gesturing holding the steering wheel of a car as one says "driving along", etc.).

Finally, Efron distinguishes what he calls 'symbolic' or 'emblematic' gestures, "representing either a visual or a logical object by means of a pictorial or non-pictorial form which has no morphological relationship to the thing represented" (ibid., p. 96). These gestures tend to be standardized in meaning within a community and are not necessarily obviously descriptive or pantomimic. As examples, Efron provides, from his Jewish examples "Poking with the index finger on the palm as signifying 'impossibility'. This will happen only when grass grows on this" (see Fig. 33 in Efron 1972), palm on cheek or behind ear to indicate bewilderment, rejection (see Fig. 34 in Efron 1972). From his Italian examples one might cite flat hands above brows: "Attention" (p. 215, Fig. 85); both hands open with palms up and held in front of the actor: "reading" (p. 207, Fig. 39); or wagging index finger back and forth: "pretty good" (p. 207, Fig. 40).

Efron's classification, never presented systematically (Ekman, in his Introduction to the 1972 edition of Efron's book, offers a logically ordered summary of his distinctions), is a very insightful and detailed analysis of gesture. It recognizes that, for a truly comprehensive understanding, gestures must be analysed from several different perspectives. Gesture classifications are multiple, and any given classification depends upon the perspective in terms of which it is to be set up. Further, so far as Efron's so-called 'linguistic' perspective is concerned, his analysis of the different ways in which gesturing can be related to speech is highly suggestive and remains one of the most articulated to date.

Paul Ekman and Wallace Friesen

Efron's analysis of the different ways in which gesture can be used in relation to speech and his recognition of emblematic gestures was used and modified by Paul Ekman and Wallace Friesen who offered a category system according to which different types of what they call 'nonverbal behavior' can be distinguished. Two of these refer to what here we would count as 'gesture' (it is notable that these authors do not use this term). These gesture categories (so-called 'emblems' and 'illustrators') have been very widely referred to. The category system is contained within their article, "The Repertoire of Nonverbal Behavior: Categories, Origins, Usage and Coding", published in 1969. They state that one of their main goals is that of making "it more difficult to conceive of nonverbal behavior as a simple, unified phenomenon, best explained by a single model of behavior...." (p. 93).

The paper was written in the context of certain specific investigations the authors were engaged in which included studies of how observers judge attitude or personality or emotional state from the bodily and facial attitudes and movements of people observed in social interaction (for the most part, psychiatric patients in psychiatric interviews), studies of cross-cultural differences in facial expressions, studies of how deception may be detected from body movements, and cross-cultural comparative studies of certain gestures. The paper was published at a time when the concept of 'nonverbal communication' and/or 'nonverbal behavior' had started to become popular, and seemed to many to be a new field of research, a new field that was of special interest to psychiatrists (see Chapter 5). The paper had a great success because it appeared to provide a well-articulated conceptual structure for an area which many psychologists and others had only just begun to become aware of. It came to be very widely cited and became, for many, a sort of touchstone.

The authors define 'nonverbal behavior' as "any movement or position of the face and/or the body" (p. 49). Obviously, this definition cannot be taken literally. What the authors intend as their field of interest (as do almost all others who use this term) are really only those aspects of "movement or position of the face and/or body" that are relevant for communication, primarily in situations of face-to-face interaction. Within this domain the authors propose a *typology* for bodily movements and positions that are in some way significant for communication in interaction.

The authors propose that there are three fundamental considerations for understanding "fully any instance of a person's nonverbal behavior". These they call *origin, usage* and *coding. Origin* refers to whether the act in question was learned or derives from some inborn form of action. Facial expressions of emotion would be examples of behaviour patterns that are heavily shaped by inborn tendencies although, as Ekman and Friesen show in their deservedly well known discussion of 'display rules', also to be found in this paper, when and how and to what extent the various emotions are displayed is shaped by learning in important ways.

Usage includes several different issues: (1) the nature of the external conditions found when the act being considered occurs. (2) How the act in question is related to "the associated verbal behavior". (3) Whether the action is done consciously. (4) Whether the person intended to communicate. (5) The nature of the feedback from "the person observing the act". (6) The type of information conveyed by the act. Under this last heading the authors distinguish, first, between information that is *idiosyncratic* (that is, it has significance only for a single individual or it is interpreted in a certain way only by one person) and information that is *shared* (that is, that groups of people agree on how the act is to be interpreted). They then distinguish *informative, communicative* and *interactive* actions. To be *informative* the act must be interpreted in a shared way by others, but the information derived from the act is independent of whether or not the actor intended to convey any information or not. To be *communicative*, however, the act must be "clearly and consciously intended by the sender to transmit a specifiable message" (pp. 55-56). To be *interactive* an act must be "by one person in an interaction which clearly [modifies] or [influences] the interactive behavior of the other person(s)" (p. 56).

Under *coding* the question of what principle governs the "correspondence between the act and its meaning" (p. 60) is discussed. Here Ekman and Friesen distinguish whether this correspondence is arbitrary, iconic or intrinsic. If the act is intrinsic (in Ekman and Friesen's sense of this term) there is no separation between the act and its significance. Whereas to wave a fist at another as if to strike them may be an example of an iconically coded action which 'means' threat, in actually hitting someone there is no distinction between the act and its meaning. The punch does not stand for aggression, it *is* aggression. They then add (pp. 61f) an account of "further ways in which a nonverbal act is related to its significant" pointing out that it may be *pictorial* ("a movement which shows its meaning by drawing a picture..."), *spatial* ("the movement indicates distance between people, objects or ideas..."), *rhythmic* ("the movement traces the flow of an idea or accents a particular phrase"), *kinetic* ("the movement executes all or part of an action performance, where that performance either signifies or is the meaning, at least in part") or *pointing* ("...some part of the body, usually the fingers or hand points to some person, some part of the body, to an object or place").

The authors then suggest that, as their discussion has made clear, "nonverbal behavior is not a single unified phenomenon with but one type of usage, one origin and one form of coding" (pp. 62-63). There are, rather, various kinds or types. They offer five categories and it is this part of the paper that has been most widely referred to. The categories proposed are well known. They are: (1) *Emblems* defined as "those nonverbal acts which have a direct verbal translation, or dictionary definition, usually consisting of a word or two, or perhaps a phrase" (p. 63). To use an emblem is deemed to be a deliberate attempt to communicate and the user takes "communicational responsibility" for it. (2) *Illustrators* "are movements which are directly tied to speech, serving to illustrate what is being said verbally" (p. 68). Illustrators, according to Ekman and Friesen, "are quite similar to emblems in terms of both awareness and intentionality. The person using an illustrator may be slightly less aware of what he is doing, and his use of illustrators may be somewhat less intentional" (p. 69). However, they are probably always informative and they are sometimes communicative. "[T]hey are probably at least as intentional as the words spoken when the speaker is excited and not exercising forethought and care about his choice of words" (ibid.).

Six types of illustrators are then distinguished (and it is here that Efron's influence is most clearly to be seen), named as *batons* which "time out, accent or emphasize a particular word or phrase" (ibid.); *ideographs* which "sketch a path or direction of thought" (ibid.); *deictic movements* which point to a present object; *spatial movements* which depict a spatial relationship; *kinetographs*, which depict a bodily action; and *pictographs*, which draw a picture of their referent.

The other categories are: (3) *Affect displays*, which are mainly comprised of facial expressions of emotion. (4) *Regulators* which "are acts which maintain and regulate the back-and-forth nature of speaking and listening between two or more interactants" (p. 82). (5) *Adaptors* which are "movements...first learned as part of adaptive efforts to satisfy self or bodily needs or to perform bodily actions or to manage emotions or to develop or maintain prototypic interpersonal contacts or to learn instrumental activities" (p. 84). Different types of adaptors are thus distinguished, according to their functions, as self-adaptors, alter-adaptors or object-adaptors.

It will be seen that Ekman and Friesen's categories have not been established according to a common set of criteria. Thus, while emblems are distinguished in virtue of their socially acknowledged communicative status, illustrators are recognized because of the contribution they are said to make to something that is spoken; affect displays are distinguished because of the type of information they convey; adaptors are distinguished on the basis of the presumed motivation that lies behind them; regulators are distinguished in terms of function. What makes it difficult to apply this typology, however, is the fact that acts that are members of one category are also members of another category, depending upon the point of view of the analyst. For example, as the authors say, "[i]llustrators can also include the use of an emblem to substitute for, repeat or contradict a word or a phrase; and similarly, illustrators can include a facial affect display..." (p. 68). Again "affect displays can be emblems, in that a particular social group or culture may select an entire affective display or an element of an affective display and code it so explicitly that it is recognized and used as an emblem; the smile in many cultures is such an emblem" (p. 77). As for regulators, the authors say that "affect displays, and...adaptors, can also serve as regulators". The authors go on to say, indeed, that "almost anything that one individual does and another observes has a regulative function, in that it can influence the communicative behavior of another" (p. 82). They then add "...though a whole variety of behaviors can serve regulative functions, we reserve the label *regulator* for those behaviors which do not fit into one of our other categories; that is, for behaviors which seem only to regulate" (ibid.). However, they offer no guidelines as to how we might identify such behaviours.

The more carefully one reads this famous paper, the more confused and confusing it seems to become. It is full of interesting theoretical points but the attempt to fit such a diversity of phenomena into a category scheme which, even as the authors try to do so, they half-recognize is not really possible, creates a sort of mental fog. It would have been better if the attempt to set up a typology had been abandoned and instead it had been recognized that behaviour in interaction is best analysed in terms of a multiple set of scales or dimensions of comparison. Had they proposed, for example, that behaviour can be compared in terms of the degree to which it is conventionalized, the nature of its link with speech, the extent and nature of the affectivity it shows, the role it plays in the regulation of the interaction, and the like; and also to recognize that behaviour can also vary in the degree to which it may be said to be *specialized* with respect to these functions, many of the difficulties this paper presents could have been avoided.

Despite the popularity of Ekman and Friesen's article and notwithstanding that the terms 'emblem' and 'illustrator' have been widely accepted, the more detailed categorization offered for 'illustrators' has not been used. This is probably because the authors themselves did not publish any research on illustrators. Except for a few publications on emblems, Ekman and his colleagues, in their subsequent work, focused on the study of affect displays and deception.

David McNeill

David McNeill, whose background is psychology and linguistics, has been primarily interested in the cognitive foundations of language. As we saw in Chapter 5, he has argued that gestures that co-occur with speech are so intimately bound up with it that speech and gesture must be seen as inseparable components of the act of utterance. For him, what he has called the co-expressive relationship of gesture and speech shows that in the thinking processes that are involved in speaking, imagistic thinking and linguistic categorial thinking are conjoined in a dialectic relationship. The utterance is said to unfold from a 'growth point' and in the course of this unfolding the imagistic aspect is manifested in gesture while the linguistic categorial aspect is manifested in speech. In developing an account of the relationship between gesture and speech, interpreted in accord with these ideas, McNeill has developed a category system for gesture that has been quite widely adopted. In giving an account of this we follow the exposition given in McNeill (1992).

The gestures that McNeill has studied are in all cases gestures that occur as a part of discourses recorded in a laboratory setting, where people give an account of a cartoon film, or some other type of film they have just seen, to another person, who is presented to them as someone who has not seen the film. The discourses studied are, thus, almost always *narrations* in which concrete events witnessed by the speaker as they were depicted in visual images are being described from memory for the benefit of another person who has not witnessed them. This has heavily influenced the kinds of distinctions McNeill has noted in the use of gesture and the range of phenomena he has hitherto been concerned with.

McNeill has stated explicitly that he is interested only in the spontaneous gesturings that are used by speakers as, in his words, "unwitting accompaniments of speech" (1992, p. 72). He defines his domain of interest by reference to an ordering of gestures referred to as "Kendon's Continuum" (see below). Placed at one end of this continuum are gestures that function independently of speech and are highly conventionalized, as in sign languages. Placed at the other end of the continuum is "gesticulation" or "idiosyncratic spontaneous movements of the hands and arms accompanying speech" (ibid., p. 37). Conventionalized gestures or 'emblems' and 'pantomime' are placed in between. McNeill is concerned only with the "idiosyncratic spontaneous movements" of 'gesticulation' and the classification of gestures that he offers is intended to apply only to these. The reason for this restriction of interest is theoretical. For McNeill, it is gestures of this sort that "can be taken to reveal the utterances's primitive stage" (ibid., p. 40). He believes that with these kinds of gestures "people unwittingly display their inner thoughts and ways of understanding events of the world. These gestures are the person's memories and thoughts rendered visible. Gestures are like thoughts themselves. They belong, not to the outside world, but to the inside one of memory, thought and mental images" (p. 12). Elsewhere he has written (McNeill and Duncan 2000: 143) "By virtue of idiosyncrasy, co-expressive speech-synchronized gestures open a 'window' onto thinking that is otherwise curtained. Such a gesture displays mental content, and does so instantaneously, in real time..."

McNeill's classification is a classification in terms of the various ways in which 'gestures' (that is, hand and arm movements having the characteristics of 'gesticulation' mentioned) may be interpreted as symbolically expressive acts in relation to the context created by the content of the speech with which they occur. McNeill's first distinction is between *imagistic* and *non-imagistic* gestures. *Imagistic* gestures are those in which movements are made that are interpreted as depicting the shape of an object, displaying an action of some kind, or representing some pattern of movement. Such gestures can be thought of as conveying an *image* of some kind, whether this be an image of how something appears or of some action or activity. *Non-imagistic* gestures include gestures that point (deictic gestures) and gestures that seem to be simple rhythmic movements only, serving to mark out segments of the discourse or the rhythmic structure of the speech. These are referred to as *beats*.

Imagistic gestures are further divided into *iconic* gestures and *metaphoric* gestures, according to the status occupied in the discourse of the image the gesture depicts. *Iconic* gestures display in the form and manner of their execution aspects of the same concrete scene that is presented in speech. So, to give one of McNeill's examples, when, as a speaker said "he tries going up inside the pipe this time" he makes an upward movement with his hand, since this "depicts, in its manner of execution, a feature also referred to in speech, namely upward motion" (1992, p. 78), it is considered an iconic gesture. *Metaphoric* gestures also display an image, either of shape or of movement, but the image depicted is presented as an image that represents or stands for some abstract concept. For example, a speaker begins his narration of a film he has just seen by saying "It was a Sylvester and Tweety cartoon" and as he says this he holds his two hands up, both open, palms facing one another. McNeill suggests that this gesture presents "the idea of a genre...as a bounded container supported by the hands" (ibid., p. 14). To give one of our own examples, a speaker (who is a social worker) is describing how, in an initial interview, a psychiatric patient had, without being asked, explained some intimate details of her life with great energy and spontaneity (see Example 8 in Chapter 8). The social worker said: "She spoke very rapidly and this was all coming out quite spontaneously." As she says "all coming out", starting from a position close to the side of her waist, she moves her hand rapidly outwards and upwards in a movement that suggests the image of a substance gushing out of herself. Just as, in her speech, she refers to the contents of the patient's discourse as "coming out" (as water might flow from some container), so, in her gesture, she performs a movement that seems to depict the same idea imagistically.

It will be seen that the distinction between 'iconic' and 'metaphoric' gestures stems from the difference in the way the image the gesture depicts is being used by the speaker. If it is used to represent some possible concrete object or action then the gesture is said to be 'iconic'. If it is used as a means of presenting an image which is to represent an abstract idea, then the gesture is said to be 'metaphoric'. In both cases the gesture displays an image deemed to be of something that could be a concrete object or action in the world. It is how that image is made use of in the speaker's discourse that determines whether the gesture is labelled 'iconic' or 'metaphoric'.

Deictic gestures, as their name implies, are "pointing movements which are prototypically performed with the pointing finger" (ibid., p. 80). *Beats* are "movements that do not present a discernible meaning" (ibid., p. 80) and which are, furthermore, simple up-and-down movements in which the hand is not transported to any particular region of the space available to the gesturer for them to be performed. Finally, McNeill distinguishes *cohesives*, and *Butterworths*. *Cohesives*, which may be imagistic gestures or deictics, are noted when the speaker uses gesture in such a way that it seems to serve "to tie together thematically related but temporally separated parts of the discourse" (ibid., p. 16). *Butterworths* (named after the British psycholinguist, Brian Butterworth) are gestures that are made when a speaker is trying to recall a word or other verbal expression (ibid., pp. 76-77).

Once again, we may note similarities in the distinctions McNeill has drawn with those of other writers. His recognition of pointing or deictic gestures as a separate class is similar to that shown by all the other writers we have considered. Likewise, several writers, as we have seen, have noted the way some gesturing seems more related to the structuring of the discourse as an activity than it is to its content. McNeill's *beats* recall Efron and Ekman and Friesen's *batons* and some of Austin's *non-significant* gestures. McNeill's recognition that there are gestures that express *images* reminds us of Wundt's broad class of *depictive* gestures or of the *pictographic* and *kinetographic* gestures distinguished by Efron and Ekman and Friesen. However, McNeill's concept of the *metaphoric* gesture appears not to have been formulated in this way before, unless we can understand Engel's notion of *figurative* or *analogous* gestures as having some similarities to it.

A comparative discussion

The schemes reviewed may be compared for their scope or range of actions they refer to; for how the actions of gesture are related to speech; and with regard to the kinds of semiotic distinctions that are made.

First of all, with regard to scope, Quintilian, Engel and Ekman and Friesen discuss the full range of what might be included under the term 'bodily expression'. Austin's discussion is more focused on expression in the hands and arms (although not exclusively). Efron, although he describes head movements as being important in 'traditional' Jewish gesturing, in his semiotic classsification he deals only with the hands and arms, while McNeill concentrates exclusively on hands and arms.

All writers appear to recognize the hands and arms as a separable expressive system, however. Quintilian devotes separate sections to the head, the glance, the face, the neck, the hands, stance and movement, and clothing. He gives special recognition to the hands, not merely as helping the speaker but because, as he says, they almost speak in their own right.

Austin devotes separate chapters to the face (or 'countenance', as he calls it), where he also deals with the glance. Most of his book, however, is taken up with a discussion of the hands, although it is important to note that Austin often describes gestures as ensembles of actions involving various parts of the body - the head, the trunk, the hands and the feet.

Engel makes no clear distinction between the different parts of the body. His classification of bodily expression, in the first place is in terms of *cause* - he contrasts 'mechanical' and 'physiological' causes with 'expressive' causes. In the second place the 'expressive' is classified in terms of semiotic distinctions.

Ekman and Friesen also do not establish their distinctions on an anatomical basis. Their divisions are based partly on motivation ('adaptors'), partly on function ('regulators'), partly on the type of information conveyed ('affect displays'), and partly on relationship with speech and social conventions ('emblems' and 'illustrators'). They note some tendency to anatomical specialization. Thus 'emblems' and 'illustrators' are mainly *manual* activities, whereas affect displays are almost entirely treated as actions of the face. The remaining writers we discussed either explicitly, as in the case of McNeill, or by implication, as in the case of Wundt and Efron, treat only of manual activity.

Now consider the way in which the schemes described differ in how they attend to the relationship between bodily expression and speech. So far as manual expressions are concerned this relationship is of special interest to Quintilian and Austin because they are both dealing with Delivery, that is, the manner in which a spoken discourse is to be performed, so how the hands relate to speech is obviously of crucial importance. This relationship is also of central interest for Efron, Ekman and Friesen, and McNeill, but in each case, it would seem, for slightly different reasons. Efron's interest derives from his observation that these relationships may differ according to cultural group. Ekman and Friesen pay attention to this relationship partly because it is in terms of it that they differentiate 'emblems' from 'illustrators' and partly because, in the light of this, it becomes important to distinguish the various ways in which speech and these forms of action are related. McNeill is interested in this relationship for specific theoretical reasons which have to do with his ideas about thought processes and the relationship between these and linguistic expression.

Engel, on the other hand, does not seem to build in a consideration of how manual actions relate to speech. His main interest is in delineating the various expressive forms useful for actors that operate as the succession of attitudes out of which a drama is constructed. Words are subordinate to this to a large degree and serve as the content for frameworks of expression that have quite general significance. Finally Wundt, although he writes of 'gesture' as a step toward spoken language, is interested in the linguistic properties of gesture as an autonomous medium, and he does not discuss the relationship between speech and gesturing at all.

Finally, consider the kinds of semiotic distinctions that are made in these schemes. Here we deal with those parts of the classification systems which deal with 'gesture' in the narrower sense in which it is being treated in this book. This overlaps to a considerable degree, but by no means completely, with the expressive activities of the hands and arms and it is in respect to this that we can find that all of the writers treated in this chapter have something to say.

All writers, from Quintilian to McNeill, as noted already, make a division between gestures that refer to an object by pointing at it and gestures that characterize the object in some way. Several writers make a threefold distinction: indicative, demonstrative or pointing or deictic gestures; imitative, depictive or imagistic gestures; and expressive gestures, that is, gestures that express a state of mind or mental attitude. Quintilian, Austin, Ekman and Friesen and McNeill also all discuss in an explicit fashion gestures that mark out, punctuate or in some other way make reference to aspects of the structure of the discourse, either in respect to its phrasal organization or in respect to its logical structure. And such functions of gesture are dealt with separately from those functions in which gestures are said to express aspects of discourse content.

Another comparative observation that may be made is that, as we approach the modern era, the schemes we have examined seem to become more explicitly *categorical*. This is no doubt a reflection of the desire on the part of modern investigators to apply quantitative statistical methods in their research. Thus, neither Engel nor Austin sets up exclusive definitions in his discussion of the different modes of expression that he describes for gesture. Later writers, especially Ekman and Friesen, and McNeill do try to do this.

As we have seen, in the case of Ekman and Friesen, even as they try to set up clear criteria by which their categories can be defined, they seem to realize that this is not really possible. Although McNeill seems content with his categories, it is not hard to see that here, also, the different types proposed are not nearly as easily differentiated from one another as they seem. For example, co-speech gestures are always coordinated rhythmically with the speech they are associated with, and since there is much variation in the hand shapes seen in such gesturing it is sometimes quite difficult to decide whether a given unit of hand action should be considered a 'beat' or a gesture with some imagistic features. Often it must be considered to be both. Likewise, although it is true that there are gestures that appear specialized as pointings, it is also true that these features can be blended with other features (see Chapter 11). Gestures in which features of the object being referred to are characterized can be combined with a direction or spatial displacement of the gesture so that we have to say that the gesture is at one and the same time deictic and characterizing.

As we suggested above, the difficulties (and dangers) inherent in a typological approach perhaps can be overcome by an approach which does not try to set up gesture types as mutually exclusive categories but which recognizes, instead, a series of dimensions in terms of which gestures can be compared. A hint of such an approach is evident in McNeill's formulation of what he has called "Kendon's continuum".

Dimensions of comparison: "Kendon's continuum" revisited

In 1988 I published a paper in which I drew attention to the different ways in which gesture can be used as a component of an utterance (Kendon 1988a). I suggested that "gesture may encompass a full range" from being like words in a language to graphical or pantomimic representations. When used in association with speech I noted that gesture serves to represent aspects of meaning in a picture-like or pantomimic manner. I also noted how it can be used in alternation with speech, serving as the functional equivalent of a word or a phrase. When it is so used on a regular basis, forms of gesture can be established which are highly stable and, under some circumstances, generally when speech is entirely absent, it may assume all of the functions of spoken language and come to have structural properties that are analogous to it. In these circumstances, I said, gestures "may become like words". The theoretical point intended was that gesture, as a medium of expression, could assume different properties, depending upon the communicative demands that were laid upon it. In particular I wanted to suggest that many of the properties that have been proposed as distinguishing features of spoken language - such as compositionality and lexical forms - are not peculiar to the spoken medium but can be found in gesture as well and that, when examined in gesture, we can see how non-compositional and non-lexical forms can, in the right circumstances, become transformed into forms which are compositional and lexical (for further discussion see Chapters 13 and 14).

McNeill published an interpretation of this paper in which he proposed that gestures could be arranged along a *continuum* (which he generously called "Kendon's continuum"). At one end of this continuum gesture is used in conjunction with speech, it is global and holistic in its mode of expression, idiosyncratic in form and users are but marginally aware of their use of it. At the other end, gesture is used independently of speech, it is compositional and lexical in its structure and organization and users are fully aware that they are using it. In between he places 'mime', which can be used in alternation with speech, and 'emblems' which are standardized gestures which can function as complete utterances in their own right but which do not constitute the components of a *language system*, as is the case with signs. The point McNeill wished to make by this formulation was that one should not think of 'gesture' as all of a piece, that there are different kinds and that each must be dealt with theoretically in a rather different way. The *continuum* was useful as a way of defining his particular domain of interest - which is 'gesture' found at the extreme left end of the continuum, or 'gesticulation' as Kendon once called it.

Marianne Gullberg (1998) proposed an expansion for Kendon's continuum. She made this suggestion in the course of developing a coding scheme to be used in a study of the use of gesture as a communication strategy in speakers who were using a language they were learning. She took as her starting point the typology offered by McNeill but found it necessary to undertake a more detailed analysis of 'iconicity' in gesture which would allow her to deal with mime. In many reports of studies in second language acquisition, mime was often referred to as being resorted to as a means of overcoming a lack in vocabulary or other linguistic means of expression and hence it was important for Gullberg to be able to take account of it.

Gullberg points out that if one considers gestures in terms of the degree to which they are iconic it is possible to range them on a scale that extends from beats, which have no representational character, to fully iconic gestures. In between she proposes "abstract deictic gestures", "metaphoric gestures", and "concrete deictics" (deictics that refer to concrete entities, that is to say) as steps along the scale toward "iconic gestures" at the far end. Noting, then, that iconics have been divided into those in which the hands are being used as if they represent objects or to describe objects - so-called Object-Viewpoint Iconics - and those in which the hands are being used as if they are the hands of some character in a narration - so-called Character-Viewpoint Iconics (see Cassell and McNeill 1990 and Tuite 1993), she then realizes that all that is needed for a Character-Viewpoint Iconic gesture to become a mime is for more than the hands to be involved in the action. Once a person starts mobilizing the trunk and, especially, the head into the action of the gesture, the gesture becomes mime. Thus it is that Character-Viewpoint Iconics merge into mime. She presents, in the form of a diagram, what she refers to as "Kendon's expanded continuum". First of all, there is a scale that runs from No Convention and Speech (this presumably means that for the gestures at this end of the scale speech is always present) to Convention and No Speech. To this she then appends another scale within the category of gesticulation, which runs from non-iconic or non-representational beats to iconics. Then, within the category of iconics she appends yet another scale, which runs from Object Viewpoint to Character Viewpoint to Character Viewpoint Expressions to which other bodily articulators have been added - the more such body articulators are added, the idea seems to be, the more complete the mime.

It will be seen that these scales that Gullberg has appended to Kendon's continuum are not really expansions of it. In effect, Gullberg has introduced some other kinds of scales in terms of which gestures can be classified or arranged. The scale of iconicity could equally well be applied to the conventional end of the scale, and mime itself can be created on the spot or it can be highly conventionalized.

Again, we might arrange gestures on a scale which goes from newly created to conventionalized yet this is not necessarily coordinated with a scale which goes from iconic to non-iconic. We may find among any repertoire of conventionalized gestures iconic forms as well as forms that do not seem to be so. Among Neapolitans, for example, a gesture in which the two extended index fingers are held so they parallel one another and are in contact, which may express the idea that two things are equal or that two people have a very close relationship (de Jorio 2000, p. 90, No. 9), seems iconic, in comparison with a gesture in which the hand with index finger and thumb extended and held at right angles to one another is rotated rapidly back and forth on the forearm which serves as an expression for 'nothing'. (Collett and Contarello 1987, p. 82). And it is far from being the case that gestures that are always associated with speech are less conventionalized than those that are not. For example, a gesture that serves to mark the logical centrality of a point being made in a discourse in which the so-called 'ring' hand shape is used (tips of the index finger and thumb placed in contact so they surround a circular space), is, it would seem, a conventional form, yet it does not function separately from the spoken discourse it serves to mark (see Chapter 12 for further discussion). In short, it seems that rather than expanding Kendon's continuum we should multiply it.

McNeill has reached a similar conclusion. In McNeill (2000b) he shows how it is necessary to set up a number of different continua for gestures. He suggests four, in which types of gestures (which he labels as "gesticulation", "pantomime", "emblems" and "sign language") may be contrasted with one another in terms of (1) how they relate to speech, (2) the extent to which they have linguistic properties, (3) the extent to which they are conventionalized, and (4) how they contrast in terms of their semiotic properties.

Conclusion

From the survey undertaken in this chapter - which has aimed to discuss representative schemes rather than to survey all that have been proposed - we have to conclude that the various comparisons and classifications that have been proposed are useful, indeed indispensable, for articulated discussion, but no one of them can be established as a single universal system, equally useful for all investigations. Humans have at their disposal the *gestural medium* which can be used in many different ways and from which many different forms of expression can be fashioned. What forms are fashioned will depend upon the circumstances of use, the communicative purposes for which they are intended, and how they are to be used in relation to the other media of expression that are available. It is useful to distinguish the different ways in which gesture can be used, to study the different conditions which constrain or facilitate the different forms that can be created by it and to examine the processes by which forms can become established that are socially shared. However any categories that may be proposed must be seen to be but temporary devices useful locally, as it were, for the purposes of a current scientific discourse. Given the nature of gesture as a form of human expression, we cannot establish permanent categories that represent *essentially* different forms of expressive behaviour. That is, we have to think of the different gesture typologies that have been proposed as provisional working instruments which may be useful within a certain research perspective or interest but are not at all to be supposed as universal or general schemes that show, in a fashion that is independent of any particular observer, or independent of any particular circumstance of interaction or occasion of use, how the activities of gesture are organized.

At the same time, our survey has also shown that, despite differences in terminology and emphasis, there is broad agreement regarding the different ways in which gesture is used. Everyone seems to recognize that gestures may be used in pointing, for representing through some form of depiction or enactment something that is relevant to the referential content of what is being said, and many have recognized that there are also important functions for gesture in respect to marking up or displaying aspects of the logical structure of the speaker's discourse. All of those whose work we have reviewed have looked upon gesture as an activity that is significant for the understanding of a speaker's expression, they regard it as having an important role to play in this and all agree that it is not without significant social meaning.

7   Gesture units, gesture phrases and speech

The survey in Chapter 6 showed that most writers accept that speakers use gestures in several different ways, including deictic reference, as a means of depicting objects or actions and as a way of punctuating, marking up or displaying aspects of the structure of their spoken discourse. However, if we are to have a better appreciation of the significance of this, we need to know in more detail how and when it is that speakers do these things. Without detailed analysis of how speakers deploy gestures as a part of their utterances we shall not have precise ideas about how speech and gesture function in relation to one another. Audio-visual technology, easily available only very recently, and available only to some of the writers whose classification schemes we have considered, now makes possible the kind of descriptive analysis of gesture use that we believe is needed. It is this that will be offered in the chapters that follow: a descriptive survey of gesture use, based upon the analysis of specimens drawn from a large collection of video recordings of occasions of conversational interaction in many different settings.

In this chapter and the next one, we look at aspects of how gesturing and speaking are organized in relation to one another. The units of gestural action we consider are the *gesture phrase* and the *gesture unit*. These are defined in terms of changes in how the body parts involved in gesturing are posed and moved, as will be explained below. Speech is analysed into *tone units*, following the criteria given in Crystal and Davy (1969). We begin by examining how these units are related to one another in time. However, we shall also consider them from the point of view of their meanings. Tone units are packages of speech production identified by prosodic features which correspond to units of discourse meaning. In the same way, gesture phrases are units of visible bodily action identified by kinesic features which correspond to meaningful units of action such as a pointing, a depiction, a pantomime or the enactment of a conventionalized gesture. When we look at the temporal coordination of gesture phrases and the tone units in any discourse we also look at the meaning relationships between these two aspects of utterance action. We shall see that speakers create *ensembles* of gesture and speech, by means of which a semantic coherence between the two modalities is attained. This is not to say that speech and gesture express the same meanings. They are often different. Nevertheless, the meanings expressed by these two components *interact* in the utterance and, through a reciprocal process, a more complex unit of meaning is the result. This is examined in Chapter 9. In Chapter 10 we illustrate the main ways in which gesture makes its contribution to the referential meaning of the utterance, at least as we have observed them in the material at our disposal. This theme is continued with a study of pointing in Chapter 11.

In Chapters 12 and 13 we explore how gesture is involved in pragmatic meanings in the utterance. We look at gestures as performatives (gestures that indicate a request, a plea, an offer, an invitation, a refusal, and so forth), as operators (as in gestures that serve as negatives or indicate the evidential status of something that is being said), and gestures that have parsing or discourse structure marking functions (for example, indicating the distinction between topic and comment or marking what is prominent or focal in a unit of discourse).

The examples used in this work to illustrate how speakers use gesture are drawn from a large number of video recordings made in everyday settings in various circumstances and various locations, almost all of them between 1991 and 2001. These include recordings made in Naples and Salerno and adjacent cities in Campania in Italy, in a small town in Northamptonshire in England which we will refer to as 'Northant', and in several locations in the United States.

All of the recordings from Campania and all those from England were made in the course of collecting material for the study of gesture and other aspects of communication conduct in face-to-face interaction either by myself or by students under my direction. Many of the occasions recorded were occasions that were taking place for the participants' own purposes. These included dinner parties, committee meetings, casual card games, interactions between customers and vendors at market stalls, semi-public presentations by tour guides, and informal conversations. However, we have also used recordings of conversations which took place at our request. In these the participants were asked to reminisce about their childhood and youth, to discuss the state of the city they live in, or to talk about what they considered to be important aspects of their own local culture. The recordings made in the United States include some that were made by students under my direction and some that were made within the context of social occasions within my own family. A few recordings kindly made available to me by colleagues have also been used. Full details of the recordings used are given in Appendix II.

All recordings were made openly, with the full knowledge and consent of the participants who knew that the recordings would be studied later and used for academic purposes. In some cases it was explained that we wanted to make the recording as a documentation of aspects of communication style in everyday life. Although it was often mentioned that we were interested in communication or conversation, our more specific interest in how conversationalists use gesture was never explained in advance. In all cases the participants were always much more interested in what they happened to be doing or what they were talking about than they were in the fact that they were being recorded.

The participants include both men and women. They vary in social and educational background. Most are above forty years in age, although some younger participants and, in a few cases, children are also included. We have made no attempt to stratify or systematize the sampling of participants. Examples have been selected for the clarity with which they illustrate different kinds of gesture usage. Questions about how gesture usage might vary systematically by age, sex, setting, discourse circumstance and the like, although of great potential interest and importance, have not been explored.

We observe the following terminological conventions. The term *utterance* (as stated in Chapter 2) is used to refer to the ensemble of actions, whether composed of speech alone, of visible action alone, or of a combination of the two, that counts for participants as a 'turn' or 'contribution' or 'move' within the occasion of interaction in which they are engaged. *Speech* will be used to refer to the vocal activity engaged in when a spoken language is employed. *Gesture* refers to visible bodily activity that is regarded as serving as an utterance or as a component of an utterance. Utterances will be said to be able to have both a spoken component and a gestural component. The spoken component may be analysed in terms of the speech phrases (defined as tone units) it contains. When the spoken component alone is referred to, it is convenient to use the term *locution*. The gestural component may be analysed in terms of the *gesture units* and *gesture phrases* it contains, as will be explained in greater detail below.

The person who engages in the production of an utterance (in whatever modality) is referred to as a *speaker*. Utterances are always *addressed* and the addressee or addressees will be referred to as *recipients* or *interlocutors*. *Participants* are those who are members of any occasion of interaction and, at least in small conversational gatherings, are those present who are treated by members of the occasion both as potential hearers or recipients and as potential speakers, that is, as having a right to engage in 'turns' or 'contributions' or 'moves'.

In the present chapter we examine gesturing as flow of action. We describe its phrasal organization and we introduce a terminology in terms of which this may be discussed. In the chapter to follow (Chapter 8) we continue with a description of further examples to illustrate some of the different ways in which speakers may organize gesturing in relation to the phrases of speaking within the same utterance. These illustrations may not cover all possibilities but they do show that there can be no simple and invariable rule governing this relationship. It appears that there is flexibility in the gesture–speech relationship and this, it will be suggested, is best understood in terms of a point of view that sees gesture and speech as two different kinds of *expressive resource* available to speakers, and that the gestures employed within an utterance, like the words that are employed, are components of a speaker's *final product*. Both the gestures and the verbal expressions used are to be accounted for in terms of such factors as the speaker's immediate aims, the speaker's knowledge of various expressive resources and possession of skills needed to use them, as well as the constraints and possibilities existing within the context of the given moment of interaction, including its various structural and ritual requirements. That is to say, the gestures that are used together with speech in the same utterance are not part of the processes that, in due course, lead up to *verbal* formulation. They are, rather, an integral part of what a speaker does in fashioning an object, the utterance, that is shaped to meet the expressive and communicative aims and requirements of a given interactional moment. Gesture is a *partner* with speech in the utterance as finally constructed.

Whether or not the utterance constructed meets those aims and does so effectively is another question. People do not always manage to get their meanings across, no matter what mode of expression or combination of modes they may use. This does not alter the fact that when people create utterances, whether in gesture, or speech, or both together, they do so with the aim of conveying meaning. Gestures, like words, are produced *for* communication even if they do not always succeed in communicating something or are not interpreted by all recipients in just the same way.

Gesture units, gesture phrases and the phases of gestural action

When a person engages in gesturing the body parts that are employed in this activity undertake a *movement excursion* or a succession of such *excursions*. That is, in the case of forelimb gesturing, for instance, the articulators are moved away from some position of rest or relaxation (this is sometimes called the 'home position' after Sacks and Schegloff 2002) toward a region of space (or sometimes toward some location specifiable with reference to the speaker's body), and then, eventually, they are moved back again to some position of rest or relaxation. This entire *excursion*, from the moment the articulators begin to depart from a position of relaxation until the moment when they finally return to one, will be referred to as a *gesture unit*. Within the course of such an excursion, or gesture unit, we may distinguish one or more phases in which the articulators reach points of furthest remove from the position of relaxation. As these apices of the excursion are approached, the hand or hands tend to assume postures or *hand shapes* that, relatively speaking, are better defined than elsewhere in the excursion, they may perform a pattern of movement that, again, relatively, is well defined, or movement may cease briefly, the articulators being held still for a moment before beginning to be relaxed and returned toward a position of rest.

The phase of the movement excursion closest to its apex is usually recognized as the phase when the 'expression' of the gesture, whatever it may be, is accomplished. It is the phase of the excursion in which the movement dynamics of 'effort' and 'shape' are manifested with greatest clarity (see Laban and Lawrence 1947; Dell 1970; Bartinieff and Lewis 1980). This phase is called the *stroke*. The phase of movement leading up to the stroke is termed the *preparation*. The phase of movement that follows, as the hand is relaxed, or is withdrawn, is referred to as the *recovery*.

The *stroke* may sometimes be followed by a phase in which the articulator is sustained in the position at which it arrived at the end of the stroke. This has been referred to as the *post-stroke hold* (Kita 1993). When a speaker employs a post-stroke hold, that is, when a speaker sustains the articulator of a stroke in position after performing the stroke action, this seems to be a way by which the expression conveyed by the stroke may be prolonged. As we shall see below, stroke and post-stroke hold together usually bracket a semantically complete phrase of speech. We shall refer to the phase of action that includes the *stroke* and any *post-stroke hold* as the *nucleus* of the gesture phrase. It is this part of the gesture phrase that, as a rule, is interpreted as that part of the action that carries the expression or meaning of the gesture phrase.

The *stroke*, then, and any *post-stroke hold* that there may be, as well as any *preparation* that leads up to the stroke, including any pauses or holds there may be in this phase of movement, define the *gesture phrase*. That is to say, the gesture phrase always and only contains but one *stroke*, but it also contains any *preparation* that leads to the stroke and, as just mentioned, any period that follows in which the gesture instrument (hands or head, for example) is *held* or otherwise maintained in the position it reaches at the end of the stroke. The *recovery* movement, when the hand (or other body part) relaxes and is returned to some position of rest is not considered to be part of the *gesture phrase*, although it is, of course, part of the *gesture unit* which contains the *gesture phrase*.

The *gesture unit*, as we have already said, is the entire excursion of the articulator of the gestural action. This excursion may contain one or more *gesture phrases*. It is, generally speaking, the *strokes* of such gesture phrases that are picked out by casual observers and identified as 'gestures'.

Although this casual identification may be good enough in the contexts of some discussions, for a proper understanding of just how speakers organize their gestural and speech components together within a given utterance it is very important to take the phases of gesture units and gesture phrases into consideration. Only in this way can we arrive at an understanding of the nature of the coordination that obtains between these two modes of expression. A proper account of this is an essential starting point for any theoretical account we might give regarding how this coordination is achieved and what this might imply for a theory of the utterance, whether from a semiotic, communicational or psychological viewpoint.[1]

The phases of gestural action illustrated[2]

We now describe three examples to illustrate what has been outlined. The first two show a gesture unit which contains but one gesture phrase. The third is an instance of a gesture unit which contains several gesture phrases. In discussing these examples we shall also consider the way in which the gesture units and their component gesture phrases are related to the spoken component of the utterance, both from the point of view of how phases of gestural action appear to be coordinated with the phrasal organization of the speech, and also from the point of view of how there is a semantic relationship between gesture and speech. The observations offered here will set the stage for the discussions that follow in later chapters.

Our first example, Example 1, is taken from Part III of the recording known as Crick (Crick III 17.42.02). It is taken from a passage in which M is explaining how his father, once the proprietor of a grocery shop, managed the cheeses that he kept ready for sale. He is explaining how his father used to wait until the cheeses stored in the cellar of his shop were "absolutely ripe". When a cheese (such as a Stilton or a Gorgonzola) is fully ripe it starts to 'sweat' or 'run' and to dry this off it was the custom to scatter ground rice over the cheeses.

In Example 1 M says "And he used to go down there and throw ground rice over it." At the beginning of this locution M is standing in front of a small table, his arms slightly forward with both hands, palms down, resting

---

[1] A lack of clarity and consistency in how investigators have defined the units of gesture they are measuring has been responsible for much confusion in the field. For example Nobe (2000) shows how widely quoted claims about the relationship between speech pauses and gestures such as those based on Butterworth and Beattie (1978) must be questioned because the units of action involved have not been defined in a consistent manner.

[2] Transcription conventions used in the Examples for both speech and gesture are described in Appendix I.

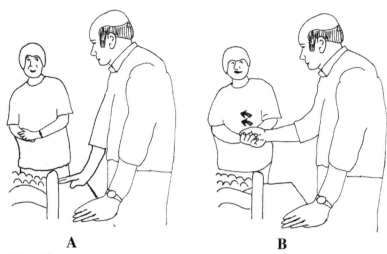

A   **B**

Fig. 7.1   M's rest position before and after his 'stroke' is shown in A. B shows the 'stroke' of M's gesture phrase.

Example 1   Crick III 17.42.02

RH right hand; ~~~ preparation; *** stroke action; -.-.recovery; (...) indicates a pause in speech. Length of pause in tenths of a second. Tonic syllables in SMALL CAPITALS.

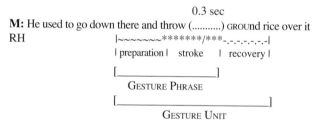

0.3 sec
M: He used to go down there and throw (..........) GROUnd rice over it
RH |~~~~~~~~*******/***-.-.-.-.-.-.-|
              | preparation | stroke | recovery |

              [_____]
                  GESTURE PHRASE
              [_____]
                   GESTURE UNIT

on the table (A in Fig. 7.1). As he is saying "throw" his right arm is extended forward with his hand oriented with palm uppermost, with the fingers flexed inward to be in contact with the palm, the tip of the thumb resting on the first joint of the index finger. The hand, so shaped, is moved by wrist extension, outward, rapidly, twice (B in Fig. 7.1). This double action of the hand has all the appearance of the kind of action one would perform if one were scattering a handful of dust or powder over a somewhat extended surface. Once this hand action is finished, M returns his hand to the position it was in before - palm flat on the table before him (A in Fig. 7.1).

We see, thus, an entire *gesture unit*. It begins the moment M commences to move his hand away from its position on the table and it ends the moment it returns there. During the course of this excursion or gesture unit M performs the hand action that we have described - this is the *stroke*. Before he performs that hand action, however, he must lift his hand away from the table to the position in front of him where the action is to be performed and he also must change the orientation of his hand and the position of the fingers. This phase, during which M in this way gets ready to do the action of the stroke, is called the *preparation*. The *preparation* and the *stroke* together constitute what we here call the *gesture phrase*. Following the hand action there is a period when the hand is returned to its rest position, and this we term the *recovery*. The *recovery* is included in the gesture unit but it is not part of the gesture phrase. The relationship between these phases of action within the gesture unit and how they are related to speech is shown in the transcription.

It will be seen that the first phase of hand action just described, identified as the *stroke* of the gesture phrase (marked as a row of asterisks in the transcript), occurs while the speaker says "throw", with the second phase being performed during a very brief pause in the speaker's speech following "throw". Note that in order for the speaker to perform the action of the stroke so that it is associated with the pronunciation of the word "throw" in this way, he has to *prepare to do so in advance of the production of this word*. Before he comes to say "throw" his hand must already be in an appropriate position to do the action that is to coincide with it. As will be seen from the transcription of Example 1 the speaker begins the *preparation* for this action (i.e., moving the hand away from its rest position and lifting it up so the hand is in the forward position used when the 'scatter' action of the stroke is performed) well in advance of "throw" - indeed he begins it just as he finishes saying "down", the final word of the phrase where he is describing where his father used to go. Thus the gesture unit, and in this case also the gesture phrase, begin just at the moment the speaker finishes the word "down". The *stroke* is begun just with the beginning of the vowel of "throw". The stroke, which in this case is a stroke with two action phases, continues during "throw" and during a brief pause in the speech that follows. Immediately the stroke is finished the *recovery* begins and, in this case, towards the end of this phase, the speaker resumes speaking, pronouncing "ground", the next word in his locution.

Two points may be made in relation to this example. First, the 'scatter' action performed in relation to the verb 'throw' is *semantically coherent* with the meaning of the verb. Thus, at the same time as the speaker uses a verbal expression for an action of a certain sort, he *also* does something with his hand that seems to exemplify this action. However, it is not the case that the speaker expresses the *same thing* with his word as he does with his gesture. The verb 'throw' has a general, abstract meaning. It means that some object is freed from a grasp and the grasping organ, usually the hand, imparts momentum to the object as it lets go of it, so that the object flies through the air. However, according to the shape, size, weight and material character of what is being thrown, the way in which the action of throwing is done will be different. Here the action of the gesture seems adapted to the sort of action one would perform were one to be scattering a handful of dust or powder over something. The gesture, thus, provides a representation of a specific type of throwing action. In doing so, the action of the gesture makes what is expressed by the verb 'throw' much more precise. As will be discussed in more detail in Chapter 8, this is a very common way in which gestures can contribute to the referential meaning of an utterance.

Second, the speaker, well in advance of the part of his locution where he is to make reference to the action of 'throwing', has *already* embarked on the preparation for the action that, in conjunction with the verb, will create a combined expression. From this it seems clear that, even as the speaker was getting ready for the verbal component of the utterance he was *also* getting ready for its gestural component. The way in which gesture and speech are employed together in this example can only be understood if it is agreed that they are planned for together. Gesture and speech, thus, are *integral components* of the utterance. The gesture could not have been organized as a *consequence* of the speech and there seems nothing in the relationship between the two components that could suggest that the action of the gesture somehow prompts the verbal structure of the phrase. The gestural action must have been got ready at the same time as the speech was got ready. It is used as an expressive device that *complements* the expression achieved in words. By using gesture with speech together, in this way, the speaker achieves a more complete account of his father's action than he otherwise might have done.

Our second example, Example 2 (see Fig. 7.2 and the transcription for this example), again shows a single gesture phrase within a gesture unit. It is also taken from Crick III (Crick III 15.55.21) and also from the part of this recording where the protagonists were recalling the way in which grocery shops used to be run. In the course of this discussion one of them, S, recalls the window decorations that the local shops used to have. She says: "And they used to have wonderful window displays in there, didn't they?" In association with saying this she raises both her arms so that her hands are level with her eyes, the hands being open and oriented so that the palms are facing obliquely downwards. Then she moves both arms together, in a symmetrical way, so that the hands each trace an outward–inward vertically downward path. This is done in a manner that suggests that she is outlining something, perhaps outlining the form of a display of goods in a shop window in which, as was the custom in the times of which she was speaking, grocery goods were often set up in quite tall and elaborate constructions. This outward–inward–downward

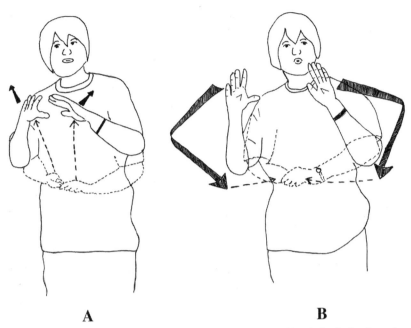

A   **B**

Fig. 7.2 A shows movement of S's arms from rest position to the position for beginning the stroke. B shows movement of S's arms from the beginning stroke position. Solid arrows show the path of movement of the stroke. Dotted arrows show path of movement of recovery.

Example 2 (Crick III 15.55.21)

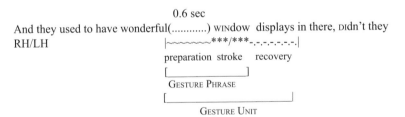

vertical movement of both hands ('outlining' as we will call it, for short) is performed in precise association with the word "window". The relationship between these hand movements and the speech is given in the transcription. The movements made by the hands in this action are depicted in A and B in Fig. 7.2.

    The first point to note is that, as this passage begins, S is holding her hands in a relaxed manner, one lightly resting upon the other, in front of her lower body (see arms drawn in broken lines in A in Fig. 7.2). Then her hands move away from this *rest position*, and they are lifted up and moved so that they perform the 'outlining' movement we have described (see A and B in Fig. 7.2). Then they return to rest lightly one upon the other, as before (see B in Fig. 7.2). We may thus again delineate a *gesture unit* that begins the moment the hands begin to move away from their position of rest in front of the body and which continues until they are returned there. Once again we see how the hands make an *excursion* away from a position of rest to which, in the end, they return, an excursion which, in accordance with our terminology, we refer to as the *gesture unit*. During the course of this excursion we see how, as before, the hands perform what we term a *gesture phrase*.

This gesture phrase is recognized in the well-defined action of the hands - here referred to as 'outlining' - in which they move, each mirroring the movement of the other, in a downward outward–inward fashion (depicted in B in Fig. 7.2). This movement may be recognized as the phase of action within the movement excursion through which is effected the expression that these movements accomplish. In this case, that is, 'outlining'. This is the *stroke* of the gesture phrase. Here the hands not only move along the outward–inward–downward vertical path we have described but they do so with an evident acceleration and in a well-defined manner that seems distinctive (in effort–shape terms we may say that in this phase the 'effort' as well as the 'shape' of the movement become very clear).

Again we see that, in order for this stroke to be performed, the hands must be positioned so that they are ready to do the movement of the stroke. We see, accordingly, that the *stroke* is preceded by a phase of movement which prepares the articulators for its performance. So again we have a *preparation*, in the present example constituted by the movement in which the hands are lifted up in front of the chest, so that the vertical outward–inward–downward movement of the 'outlining' action may be performed (see A in Fig. 7.2). Once this outlining movement is finished, the hands then relax slightly and are moved somewhat more slowly back to their position in which one is at rest upon the other (dotted arrows in B in Fig. 7.2). In this phase we may note a diminution in speed of movement and a diminution in the definiteness with which the movements are performed. Here the hands 'merely' return to their rest position. This is the *recovery* phase. In this case, again, then, we have a gesture unit that extends from hands-at-rest to hands-at-rest, within which a single *gesture phrase* is contained, consisting of a preparation and a stroke.

Now let us consider how, in this example, the speech is associated with the gesture unit and the gesture phrase it contains. We may note, first, that the speech is organized into two tone units: "They used to have wonderful wiNdow displays in there/DIDn't they." The second tone unit is a 'tag' - the voice is much lowered in volume and there is much less change in pitch level in the tonic syllable than there is in the first. That is, it is subordinated to the first tone unit (Crystal 1969), the two tone units being performed together as a single turn (or single locution). The gestural expression occurs in association with only the first of these two tone units.

It will be seen that the *stroke* of the gesture phrase is performed precisely in association with "window". As the speaker says "WIN" (the tonic syllable of the phrase) she moves her hands rapidly downwards and outwards (B in Fig. 7.2). Over the second syllable of this word she moves her hands rapidly inwards, the movement over the entire word thus describing a downward and outward–inward path which, done by the two hands mirroring each other's actions, we have described as 'outlining'. As she says "displays" the hands lose their acceleration and there is an evident relaxation as they return to their rest position (dotted arrows in B in Fig. 7.2). We see, in short, how the stroke of the gesture phrase is performed very precisely in association with "window". This word occupies the nucleus of the first tone unit and is here, also, the high information word of the phrase, specifying the type of display that the speaker is referring to. In this example, by this coordination of the stroke with the word "window", the speaker achieves an ensemble of expression in which, at one and the same time, she specifies the type of display she is referring to and, through the gesture, performs an action that seems best interpreted as an action that outlines an area that presents itself immediately in front of the speaker as the large expanse of a shop window. It seems reasonable to say, once again, that the gesture–speech ensemble the speaker creates here also has *semantic coherence*.

In this example, then, as in Example 1, we see how the gestural action can be analysed as a gesture unit within which we can distinguish a gesture phrase. We see how the stroke of the gesture phrase co-occurs with a verbal expression with which it may be said to be semantically coherent and we see how in achieving this coordination the speaker begins the preparation for the stroke in advance. It is notable, however, that in this second example the speaker inserts a pause between "wonderful" and "window" and it is in this pause that the hands are finally positioned so that they can perform the rapid 'outlining' action that we have here identified as the stroke. Whereas, in the first example, we noted a pause in the speech immediately after "throw" during which the speaker completed the second part of the two-part action that constituted the 'scatter' action of the stroke, in the present example there is a pause in the speech before the word that takes the stroke. These pauses do not appear to be word-search pauses, for in both cases the speaker's flow of action is fluent and there is no withdrawal of visual attention. They appear, rather, to be pauses introduced to permit a coordination between word and stroke that produces the semantic coherence we have noted. In both cases, however, in terms of how the spoken and the gestural components are organized in relation to one another, this coordination, in each case, is achieved in a somewhat different way.

Example 3, our third example, shows how a single gesture unit may contain several gesture phrases. This is taken from a recording made in Northant of a guide, GB, who is giving a tour of the town, describing points of historical and architectural interest. In this extract (GB 2.22.45) GB has been explaining how certain buildings in the town had been demolished and new ones put up using, as he is explaining, stone from these demolished buildings. In the extract examined here he suggests that the re-use of good building stone is a common practice. He then expresses this idea in a somewhat more concrete fashion. It is during this part of his discourse that he uses his right arm and hand in gesturing. He also uses his head, as we shall see.

The relationship between words and gesture in Example 3 is shown in the transcription. The four strokes of the manual gesture units are depicted in Fig. 7.3 (p. 122). In this Example we see but one *gesture unit* - here labelled as a *forelimb gesture unit* (fgu) since, in this example there is also a gesture unit performed by the head. The single forelimb gesture unit extends from the moment the right hand begins to be raised (four-tenths of a second before GB begins tone unit 6) to the moment the hand begins to relax (seven-tenths of a second after the end of tone unit 9). Within this forelimb gesture unit, however, there are four *forelimb gesture phrases* (fgps). The *strokes* of the forelimb gesture phrases are as follows: In the first of these, fgp 1, GB lowers his right hand by moving his forearm vertically downwards by an extension movement from the elbow joint, with the hand held rigid at the wrist, its digits partially extended and held in contact with one another (Fig. 7.3B). In the second, fgp 2, GB moves his right hand rapidly to the right in a horizontal movement, at the same time slightly extending his wrist (Fig. 7.3C). In fgp 3 he moves his hand vertically downwards, at the same time changing the orientation of the forearm so that the palm of the hand comes to face downwards (Fig. 7.3D). In fgp 4, there is a rotation of the forearm so that the palm of the hand turns to face upwards (Fig. 7.3E). Each of the strokes of the first three of these phrases is preceded by a phase of *preparation*. For each, that is, there is a phase in which the hand is lifted in readiness for the movement of the stroke. In all four phrases the *stroke* is followed by a *hold*. That is, the hand, after being moved downwards or laterally, as the case may be, is held still in the position it has reached at the end of this movement. The fourth gesture phrase, it is to be noted, has no preparation, for in this case the movement, a forearm rotation, is done within the position the forearm had reached at the end of the previous stroke. The different movements of the hands just described are not separated by periods in which the hand *recovers* or returns to its rest position or even begins to be relaxed and begins such a return. It is for this reason that these movement phrases we have identified as *gesture phrases* are all united together in a single *gesture unit*.

In the head, head gesture phrase (hgp) 1 is a once repeated lateral head turn or 'head shake'. Hgp 2 is a lowering of the head. Note that hgp 1 is performed during the *hold* of the last of the forelimb gesture phrases, whereas the final head gesture phrase, a head lowering, is coordinated with the fourth fgp, in which the forearm is rotated so that the palm of GB's open hand now faces upwards.

Example 3 (GB 2:22:45)

fgp: forelimb gesture phrase; fgu: forelimb gesture unit;
hgp: head gesture phrase

```
     (1)     (2)                    (3)
     AGAIN/ good quality STONE/It is like a LOT of stone/ um
     (4)                    (5)
     Throughout the WORLD /If it's a good BUILDing material/
        (6)                         (7)                 (8)
     (0.4)When you KNOCK something down /you don't THROW it away/ you USE it again/
RH|~~|*********/**************|~~~~~~|******/*******|~~~~~~|******/******
     prep  stroke       hold       prep   stroke   hold   prep   stroke    hold
     [_____][_____][_____
           fgp 1                       fgp 2                 fgp 3
     [_____
                              fgu 1
        (9)
     (..0.7.)because it will last forEVER/(...0.7...)
RH  *********************/*****/*******|-.-.-.-.-.-.-.-.-.|
           hold (continues)   stroke     hold      recovery
     _____][_____] (hand relaxes, lowered)
           fgp 3              fgp 4
HD|~~~~*******/****/***|******|_____|
     [        hgp 1    ][  hgp 2    ]
     _____]
                    fgu 1 (continued)
```

Now consider how these gesture phrases are coordinated with the tone units into which we have divided the locution. There are nine tone units - in each case the tonic syllable is indicated by small capitals. The first five introduce the idea that good quality building stone is recycled. GB does not use his forelimbs in gesture during this part of his discourse (he does employ his head, but for the sake of simplicity of exposition we shall not discuss this here). With the final four tone units, where he does use both forelimbs and head in gesture, he expresses the idea of recycling old stone in new buildings in a more concrete way. It is notable that in the first three of the tone units which are associated with forelimb gesture phrases, we have a verb phrase which expresses a kind

A
If it's good quality stone

B
when you knock something down

C
you don't throw it away

D
you use it again

E
because it will last forever

Fig. 7.3   The four strokes of the four forelimb gesture phrases in Example 3. B: Hand lowered sharply. The dynamics of this movement suit the idea of making a sharp impact on something. C: Hand and arm 'flung' outwards. The dynamics of this movement are coherent with the idea of 'throwing' something. D: Hand with palm facing down lowered slowly. The dynamics of this movement suit the idea of placing an object on something. E. Forearm rotates so palm faces upwards. This is an action of 'discourse presentation'. See Chapter 13 for further discussion of this kind of gesture.

of action. The final tone unit, associated with a head gesture, describes a state of being, not an action.

First, it is to be noted that each gesture phrase is associated with a separate tone unit. It is also to be noted that the preparation for the stroke in each case *precedes* the tone unit with which it is associated. Thus, the preparation for forelimb gesture phrase (fgp) 1 begins during the four-tenths of a second pause that precedes the beginning of tone unit 6; the preparation for fgp 2 begins over "down", the last word of tone unit 6; that for fgp 3 begins over "away", the last word of tone unit 7. And between the end of tone unit 8 and tone unit 9 there is another pause of seven-tenths of a second during which GB prepares for the gesture that he makes with his head. Note further that, in each case, the stroke is followed by a *hold* which, when combined with the stroke, ensures that the *nucleus* of the gesture phrase (stroke and post-stroke hold together) is so organized that it extends over the major part of each unit of speech that conveys a new idea.

Now note how each gesture phrase is differentiated from the other so that the actions are interpretable as forms of expression which, when considered from the point of view of what they express, show a *semantic coherence* with the verb phrase with which they co-occur. Thus, in the stroke of fgp 1 (associated with "knock something down"), the hand is held tense, with fingers extended and together, it is moved downward sharply immediately before the speaker says "knock" in a form of action consistent with the notion of hitting something in a brusque manner as one would if one were to knock something down. In the stroke of fgp 2 (associated with "you don't throw it away"), in contrast, again immediately before "throw" the arm moves laterally, outward, and the hand, while 'open' as before, is now lax, and at the end of the outward movement the wrist is extended. This has the consequence of 'throwing' the hand outward. This movement seems consistent with the idea of 'throwing away' something. In the stroke of fgp 3 (associated with "you use it again"), again in contrast, the hand, again open, is now oriented so that the palm faces downwards and the hand is lowered (this time as he says "use"), but with a deliberate precision, rather than brusquely. Perhaps this may be interpreted as being consistent with placing something and, if so, it could be seen as consistent with the idea of 'using something', especially using something in the context of building something. As for the head shake over "because it will last forever", this may be seen to be semantically coherent if we accept the idea that the negation expressed here in the head shake is the negation that is implied by the words uttered, namely that there is no exception to the state of affairs that has been characterized (see Chapter 13 and Kendon 2002).

The two final gesture phrases, which occur simultaneously, the head lowering (hgp 2) and the forearm rotation that turns the palm of GB's open hand so it faces upwards (fgp 4), do not relate to the content of the speaker's discourse. The lowering of the head here is a unit of movement characteristically associated with the falling intonation tone that comes at the end of a discourse unit or locution (it thus marks an aspect of discourse structure), while the turning of the hand so the palm faces upwards is a gestural form often seen in a context such as this one, where it can be interpreted as an 'offer' or a 'presentation' of the discourse object to the recipients, commonly to be seen at the end of a discourse, where it serves as a terminal marker.

Gestures of this type, which are considered to belong to the so-called 'Open Hand Supine' family and which have a range of discourse marking and other pragmatic functions, will be discussed further in Chapter 13. See also Müller (In Press).

Discussion and conclusion

In this chapter we have aimed to provide a terminology in terms of which the organization of manual or forelimb gesturing may be described. We have also made observations on how the phrasal organization of gesturing is organized in relation to the phrasal organization of the speech of the utterance of which it is a part.

We have shown that forelimb gesturing is best regarded as movements that are organized as *excursions* and that it is in terms of this that the units of gestural activity may be defined. We defined the *gesture unit* as the entire movement excursion, which commences the moment the gesturing limb or limbs begin to leave their position of rest or relaxation, and which finishes only when the limbs are once again relaxed. Within the gesture unit one or more *gesture phrases* may be discerned. A gesture phrase is identified for every *stroke* of gestural action that may be observed, the *stroke* being that phase or those phases of the excursion in which the poses and movement patterns of the gesturing body parts are most *well defined*, relative to the entire excursion. The stroke phase, as we noted, often is not carried out until the limb has been moved to some particular position, relative to the speaker's body, and the phase during which this positioning occurs is referred to as the *preparation*. The *stroke*, and any *preparation*, together constitute the *gesture phrase*. Also considered part of the gesture phrase are any phases either during the preparation, or following the stroke, in which the gesturing body part is *held*, that is, in which it stops moving but is sustained in a position that requires muscular action if that position is to be maintained. As we saw, a gesture unit may contain only one gesture phrase, or it may contain two or more of them.

We then discussed, for the three examples, how the phrasal organization of the gesturing in each case was organized in relation to the speech. The principal feature in this organization that we noted is how what is distinguished as the *stroke* of the gesture phrase is performed in close temporal proximity to that part of the associated tone unit that expresses something that can be regarded as semantically coherent with it. The *nucleus* of the gesture phrase, that is, the stroke and any hold that may follow it, tends to be performed in such a way that it is done at the same time, or nearly at the same time as the pronunciation of the word or word cluster that constitutes the nucleus, in a semantic sense, of the spoken phrase. This means that, by coordinating temporally the nucleus of the gesture phrase (i.e. the stroke and any post-stroke hold) with the semantic nucleus of the spoken expression, the speaker achieves a *conjunction* of two different modes of expression which, as we have said, also have semantic coherence one with the other.

To achieve this, however, we noted that the *preparation* of the gesture phrase begins in advance of the parts of the spoken expressions to which it is to be linked semantically. This means that, when using gesture, the speaker must already have organized it at the same time as the plan for the spoken phrase with which it is to co-occur is organized. Gesture and speech, thus, are planned for together and gestural expression is a fully integrated component of the utterance's construction.

As already mentioned in Chapter 5, it is this integration of gesture and speech that led Kendon (1980a) to claim that these two modes of expression must be considered as "two aspects of the process of utterance" and that led McNeill (1985) to ask, ironically (in the title to his first article on gesture), "So you think gestures are nonverbal?" and to propose that gestures, rather, must be regarded as a part of language. McNeill's growth point theory is his attempt to work out the implications of this integration for cognitive theories of utterance production (McNeill 1992, 1999, 2000; McNeill and Duncan 2000). De Ruiter (2000) and Kita (2000) and Kita and Özyürek (2003) offer alternative theoretical frameworks which, nevertheless, also take the integration of gesture with speech as a starting point (see Chapter 5).

The phrasal analysis of gesturing followed in this chapter was first developed in Kendon (1972) and the associated terminology (since only slightly modified) was first proposed in Kendon (1980a). The way in which the components of gesture phrases are organized in relation to speech phrases considered as tone units and the semantic coherence of these two modes of expression was also described in these papers (see also Schegloff 1984 and McNeill 1992 for similar descriptions). It was said in those papers, however, that the stroke of the gesture phrase was always completed either before or at the same time as the tonic syllable of the co-occurrent tone unit, as if there was some kind of invariable association between the tonic centre of the tone unit and the stroke of the gesture phrase. Furthermore, it was suggested that the tonic centre of the tone unit was also the 'high information' word of the phrase, so that the stroke of the gesture phrase, the tonic syllable, and the information centre of the speech phrase, were all co-occurrent. As will be evident from the examples described in this chapter, however, it does not seem that we can make so easy a generalization. Although in Example 2 the stroke is performed simultaneously with the tonic centre of the tone unit and this is also the high information word, in Example 1 the speaker performs the stroke as he says "throw", but he continues his stroke *after* this word is finished. As he says "ground", which in this case is the tonic centre of the tone unit, he is completing the recovery phase of the gesture phrase. In Example 3, where we saw a succession of gesture phrases associated with a succession of tone units, while for each tone unit we could find an associated gesture phrase, how the strokes of those gesture phrases are placed in relation to both the tonic syllable and the semantic structure of the speech phrases is variable. In speech phrases 6 and 7 the stroke is performed well in advance of the tonic centre, whereas in 8 and 9 it co-occurs with it. And we also noted that the gesture phrase associated with speech phrases 7 and 8 began before the preceding speech phrase was completed.

We also saw that, in all three examples, pauses in the speech occur which are not pauses that arise from word searches or other difficulties in speaking. They appear to arise, rather, as adaptations to the production of the associated gesturing. However, the placement of these pauses in relation to the associated gesturing is also variable. In Example 1 there was a pause in speech while the speaker was completing his stroke, whereas in Example 2 there was a pause in speech that preceded the stroke, inserted while the speaker was getting her hands ready to perform the stroke. In Example 3, on the other hand, although there were two pauses in speech that were associated with preparation phases of gesture phrases (one preceding speech phrase 6 associated with the preparation of fgp 1 and one preceding speech phrase 9 associated with the preparation phase of head gesture phrase 1), there were no pauses between phrases 7 and 8 and there, as we noted above, the preparation for the next gesture phrase began during the end of the preceding speech phrase.

To sum up, when a speaker speaks, the speech is organized into a series of packages, here identified as tone units marked in terms of variations in voice, pitch level, loudness and pacing. These packages tend to correspond to units of meaning that are at a level above the lexical level, and which, for convenience, may be referred to as 'idea units' (Kendon 1980a). Gesture is also organized into packages of action, here termed 'gesture phrases', which coincide with and tend to be semantically coherent with the units of phrasal meaning or 'idea units' expressed in the tone units. However, the gestural expression typically takes up just a part of the idea unit the tone unit expresses. For example, it may bring out an aspect of meaning associated with the verb in the phrase (as in Example 1 or Example 3), or it may add an imagistic dimension to something referred to by a noun (as in Example 2). The precise way in which a coincidence is achieved between a gesture phrase and that part of the tone unit to which it is related semantically appears to be variable. In our interpretation, this means that the speaker can adjust both speech and gesture one to another as if they are two separate expressive resources which can be deployed, each in relation to the other, in different ways according to how the utterance is being fashioned. In the next chapter we shall review a further series of examples which will illustrate this in greater detail.

8   Deployments of gesture in the utterance

In examining examples of utterances in which speech and gesture are employed together, we have seen how the gesture phrases commence in advance of the words to which their strokes appear to be connected semantically. We suggest that this is best accounted for by supposing that it is only in this way that the *strokes* of the gesture phrases can be produced so that they are coordinate with what is expressed with the semantic nuclei of the co-occurring spoken phrases. This semantic coherence (or "co-expressiveness" as McNeill has called it)[1] of gesture phrase stroke with spoken expression is evidence that the gestural component and the spoken component of an utterance are produced under the guidance of a single plan. We suggest, however, that the conjunction of the stroke with the informational centre of the spoken phrase is something that the speaker *achieves*. In creating an utterance that uses both modes of expression, the speaker creates an *ensemble* in which gesture and speech are employed together as *partners* in a single rhetorical enterprise.

Consider again Example 1 and Example 2 from Chapter 7. In both the speaker introduces a pause in the speech which appears to be related to the process of organizing the gestural component. In Example 1 the speaker paused for a moment after he had finished pronouncing the word that was semantically coordinate with the stroke, so that the two-part stroke could be completed before he went on to the next words of the spoken component. In Example 2 the speaker inserted a pause immediately before the word with which the stroke coincided ("window"), in this way allowing the hands to be fully ready for the stroke at the same time as the word was uttered. In Example 3, on the other hand, the speaker's utterance included a series of phrases without intervening pauses. In this part of his discourse, the speaker embarked upon the preparation for his next stroke before he had finished a current tone unit. These variations in how the speech and gesturing are organized in relation to one another suggest that speakers continuously adjust one utterance component to the other. This is why we prefer to say that the semantically coherent gesture–speech *ensemble* is a speaker *achievement*. The relationship between the gestural component and the speech component in the utterance does not seem well understood as a simple causal relationship, where the one is dependent upon the other in some kind of unchanging way. Speakers, rather, can control these two components and can orchestrate them differently, according to the occasion.

[1] E.g. McNeill 1992, p. 23.

We now examine a series of examples which show this in more detail. We begin with two examples which show the integrity of the gesture–speech ensemble but which show, further, that the gestural component is as much a part of the unit as the speaker constructs it as are the words. In these two examples we see a speaker repeat something that he has just said, in one case for the benefit of his interlocutor, who had not fully grasped what had been said, and in the other case as a revision of what had been said the first time. In both of these examples it is the gesture–speech ensemble as a whole that is repeated or revised, not just the verbal component. This means that, from the speaker's point of view, the unit that had been constructed was constructed of both a spoken action *and* a gestural action, and that each was as important as the other in the total expression. If the gesturing in these examples was not fully a part of the utterance as the speaker intended it to be fashioned, it would not have been repeated with the utterance's re-doing.

The examples that then follow illustrate how speakers can adapt the performance of the gestural component and the spoken component of an utterance, one to another, in accordance with what may be required to produce them. First we present examples which show how the execution of a gesture phrase or a series of gesture phrases can be modified so that it is adapted to the phrasal structure of the associated spoken discourse. Then we present examples which show how, on the other hand, the execution of the spoken discourse can be modified to accommodate the structure of the associated gesture phrases. This is then followed by examples which show how speakers, in repeating an utterance with variations for rhetorical effect, may change the way gestures are used, even as the words stay the same. In our view, such examples show that speakers have flexibility in how they organize their verbal and gestural components as they construct their discourses. Speech and gesture are partnered in the common enterprise of discourse construction. Neither is the cause nor the auxiliary of the other, nor is there an obligatory link between them.

Repeating and revising the gesture–speech ensemble

The two examples described in this section show how a speaker, in repeating an utterance or in revising an utterance, may repeat or revise the gestural component as well as the verbal component. Examples of this sort reinforce the idea that both components are constructed components of the utterance. The gestured component, like the verbal component, is guided by the output the speaker is aiming at.

Example 4 is taken from a recording made during a lunch-time in a family home (Takoma Park 2000: 01/7.39.35). The speaker is describing to a guest an old sausage and pastry factory which had been taken over by some new proprietors for a new purpose. He is talking about the state of the factory when it was taken over. He says of the former owners of the factory that "they made everything greasy" which meant that the new owners had a lot of cleaning up to do. He utters the phrase "they made everything greasy" twice, the second time in response to his guest's request because, evidently, the guest had not fully heard what was said the first time. The guest then indicates that it is, specifically, the word "greasy" that he had not heard and R then repeats just this word. The first point of interest in this example is that when the speaker, R, says again the same phrase he had said before, he also repeats the gesture he had used before, as if it is a fully integral part of the entire unit of discourse. The second point of interest arises from the nature of the gesture R uses when he repeats just the word "greasy" and how this is performed in relation to both his own speech and the speech of his interlocutor.

Example 4 TP-1-2000. 7.39.35.

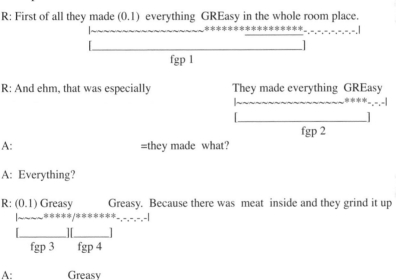

In the transcription for this example four gesture phrases are shown. The appearance of the stroke of the first two gesture phrases is shown in Fig. 8.1, that of fgp 3 and 4 is shown in Fig. 8.2. These will be discussed later. Regarding fgp 1 and 2, the stroke is, in each case, performed in association with "greasy" which is also the tonic centre of the phrase. The movement is almost identical in both cases (in fgp 2 the movement is slightly more rapid and has slightly less amplitude than it does in the first). The hands are held open, fingers slightly spread and are lifted so that they are held opposite one another in front of the speaker's chest (this is the preparation) and in the stroke they are moved in unison in a downward curvilinear fashion as a consequence of forearm rotation and a slight outward rotation of the upper arms. The hand shapes and movement combination here employed suggest an image of a three-dimensional surface which is being covered over or is covered over.

In the first part of this example, thus, the speaker describes what some people did ("they made everything greasy"), using gesture and speech together to do so, the gesture conveying an image, as we have suggested, of something that has spatial extent - in this context, perhaps, that of a bounded area being covered over. He is then interrupted by his interlocutor who indicates that he has not heard what it is that these people did. At this, the speaker repeats that part of his previous utterance in which he describes the activity of the people involved. The point here is that in this repetition it is the entire gesture–speech construction that is repeated, not just the verbal component. That the speaker does this shows that, for him, the verb phrase was a *gesture–speech ensemble.* That is, he had *constructed it as such* and the gesture, thus, is as much a part of this construction as are his words.

A, R's interlocutor, when he asks for clarification the first time, says: "They made what?" and in response to this R repeats the whole phrase, verbal and gestural components together, as we have just seen. The problem for A, however, appears to have been, quite specifically, the word 'greasy' and this he makes clear when he re-requests clarification. A now says: "Everything" - here using a raised but level intonation and leaning forward but then holding his posture. By repeating the speaker's word that immediately precedes the word he had not heard, as well as through the intonation and the held posture he employs, he makes it clear that it is just the word 'greasy' at the end of R's sentence that he had not heard. R replies by supplying this word - he repeats "greasy". But as he does so he now uses a completely different gesture (Fig. 8.2). He uses his right hand only, held with palm obliquely up, fingers extended and slightly spread in an 'open bunch' formation, the hand being moved downwards twice in rhythm with the syllables of 'greasy' (fgp 3). He now focuses on the word 'greasy' and this focus is seen not only in the way he says the word, but also in the gesture employed with it. It is as if he is holding the word as an object and exhibiting it.[2] As soon as he finishes saying the word 'greasy' he embarks on a new gesture phrase, which, in this case, is not associated with any words on his part, but with what he now expects from his interlocutor. In this gesture phrase

[2] The oscillatory movement we see in R's gesture here may well be related to gesture-oscillations seen in other contexts where an object, whether real, virtual or (perhaps as in this case) metaphorical, is being shown in position (as we shall see in Chapter 9) or held up for inspection (as will be suggested in Chapter 12 in connection with a well-codified Neapolitan gesture that marks a type of question).

Fig. 8.1   Example 4. In the stroke of fgp 1 and fgp 2 R moves spread hands away from one another and downwards. The amplitude of the movement in fgp 2 is slightly reduced.

Fig. 8.2. Example 4. In fgp 3 R uses right hand only, moving it downwards twice with restricted amplitude, in coordination with the syllables of "greasy".

he changes the orientation of his hand so that the palm now faces fully upwards and, as A repeats the word 'greasy', thus indicating that he now has heard it, R moves his hand up and down, this time in coordination with A's pronunciation of the word (fgp 4). It is as if, having repeated the word 'greasy' in response to A's request (which he 'holds and exhibits' in his hand as he does so, as we just noted), he now awaits A's confirmation and shows that he does so with the upturned palm position of his hand (see Chapter 13). Following this, R then repeats "greasy", so confirming the correctness of A's hearing. Now, however, as he does so, his hand relaxes and 'recovers' to a rest position. There is no gesture phrase associated with this last word.

Thus, in the first case, R constructed a gesture–speech ensemble which expressed the notion of the spreading of the grease, and when he interpreted A's first request as a request to repeat what he had just said, he repeated the whole ensemble, not just the words. This means, thus, that the gestural component is as much a part of the finished construction as the words and, from the point of view of the structuring of the utterance, the gesture has the same status as the words here. It is a *partner*, thus, in a constructed object.

A's second request, however, changes the focus away from the full statement that R had made to just one specific word. Now R's employment of gesture changes. As he repeats the word for A he holds his hand as if holding a small object - holding and exhibiting the word, as it were. And this 'container' for the word is then re-oriented as if to receive the confirmation that R expects, and gets, from A. Once it is clear that A has heard the word, however, it is only necessary for R to repeat it as a confirmation of correct hearing. No gesture is needed now, for this.

This example shows, thus, how the speaker employs gesture as a partner in the utterance he constructs, but it also shows how the nature of that partnership changes according to the focus and aim of the utterance. And we may also note how, in fgp 4, we have an example that reminds us that speakers may also use gesture separately from words, in this case as a part of displaying a quite specific expectation regarding the response of the interlocutor.

Now consider Example 5. Here we have an instance of someone repeating an utterance because the first version was, for him, erroneous. As we shall see, the utterance in its first version was a gesture–speech ensemble and it is so again in its second version. We shall see, too, how both components of this ensemble are corrected, so that both gesture and speech are altered for the second version. Once again this shows that the speaker attends both to words and to gesture, using them together to create a complete expression.

The recording is taken from a video tape of a teaching encounter between a medical intern and his supervising physician (Preceptor VII, 2.37.89). The intern is giving an account of a patient he has just examined. He has just

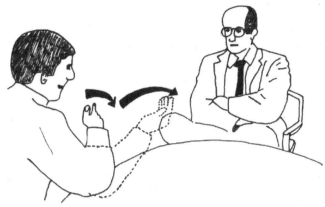

Fig. 8.3a   Example 5. Speaker moves hand outwards as he says "following my tail".

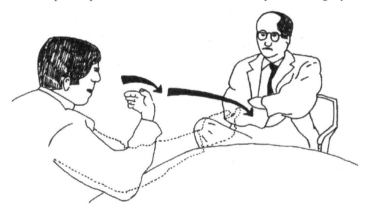

Fig. 8.3b   Example 5. Speaker repeats with modification his outward hand movement as he says "following their tail". Note the greater degree of arm extension and lateral displacement as compared to 8.3a. Note also change in hand shape.

Example 5 Preceptor VII 2.37.89

I feel like I'm just FOLLOWing my tail/ or (0.33) following THEIR tail/what they've

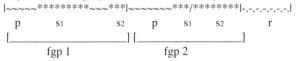

ALready initiated/ but I think we can we can (0.46) we can do something for her/ here today

explained the tests and procedures he would recommend for this patient and is now expressing his opinion that what he is proposing is not very new, since it will just be continuing with something that previous doctors had already begun. He says: "I feel like I'm just following my tail" - and then he immediately corrects himself, saying "or following their tail, what they've already initiated". The gesture–speech relationships are shown in the transcription. As he says "following my tail" he twice flexes then extends his wrist, thus twice moving his opened hand in an outwardly directed semicircle, at the same time displacing his forearm away from himself slightly (S1 and S2 in fgp 1 in the transcription for Example 5 and Fig. 8.3a). With "or" and the pause that follows, the hand is moved back slightly toward himself in a movement that is preparatory to a repetition of the movement he has just done which is now performed over "following their tail". However, as he says "their" - the word is given extra tonal prominence - he moves his arm so that his hand is now displaced *away* from himself (S1 and S2 in fgp 2 in the transcription for Example 5; Fig. 8.3b). It is to be noted, also, that his hand shape changes, so that instead of an 'open' hand there is an index-finger-extended hand shape. Whereas the dynamic image of 'following' that the first gesture provides is produced near to the speaker, the dynamic image of 'following' that the second gesture provides is performed away from the speaker in a more distal space that is thus appropriate for "them" in contrast to the proximal space used previously that is appropriate for "my".

In this example, thus, what is revised is not just the words. The gesture is revised as well. That is, what is revised is the *gesture–speech ensemble*. It seems evident, in this case, that the utterance has two aspects that are produced together. The gesture, like the words, is a component of the speaker's *final product* and, accordingly, if it is this final product that is to be revised, all of its components are revised together, as a unity.[3]

---

[3] At the Max Planck Institute for Psycholinguistics in Nijmegen, Mandana Seyfeddinipur has been studying what happens to gesture in association with various kinds of speech disfluencies. She finds that when a speaker self-interrupts and subsequently re-starts with a repair of some kind, any associated gesture is also interrupted and gesture does not resume until fluent speech resumes. She also finds that speakers sometimes interrupt their own gestures which are then repaired and when this happens speech is also suspended (compare the example of gesture repair in Example 65, pp. 219–220). Evidently, just as gesture is suspended when speech is suspended prior to a speech-correction, so speech is suspended when gesture is suspended prior to a gesture correction. Speakers, thus, maintain the integrity and consistency of the gesture–speech ensemble, monitoring both components simultaneously for correctness and appropriateness. These findings support the view that speech and gesture are partnered components in the gesture–speech ensemble of the utterance and both are parts of the speaker's final product. At this writing (December 2003) this work is still being prepared for publication, but for gesture suspension associated with speech suspension see Seyfeddinipur and Kita (2001). The *Annual Report* for 2002 of the Max Planck Institute for Psycholinguistics, Nijmegen, pp. 60-61 summarizes Seyfeddinipur's observations on gesture repair.

Mutual adaptation of gesture and speech

The examples we have given so far illustrate how the speaker plans for and produces the gestural and the verbal component together. We have seen that the gestural component is organized so that the *stroke* of the gesture phrase is placed in relation to the spoken component so that what is expressed in gesture is semantically coherent with what is expressed in words. The examples described in the previous chapter suggested, indeed, that the speaker can adjust one component in relation to the other, adjusting the onset of the gesture unit, for example, so that it is early enough to ensure that the stroke can coincide with the appropriate part of the spoken phrase, but not too early, so that the gesture has to wait, nor too late, so that it lags behind. Further details of this process of adjustment will now be illustrated. First we give examples that show how the execution of a gestural expression can be modified to fit the structure of the spoken expression. Then we give examples that show the reverse of this: the organization of the spoken expression being modified to accommodate the requirements of the gestural expression.

Gesture performance adapted to the structure of spoken discourse

We begin with Example 6 that has been taken from a recording of someone telling the story of Little Red Riding Hood (Pollack Red Riding Hood 20.01.16). The speaker had been asked to tell this story as if she was telling it to children. In the extract here examined the Big Bad Wolf has already swallowed Little Red Riding Hood's grandmother, and the hunter, who has come to rescue Little Red Riding Hood, has just cut off the Wolf's head. Little Red Riding Hood then tells the hunter that the Wolf has eaten her grandmother, whereupon the hunter again takes his axe and slices open the Wolf's stomach. The speech in the passage in question is as follows: "And the hunter said, oh well, that's soon remedied, and he took his hatchet, and with a mighty sweep, sliced the wolf's stomach open, and the grandmother popped out." (See the transcription and Fig. 8.4.) As the passage opens the speaker's hands are resting on her knee (Fig. 8.4A). Just before she begins the segment of discourse in question, she begins to move first her left hand, then her right hand, so that as she says "and he took his hatchet" the hands come together as if grasping an axe handle (Fig. 8.4B), they are lifted up to a position just above the speaker's right shoulder (Fig. 8.4C). This is clearly preparatory to what follows, a rapid leftward horizontal movement of both arms, an enactment reminiscent of the sort of action one might make if swinging an axe to make a longitudinal cut in something. At the end of this movement the hands are held (post-stroke hold) until the end of the phrase "sliced the wolf's stomach open" (Fig. 8.4D). The

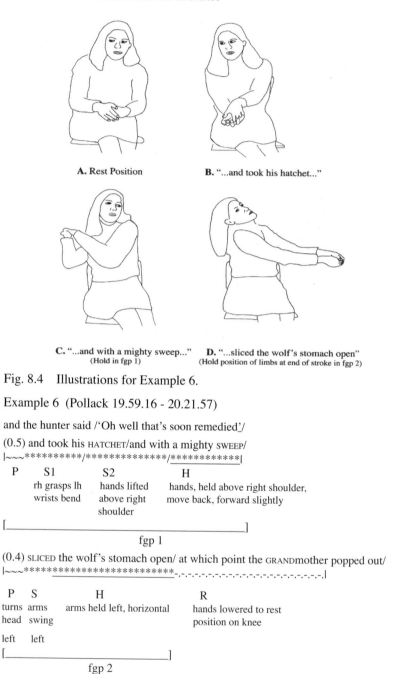

A. Rest Position   **B.** "...and took his hatchet..."

C. "...and with a mighty sweep..."   **D.** "...sliced the wolf's stomach open"
(Hold in fgp 1)   (Hold position of limbs at end of stroke in fgp 2)

Fig. 8.4   Illustrations for Example 6.

Example 6 (Pollack 19.59.16 - 20.21.57)

and the hunter said /'Oh well that's soon remedied'/

(0.5) and took his HATCHET/and with a mighty SWEEP/

|~~~***********/***************/************|

P	S1	S2	H
	rh grasps lh	hands lifted	hands, held above right shoulder,
	wrists bend	above right	move back, forward slightly
		shoulder	

[_____]

fgp 1

(0.4) SLICED the wolf's stomach open/ at which point the GRANDmother popped out/

|~~~****************************_._._._._._._._._._._._._._._._._._.|

P	S	H	R
turns	arms	arms held left, horizontal	hands lowered to rest
head	swing		position on knee
left	left		

[_____]

fgp 2

rapid leftward swing of the arms, however, occurs *precisely* as the speaker says "sliced". Note, however, that the speaker is all ready to perform this action by the time she has said "and he took his hatchet". Yet, she holds up the execution of this gesture while she completes the adverbial phrase that follows: "and with a mighty sweep". It is clear that the speaker has full control over just when she will perform the sweeping movement associated with "sliced". She has chosen a particular gestural expression for this passage but she has also chosen a particular discourse structure - and she paces the performance of the gestural expression so that it fits precisely and appropriately with this discourse structure.

In Example 7 (Napoli Sotterranea 10.30.45) we see how a speaker inserts a parenthetical passage into his discourse, a discourse in which he is also using gestures. During the parenthesis the movements of the multi-stroke gesture phrase in progress are suspended, but the hands do not return to a rest position. They remain in place ready to resume the performance of the gesture phrase, which they do as soon as the parenthesis is completed and the speaker returns to his main discourse.

The example is taken from a recording of a guide who is giving a tour of the ancient subterranean aqueducts of Naples. He describes how the well-workers climb up the wells into the houses or courtyards where the well-openings were situated to collect the money that was due them. He comes to a passage where he is explaining that in the walls of these wells there are holes on either side which allow the well-worker purchase with both hands and feet so that he can climb up and down the wells. He says in the pertinent passage: "*Sulle pareti di questi pozzi, ve li farò vedere poi nella visita, di qua e di là vedete, ci sono dei fori*" ('On the walls of these wells, I will let you see them later in the visit, here and there you see, there are some holes') (Fig. 8.5).

Example 7 Napoli Sotterranea 10:30:41

I told you at the beginning that the well is one metre by one metre
Io vi ho detto all'inizio che il pozzo è un metro per un metro

On the walls of these wells/I'll let you see them later in the visit/here and there you see/
(0.3) Sulle pareti di questi pozzi/ ve li farò vedere poi nella visita/ di qua e di là vedete/

|~~~~~**********************/_____/***************|

P   S1   hands remain positioned for S   S2
                               but movement suspended

[_____]
                      fgp 2 (rh&lh)

there are some holes
ci sono dei fori

Fig. 8.5   Example 7. A: Hand movements in S1 that suggest the walls of the well. B: Hand movements halted during parenthetical phrase.

As he says "*Sulle pareti di questi pozzi*" ('On the walls of these wells') he is holding up both forearms, elevated so that they are level with his shoulders, the upper arms vertical and the hands, open, with palms turned out (Fig. 8.5A). He moves his forearms outward and back alternately in movements of small amplitude in a gesture that suggests the narrow space of the well, bounded by vertical walls. The hands are positioned ready for this alternating movement by the time he begins to speak and immediately he commences their alternating movement which is repeated three times as he says "*Sulle pareti di questi pozzi*" (S1 in the transcription). The movement is halted during the parenthetical phrase "*ve li farò vedere poi nella visita*" ('I will let you see them later in the visit') but the arms and hands maintain their position (Fig. 8.5B). These movements are then resumed, accomplishing two back and forth movements the same as before the parenthesis, just as he says "*di qua e di là vedete*" ('here and there you see') (S2).

Once again we may see that for a speaker to be able to do this he must have full control over the gestural expression he is using. As in the previous example, the speaker is able to adjust the performance of the gesture in a way that is fully adapted to the structure of the spoken discourse.

Speech performance adjusted to the requirements of gestural expression

Speakers may adjust the production of speech so that a gestural expression may be performed in an appropriate relationship with it. The examples presented in this section illustrate three different ways in which this may be done: (a) speech is held up to allow the *preparation* of a gesture phrase to be completed; (b) speech is held

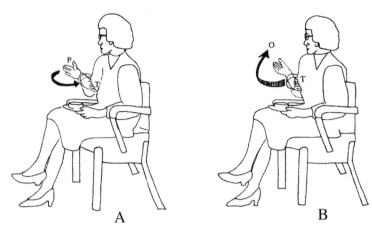

Fig. 8.6   Example 8. In A F says "and this was" directing her right hand outwards in an 'abstract point' when saying "this". In the pause that follows "was" she moves her hand toward herself (T) in readiness for the outward movement to O that follows shown in B.

Example 8 ISP 00161 10821.

D: She told she tell you this on the phone?
F: This was all in on my first contact with her
D: But she didn't say what the sexual experience was?
F: No. (0.4) She talked very rapidly and this was (0.3) all coming out very spontaneously

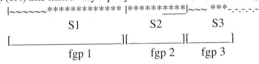

up to allow the *stroke* to be completed; (c) speech is held up to allow a gestural expression to be foregrounded. In these cases the speaker stops speaking for a moment so that the gesture being employed is now the only expressive action.

(a) *Speech held up to allow the completion of the preparation phase of the next gesture phrase.* The first example, Example 8, is taken from a film of a psychiatric discussion (ISP00161: 10821). A psychiatrist had been asked to present a case to a group of three psychiatric interns who were asked to discuss it. Present also were another supervising psychiatrist, and a social worker who was the original person the patient in question had contacted at the psychiatric clinic where she was being treated. The psychiatrist presenting the case starts by reading from the notes made by the social worker from the original phone call. The patient had, apparently, talked very freely about her problems in a way that struck the supervising psychiatrist as unusual. He interrupts the presenting psychiatrist's discourse and turns to the social worker and says: "She told she tell you this on the phone?" The social worker replies "This was all in on my first contact with her" to which the supervising psychiatrist responds: "But she didn't say what the sexual experience was?" The social worker then says: "No. She talked very rapidly and this was all coming out very spontaneously." Over "no" she shakes her head. She then lifts her hand slightly and performs a series of wrist rotation movements as she says "she talked very rapidly" (S1 in the transcription). As she says "and this was" she lifts her hand and directs it outward to her right (Fig. 8.6A - this is a pointing movement, an example of 'abstract deixis' as McNeill, Cassell and Levy 1993 call it). As she says "all coming out" just in association with "all" she moves her hand from a position close to her body outwards in a sweeping movement. The hand is then returned to a rest position in her lap (Fig. 8.6B). It will be seen that, in order for her to be able to perform the outward sweeping movement that is done in association with "all", it is necessary for the hand to be moved back inwards close to her body from the position it had reached when she says "and this was". This is indicated by the arrow P→T in Fig. 8.6A. It is during the very short pause between "was" and "all" that this move is accomplished. The speaker, thus, holds up her speech for a moment to make it possible for her hand to make the necessary transition from the one position to the other, so that it is ready to begin the stroke of the next gesture phrase in an appropriate relationship with the speech with which it is associated.

The next example, Example 9, is taken from a recording made in Northant during a meeting of the management committee of a small museum (OMMC: 1:46:45). The speaker, JH, is talking about a disused chapel and he is explaining how an attempt is being made to persuade the trustees of the property of which this chapel is a part to agree to let the chapel be used as an occasional exhibition hall and lecture room. He says: "We're trying to uh we're going to try to persuade the Creed Charity to appoint a management committee to make use of it for educational purposes, in other words turn it into a small museum cum display area cum lecture hall cum activity centre." Over the last part of this discourse, where he lists the proposed possible uses, he holds both his hands up in front of him, hands open, palms facing one another, and he lowers both hands in a well-defined downward movement as he says "museum", "display area", "lecture hall" and "activity centre".[4] In each case the lowering movement is made in conjunction with the stressed syllable of each of these

---

[4] The gesture JH uses here is common in contexts where a speaker is specifying the topic or domain of concern of subsequent discourse or, as in this case, setting the limits on something, here the potential range of uses to be proposed for the Ashton Chapel. We deal here with gestures that belong to the "open hand palm vertical" gesture family. The semantic theme of this family seems to be that of setting a boundary to something (perhaps ultimately related to the idea of cutting something into segments. See Calbris 2003). For the concept of 'gesture family' see Chapters 12 and 13.

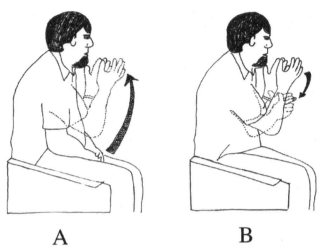

A   B

Fig. 8.7   Example 9. JH lifts his hands during the pause between "small" and "museum" (A), then lowers his hands as he says "museum".

Example 9 OMMCM 1:47:00 JH Ashton Chapel

Uh and we're tryin' to/ or we're going to try and persuade the Creed Charity /
to appoint a management committee/ to make use of it /for educational purposes/
in other words turn it into
a small (..... 1.125.....) museum/ cum display area/ cum lecture hall /cum activity centre/

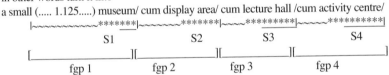

words. In the previous part of his discourse his hands have been resting in his lap. There must, therefore, be a preparatory movement, a lifting of the hands to the position from which they can perform their first downward movement. This is done between "small" and "museum". It is remarkable that as soon as JH reaches the word "small" in the phrase "in other words turn it into a small museum" he pauses his speech for one and one-eighth of a second. During this very long pause he lifts his hands, readying them for the first of the four emphatic downward movements just described. There is no evidence that JH is here pausing to search for the next word. The pause is here a rhetorical pause, serving to bring out and make very clear the list of uses he is proposing. However, the pause also allows him to lift his hands in the manner described - a movement that now becomes in itself conspicuous for his interlocutors and can serve as a means of indicating that something emphatic and important is about to be said.

You'll notice...   ...that's also part of...   (0.3) LAXton Junior School

Fig. 8.8   Example 10

Example 10 GB 2.28.48

GB: You'll notice that's also part of (0.3) LAXton Junior School
|*~*~*~*****|~~~~*********|~~~~******_.-.-.-.-.-.-.-.-.|
　　　　S1　　　　　　S2　　　　　　S3
　[_____][_____][_____]
　　　fgp 1　　　　　fgp 2　　　　　fgp 3

The third example to be presented in this section, Example 10, is similar. It is taken from the recording of GB who is giving a guided tour of Northant (GB 2:28:52). One of the features of this town is an ancient and important public school and much of the tour is devoted to showing the buildings of this school and expounding its history. There are other old schools in the town as well, and in the example here described we deal with a moment in which, as the guide is passing the entrance to one of these other old schools, he points it out to his party of tourists. He says: "You'll notice that's also part of Laxton Junior School." When he says "Laxton" he raises his voice and makes this word prominent. This word is preceded by a pause of 0.25 seconds inserted immediately after "of" and is accompanied by a vertically directed extended index finger (Fig. 8.8C). This gesture is what might be called a 'nomination deictic' in which the speaker points with an extended index finger, not to any object in the real environment but, as it were, to a word or a phrase that nominates something. What we see in this example is how the quarter-second pause inserted before the gesture–word combination 'Laxton + vertical index finger' is occupied by the speaker adjusting his arm and hand position so that he can perform this vertical index finger gesture as he says "Laxton".

In the preceding part of his utterance he has directed a palm-vertical index finger toward the building in question as he says "you'll notice" (Fig. 8.8A). Still with his arm extended toward the building, he changes his hand shape to an open hand palm up as he says "that's also part of" (Fig. 8.8B).[5] As he says "Laxton" he now uses the extended index finger directed vertically, as we described above (Fig. 8.8C). In order to perform this gesture in association with "Laxton", however, the speaker must flex his elbow somewhat to bring the forearm into a vertical position. He must also change the shape of his hand from palm-up open hand to extended index finger. These changes are accomplished during the quarter-second pause that is inserted after "of" - a moment of non-speech which allows the speaker time to adjust his limb for the new gesture phrase.

Finally, let us refer back to Example 2, described in the previous chapter (pp. 116ff). It was noted there how the speaker performs what we described as an 'outlining' movement with both her hands, beginning this movement with the stressed syllable of "window" in the phrase "window displays". To do this, however, her hands must be lifted up and readied to make the outlining movement. She inserts a pause of eight-tenths of a second between "wonderful" and "window" and within this pause she completes the preparation for the stroke of the gesture phrase carried out in association with "window". Note that this example is very similar to Example 10, just described.

These four examples illustrate how, in certain circumstances, a speaker may hold up or pause speech to allow for a stroke to be prepared for so that it will fall just on the appropriate syllables. Such examples show that a speaker has fine control over both gesture phrases and speech, and that in the process by which the utterance is created a reciprocal relationship is maintained between the immediate planning for the speech phrase and the immediate planning of the gesture phrase. Furthermore, examples like this make it clear that speech phrase and gesture phrase are *executed conjointly* - and we cannot say that gesture has a causative, provocative or dependent role in relation to speech.

(b) *Speech held up to allow the completion of a complex gesture phrase.* Sometimes it happens that the gesture phrase employed includes a stroke that comprises two or more movement phases. Where such multi-stroke gesture phrases are done as a part of a gesture describing the shape of something or exhibiting an action pattern involving more than a single phrase of action, we

---

[5] These are real-object pointing gestures. The significance of different hand shapes used in pointing (such as the difference between pointing with the index finger or with a palm-up open hand noted in the present example) is discussed in Chapter 11.

find that while the first part of such a gesture phrase may be done in association with a verbal expression to which it is related semantically, speech is then paused immediately afterwards, long enough for the gestural expression in question to be brought to completion. We saw this in Example 1 described in Chapter 7. Here are three further examples.

Example 11 is taken from a recording made of a meeting of the committee of Northant Cricket Club (OCC 8.13.39). At the time of this example the discussion has focused on a new pavilion that the Club has just finished building and the problem of choosing an appropriate pattern for the curtains is being discussed. JJ, the secretary of the Club, has brought with him some books of cloth samples. These are elongated books with large strips of cloth bound together at one end. One can 'leaf' through them, lifting up a page of cloth and throwing it back to reveal the next one. In the extract considered here, after mentioning that he has brought the cloth sample books along to the meeting he says: "Actually there's three that seem to go with everything. There's a choice of three, basically. What with going through reams of curtain material books." (See the transcription for Example 11.) As he says "reams" he raises his right hand and moves it rapidly upwards and forwards, but then he does this again - that is, he flings his hand upward and outward twice in a manner that recalls rather vividly the sort of action one would perform if one were leafing through the books of material of the sort he has brought (Fig. 8.9). The time required to do the whole of this two-stroke gesture phrase, however, is much longer than the time required to pronounce the syllables "reams of". Immediately after "reams of", accordingly, JJ pauses in his speech (for nearly one-half of a second) and during this pause he carries out the second stroke of this two-stroke gesture phrase. Speech is paused, thus, to allow for the completion of a gestural expression.

In Example 12 a woman is describing her office (Takoma Park 2000: 01/ 8.25.20). She is describing her desk and how she arranges lots of personal photographs along the sides of her desk. She says: "My desk is a very tiny little metal desk that I put my photographs all along the sides of the desk." In association with "sides of the desk" she performs two strokes to provide a diagram in space of her desktop (S2, S3 in the transcription). She moves her hands (open hands, palms oriented outward, fingers upward) laterally in a horizontal fashion as she says "the sides" (Fig. 8.10A) and then follows this immediately with a forward movement of her right hand, now with the fingers oriented so they point horizontally away from her (Fig. 8.10B). Her two-stroke movement here shows that she refers not just to the side of the desk that faces her as she sits at it, but also the side of the desk that extends away from her. She describes with her gesture, that is, two of the sides of her desk. The second forward movement, which completes the gestural description, is performed during a pause in her speech which immediately follows "the sides". Once again, the

Fig. 8.9   Example 11. Hand moved from A to B in preparation as speaker says "going through". Hand flung B to C (S1) as he says "reams of" and B to D (S2) in the pause that follows. He utters "curtain material books" while hand returns to rest position.

Example 11 OCC 8:19:39.

There's a choice of three basically/
                            0.5
what with going through reams of (. . . . .) curtain material books
|~~~~~~~~~~~~*****~~~*****-.-.-.-.-.-.-.|
              S1   S2
[_____]
           fgp

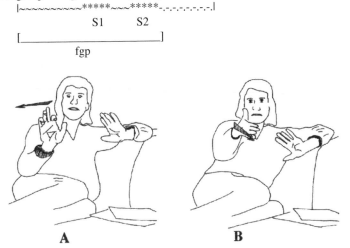

A   **B**

Fig. 8.10   Lateral hand movement of S1 (A) and forward hand movement of S3 (B).

Example 12 Takoma Park 01/2000. 8.25.28.

My desk is a very tiny little metal desk
                      0.2   0.5
that I put my photographs all along (. .) the sides (. . . . .) of the desk
|~~~~~~~~~~~*********|~~~~~~~********|*****|-.-.-.-.-.-.-.|
          S1   S2   S3

complex two-stroke gesture phrase is too long to be done simultaneously with "the sides", which is what it connects to, so the speaker holds up her speech to allow for the completion of the second stroke and so allow her diagram of the desk to be completed. As she completes her phrase with the words "of the desk" her hands have already completed their recovery.

The third example, Example 13, is taken from the recording made of the Museum Management Committee already referred to (OMMC 1.27.59). In this extract, the problem being discussed is that one of the exhibits that has been part of an exhibition has appeared to have developed a crack. It is a piece of wood on which there is some old writing, which is held in a wooden frame. J, who is skilled in woodwork, is describing a possible way in which the crack in this piece of wood could be cured. He says: "Um what I could try, I could try taking it out of there [i.e. taking the board out of its wooden frame] and then getting some large clamps and just see if it would pull. Now if it would pull up again that means we can possibly trickle some glue in you know and glue it up again." The gesturings associated with this extract are complex. What is pertinent for the present discussion is that as he says "possibly" with his right hand held with index finger extended, palm facing towards himself, he begins a succession of lateral diagonal downward movements, each of very restricted amplitude (S1a), which is then followed by another series of movements, similar, but now in the opposite direction, accomplished as he says "trickle" (S1b). The movement begun with "possibly" appears to be an enactment of the sort of movement one would make if holding a tube of glue and running it along a linear path, wiggling it at the same time to ensure the glue spreads into the place where it is needed. It is to be noted, however, that in order for this movement to have some proportionate relationship to the crack in the object that is the focus of J's discourse here and which is depicted in the space before him through the gestures he performs, this 'trickling' enactment must be prolonged beyond the time needed to utter the word "possibly". And indeed he does prolong it, and inserts a pause in his speech just after "possibly", a pause which allows this movement to be completed.

Example 13 OMMC 1.27.59.

Um what I could try /I could try taking it out of there/
and then getting some large clamps/ and just see see if it will pull/
now if it will pull up again/
that means we can possibly (..............) trickle some glue in/you know/ and glue it up again/

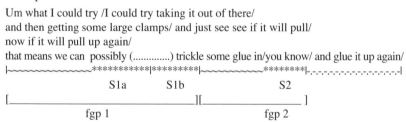

Here, then, in these three examples, we see how a complex gesture phrase may be given time for its completion. The flow of speech is adjusted so that the complex phrase may be accomplished, yet preserving its relationship of semantic coherence with the verbal expression to which it is linked.

(c) *Speech is paused to allow a gesture to stand on its own.* Here we describe examples in which a gesture is performed within a pause in speech because, in these cases, the gesture is either being employed to create a certain effect or, as in one of the examples to be described, the gesture itself is an object that must be perceived in its entirety before any speech associated with it can be intelligible. In these examples the gesture is *foregrounded.* This is accomplished by holding the speech back to give 'space' for the gesture so that it may be fully attended to on its own.

The first example considered here, Example 14, is taken from a conversation recorded in a shop where clay figurines for the Neapolitan *presepe* (Christmas crib) are made and sold (LB 11.56.21). In the course of this conversation, the woman who owns the shop was asked to talk about things that are typically Neapolitan. M, who is conducting the conversation, says: "*Quando si parla di Napoli si parla di due cose essenziali. La cucina e...*" ('When one speaks of Naples one speaks of two essential things. Cooking and...') (Fig. 8.11). The speaker does not complete his list here because he is interrupted by the woman he is speaking with.

What is of interest here is that, immediately after M says "*due cose*" he pauses in his speech for three-quarters of a second and during this pause he holds up his hand with index and middle finger extended in a gesture of 'two' and moves the hand back and forth twice with small amplitude movements (see footnote 2). The gesture is thus *exhibited* and speech is withheld during this exhibition. Of particular interest is the fact that the preparation for this gesture begins as he is saying "*cose*" but the stroke, as we have just described, is accomplished in the pause that follows. It is to be noted that in this example the gesture is exhibited *after* the words to which it is linked have been uttered, not beforehand.

The second example, Example 15, is taken from the conversation recorded in Northant in which S and M are reminiscing about traditions from their childhood. M suddenly recalls something that happened at Christmastime. His father was proprietor of an important grocery store in Northant and in this extract he describes how, at Christmastime, a very large Christmas cake would be sent to his shop and customers would be able to buy pieces of it (Crick III, 15.26.04). He says: "And another uhm like uhm I suppose like a tradition, in me father's shop, every Christmas, he used to have sent down from London a Christmas cake, and it was this sort of size." Between "was" and "this" there

Fig. 8.11   M's gestural presentation of *due* ('two') in Example 14.

Example 14 LB 11.56.21.

Ehm when one speaks of Naples/   one speaks of two things   essential
                                                0.4
M: Ehm quando si parla di Napoli/ si parla di due cose (. . . .) essenziali/

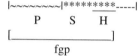

```
|~~~~~~~~~|*********_____|
          P      S      H
         [_____]
              fgp
```

Fig. 8.12   Example 15. M acts as if to sketch a large rectangular object lying on the table in front of him, understood as a depiction of the Christmas cake he refers to verbally.

Trans. 8.12. Example 15 Crick III, 15.26.04.

I mean another uhm like uhm I suppose like a tradition/in me father's shop/
every Christmas/(..1.3..)he used to have sent down from London/ (0.6)
a Christmas cake/ an' it was (....1.02....) this sort of (0.4)size

```
|~~~~~~~~****/*******/*********|-.-.-.|
          S1      S2      S3
        [_____]
                 fgp
```

is a pause in speech which lasts a whole second (see the transcription). As he says "it was" he leans forward over a table he is standing in front of and extends his arms forward, both hands with index fingers extended, positioning the hands so that the two fingers point at adjacent spots on the table. During the pause he moves both arms apart, then moves them towards himself, as he leans backwards, finally moving the hands together again so that they are again in a position similar to that which they were in at the beginning (Fig. 8.12). In other words with these movements he outlines a large rectangular object. The outline provides an image for the cake. From his gesture we have a clear idea of the form of the cake and how it would have lain on the counter of the shop. However, for his utterance to be intelligible, this diagram of the form of the cake has to be available to the onlookers. M does the gesture without speech, thus foregrounding it so that it becomes the main object of attention and thus can be understood as referring to the "Christmas cake" named before the gesture and to the aspect of the size of the cake referred to in "this sort of size" that follows. It is notable that in this case the two other participants in the situation both can be seen to be directing their gaze toward the table where M makes these movements and his wife, S, says during the one-second pause, but only after the gesture has designated three of the four sides of the object: "Oh I remember that!" It seems clear that S thus treats the gesture as a part of the utterance M is constructing and waits until the image of the cake is almost completed before inserting her turn.

The last example we present in this section, Example 16, is another from the recording of the Cricket Club Committee meeting (OCC 8.11.21). C is discussing the way the money had been spent in relation to the new pavilion the Club had erected. He says: "Uhm overall our cash spend is going to be very close to the budget of fifty thousand five hundred."

This utterance is addressed to the Chairman of the committee who, however, makes no response. Neither do any of the others who are sitting round the table. So C continues, re-stating with a further explanation what he has just said. He says now: "That the overall budget for the project was sixty-one thousand five hundred but if you recall there was eleven thousand pounds' worth of contribution in kind, so the cash budget for the project was fifty thousand five hundred."

Between "overall" and "budget" there is a pause in his speech of one-half second. During this pause, with his hand in an 'open' form, he rotates his hand inward–outwards (S1). This movement, the stroke, is performed in this pause, the preparation (a lifting of the hand combined with an adjustment of the hand to an 'open' hand shape) co-occurring with the first three words of his phrase. The action of this gesture phrase is a version of a 'presenting' gesture (a PP gesture, as described in Chapter 12) which here serves to 'present' the concept of "overall" referred to lexically immediately before, and which is the tonic centre of the phrase. That this PP gesture seems to incorporate a reference to the concept of "overall" is suggested by the upward and inward–outward arching trajectory of the movement.

A similar pattern is observed in relation to locution (4). There, it will be seen that again the hand is lifted in preparation for a stroke that is performed in a quarter-second pause following the tonic centre of the phrase, in this case the word "cash". Here the hand, which has remained in its PP pose, is lifted (in the preparation) and moved outward by wrist extension in the stroke (S3). In this case there is no arc-trajectory to the movement, so here the gesture is a simple 'presentation' or PP gesture. Here what the gesture appears to do is to 'present' the concept of the 'cash budget' which the speaker wishes to characterize.

Example 16 OCC 8.11.09

(1)

Uhm OVERALL our cash spend is going to be very close to the budget
of fifty thousand five hundred
[No response from Chairman - interval of 3.0 seconds]

(2)

That the OVERALL (..0.5..) budget for the project was sixty-one thousand five hundred
|~~~~~~~~~~~~~*******/**

       P   S1   S1hold

[_____

                            fgp 1

(3)

but if you recall there was eleven thousand pounds' worth of contribution in kind
/***|

                      S1hold   S2

_____]

                       fgp 1 cont.

(4)

so the CASH (0.27) budget for the project was fifty thousand five hundred (...0.5...)
|~~~~~~~~~~*****/***_._.-.-.-|

       P   S3   S3hold   r

[_____]

                            fgp 2

What we appear to have here are two instances of something very similar to Example 14 ("*due cose*") previously described. In each instance, the central idea of the phrase is first expressed verbally (that is, the *overall* budget in the first instance, or the *cash* budget, in the second instance) and then it is 'presented in gesture', the speech being withheld as this is done, so that the gesture can be foregrounded as the object of attention.

Adding and changing the gestural component of the utterance

It is notable how, in the example just described, during his first exposition, C uses no gesture at all. C only brings it in when he re-explains his point, which he does in response to the Chairman's apparent non-response. C's use of gesture, that is to say, is brought in as a part of an utterance re-design, here undertaken as a way to get the Chairman to show that he has heard and understood what C is saying.

Example 17 is a similar case. Here a speaker tells again something she has just told, using the same words, but in her second telling uses a gesture that illustrates the telling, whereas in the first telling she uses none. This again illustrates how a speaker may redesign an utterance to include gesture. In this case this is done in a context in which the interlocutor had requested a re-telling, as if it were important for him to take account of every detail of the narrative. The gesture is brought in on the second telling as part of the speaker's strategy to make what she is saying more vivid and thus, perhaps, more easily attended to by her interlocutor.

The example comes from a recording of a discussion between a medical intern and a supervising physician (Preceptor II: 00.32.03.48/00.35.31.04). The medical intern is describing the patient she has just examined to the supervising doctor and is giving an account of the circumstances that originally led the patient to receive medical attention. In this case the re-telling is requested by the supervising doctor for whom it is evidently important that he be quite clear about the sequence of events being described. The first time she gives her account of the events that led to the patient's visit to the hospital, she gives it as part of her opening presentation of the case she had charge of. The second time she gives her account is when the supervising doctor asks for a new account of this sequence of events. On both occasions she begins by telling how, when the patient got up in the morning, he fell down, hitting his hip on something. Thereafter he does various things, which include driving a car to a neighbouring city. As far as he was concerned he seemed all right. However, when his wife returned home that evening she noticed certain problems and he himself, when eating, complained that "that spoon kept turning over". That is, he was suffering from a lack of control of his right hand.

In the first account of this episode the intern says: "And then he said that when he was eating dinner that night 'that spoon kept turning over'". As she says this she uses no gesture. In her second account, she again quotes the patient's words. She says, in this second account, "He says 'That spoon kept turning over' you know, and that he had fallen out of bed." In this second account she now uses a gesture in which she lifts her right hand, fingers partially flexed, and rotates it - 'turning over' her hand - as she quotes

Example 17 Preceptor II Part I: 32.47.63; Part II: 35.05.76

Part I

I: And then he said/ when he was eating dinner that night /

"that spoon kept turning over"   okay?
P: [NOD]

Part II

P: Now, his deficit was uh left sided

I: What his deficit was   according to his wife   yes left face

P: right   right. She was here today

P: but we don't have his old record I: right, we don't have his old record. She's here today.

I: Left face   Disarthria. And the right clumsiness of the hand. P: So left face and right hand.

I: Right. So. Looks like mid-brain. Okay.

I: So he That's what

I: He says "that spoon kept turning over" you know and that he had fallen out of bed
   |~~~~~~************|*****|-.-.-.-.-.-.-.|~~~~~~~*****************|
        P   S1   S2   S3

So that makes you think he's a right handed person
|~~~~~~*************|-.-.-.-.-.-.-.-.-.-.-.-.-.-.-.-|
      S4

In S1 (fgp 1) speaker holds right forearm vertical and rotates it rapidly, thus rotating her hand in a turning movement. In S2 an open hand, palm facing outwards, is moved forward briefly (probably this is the speaker's comment that this is what he had said to her, and is not her interpretation). Note the "you know" that immediately follows, which also has this function. In S3 the speaker moves her right hand outward in an arc-movement of broad amplitude, seemingly a reference to something falling outward. S4 is a (vertically oriented) open hand palm up gesture (see Chapter 13), 'presenting' her interpretation. The interval between Part I and Part II of this extract is three minutes, during which I finishes her first account.

the patient's words. The speaker thus uses just the same words in the two instances, words which, evidently, are to be understood as quotations from what the patient had said to her. The first time she gives this quotation she does so as a part of her first account of this patient to her supervisor. No gesture is used during this discourse. The second time she gives this quotation she does so as a re-telling, in response to the supervising physician's request for this, and now she does use a gesture. As we have already suggested, this shows how a speaker may introduce gesture as part of an utterance re-design, in this case where the recipient has shown a need for a more detailed, more analytic account of the sequence of events.

In the next example, Example 18, we see a speaker using the same words twice, but with different gestures in each case. He thereby achieves two different expressions. Then he repeats something he has just said, in this case as a means of showing he agrees with a comment someone else has just made, but in the repetition he uses a gesture as part of the phrase instead of a word. The utterance unit is repeated, that is, with the same meaning, but in its second production this meaning is achieved through a different combination of the gestural and spoken components of the utterance.

This Example comes from a recording made in Torre del Greco of a *commerciante* (trader, dealer, businessman) who sells shirts in an open market who, because of the slowness of business, is spending his time playing cards with three friends (Commerciante II, 00.29.59). Peppe (the shirt-seller) has been arguing with Vincenzo about how many points he has earned in the game. He claims more than Vincenzo wishes to allow. Aniello (Vincenzo's partner in the game) supports Peppe, however, and Salvatore, Peppe's partner, tells Vincenzo not to be so argumentative. Vincenzo then turns to Rosaria, who is standing beside the video camera as part of the team who is making the recording, to make a comment about Peppe. He points to him and then says "*è commerciantë a verë* " ('he is a true businessman').[6] He makes this comment to indicate that Peppe is the type who drives hard bargains. Vincenzo then repeats this comment, saying again "*è commerciantë a verë* " and then he says "*è commerciantë proprië*" ('he really is a businessman'). Rosaria then comments: "*chi è commerciante lo vedi in tutto*". Freely translated, this is the equivalent of an expression such as "once a businessman always a businessman". Vincenzo responds by directing his hand toward Peppe and then he says, as a sort of confirmation of Rosaria's comment, "*è commerciante*" ('he's a businessman').

Consider first the two occasions when Vincenzo says "*è commerciantë a verë*" These might seem to be mere repetitions. However, this is not so,

---

[6] In much of the material recorded in Campania speakers use both varieties of Neapolitan and regional varieties of Italian. The conventions followed in transcribing the speech in these cases are described in Appendix I.

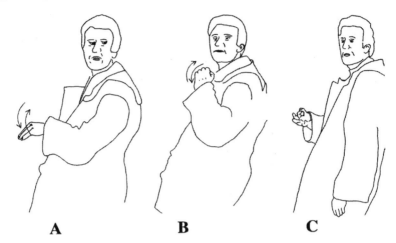

A   B   C

Fig. 8.13   Example 18. Vincenzo uses a different gesture each time he asserts that Peppe "is a business man" (*è commerciante*).

because each time he utters the phrase he uses a different gesture. If we take this into consideration we see that he says something different in each case. As he says "*è commerciantë a verë* " ('he is a true businessman') the first time, he lifts his left hand up, held open with palm towards himself, and moves it up and down by means of a succession of forearm rotations (Fig. 8.13A). This is a widely used gesture that indicates that something is excessive or 'too much'.[7] Here Vincenzo combines 'he is a true businessman' with an expression to indicate that one should regard his character as a businessman as being too strong or in some way too fully developed. He then follows immediately with the same verbal phrase "*è commerciantë a verë* " but this time he moves a clenched fist up and down in front of his chest. This gesture probably makes a reference to the idea that Peppe is a "tight-fisted" businessman, tough, that is to say that he drives a hard bargain[8] - while the rhythmic downward movements add emphasis to this (Fig. 8.13B).

Now comes a slightly different phrase: "*è commerciantë proprië*" ('he really is a businessman'). Here Vincenzo uses no gesture. However, in response to Rosaria's comment - "*chi è commerciante lo vedi in tutto*" ('once a businessman always a businessman') - Vincenzo points to Peppe and then says "*è commerciante*" ('he's a businessman') but as he says this, he does another gesture - now with his right hand held so that thumb and forefinger are in contact at the tips forming a 'ring' shape (the so-called 'ring' hand), in this case moved up and down with a tightly

---

[7] For one published example see Poggi and Caldognetto (1998, p. 186, No. 45).
[8] Cf. de Jorio (2000, pp. 104-105) for a description of two gestures for *Avarizia* ('Avarice') which share features in common with the present gesture.

restricted amplitude (Fig. 8.13C). This gesture is used to mark what is being said as precisely meant, when the speaker specifies that what is being said is exactly what is meant. It can, as here, express the same thing as the word *proprio* ('truly, really').[9]

In this case we have an instance of a repetition in which, however, the *means of expression* is varied. The second time, part of what Vincenzo says is said in gesture. By shifting part of his expression into gesture he alters in some way the effect of his utterance. Perhaps the gesture used here serves as a means of attenuating the expectation of a further response that his utterance might create because, by adding a gesture that expresses the idea that P 'really is' a businessman, he displays his agreement with what Rosaria has just said and makes his own comment complete. In this way he shows that he is about to withdraw from the exchange with Rosaria. Indeed, almost immediately afterwards he returns his attention to the card game.

The next example, Example 19, is taken from a recording of a meeting of the committee of a Bocce Club in a small town not far from Salerno (Bocce II, 8.10.48). In the part of the discussion we are concerned with here, Enzo has said that on the poster announcing the competition, all the various sponsors will be listed. Peppe, for some reason, objects to this idea. To press his case, Enzo now takes a specific example, the poster for the competition held at San Severino which he then describes. He does this by stating what the headings were on the poster and then he says: "*stevënë cinquanta sponsorizzazionë a sottë, cinquanta sponsorizzazionë, non una sola*" ('There were fifty sponsors below, fifty sponsors below, not one only'). As he says "*stevënë cinquanta sponsorizzazionë a sottë*" ('there were fifty sponsors below') he looks at Peppe, and as he does so, with his two hands held open with palms vertical, he traces out, on the table in front of him, a sort of oval shape which seems to suggest the spatial arrangement of all the names on the poster. Peppe remains rigid at the conclusion of this utterance, he shows no change in expression whatever. Enzo now repeats what he has just said - but this time he looks away from Peppe, actually in the direction of Giovanni, who is at the other end of the table. And now he holds up both hands, spread, palms out, moving them laterally and slightly downward as he does so. Thus the utterance has been re-designed and now, in gesture, instead of referring to how all the names were arranged under the poster, he uses a gesture which expresses the notion that what is being asserted blocks whatever anyone else might offer to counter it.[10]

The gesture Enzo uses with this repetition is quite different from the one he used before. Once again we have an example of how gesture, along

---

[9] See Kendon (1995) and Chapter 12.
[10] We interpret Enzo's gesture here as an instance of the 'vertical palm' (VP) group in the Open Hand Prone family of gestures. See Chapter 13, where the Open Hand Prone family is discussed at length. The semantic theme of such VP gestures is halting or stopping a line of action of the speaker or of the speaker's interlocutor(s). This line of action may be past, present or , as in the present case, potential.

with intonation and voice level, is all part of the re-design of the utterance, notwithstanding the fact that, from the point of view of propositional content, it is a repetition. As a conversational move it is not a repetition, but something new, and there is something new in the gesture as well. Thus we may say that the gesture is part of the speaker's design for the utterance.

Conclusion

In this chapter we have reviewed a series of examples which illustrate some of the different ways in which gesture and speech may be organized in relation to one another when they are used together in the same utterance. First, we considered two examples (Example 4 and Example 5) which demonstrated that when a speaker constructs an utterance as a gesture–speech ensemble it is treated as a unit. Where the utterance was repeated, for instance, or where it was corrected, both components were repeated or both components were corrected as if they were equally important partners in a single unit. We then gave two examples which showed how a speaker may delay the execution of the stroke of a gesture phrase as an accommodation to the insertion of spoken phrases which do not directly advance the narrative line of the discourse. In Example 6 we saw how the speaker delayed the stroke that coincided with a verb during an adverbial phrase that preceded it, while in Example 7 we saw a case in which the speaker inserted a parenthetical sentence in a discourse, and suspended the actions of the stroke during this parenthesis. Then we gave examples that showed the opposite: that is, cases in which the speaker holds up speech to accommodate the performance of the stroke. Example 8, Example 9 and Example 10 showed speech being held up while the gesture articulators were moved into position to carry out the stroke (something we also saw in Example 2, in Chapter 7), while in Example 11 and Example 12 we saw how a pause in the speech may be inserted so that a complex or two-part stroke can be completed. Examples 14, 15 and 16 presented cases in which speech was halted so that the stroke was thereby foregrounded. Finally in four examples, Examples 16, 17, 18 and 19, it was shown how a speaker, in re-saying something, either uses or does not use gesture, or changes the kinds of gestures used, according to shifts in the overall rhetorical aim to be accomplished through these re-sayings or re-statements. These examples illustrate well, thus, how speakers can *orchestrate* the gesture and speech components of an utterance, changing these orchestrations in relation to the momentary demands of the communication moment or shifts in the speaker's aim.

In our view, these observations suggest that the gestural component of the utterance is under the control of the speaker in the same way as the verbal component and that it is produced, as spoken phrases are produced, as part of the speaker's *final product*. These examples suggest that gestures should be looked upon as fully fashioned components of the finished utterance, produced as an integral part of the 'object' that is created when an utterance is fashioned. Gestures are deployed by speakers in different ways for different aims, and what is created through gesturing can differ from one occasion to the next but, in each case, gestures are deployed and fashioned as they are because, in some way, they make it possible for the speaker to accomplish a more complete expression.

9 Gesture and speech in semantic interaction

Utterances, we have suggested, are like objects that are constructed out of spoken and gestured materials and, accordingly, may be said to have two components. In the preceding two chapters, we showed, through a series of examples, some of the different ways in which these may be put together. With this chapter we begin a consideration of how the gestured component contributes to the meaning or expression of the utterance.

The gestured component of an utterance can be a part of its *referential* content. For example, when JJ, in Example 11, moves his hand forward as if he were leafing through a book of cloth samples as he says "what with going through reams of curtain material books" his gesture makes reference to actions involved in looking through the curtain material books, which is part of the content of his utterance. Likewise, the 'throwing away', 'knocking down' and 'placing' gesture phrases in Example 3, or the gesture in Example 4 that was associated with R saying "they made everything greasy", the so-called 'outlining' movement of SM in Example 2 as she refers to "wonderful window displays" or M's raised two-finger action in Example 14 which gives prominence to the idea that there are "two things" typically referred to when one speaks about Naples, are all instances of gestures that are a part of the referential content of their respective utterances.

On the other hand, Enzo's raised spread hands which we see when, for the second time, he says "*sponsorizzazione*" in Example 19, or the vertically raised index finger of GB as he says "Laxton Junior School" in Example 10, are not part of the referential meaning of what is being said but are gestures that indicate something about the speaker's attitude to the referential meaning or that contribute to the interpretative framework in terms of which this meaning should be treated. In Example 19 Enzo's hand action is an indication that, for the speaker, what he is asserting cannot be denied (see Chapter 12). In Example 10 GB's raised index finger singles out the name that he is pronouncing as the component of his utterance that deserves particular attention (we called this a 'nomination deictic').

The functions of the gestures in these examples are instances of what will be referred to as *pragmatic* functions, by which we mean any of the ways in which gestures may relate to features of an utterance's meaning that are not a part of its referential meaning or propositional content. Three main kinds can be distinguished. There are *modal* functions, as in Enzo's gesture in Example

158

19 above, for here the gesture alters in some way the frame in terms of which what is being said in the utterance is to be interpreted. Other examples include gestures that indicate whether the speaker regards what he is saying as an hypothesis or an assertion, and the like. In other cases a gesture may have a *performative* function, as when it is used to indicate the kind of speech act or interactional move a person is engaging in. For example, the palm-up-open hand may be used as a way of indicating that what the speaker is saying is being 'offered' to the interlocutor, perhaps as an example to be discussed, or as a proposal. Finally, gestures are often used as if they are punctuating the spoken discourse, or as if they are marking out its different logical components. This appears to be the function of GB's gesture in Example 10. We say of such gestures that they have a *parsing* function. These *modal, performative* and *parsing* functions of gesture, which are very important and widespread, will be illustrated and discussed in Chapters 12 and 13.[1]

Interactive or *interpersonal functions* of gestures should also be mentioned. These include, for example, the use of gesture as a way of indicating to whom a current utterance is addressed, to indicate that a current speaker, though not actually speaking, is nevertheless still claiming a role as speaker (still 'holding the floor'), and gestures that regulate turns at talk, as in raising a hand to request a turn, or pointing to someone to give them a turn, as happens at formal meetings or in the classroom. Important and interesting though these functions are, for reasons of space, a separate, systematic discussion of them will not be included here.[2]

In this chapter, and the two that follow, we will deal with the *referential* functions of gesture. There are two ways in which these may be fulfilled.

[1] The term 'pragmatic' used here for gestures that relate to aspects of meaning other than those that are 'referential' is not very satisfactory, but no other term seems available. Austin (1802) would have called these gestures 'non-significant', while Efron (1972) would probably have referred to them as 'logical-discursive' gestures (see Chapter 6). Gestures that appear to display structural relationships between different parts of a speaker's discourse have been referred to as 'cohesives' by McNeill (1992). See also his concept of 'catchment' (McNeill, Quek et al. 2001).

As for the three main functions of pragmatic gestures here distinguished, note that previously (Kendon 1995b) I used the terms 'illocutionary marker gestures' and 'discourse structure marker gestures' for what I now call 'performative' and 'parsing' gestures, respectively. I use the term 'performative' at the suggestion of Cornelia Müller. My use of the term 'parsing' is an adaptation of a term that, hitherto, has been mainly used to refer only to the process of grammatical analysis of sentences, or (more recently) to the logical or syntactic analysis of strings in computer programs, although it is used occasionally in a more extended way to mean 'make sense of something' or 'understand something'. It apparently derives from the Latin word *pars* 'part' or from the French *pars* 'part' and refers, thus, to the action of dividing something into parts. Although the various 'discourse structure marking' functions that gestures may serve cannot be said to be 'parsing' in a strict sense, if we take it to mean 'dividing into and indicating the structural parts of a discourse' our use of the term here seems justified.

[2] These functions of gesture have often been acknowledged (see, for example, Kaulfers 1931, Goodwin 1981, Heath 1992, Streeck and Hartege 1992) but a systematic discussion seems lacking.

Gestures may provide a *representation* of an aspect of the content of an utterance. JJ's hand and arm actions in Example 11, which appear to act out the movements involved in turning the pages of a curtain-material sample book, are an example of a representational gesture as is, also, in Example 8, the outward sweep of F's hand as she says "was all coming out". On the other hand a gesture may contribute to the propositional content of an utterance by *pointing* to the object of reference in the discourse (which may be a concrete object or it may be a virtual or abstract object). Gestures that serve as representations of utterance content are considered in this chapter and in Chapter 10. Features of pointing are considered in Chapter 11.

Regarding representational gestures, there are three questions to be discussed. First, what are the various techniques employed by which representation in gesture is achieved? Second, how is the object identified that is purported to be represented by a gesture? Third, what kinds of contributions do representational gestures make to the meaning of the utterance they are a part of?

So far as techniques of representation used in gesture are concerned, various attempts have been made to classify them (see Wundt 1973, Mandel 1977, Kendon 1980b, 1988b, Poggi and Caldognetto 1998, Calbris 1990, Müller 1998). Although there are differences between these classifications, they all provide for a division between *modelling, enactment* (or *pantomime*) and *depiction*. In *modelling* a body part is used as if it is a model for some object. When the hands are used in this way, they sometimes may be shaped so that the form of the hand bears some relationship to the shape of the object the gesture refers to (as in Example 13, p. 146, when the speaker uses his hand as if it is a tube from which glue is being trickled). In *enactment* the gesturing body parts engage in a pattern of action that has features in common with some actual pattern of action that is being referred to (as in Example 1, p. 114, in which M poses and moves his hand as if he is scattering a handful of something that has a granular character). In *depiction* the gesturing body parts - which are almost always the hands, which may be shaped in different ways according to what is being depicted - engage in a pattern of movement that is recognized as 'creating' an object in the air. Effectively, in these cases, the gesturer sculpts or sketches (or sometimes does both at the same time) the shape of something (as in Example 15, pp. 147–149), in which M outlines the shape of the cake he is talking about).[3]

These classifications all take for granted the process by which a gestural action comes to be recognized *as* a representation. If one considers any particular example, it is clear that the movements, even if perceived as modelling something, acting something out or depicting something, can be

---

[3] These techniques of representation can often be combined, as may be seen in Example 13 where the speaker's hand is the tube of glue, but its orientation and pattern of movement *enact* the action of trickling the glue onto a particular surface.

recognized as doing so almost always in only a quite perfunctory or sketchy fashion. Their recognition as representations and the recognition of the objects or actions they represent, requires an understanding of the contexts in which they are employed and how they relate to them. Very often the contexts are those provided by the meanings expressed in the verbal part of the utterance of which they are a part. The forward flinging arm movements of JJ in Example 11, p. 144, for example, are only recognizable as representations of the movements of someone turning the pages of a book of cloth samples (curtain material) once the understanding that JJ's words provide is available. This does not mean, of course, that words provide *all* of the meaning of the gesture. JJ's words could not transform *any* sort of action into a representation of cloth-sample-book page turning. JJ's movements here, although not by themselves recognizable specifically as cloth-sample-book page turning actions, nevertheless have characteristics that allow them to be recognized as *enactments* - they would not be seen as pointing, as sculpting or drawing movements, for example. In many cases, as we shall see, the gestural actions that are interpreted as being representational are drawn from repertoires of forms of action that are widely used. These actions have very general meanings - perceived on their own, the user may be recognized as 'pointing to something', 'describing the shape of something' or 'acting out an action of some sort'. When the way such actions are used is taken in conjunction with the utterance's verbal component, however, they are then understood in a much more specific way.

Finally, once we understand the various techniques of representation employed in gesture, and once we understand how these come to be recognized, we may then consider what difference, if any, the gestural component makes to the meaning of the utterance. As we shall see in Chapter 10, no simple statement is possible. Gesture contributes in many different ways. In some cases it may seem as if a gesture provides an expression parallel to the meaning that is provided in words. In other cases gesture appears to refine, qualify or make more restricted the meaning conveyed verbally, and sometimes we encounter the reverse of this. In yet other cases gesture provides aspects of reference that are not present at all in the verbal component. In other cases, again, gesture may serve to create an image of the object that is the topic of the spoken component.

An illustration

In order to develop the issues just outlined in more detail, we offer an illustration (Example 20). We describe a passage from Crick III (16.59.58 - 18.09.08), a recording, made in Northant, in which M and his wife S are reminiscing about earlier times in a conversation with A, who is a representative of the Historical Society of the town. In the passage to be described here, M is talking about his

Example 20 Crick III (16.59.58 - 18.09.08).
Transcription continues on next page.

(1)   (2)   (3)   (4)
M: We used to have thu We used to have them The che 'Coz you've been in Oxfam haven't you?

                (5)
A: Been?   M: In Oxfam   A: In Oxfam. Oh yes, lots of times.

(6)
M: You know the cellar? (....1.50....)   A: Yes I have once been down there, yes
   |~~~~~~*****************| |~~~~~~~****************|
                 [1]

(7)
M: Well that's where he used to keep all the cheeses down there A: Oh yes

(8)
M: And the cheeses used to come in big crates about as long as that
              |~~~******************|~~
                         [2]

          (9)
and they were shaped like a threepenny bit at the ends   A: Mhmm
~~~~~~~~~~~~~*******************|********|
                  [3]   [4]

(10)   (11)
M: With slats on. There used to be two cheeses in each crate
   |~~****|~~~~~~~~~~~~~~~~****************|
      [5]   [6]

(12)   (13)
And they used to send these down from London. And he'd wheel 'em down the cellar

(14)   (15)
and put 'em up on the (....0.67...) There's a a stone floor going right along.
        |~~~~~~~***********/*******/********_._._._.-|
                    fwd   back   fwd
                              [7]

(16)   (17)
And he'd set 'em all An' his Stilton cheese and Gorgonzola he'd put down there

(18)
And he w- wouldn't sell it until it was absolutely ripe.

(19)
And he used to go down there and throw (0.3) ground rice over it.
        |~~~~~~~****/*****_._._._.-|
                     [8]

(20)
And when it started to run he knew it was thereabouts
        |~~~~~~~*********************|
                    [9]

Transcription for Example 20 continued from previous page.

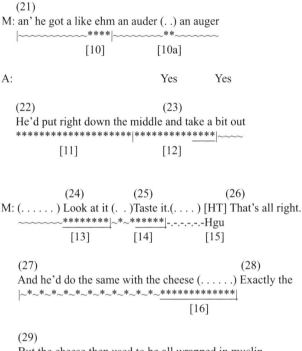

(21)
M: an' he got a like ehm an auder (. .) an auger
|~~~~~~~~~~~~~****|~~~~~~~~**~~~~~~~
        [10]   [10a]

A: Yes   Yes

(22)   (23)
He'd put right down the middle and take a bit out
*********************|**************|~~~~
     [11]   [12]

        (24)   (25)   (26)
M: (. . . . . .) Look at it (. .)Taste it.(. . . .) [HT] That's all right.
~~~~~~~*******|~*~******|-.-.-.-.-Hgu
    [13]   [14]   [15]

(27)   (28)
And he'd do the same with the cheese (. . . . . .) Exactly the
|~*~*~*~*~*~*~*~*~*~*~************|
                 [16]

(29)
But the cheese then used to be all wrapped in muslin.

A: Yes, Mhmm. I think I remember seeing that.

(30) (31)   (32)
M: Yeah. But ehm. Oh he was very particular about his cheese.

A: Mhmm.

father, who was the proprietor of the most important grocery shop in the town. In the present example, M is describing how his father received and stored cheeses and how he prepared them for sale.

As we shall see, M uses in his gesturing a number of different techniques to represent the objects and actions that he refers to and the ways in which these gestures are related to co-occurrent speech and how they contribute to utterance meaning are various. The gestures he uses, when taken on their own, can be seen to bear very general meanings. The contribution they make to the meaning of the utterance of which they are a part is only realized through an *interaction* between the meanings of these gestures and the meanings of their associated words.

M: "You know the cellar?"   A: "Yes, I have once been down there!"

Fig. 9.1   M's depictive point. A's index finger gesture combining enumeration and deixis.

A transcription of this passage is provided on the two preceding pages. In this passage M first establishes where, in the grocery shop, the cheeses were stored - this is the cellar. He then describes how the cheeses were packaged when they arrived, then he explains where they were placed in the cellar, and then he describes how his father tested the cheeses to see if they were ripe and ready to be sold.

To establish where the cheeses were kept M first asks A, his interlocutor, if she has "been in Oxfam". This refers to a charity shop operated by Oxfam (the Oxford Committee for Famine Relief) which, in Northant, occupies the space that was once M's father's grocery shop. When A agrees that she has been in that shop, he then says "You know the cellar?" As he says this he extends his right arm forward, flexes his wrist and lowers his arm rapidly so that his extended index finger is directed downward and somewhat toward himself (fgp [1], and see left drawing in Fig. 9.1). This movement can be identified as *pointing* because it shares with other pointing gestures the character of a final linear movement in a well-defined direction (see Chapter 11). However, the lowering of the horizontally extended forearm, combined with a wrist flexion that directs the index finger downwards, adds, in this case, an additional feature which suggests that the speaker is not just pointing to something below him (indicating the relative location of the cellar) but he is also describing a movement through space that is downwards and underneath. In this movement there is added the element of a descent through space. Note that M is not suggesting a path of movement that could be carried out in the actual space which the speakers are currently occupying. Through this movement he creates or, as we might say, *animates* the notion of a space underneath, the cellar space. In this pointing, then, we have an illustration of how a pointing action can create or bring to life a notional space (cf. Haviland 1993, 2000).

M's interlocutor, A, responds by saying "Yes I have once been down there, yes" and as she says "I have once been down there" she extends her index finger, directing it forward, lowering her forearm so that the finger is directed straight in front of her (see right drawing in Fig. 9.1). This also has the character of a pointing gesture, but it lacks a movement component that might suggest that a path through space is being described. Here, because A's finger remains horizontal and is not directed downwards, if it is an act of pointing, it is pointing in the direction of M's action that has animated this notional space (she points, that is, to the *idea* of the cellar that M has conjured up). It may also be that the horizontal positioning of the index finger here marks the idea of a unique occasion expressed by the word "once". [4] There seems to be nothing here that can allow us to decide between these two interpretations and, indeed, there may be no need to do so, since they are not mutually exclusive. A, in this gesture, can simultaneously be pointing to M's notion of the cellar and marking the idea of uniqueness, in this case the unique occasion on which she has visited the cellar.

Now that the cellar as a space has been jointly oriented to, M can say "Well that's where he used to keep all the cheeses down there." He now proceeds to explain how the cheeses arrived and where in the cellar his father put them. He begins with (8): "And the cheeses used to come in big crates about as long as that". As he says this, he places his two hands before him, palms facing one another, and held apart a certain distance (Fig. 9.2A). This action is done in conjunction with the deictic phrase "as long as that" and it is to be noted that as M performs this gesture, he also looks down and appears to glance from one of his hands to the other. This placement of the manual action in relation to the word "that", combined with M's directing his gaze towards his hands in the way that he does, are probably the features that mark the action as the referent of "that". [5] From characteristics of the hand action itself we may see that in this case what is being referred to is an object that is elongated and oriented horizontally. It is also shown to be a thick object, for M uses 'spread' hands (had he used extended index fingers instead, the object indicated would be thin, like a rod), and from the 'reach' of the hands M uses here, the object designated is large. All of this leads us to interpret the gesture as referring to the object referred to by "that" so that, in this context, it is the features of the length and volume of the crate in which the cheeses used to arrive which is being designated by this gesture. We might say here that through this action

---

[4] No systematic study has been undertaken, as far as I know, but there is good reason to think that the index finger is used in a variety of contexts in which the concept of singularity is being marked. In Chapter 11, where the different hand shapes used in pointing is studied, we show that index finger pointing is usually done in contexts where some object is indicated because it is an object to be distinguished from other objects, rather than because it is an exemplar of some class of object or of a concept.

[5] Streeck (1993) has described examples in which speakers look at their own hands when these are used as gestures in discourse contexts that are very similar to the context described here. He suggests how this act of looking serves to draw attention to the relevance of the gesture for the discourse at these junctures.

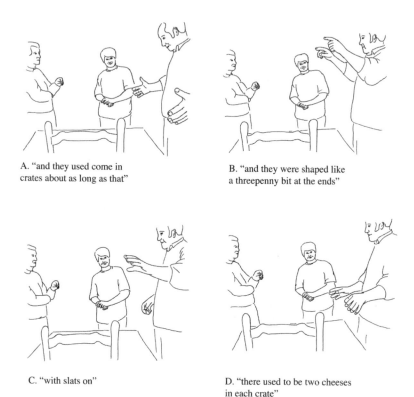

A. "and they used come in
crates about as long as that"

B. "and they were shaped like
a threepenny bit at the ends"

C. "with slats on"

D. "there used to be two cheeses
in each crate"

Fig. 9.2. Gestures specifying size, shape and structure of the cheese crates and how the cheeses were placed within them. A. Size-shape-specifier gesture serving as a referent for the deictic pronoun 'that'. B. Outline sketching gesture, describing the shape of the ends of the crate. C. Extended spread fingers moved laterally and horizontally depict the lateral horizontal arrangement of multiple long thin objects - the slats on the crate. D. Spread hands perform 'object-placement' movements and thus indicate the relative position of the two cheeses packed in the crate.

an image of the size and shape of the cheese crate is *enabled*, but it is only enabled when it is taken in combination with the verbal component.

It is our contention that the hand action here is a specific instance of a kind of hand action that is very commonly seen when the size and shape of an elongated object with thickness is being depicted. The hand action of M, that is, is here an instance of the use of a form of gestural expression that is widely used when the outer limits of some horizontally oriented object are being referred to. It could be called a 'size-shape-specifier' gesture and it is not unlike the 'size-shape-specifiers' that have been described in use in sign languages (see Klima and Bellugi 1979; see also Chapter 15). More generally, it may well be a version of a gestural expression that is often used when a speaker wishes to *delimit* the boundaries of something. As we saw in reference to Example 9 in Chapter 8, it can be used to specify the boundaries or limits of some abstract concept, and it is also used as an indication of the bounded or delimited nature of some topic of discourse a speaker is proposing to discuss. Used in the present context, it gains its specific interpretation as a *designation* of the size and shape of the cheese crate only from the way in which, in this context, it is related to the verbal component and to other aspects of what M does here, including his looking from one hand to the other.

M's next unit of speech is (9) "and they were shaped like a threepenny bit, at the ends" and here, in fgp [3], he lifts both hands up to the level of his face, now with single index fingers extended, and moves his hands in a symmetrical fashion, rapidly outwards, downwards, then inwards (Fig. 9.2B). The use of extended index fingers combined with continuous movement with a well-defined path is a form of action used in contexts where an outline of something is being depicted (compare Example 15 in Chapter 8 and Example 42 in Chapter 10). Combining such manual action with the words "shaped like a threepenny bit" establishes the interpretation of this action here as an 'outlining' of the polyhedral shape of the cheese crates.[6] Here M uses another well-established gestural technique of representation. Again, the way it is to be understood is a consequence of our common understanding of the 'outline' gesture technique, in interaction with the reference to shape made in the verbal component.

In (10), "with slats on", M continues his description of the cheese crates, here making a reference to how they were constructed - a 'slat' being a relatively narrow strip of wood. As he says "with slats on" he moves a spread hand - five digits held separated - in a linear horizontal well-defined outward direction (Fig. 9.2C). The hand movement here, well bounded and horizontal as it is, again is a type that is widely seen when a horizontal straight line is depicted. The spread hand used here, however, suggests not a single line but multiple parallel lines. When combined with the verbal component, "with slats on" it is interpretable as a reference to the slats. It is to be noted that the action suggests that the slats were affixed lengthwise along the crate, not as crosspieces nor as attachments at the ends of the crate.

With (11), "There used to be two cheeses in each crate", M extends both arms forward, hands spread, fingers slightly curved, palms oriented slightly outward, the hands being held so they are at or slightly below the speaker's waist. Once the hands are positioned in this manner, they are then moved

---

[6] From 1939 until 1971, when Britain decimalized its coinage, a twelve-sided brass coin was in circulation with the value of three pennies (one-quarter of a shilling). It was known as a "threepenny bit".

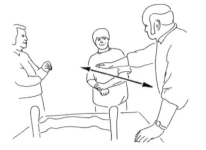 

Fig. 9.3.   M: " There's a stone floor going right along." M moves an open-hand-palm-down forward and back in an area to his side. A 'flat surface' gesture showing the relative position and orientation of the section of stone floor in the cellar where M's father used to set up his cheeses.

Fig. 9.4   M: "And he used to go down there and throw ground rice over it."

downwards in a short, rapid but abruptly terminated movement, which is repeated several times (Fig. 9.2D). These movements are characteristic of actions performed when the spatial *location* of some object is being indicated. These repeated movements are, it seems, *location establishing* movements. They are often used to indicate that the position to which a hand or the hands have been moved is the *location* of some object in virtual space. In this case, such location establishing actions, combined with a hand shape that suggests the shape of the objects being placed, and done in association with the words "There used to be two cheeses in each crate", favours the interpretation that the actions of the hands make reference to the positioning of the cheeses relative to one another. In this way we may say that fgp [6] depicts the two cheeses as packed in the crate. Note that the positioning of the hands, in this case, suggests that the cheeses were packed in the crate one beside the other, not one on top of the other, for example.

M then explains how his father would "wheel 'em [the cheeses] down the cellar" and he begins to say where he put them. He says "and put 'em up on the" but he breaks off this sentence and inserts the explanation (15): "There's a stone floor going right along." The meaning of this is not very clear until we take into account the hand action that accompanies it. In this M lifts his hand up (all fingers extended and adducted, palm down), which he then moves forwards, backwards and forwards again, ending with a brief hold (Fig. 9.3). Here the open hand, palm facing down, combined with a steady horizontal movement, is a form of action commonly used to evoke the idea of a flat surface. In this case, of course, combined as it is with the words "stone floor", the movement serves to specify a stone floor - and from the relative space in which this action is performed, rather to M's right, forward and backward in the sagittal plane, what is suggested is a flat surface running along the right side of the room that is the cellar. From the way in which this surface-depicting action is performed, the hand being positioned so the depicted surface seems to be at or below M's waist level, this conveys the idea of a raised strip of stone floor, like a low shelf - and it was upon this that his father placed his cheeses (a visit to the cellar M refers to confirms the presence of this raised stone floor).

After (16) and (17), in which M explains how his father used to set the cheeses on this raised floor, he continues by saying that his father would not sell any of his cheeses until they are "absolutely ripe". Now comes (19): "And he used to go down there and throw ground rice over it" - an extract already discussed in Chapter 7 (see Example 1, Fig. 7.1 and also Fig. 9.4). As we pointed out in our discussion of this example, the action that M performs in association with "throw", at least when taken in conjunction with the verb, is interpretable as a stylized extraction from an enactment of the pattern of action you might engage in if you were to scatter a handful of dust or sand - or ground rice - over a surface of some sort. Like almost all enactments, when used in gesture, it is a stylized extraction or abstraction. It picks out only some salient feature of the action complex that would be involved in actually scattering a sand-like or powdery substance. It is not a representation of a specific concrete action performed on a specific occasion, but an action that makes reference to a *class* of throwing actions. Once again we may note that the action of this gesture phrase cannot be precisely interpreted until it is perceived as part of the gesture–speech ensemble in which it is employed. The action has a general, abstract, significance which is made specific by the verbal component with which it is associated. At the same time, as we noted in our previous discussion of this example, the action of the gesture makes more specific the verb "throw" here used in the verbal component. There is, thus, a *reciprocal* relationship, semantically, between word and gesture.

Following this, as M says "he knew it was thereabouts", we have fgp [9], in which the two hands, with fingers extended and partly spread, palms facing one another, are oscillated alternately up and down. This is a version of a gestural expression that is often used in environments in which the idea of 'more or less', 'approximately', and the like, is being expressed. There are several variations. In the Neapolitan repertoire there is a gesture that may be glossed as 'more or less' or 'approximately' or 'it could be this or it could be that', in which the hands, fingers spread and held palm down are oscillated in a manner very similar to what is seen here (de Jorio 2000, pp. 182–183). Here the gesture is used in association with the word "thereabouts". This is an example of a *modal* gesture, to use the terminology proposed above, for it expresses the attitude of the speaker towards something, it refers to his estimate or evaluation of something, rather than describing something. Here, however, since it is part of a report of M's father's actions, it has a referential function. From the point of view of the technique of representation used, the gesture can be understood as a form of what we shall call *dynamic depiction*, for it seems to provide an image of something that is to be found at a certain level, but which oscillates around a certain level, rather than remaining fixed at it.[7]

We come now to the final sequence of gesture phrases in which we see the speaker switch rapidly and fluently from one technique of representation to another. We see illustrated body-modelling combined with enactment, object manipulation enactment, pointing, and the acting out of a character's reaction to a sensation, all within a very short segment of discourse and all in a manner that is perfectly suited to its aim. In (21) and (22) M names the instrument his father used to test the cheese, an auger, and describes how he used it. In the associated gesture phrases he uses his right hand to model the auger and his left hand to model the cheese into which the auger is inserted, and in fgp [10] and fgp [11] he acts out the insertion of the auger into the cheese. Thus, with his right hand, he folds his fingers to the palm, leaving only the index finger extended, but his hand is oriented so that the index finger is directed vertically downwards. At the same time his left hand forms an 'open' fist. He lowers the right hand so that the index finger is inserted into the space between the curled fingers of the left hand. (Fig. 9.5A).

It is to be noted, in this case, how the first time that M arranges his hands in this way and moves his index finger toward his left hand to penetrate it, this entire action is carried out *before* he says the name of the instrument. The first gesture phrase complex, that is, is acted out as he says "an' he got a like ehm ". The gestural complex here thus becomes intelligible *retrospectively*, once the instrument is named. Once the instrument is named, the gestural complex becomes immediately intelligible only because the meaning of the word "auger" is known. Knowing the name of this instrument (as A certainly does, as is made evident by her pattern of "yes" utterances) means knowing how it is used - in this context of talk about cheeses it is immediately clear how it would be used, a use which M's gesturing illustrates.

M is himself not quite certain of the word he should use - he first says "auder" which is incorrect, although A immediately understands him. Nevertheless, after a brief and incomplete re-doing of the action of fgp [10] (seen in [10a]), M now says the word correctly ("auger") and then immediately embarks on fgp [11]. This is very similar to fgp [10] and [10a], although it is notable that

---

[7] The image of a fluctuating level is being used as a metaphor for the idea of approximation. According to McNeill's (1992) terminology this would be a 'metaphoric gesture' although, of course, it is not the *gesture* that is metaphoric but the image it evokes which is being used in a metaphoric way.

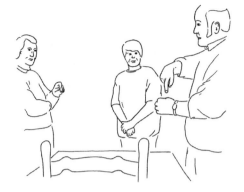

Fig. 9.5A   M: "An' he got like ehm an auder an auger"

M's right hand models the instrument while his left hand models the cheese. The gesture is used here as a way of naming the instrument.

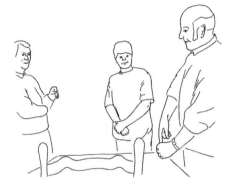

Fig. 9.5B   M: "He'd put right down the middle"

M plunges index finger into the fist of his left hand, lowering both to the table as he demonstrates the action of boring into a cheese with an auger.

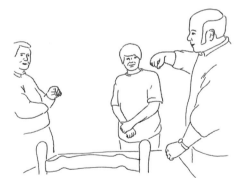

Fig. 9.6C   M: "and take a bit out."

Right hand is lifted up. Note the change in hand shape to a shape one would use when holding the handle of something. M enacts pulling the auger out of the cheese.

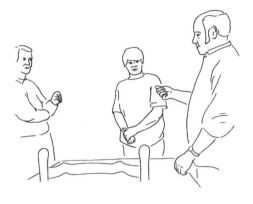

Fig. 9.5D   M: "Look at it"

M with hand posed as if holding
the handle of the auger positions
his hand as he would if he were
holding the auger so that the end
of it with a piece of cheese on it
can be easily inspected.

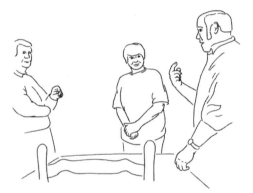

Fig. 9.5E   M: "Taste it"

M directs index finger towards
his mouth, in part as if moving
something towards it, in part as
pointing to the mouth as the site of
the action of tasting.

the penetration of the index finger into the fist is prolonged and the hands are
lowered all the way to the table in front of him (Fig. 9.5B). Fgp [10] and [10a],
it would seem, are more schematic as representations of auger-use than fgp
[11] which is closer to an acting out of using the instrument on a particular
occasion. Note that the first auger gesture, which is schematic in character,
is associated with words in which the name of the instrument is being given.
The action of fgp [11], which is closer to an enactment of actually using the
auger, is associated with speech in which the actions of M's father are being
described.

M then continues with phrases (23)–(26) in which each step of the process
of examining the cheeses is described, with a gesture phrase corresponding to
each speech phrase. As M says "and take a bit out" he lifts his hand up again,
changes from extended index finger to a closed hand shape. The hand is lifted
up in an action which is similar to the action one would perform if, holding

the handle of the auger, one were to lift it out of the cheese (Fig. 9.6C). Thus whereas, in fgp [11] M's right hand *modelled* the auger (the 'model' of the auger was employed in an enactment of using the instrument), in fgp [12] M's hand now acts out holding the handle of the instrument - a shift from body-modelling to enactment. This continues with (24) where in fgp [13] M positions his hand as he might if he was holding the auger in front of him so that he could look at the cheese on the end of it (Fig. 9.6D). But in fgp [14] M *points* to his mouth, thus indicating the location of the act of tasting (Fig. 9.6E). The final gesture phrase in the sequence, [15], is a *head* gesture phrase. Here, without speaking, M enacts an approving head nod - acting out, thus, his father's response to tasting the cheese.

Discussion and conclusion

In the foregoing account we have sought to illustrate, through a single example, some of the different techniques of representation that may be used in representational gesturing. We have discussed how, through a collaboration with the verbal component, these gestures come to be recognizable as representations of objects and actions. We have also sketched in some of the different ways in which the gestures in this example appear to contribute to the meanings of the utterances of which they are a part.

We have seen that M uses several different representation techniques. He uses techniques of *depiction* as he describes the crates the cheeses came in. These include the use of a *size–shape specifier* and an *outliner*, as when he employs his extended index fingers to outline in the air an aspect of the shape of the cheese crates. He uses his hands to indicate the shape of objects which, through how he moves his hands, are shown to be *in position*, the relative positions of the hands showing the relative spatial positions of the cheeses in the crate. He *acts out* actions that he describes of his father as he does things with the cheeses, and in referring to the instrument his father used to test the ripeness of the cheeses he uses his hands to *model* the objects in question and to show how they are used in relation to one another.

It is interesting to note with what fluency M moves from one mode of gesturing to another. This fluency is comparable to the fluency with which he shifts in his speech from one perspective to another. Thus he shifts from an *observer viewpoint* describing the cheeses in their crates as if they are objects in front of him to a *character viewpoint* when describing the actions of his father - his enactment of throwing ground rice over the cheeses and his demonstration of how his father used the auger to penetrate the cheese, and how he examined the sample of cheese so obtained are done from his father's viewpoint (see McNeill 1992, pp. 118ff). We note how, accordingly, as M shifts from one perspective to another in his spoken discourse, so he shifts in his gesture in a coordinate fashion from one representational technique to another.

This extreme fluidity of use and the detailed way in which the hands can change their symbolic role from one part of the discourse to another shows how the gestures produced by this speaker are shaped by his *semantic aims*. It shows how his gesturings, like the words with which they are associated, are fashioned under the guidance of *meaning production*. It also suggests that they are shaped as *displays* - we would not expect the kind of detailed and exquisitely adaptive complexity in techniques of representation we see here, so typical, as it is, if gestures were not being created as parts of an *object that is being created for public presentation*.

In the foregoing account we have also sought to show what makes possible the interpretation of the gesturings as representations and how the object or action in any given case comes to be recognized. We have shown that the gestural actions can only be given a precise interpretation when taken in conjunction with the words associated with them and yet, at the same time, we have shown that the gestures are forms of action that are widely used. They are forms of action that appear to be drawn from a vocabulary of expressive actions which have very general or very abstract significances.[8] When brought into use in a gesture–speech ensemble, however, they take on quite specific meanings and make a strong contribution to the image-like vividness with which the speaker's discourse comes to be experienced. The relationship between word and gesture is a *reciprocal* one - the gestural component and the spoken component *interact* with one another to create a precise and vivid understanding.

Lastly we considered how, as a consequence of these interactions between word and gesture, the gestural component makes its contribution to the utterance's meaning. In the passage analysed here there are at least three different kinds of contribution that are made by the gesturing. First of all, there are instances where the gesture does not seem to alter the semantic content of the utterance, yet it adds, nonetheless, to the way what is conveyed is experienced and this may have consequences for how recipients may conceive of what has been conveyed, the kinds of memories this may evoke for them

---

[8] See Calbris (1990). Note that if it is true that speakers, when using gestures descriptively, draw from a repertoire of widely shared techniques, they must, at some stage, have *learned* to use these techniques. The issue of how techniques of gesturing are learned remains barely investigated. Preliminary and informal observations made from recordings of children of various ages in Naples suggest that by the age of about twelve years the art of using gestures descriptively has largely been mastered. At earlier ages such gestures lack precision and clarity in their execution.

and how what is said is fitted with their own experience. All this can have consequences for their understanding. Thus, the dynamic point of fgp [1] as M says "You know the cellar?" does not add to or modify the content of the words, but it may serve to evoke an image of a space below, a space into which one might descend. This is, of course, a component of the meaning of the word 'cellar' but with this action it is as if M gives this component of the meaning of the word a more direct experiential dimension than it otherwise might have. Likewise, the enactment of [12] and [13] (associated with "and take a bit out" and "look at it"), the pointing action of [14] (associated with "taste it") and the head gesture of [15], that just precedes "that's alright", while they do not appear to add information that is not already given verbally, they serve to animate and enrich M's account, and show more precisely what is being looked at, how the tasting might have been done, and the kind of response to the taste test his father might have given.

In fgp [2] (associated with "crates as long as that"), on the other hand, we have an example of a gesture that is deployed as the object of reference of a deictic sentence which would be incomplete without it. The gestures of fgp [5] (associated with "with slats on"), [6] ("two cheeses") and [7] ("stone floor") provide additional information about the spatial orientation, spatial relationships or relative positioning of objects referred to.

Fgp [8] ("throw ground rice"), makes clear the *kind* of throwing action M is referring to and that his father must have employed, while in fgp [11], given that the right hand is a model for the auger and the left hand a model for the cheese, it is only if this gesture is taken into consideration that the sentence "He'd put right down the middle" comes to be fully intelligible.

We thus see how, in this example, M's gestures, in different ways, provide spatial and orientational information that is not referred to in the words, they add precision to the meaning of verb phrases, or may also provide a dimension of visual animation to the account being given which, in this context, may result in a much richer experience of this account than would have been provided without these gestures.

In the next chapter a more complete and systematic account of the different ways in which gesture appears to make a contribution to the referential meaning of the utterance of which it is a part will be attempted. In this way we shall explore the diverse ways in which these two different modes of expression, verbal and gestural, may collaborate with one another.

10   Gesture and referential meaning

In the previous chapter, using a single example as an illustration, we noted at least four different ways in which representational gestures collaborated with the verbal component of an utterance to contribute to its referential meaning. We saw how M used a gesture as an object of deictic reference for a verbal expression, how he used gestures to contribute information about the spatial orientation, spatial relationships or relative spatial positioning of objects referred to and how he used a gesture to provide greater specificity to the meaning of a verb phrase. There were also examples in which he used a gesture that seemed to have a meaning that was the same as the concurrent verbal expression. In these cases, we suggested, the gesture may have contributed to how the recipient experienced the utterance, allowing it to be apprehended in a more enriched, vivid and evocative way than it would have been without the gesture.

In this chapter further examples are offered to illustrate the different kinds of contributions that gesture can make to referential meaning, including those already noted in the last chapter. Six different kinds of contributions are distinguished. Each will be discussed and illustrated in turn.

(1) There are gestures which have a 'narrow gloss' which are used in parallel with those words or phrases that are often said to be equivalent to them. In such cases it is as if the speaker is simultaneously uttering in gesture the very same thing that is being uttered in words. Here the semantic relationship between word and gesture appears to be one of complete redundancy. Nevertheless, as we shall see, there are various effects that speakers may achieve by using gestures of this type in this manner.

(2) Gestures with a 'narrow gloss' may also be used in parallel with verbal expressions which are different in meaning from those of the gestures' verbal glosses. In such cases the gestures are not semantically redundant but may make a significant addition to the content of what the speaker is saying.

(3) Gestures may be used to make more specific the meaning of something that is being said in words. In the cases given it will be seen how a gestural enactment, used in conjunction with a verb phrase, appears to make the meaning of the verb phrase much more specific.

(4) Gesture may be used to create the representation of an object of some kind. This may be deployed in relation to what is being said as if it is an exemplar or an illustration of it.

(5) Gestures may be used either as a way of laying out the shape, size and spatial characteristics or relationships of an object being referred to, or as a way of exhibiting patterns of action which provide either visual or motoric images of processes.

(6) Gestures can be employed to create objects of reference for deictic expressions. We saw this in Chapter 8 where M talked of "crates as long as that" and used a gesture to show the size and shape of the crate he was referring to.

These six different ways in which gesture may be employed to contribute to the meaning of an utterance are those we have noted so far in the material we have at our disposal. No claim of exhaustiveness is made. Furthermore, it should be clear that a given gesture may contribute to the referential meaning of an utterance in more than one way simultaneously (we shall discuss this point further in Chapter 11 where we point out how gestures can be simultaneously deictic and descriptive). Our purpose in offering the present account is to clarify the various ways in which gestures function as components of referential meaning in the utterance.

Narrow gloss gestures used with equivalent verbal expressions

De Jorio (2000, pp. 32-33) noted that there are a few gestures that have what he called a *significato semplice*, or 'simple meaning'. He notes that if, for example, one observes a gesture in which the tip of the index finger rubs back and forth on the tip of the thumb, everyone will know that 'money' is being referred to. If one observes the hand being shaped in the form of a hook everyone will know that a reference is being made to a thief or to stealing. Gestures of this sort will here be referred to as 'narrow gloss' gestures. They tend to be regarded as if they are the equivalent of a specific verbal expression. Such gestures would fall within the definition of 'emblem' offered by Ekman and Friesen (1969), however, this term is also used to cover a much wider range of more or less conventionalized forms than those we intend by the term 'narrow gloss'. Gestures of this type, at least among Neapolitans, are quite often observed being used as if the speaker is uttering the same meaning unit as a word and as a gesture, simultaneously.

For example, in Example 21 (Commerciante I 25.06), from a recording made of a stallholder and his friends who are playing cards while waiting for customers in the *piazzetta* of a town near Naples, the players are joking about being videotaped and one of them suggests that the videotape that the students are making will be broadcast on a certain television network. Because the students have explained that their interest is in the commercial activities of the market-place where they are making the video, Peppe suggests that the

A   B

Fig. 10.1   *Danaro* 'money' (A) from No. 2 in Plate XX and *ladro* 'thief' (B) from No. 7 in Plate XIX in de Jorio (1832).

video should be shown to the government finance minister. He tries to recall his name. He says: *"fancellë vërè 'o ministrë ëëë commë se chiammë chillë? 'o ministrë eee (.) chillë re sordë, ra finanzë"* ('Show it to the minister, how do you call him? The minister, the one for money, for finance'). As he says *"sordë"* ('money') he uses the gesture common for this: tip of index finger rubbed back and forth against the tip of the thumb.

Again, in Example 22 (La Bionda 11.55.46), taken from a recording made of a conversation with the proprietor of a shop that makes and sells objects for the Christmas Crib displays *(presepe)* that are an important part of the Neapolitan tradition at Christmastime, the proprietor is explaining that as the Christmas season approaches it gets more and more crowded and it often happens that undesirable people pass through her shop. Her interlocutor asks: *"tipo?"* ('for example?') and the proprietor replies: *"Ladri, truffatori"* ('thieves, shoplifters') and as she pronounces each one of these words with both hands she flexes her digits 4, 3 and 2, leaving the index finger extended but slightly bent, in a gesture that is commonly used to mean 'thief' (see de Jorio 2000, p. 258 and Plate XIX no. 7). Thus, in such examples, as the speaker uses the word for 'money' or 'thieves' a gesture is done at the same time and it is interpreted as being the equivalent of these words.

Although this is common practice among Neapolitans (who have a fairly large vocabulary of such 'simple meaning' or 'narrow gloss' gestures) it is by no means to be observed only among them. Example 23 shows us something like this in a British English speaker who lives in London. This example is taken from a recording known as Boardman Cousins and Actors, a videotape made at a 'talk show' organized by the British Council in Naples in which a number of English people talked about their life and work in England for the benefit of a Neapolitan audience who understood English and had an interest in Britain and its culture. One of the participants is describing the work she does in the office where she works in London. She says: "I do everything, from the accounts, to the typing, to the telephone, to the cleaning, everything." As she says "accounts" she leans her head on one side, but as she says "typing" and "telephone" and "cleaning" she does a gesture in each case that displays an abstracted fragment of the manual action involved if you type, if you lift a telephone receiver to your ear, if you rub a surface with a cloth. It is as if these gestures are kinesic equivalents of the words naming these activities.

What determines when a speaker will use such gestures in this way? A systematic study of the contexts in which we see this sort of usage has yet to be carried out. If an attempt were made to compare observers' understandings of the objects referred to in these cases, with or without the presence of the speech, it is likely that understanding would be equally good in both cases. That is, in these cases the gestures seem to add nothing to the information about referential content here. They do provide an alternative representation, however, and one of the circumstances in which people may use them may be when there are conditions which might interfere with a complete hearing by the speaker's interlocutor (such as a high noise level) or where, for some other reason, the speaker may not be sure that the interlocutor is fully attending to or fully understands what is being said (this could account for the gesture use in Example 23). However, there are other possibilities. For example, by using a narrow gloss gesture it is possible for a speaker to make physically present a representation of a concept. This representation can be positioned in space so as to be conspicuous and its presence can be prolonged beyond the brief moment of a spoken word. In this way the concept can be held present to the interlocutor during a whole passage in the discourse.

In Example 24 (from the recording PF), the speaker, PF, who was a boy during the German occupation of Naples in the Second World War, in the course of explaining his now more favourable attitude to the Germans, says "*Poi io sono stato due anni in Germania*" ('Then I have been two years in Germany'). As he says "*due anni*" he holds up his index and middle finger in a representation of the concept *due* ('two'). In Example 14, already described in Chapter 8, (see p. 147 and Fig. 8.11) M, in the course of an interview in which he is asking his interviewee about what she thinks is important in Naples, says: "*Quando si parla di Napoli si parla di due cose essenziali*" ('When one speaks of Naples one speaks of two essential things'). As he says "*due cose*" he lifts his right hand with index and middle finger only extended, again giving a gestural representation of *due* ('two').

In both of these examples the 'two' gesture seems simply to duplicate the meaning of the word *due*. However, by doing this the speaker may make the number he refers to very plain. In addition, as already noted in the discussion of Example 14 in Chapter 8, the speaker makes the 'two' gesture while he pauses his speech after he has said "*due cose*" ('two things'). In this way the gesture can preserve the idea of 'two' in visible form, and this may contribute to its prominence in the utterance.

In a third example, Example 25, taken from the recording of the stallholder and friends playing cards (Commerciante II 00.29.39), Peppe, in arguing over

Fig. 10.2   Example 25. Peppe thrusts his hand forward exhibiting in gesture the idea of *due* 'two' in arguing with Vincenzo over points he has won in the card game.

points in a card game, asserts that Vincenzo (his opponent) has won *"due"* whereas Vincenzo disagrees. Peppe lifts up his hand in the 'two' hand shape and holds it there, even moving it forward toward Vincenzo. The idea of *"due"* is thus presented visually and it can be sustained, physically, so Vincenzo is less able to ignore it (Fig. 10.2).

The next two examples, Examples 26 and 27, suggest how a speaker can prolong the presentation of an idea by prolonging the gesture that expresses it. In an ethnographic film about gesture in Naples by Diego Carpitella (1976, 1981), a street vendor is seen engaged in a long harangue about his wares. In the course of this he assures his audience that he is not cheating on the price, that he would go to prison if he were. As he says this, he holds his hands forward, resting one wrist upon the other as if they were tied together. This gesture can be glossed as the equivalent of *galera* ('prison') (de Jorio 2000, p. 348). He produces this gesture as he says *"galera"* but maintains his hands in the arrangement described for the entire piece of pertinent discourse. Here the gesture serves as a kind of physical representation of the point with which he especially wishes to impress his audience. The same speaker, a few moments later, declares that he will swear by his mother that what he is saying is true - and as he says this he crosses his hands on his chest in a gesture that means *'giurare'* ('to swear'). See de Jorio (2000, p. 231).

In both cases the gesture used is equivalent to a word: *'galera'* ('prison'); *'giurare'* ('to swear, promise'). It is brought in during the phrase in which the word is used. In both cases it is this word that carries the main burden of the information the phrase conveys - it is the word that provides the new information. That is, in these cases it is the concept conveyed by the most important word in the phrase that is selected for expression in gesture. By using the gesture, however, the speaker is able to present that concept in another way, in a way that is not fleeting, but can be held before the audience. Perhaps, because of this, the gesture can serve in assisting to fix this concept in the mind of the audience.

We may add that, when one says *'giuro'* ('I swear') and also does the gesture, perhaps one can be seen to be doing the act of swearing. In fact it might be argued that the gesture *is* the act itself, where the verbal statement 'I swear' is only a report of it. As Mary Key (1977, pp. 7-8) has suggested, many so-called performative verbs (for example, 'promise', 'swear', 'bless', 'congratulate', 'greet', 'thank', 'deny' - there are many others) have gestural equivalents and these equivalents can often be regarded as constituting the actual performance of the act, the verbal expression sometimes being not quite enough. Thus an agreement is 'sealed' with a handshake, and one does more than make a merely verbal promise to tell the truth in court when one raises one's right hand or places it on the Bible in making the promise (Hibbitts 1992).

The reader may have noted that, in this section, all of the examples we have given, with one exception, are from Neapolitan speakers. This may reflect a characteristic of Neapolitan culture. If we compare Neapolitan speakers with British speakers, for instance, where the discourse situation is similar for both, Neapolitan speakers more often use gestural expressions that are coordinate with individual words in their discourse, with the result that a Neapolitan may employ two or even three gestures in the course of a single tone unit. This is much less likely among British speakers (Kendon 2004). This tendency may in part be a consequence of the fact that, in Neapolitan culture, a much larger vocabulary of gestures that can be used as the equivalent of single words is available. We still must explain why such a large gesture vocabulary should exist in this culture, however. Some discussion of this will be found in Chapter 16.

Narrow gloss gestures with a non-matching verbal expression

Narrow gloss gestures are by no means only used in environments where the speaker also pronounces the equivalent word. They can be used on their own, without speech, either alternating with speech within a sentence or as part of an utterance composed only of gestures. They are also used in association with a verbal expression which does not match the gesture directly. Sometimes this means that the gesture serves to specify a dimension of reference that is not itself directly given in words. Sometimes the gesture serves to indicate a more general concept than is implied by what the speaker says in words.

In Example 28, taken from a recording made of someone who is giving a guided tour of certain ancient aqueducts that are under the city of Naples (Napoli Sotterranea 10.29.51), the speaker is explaining how the workers within these aqueducts, the so-called *pozzari,* who had the care of the various wells from which the inhabitants of the city could draw their water, obtained the money due to them from their clients. He introduces his explanation by

Fig. 10.3. Example 29. Peppe uses a gesture glossed as *"na mazzata"*, literally a staff or club but which here means a blow or hit. He uses this gesture as he says that the shoes he wanted to buy were *"troppo carë"* ('too dear') thereby suggesting that the price had 'hit' him.

asking members of his audience what they think the *pozzaro* did to let his clients know that payment was due. He says: *"ora quando quest'operaio, questo pozzaro che lavorava giù, e e gestiva la manutenzione, doveva essere pagato, secondo voi, da qua giù come poteva lui avvisare gli utenti sopra che dev'essere pagato?"* ('Now when this worker, this *pozzaro* who was working down below, and and seeing after the maintenance, had to be paid, according to you, from down there how was he able to advise the client above that he had to be paid?'). On both occasions, when the speaker says *"pagato"* he uses the gesture for money described above. In cases of this sort we see how a gesture like the one usually glossed as 'money' may be used when there is a reference to money even where the actual word money is not uttered. One of the references implied here is 'money' and the gesture indicates this.

In Example 29 (Commerciante II 36.57, see Fig. 10.3) a gesture that is a kinesic rendition of a Neapolitan metaphorical expression is used to link a circumstance the speaker is describing to something in which the use of this expression would be appropriate. In Neapolitan there is an expression in which one says of something that is unexpectedly unpleasant that it is *"na mazzata"* that is, a club, heavy stick or staff: something that can hit you. This can refer to any sort of sudden unpleasantness but it is often used to refer to something financial, for example an unexpectedly high price for something. Here Peppe explains to his son that he really needed to buy a new pair of shoes, however he adds that he did not do so because they were too expensive. He says: "*Giova' m'eva i' a fa nu parë 'i scarpë (.) io aggia vistë purë nun è cosë pëcchë troppë carë*" ('Giovanni I was going to go to buy a pair of shoes I had seen, but it wasn't the case [i.e. I did not do it] because too expensive'). As he says "*troppë carë*" ('too expensive') he lowers his open right hand, palm vertical, twice toward his left hand, held open, palm up. This gesture has a narrow gloss in Neapolitan as *na mazzata*. In this way Peppe shows that the discovery of the high price of the shoes was a shock for him.

Example 30 is a case in which a gesture, though not as narrow gloss as the ones mentioned so far, nevertheless can easily be rendered with a verbal expression. Here it is used so that, simultaneously with the words being uttered, it brings an additional meaning, even though there is no verbal expression of it. The example is taken from the recording PF. The speaker is talking about his boyhood in Naples and he claims to have been among the first of the street urchins who participated in the revolt against the German occupation of the city in 1943. He says "*Io sono stato uno di quei scugnizzi napoletani*" ('I was one of those Neapolitan street urchins'). As he says "*scugnizzi*" ('street urchins') he lifts his right hand up, held open with the palm facing inwards, and moves his hand backwards over his shoulder twice. This gesture is a well-known form used to make reference to things of the past (cf. de Jorio 2000, p. 312). Here the speaker's verbal expression implies a reference to time past. The gesture makes this implication explicit.

Example 31 is another illustration of the use of the gesture for past time just described. It is taken from a passage from SG (SG 11.32.13) in which the speaker, a woman, is describing some of her recipes. (Fig. 10.4). She is discussing recipes for the famous Neapolitan *sugo* or *ragù*. Having explained her own method for making it, she explains that this was the method her father taught her. She says "*però, il vero ragù è quello lì ch..., almeno penso eh, che me l'ha insegnato mio padre, mio padre cucinava (....) mamma mia facevë allëccà 'e baffë*" ('However the true ragù is that one tha-, at least so I think, that was taught me by my father, my father used to cook (....), *mamma mia* it made you lick your chops!'). As she says "*mio padre*" she throws her open hand back over her shoulder in the gesture just mentioned that refers to something in the past, thus adding the idea that her father was something in the past (Fig. 10.4A).

Note that the phrase beginning "*mio padre cucinava*" is completed with a gesture which is 'slotted in' at the end of the sentence. As she says "*cucinava*" she places her thumb and index finger in contact with her cheek and moves her hand in a forward twisting motion, a gesture that expresses the idea of something delicious (Fig. 10.4B). With this gesture she thus adds a comment on the quality of her father's cooking and also completes the phrase.

The kind of gesture usage seen in this last example is very common among Neapolitan speakers. It has also been described by Tatania Slama-Cazacu

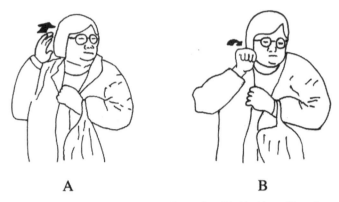

Fig. 10.4. Example 31. A: Speaker directs hand behind herself as she says "*mio padre*" indicating that she is talking about something in the past. B: Speaker completes a sentence with a gesture that means 'delicious' - a comment on the *ragù* that her father used to cook.

(1976) for Romanian speakers. A systematic study is lacking however, though it is surely deserved. In what kinds of expressions and in what linguistic and interactional contexts do we see such gesture alternation, how are alternated gestures positioned within the sentences of which they are a part and what kinds of items in sentences usually receive an alternate gestural form?

Example 32 is again one in which a 'narrow gloss' gesture is used in this case to indicate the broader concept the speaker's words imply. It is taken from a recording made of a group of middle-aged people discussing the bad behaviour of the young (AVIS 6.53.58). One of the speakers is a bus driver. He describes how young boys on his bus often write obscene phrases on the backs of the bus seats and they do this right in front of the girls they are with. He exclaims that the girls don't care, indeed they laugh about it too. He finishes his discourse by saying: "*Sono contente, quindi sono consapevoli anche loro. Gli sta bene anche a loro*" ('They are happy about it, hence they are also aware of it. It's OK also for them'). An implication of this is that the girls are equally involved in this kind of activity. That is, they are the equal of the boys in this. This implication is made clear in the speaker's gesture in which he places two extended index fingers alongside one another (Fig. 10.5). He does this as he says "*Sono contente, quindi sono consapevoli anche loro*" ('they are happy about it, they are aware of it too'). The gesture he uses is very well known and it is generally said to mean that two people are very close, either that they are close allies, very close friends or that they are lovers (see de Jorio 2000, p. 90). Here, however, it is used to express (as is also common) the more abstract idea of equality of participation.

Fig. 10.5. Example 32. Speaker uses a gesture that means that two things are 'equal' or two people are 'close'. In the context here he uses it to suggest the equality of participation of boys and girls in the writing of 'shameful phrases' on the backs of bus seats in Salerno.

Gestures as semantic specifiers

It is common for a speaker to employ a gesture when uttering a verb or verb phrase where the form of the action of the gesture is interpretable as a movement pattern extracted from the pattern of action that might be performed were the speaker actually to carry out the action referred to by the verb. However, in such cases the gesture is not a kinesic equivalent of the lexical verb but is an enactment which displays a specific form of action often, also, displaying something of the manner of the action. In such cases the gesture adds referential information for it makes the utterance have a much more specific meaning.

Example 1, described in Chapter 7 (pp. 113ff), illustrated this. As was noted, the 'throwing action' that M performs in association with the word 'throw' as he speaks the sentence "And he used to go down there and throw ground rice over it" is an action that seems highly suited to the action of scattering a substance such as ground rice. We suggested that in this way the speaker makes the meaning of 'throw' in this context much more precise. It is interesting to compare this with another occasion when the same speaker uses the verb 'throw' and again uses a gesture which, though quite different, nevertheless suggests a throwing action that is suited to the kind of throwing that is implied, given the sorts of objects involved and the purposes for which they are being thrown.

In Example 33 (Crick II 13.54.17), M is describing how American soldiers, when leaving a military base near a nearby village that they had used during World War II, left behind a great deal of useful stuff. He goes on: "and they used to come through Northant and they used to throw oranges and chewing

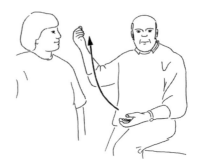

A: Example 1 (see p. 114). M's gesture as he says "And he used to go down there and throw ground rice over it."

B: Example 33. M's 'tossing' gesture as he says "throw oranges" and again as he says "and chewing gum."

Fig. 10. 6. Two different gestures associated with the verb 'throw' suggesting a different kind of throwing action in each case.

gum (...) all off the lorries to us kids in the streets." As he says "throw oranges and chewing gum" he twice lifts his hand rapidly from his lap, directing its movement over his shoulder, opening the hand slightly each time, in a manner that suggests the action of throwing things out of something, without much regard for their precise destination (Fig. 10.6B). This action appears to enact a form of throwing that seems well suited to the actions of the soldiers here described as throwing things off lorries into the street as they drove along. Here, although he says "throw oranges and chewing gum" by his gesture he displays a particular version of 'throwing' (perhaps the English verb 'toss' might have been appropriate here) and he also, by repeating the action, suggests that this was a succession of throwing actions on the part of the soldiers, not a single action of throwing. Thus many additional features of this action are provided in the gesture.

A somewhat similar pair of examples comes from the recording Pollack (Little Red Riding Hood) referred to in Example 6 in Chapter 8. Someone is telling the story of Little Red Riding Hood and she reaches the point in the narrative where the hunter sees Little Red Riding Hood running away from the Big Bad Wolf and comes to her rescue by cutting off the Wolf's head (Pollack 19.26.16). The narrator says (Example 34): "and the hunter took his axe, and with one mighty heave, sliced the wolf's head off..." As she says "and the hunter took his axe" both her hands move from her lap into a configuration suitable for holding something like an axe handle and in this configuration they are lifted up so they are held above her right shoulder. She holds them in this position as she says "and with one mighty heave" and then, exactly as

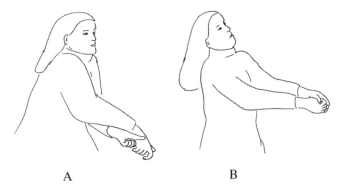

A   B

Fig. 10.7   Example 34 (A) and Example 6 (B). The arm position at the end of the stroke associated with the word "sliced" in "..sliced the wolf's head off" (A) and in "sliced the wolf's stomach open" (B). Trajectory of the enacted axe-swing differs according to the object being sliced.

she says "sliced" she swings both hands, still held as if holding an axe, in a diagonally downward motion to her right, the hands then being held still in this position until the end of the entire verb phrase. With this action, thus, she gives a representation of the action of the hunter as he cut off the Wolf's head (Fig. 10.7A). Very shortly afterwards, in the same narration, we encounter a very similar piece of discourse (Example 6, Fig. 8.4, p. 136). Immediately after the hunter has cut off the Wolf's head, Little Red Riding Hood tells him that the Wolf has eaten her grandmother. To remedy this situation the hunter then cuts open the Wolf's stomach and out pops the grandmother. The narrator says (Pollack 20.01.16): "...and the hunter took his hatchet and with a mighty sweep, sliced the Wolf's stomach open..." The structure of the verbal component is the same as before, and the pattern of gesture is also the same. As the narrator says "...and the hunter took his hatchet..." she again moves her hands so that they enact grasping an axe handle and lifts them as if holding an axe above her right shoulder. As she says "and with a mighty sweep" the hands are held in this position above her shoulder. As she says "sliced" she again swings both hands held together rapidly, arms straight, to her left, and holds them still at the end of this movement until the end of the verb phrase. But this time the movement, instead of being a downward diagonal movement, is a horizontal movement (Fig. 10.7B). Slicing off a wolf's head might call for a downward movement but a horizontal movement would be closer to what might be involved in slicing open its stomach. Note that, in English, there are various verbs for cutting, of which 'slice' is one, but one can also use 'chop' or 'cut' or 'slit', and so forth. Here the narrator uses only the verb 'slice' but,

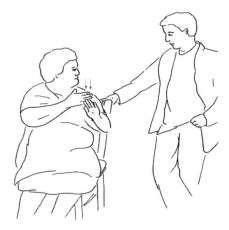

Fig. 10.8   Example 35. C makes a 'chopping' gesture against her left hand as she refers to *"carota"* ('carrot') as an ingredient in a sauce for a *spaghetti bolognese*. She shows in gesture that the carrot is chopped up when put in the sauce. It is as if she had said *"carota tritata"* ('chopped carrot').

in her gesture, she differentiates one from the other. The gestures, thus, in this case, make much more precise her account of the hunter's action.

Related to this kind of gesture use are those examples in which an object is mentioned and a gesture is made accompanying such a mention which shows how the object referred to is to be treated or is being treated in the context of what is being talked about, even though the operations carried out in relation to the object are not mentioned in words.

In Example 35 (DSGA 0.26.24), C is explaining to M what the ingredients are for the *sugo* for a Bolognese (Fig. 10.8). She lists several items: *"un po' diii sedano, na bella carota, con la cipolla, la faccio soffrigere co' olio, e burro"* ('a little celery, a fine carrot, onion, I fry it with oil and butter'). As she says *"na bella carota"* she holds her left hand forward, fingers straight and palm down, and with the right hand, also held so all fingers are straight and held together but oriented so the palm is vertical, she moves the hand rapidly and vertically downward several times against the other hand. This is a 'cutting' gesture. If you take words and gestures together this means 'chopped carrot' (*'carota tritata'*) not just 'carrot'.

Similarly, in the recording LB, the conversation with the proprietor of the shop selling items for the *presepe*, in Example 36 (LB 11.57.49), the speaker, having been asked to describe a recipe, is explaining how to make *spaghetti alle vongole* ('spaghetti with clams'). She says: *"si comprano le vongole, poi a parte si soffrigge l'aglio, un bel pepperoncino, poi si mette un poco di pomodorini, si lavano le ven.. vongole e si mettono, si riscaldono i spaghetti,*

Fig. 10.9   Example 37. UB acts as if holding a brush or pen between thumb and forefinger and writing something on the back of the seat in front of him, in front of his neighbour (here treated as if he is the girl the boy is sitting next to) in the bus he is riding in.

e si versa tutto" ('One buys the *vongole,* then on one side one fries garlic, a fine hot pepper, then one puts in a few small tomatoes, one washes the *ven-vongole,* one re-heats the spaghetti, and one puts it all together'). As she says *"un poco di pomodorini"* she holds her two hands, palm down, index and thumb extended and in contact at the tips, and she moves the thumb forward against the tip of the index finger. This is a 'squeezing'action that refers to how one squeezes the little tomatoes as they are put into the pot - they are squashed so they break open. This operation is not mentioned in words, it is given only in the gesture. The reference to this ingredient and how you operate on the ingredient as you put it in for cooking are thus combined in a single moment of the utterance.

As a last example (Example 37) in this section we take a passage from the AVIS recording already referred to (AVIS 6.53.23) in which the bus driver (UB) is describing how boys write salacious phrases on the backs of the seats of the buses with the full complicity of the girls in their company. In this example we see a very elaborate enactment which, in consequence, imports many additional details into the utterance that get no mention in the words (Fig. 10.9). The speaker says: *"e il ragazzo a fianco, il fidanzato di una ragazza che continua a designare e pennellare, e loro guardano"* ('and the boy in the next seat, the boyfriend of a girl, who continues to draw and paint, and they watch'). As he says *"che continua a designare e pennellare"* he leans leftwards in front of the man sitting next to him and extends his left hand forward, with the hand posed as if it is holding an implement such as a pen or a brush. He extends this hand forward, and aligning his gaze to his hand just as he would if he were really writing, makes slight back and forth movements 'as if' writing, enacting, thus, not just a 'writing' gesture, but one that is carefully placed in relative space so that it is just as if the writing is being done on a vertical surface opposite his immediate neighbour. By this enactment he conjures up the whole scene of the boy leaning across to write on the back of the bus seat in front of the girl he is next to. In this way a great deal of additional and specific information is added to the utterance.

Gestures as an 'exhibit' or 'specimen'

The speaker's hands are employed to create a version of some object that is being referred to. When an object is being discussed, if an exemplar is present, the speaker may pick it up and present it while it is being talked about. If an exemplar is not to hand, however, sometimes a version of it can be created in gesture. Here are three illustrations.

Example 38 is taken from a recording made in Naples known as *Piccolo Teatro*. In this recording a man is talking with the wife of the concierge of the building where he has a shop, about his memories of Naples during the Second World War. He describes how his family tried to leave the city during the bombardment of 1943 and explains that all they had with them to eat were some bags of small apples, partly rotten, fit only for horses or donkeys or pigs. He says (Piccolo Teatro 0.05.00): "*...mio padre prendeva due tre borse ma tutte di mele, ma mele marce, mele che adesso së rannëëë së rannë 'o cavallo 'o ciuccië, 'e melë 'e torzë 'e melë*" ('my father was carrying two or three bags but all of apples, but rotten apples, apples that today are given are given to horse or donkey, and apples and apple cores...'). As he says "*ma tutte di mele, ma mele marce*" ('but all of apples, but rotten apples') he holds up his right hand and forms a small circle with index finger and thumb, pointing to it with the index finger of his left hand (Fig. 10.10, p. 192). His hands in these poses are held up at about the level of the speaker's upper chest and moved forward two or three times in highly bound movements of extremely short amplitude - 'presenting' the hand to his interlocutor, which now is being used to exhibit the small apple, as it were. Note that, in doing this, the speaker shows that the apples were very small, an additional feature not mentioned in his words.

Example 39 (Crick I 12.11.00) is very similar. S is describing the huge meals that she remembers served at a Norfolk gamekeeper's house that she and her husband used to visit when they were young. She describes how, at tea-time, "out would come the little lemon curd tarts, little jam tarts". As she says this she poses both of her hands in front of her so that they show a small horizontal circle. Here the hands are used to 'create' such a little tart - the hands become an 'exhibit' that illustrates the object being referred to (Fig. 10.11, p. 192).

Example 40 is from a recording of a meeting of the Cricket Club Committee (OCC 8.28.55) where the committee member in charge of building a new pavilion for the club is explaining the security arrangements. He says: "Bear in mind that we are planning to put a bar [0.6] across the double doors on the inside." As he says "bar" he lifts up his two hands, held with palms oriented outwards, with all digits extended but held together, thumb opposed but extended, which are then moved horizontally away from one another (Fig. 10.12, p. 192). The effect of this gesture is to mould a wide horizontal elongated object, which has a certain depth. The speaker thus 'creates' the bar - and shows by the way he moulds it that it will not be rod shaped, but flat. Furthermore, he pauses in his speech immediately after "bar" for six-tenths of a second, long enough to hold his two hands still as if to ensure that the bar was not only created but sustained in its place.

In each of these examples, then, an object that the speaker refers to is 'created' so that it may be viewed by recipients. The gestures in these examples bring the object forth and exhibit it. It is interesting to note that in all the cases of this sort that we have collected, the speaker looks at his or her own hands as the action of object-creation is begun. Thus the hands have become objects for the speaker, as well as for the interlocutor, objects set out in interactional space for presentation and inspection (cf. Streeck 1993).

Gestures showing object properties and spatial relationships

Gestures are often employed in an utterance to refer to aspects of the structure or shape of something being described. This was clearly illustrated in the passage from Crick III (Example 20) described in Chapter 9. There M is describing how the cheeses sent to his father's grocery shop arrived packed in crates. As he says: "the cheeses used to come in big crates about as long as that and they were shaped like a threepenny bit at the ends, with slats on, there used to be two cheeses in each crate" he uses gestures to exhibit the length of the crate (Fig. 9.2A), to sketch the shape they had when viewed from one end (Fig. 9.2B), to display the orientation of the slats from which they were constructed (Fig. 9.2C), and to indicate how the cheeses were arranged side by side within the crate (Fig. 9.2D). In this example, as we noted, much information about the spatial organization of the crates, their shape and their size, and how the cheeses are arranged, is given in gesture. Gesture and speech together provide a much more complete picture of these objects than do the words alone.

Fig. 10.10. Example 38. With thumb and forefinger of his right hand held to form a small circle, G points to it with his left index finger as he draws attention to the size of the apples that were all that his father had for his family to eat as they fled Naples during the bombardment of 1943.

Fig. 10.11 Example 39. S refers to the lemon curd tarts she remembers from the teas of her youth and uses her hands to 'exhibit' a tart as she speaks of them.

Fig. 10.12   C uses his hands to suggest the positioning and shape of a security bar that is to be placed on the inside of the double doors of the new cricket pavilion that the Cricket Club Committee is discussing.

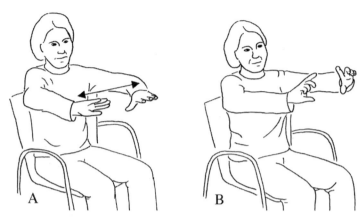

Fig. 10.13. Example 41. A: G moves her hands, open palm down, away from one another, describing a level surface, as she says "*le pietre*" referring to the gravel in the bottom of her aquarium. B: G holds her two hands up as if spanning two large objects with her fingers as she refers to the two large rocks in her aquarium. Through her gesture we gather that these rocks stand side by side.

A very similar example, Example 41, may be cited from a recording made in Portici, near Naples, of a group of young girls, members of a Parish youth group, who were describing their rooms at home, their toys and their pets. One girl describes her aquarium. She says "*e ci sono le pietre piccole, poi ci sono due pietre grandi*" ('and there are little stones, and then there are two big stones'). As she says "*le pietre*" she moves her two hands, held as open hands palms down, away from one another in a horizontal fashion, thereby indicating how the little stones (i.e. gravel) are spread out in a layer (Fig. 10.13A). As she says "*due pietre*" she holds her two hands up, side by side, each held with the thumb and index finger widely separated but partly flexed, as if to indicate two fairly large objects (Fig. 10.13B). This is very similar to M's use of his hands when he says "there used to be two cheeses in each crate". Like M in that example, so here, the speaker positions her hands to show how the two large stones are set side by side in her aquarium. Further, in this example G, in positioning her hands in this manner, moves them forward and back rapidly with a highly restricted amplitude. Like M, thus, she also employs a location establishing movement.

Examples of this sort abound. Whenever speakers give descriptions of objects, gesture is almost always employed as an integral component of such descriptions. Gestures used in this fashion undoubtedly serve to provide important information for recipients (see Beattie and Shovelton 1998, 1999a, 1999b, 2001 for experimental demonstrations of this). However, they may be useful also because they make possible a much more economical account than any that could be accomplished by words alone. This can make gesture a valuable form of expression in situations such as informal conversation, where speakers are often under some restraint not to over-occupy the floor. The time for turns at talk is time in common, and there may be competition for it. In consequence, speakers are likely to be under a certain amount of pressure to refrain from very lengthy turns. In addition, the description of the spatial structure of objects can be accomplished much more rapidly in gesture and one does not have to take out nearly as much time to think out what one has to say as one does when such a description has to be organized in words. These considerations certainly must be taken into account in any attempt to develop an explanation as to why, in any given stretch of discourse, gestures are employed.[1]

Gestures as objects of deictic reference

The speaker uses gestures to create the object to which reference is being made deictically in the spoken component. M's 'size-shape-specifier' gesture in the example from Chapter 9 just referred to, used when he says of the cheese crates "they were as long as that", is an example. We now give four further examples. The first two are examples in which the speaker, in gesture, creates or describes a shape or creates an object in gesture by sketching. This gestural description or creation then becomes the object of deictic reference. In the second two examples we see how enactments can become objects of deictic reference.

In Example 42 (GB 2.33.49) GB, who is giving a guided tour of an historic Northamptonshire town, points with index finger and arm straight to a feature on a building he is standing opposite and says "A nice Venetian window there, by the way." As he says "by the way" he retracts his arm and adjusts his glasses, and then extends his arm laterally to his right, this time with open hand palm up, in preparation for his next piece of discourse, which is to be about something else. In the interval during which he is preparing himself for this next piece of discourse, a member of his audience calls out: "A nice what?" whereupon GB, still with his arm in the position he had established for his new piece of discourse, says "Venetian window." Then he moves his hand back to re-direct it to a position in space that is opposite the Venetian window and then says "the one that goes like that at the top." As he says "the one that"

---

[1] Speakers vary in the extent to which they use gesture, some being much more likely to do so than others. In an intriguing study by Melinger and Levelt, presented at the First International Conference on Gesture Studies, Austin, Texas, June 2002 (see Melinger and Levelt 2002), it was shown how speakers who used gesture to describe for another the layout of a diagram left out spatial information from their verbal descriptions which was not left out by speakers who did not use gesture. This study is a clear demonstration of the complementary relationship that speech and gesture can have to one another in such descriptive tasks.

with his index finger he sketches a shape in the air which corresponds to an upward pointing shape, as he says "goes like that at the top" he lowers his hand to hang loosely by his side, before embarking, once again, on the piece of discourse that is to follow. Here the sketch of the window's shape is first made and then the deictic word that refers to it is uttered.

In Example 15 (Crick III, 15.21.04, see Fig. 8.12, p. 148) M explains about the large rectangular cake that was sent down from London to his father's shop every Christmas. He says: "I mean another uhm like uhm I suppose like a tradition, in me father's shop, every Christmas (1.3 sec), he used to have sent down from London a Christmas cake, an' it was (1.02 sec) this sort of (0.4 sec) size." In the one-second pause in speech that follows "was" M leans over the table in front of him and moves his two hands symmetrically in a 'sketching' movement of large amplitude to depict a large square object lying flat on the table in front of him. Thus he creates the cake for all to see. Once again note that the shape of the object is first depicted and then the deictic word that refers to it is uttered. Here also the recipients must see and retain the image created if what M says here is to be properly understood. In both of these cases, however, the object sketched in gesture had been named in the preceding discourse, as when GB says "Venetian window" and M says "a Christmas cake". [2] This makes it clear how the sketching gesture is to be interpreted.

The next two examples show a pattern of activity being displayed as an object of deictic reference. In both cases the gesture that has this status is produced as a performance separate from the performance of the associated words. In Example 43 (from Chinese Dinner, a recording of two couples eating a Chinese take-home dinner in the home of one of them)[3] the discussion has turned to smoking and the problems of quitting smoking. One of the guests is describing how, in her department (she works at a small college), someone was trying to quit smoking. She says: "Like this woman who tried to quit but she's just like you see on television where they're like this (0.2 sec) you know what I mean? (0.7 sec)". As she says "television where they're like this, you know what I mean?" she moves both hands in unison, somewhat up-raised, back and forth in rapid short-amplitude movements. This is probably a conventionalized gesture used to represent the idea of someone in a state of frustration. It is to be noted that this display, which is the object of the deictic expression "where they're like this", begins as a movement of her right hand only as she says "to quit but she's -". The movement is suspended as she changes her posture, leaning back in her chair, and resumes with both hands as she says "on television"

---

[2] See Chapter 15 where we see that the role played by gestures of this sort in spoken discourse is similar to the role played by so-called classifiers in primary sign language discourse.
[3] I am indebted to Charles Goodwin for permission to use this material.

continuing as she says "you know what I mean" and onwards for seven-tenths of a second after she has finished her speech. Here the gesture is a uniphrasal gesture unit in which, in the stroke, there is repetitive movement. It is produced as a performance that is separated from the performance of the speech with which it co-occurs. It is not tied in with the structure of the spoken discourse. The rhythmic movements of the gesture phrase, which is multi-phased, are not organized in association with the tonic centres of the phrases of her discourse, nor is it linked to the syllabic structure of the speech. The gesture phrase runs through and continues on after the entire unit of spoken discourse, as if it is an object apart from the activity of speech.

Example 43. ** gestural movement; v= hand(s) moved forward and down; ^=hand(s) moved upward; h=hand(s) held still. Each sub-stroke is labeled with a letter. A–C: only right hand is used; E–V: both hands move in unison. During D hands are held still while speaker leans back in her chair. Tone units numbered with numbers in parentheses above the line of text.

(1)
Like this woman tried to
   (2)   (3)
quit/but she's just like you see on television/ where they're like this/
|*********| |**/**/**/********/****/***/**/**/

 v ^ v   h   v ^ v   ^   v   ^   v ^
 A B C   D   E F G   H   I   J   K L
|_____

                  fgp 1
   (4)
(0.2) you know what I mean?(.......0.7......)
//**************/**/***/**/**/**/**/**|

 v ^   v   ^   v   v ^ v ^ v
 M N   O   P   Q   R S T U V
                               |
                  fgp 1

Note that the forward–back movements of the hands, each 0.2 secs in length, are not coordinated with either the syllabic structure of the speech nor to the tone unit structure. The use of conventional orthography for the speech here does not show the temporal proportions of hand movements and speech. Note the continuation of the forward–back movements after the verbal discourse is ended.

In Example 44 (Crick III 14.12.09) S is describing how, as a child, she used to go to a certain church for their harvest suppers or for Sunday School and used to enjoy watching a certain person playing the organ. She says: "She used to play the organ then and of course I think there was someone who

used to have to stand there doing this (0.9 sec) and that was sort of great fun."
Here, as she begins to say "I think there was somebody..." she holds both
hands in front of her, palms down, formed as loose fists, and she moves them
down in unison, also bowing her body forward repeatedly, in an enactment
of someone operating an organ pump. Notice that in this case, again, just as
in the example from Chinese Dinner (Example 43), the enactment which is
the object of the deictic pronominal "this" is begun as the whole sentence is
begun and the action continues for two cycles beyond the end of her speech,
continuing into the pause that is inserted between "this" and the resumption
of her speech with "and that was sort of great fun". Here, as in Example 43,
the movements that serve as the object referred to are made independently of
the structure of the speech, they are not rhythmically coordinated with it, and
continue afterwards, as if the enactment becomes an object separated from the
person who is also speaking.

Example 44. ** two-handed movement; ∧ hands raised; V hands lowered.
The succession of movements comprises a single multi-phase stroke.
fgp: forelimb gesture phrase.

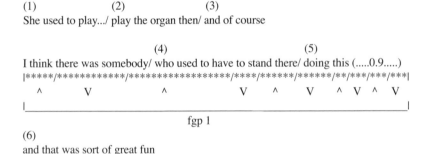

```
(1)              (2)                (3)
She used to play.../ play the organ then/ and of course

                      (4)                          (5)
I think there was somebody/ who used to have to stand there/ doing this (.....0.9.....)
|*****/***************/***********************/****/******/******/**/***/***/***|
      ∧        V                ∧                   V    ∧   V   ∧ V ∧ V
|_____|
                           fgp 1
(6)
and that was sort of great fun
```

Conclusions

This survey of different ways in which gesture can contribute to the referential
meaning of the utterance of which it is a part can only suggest the diversity
and complexity of this matter. The modes of gesture use we have described are
representative but we make no claim to have covered all of the possibilities.
Nevertheless, the examples should be enough to show that speakers have a rich
resource available to them in gesture. It is a medium which can be employed
in many different ways - to create objects, to show spatial relationships, to
exemplify actions - uses which can be brought in in relation to the verbal
component of the utterance to suit various purposes. Often gestures are used

to accomplish expressions that are in addition to or complementary to what is expressed verbally. They supply components of meaning integral to the utterance of the moment.

In regard to the use of what we have here termed 'narrow gloss' gestures, we offered a few observations that suggested how these can be useful as a means by which a symbolic object can be created and held before the recipient, serving as a way of prolonging the presentation of the idea. It is also possible, but this remains to be explored systematically, that speakers may tend to use such gestures (only if they have them available, of course) if they perceive the communication situation as one in which they may not be fully understood or in which they fear the loss of the attention of their interlocutors. However, as we also suggested, the use of such gestures can alter the way the utterance incorporating them is experienced by the recipient. There seems little doubt that speakers often use gestures for dramatic effect. Indeed, this is probably an important reason why gestures are used in some circumstances, a factor in gesture use that has received much less attention than it deserves.

We also mentioned another factor. We suggested that when a speaker is faced with the need to describe the form or size of some object, to talk about spatial relationships between objects, to describe an environment and how one might move about in such an environment, descriptive gestures, rather like drawings or pictures, can achieve adequate descriptions with much greater economy of effort and much more rapidly than words alone can manage. Given that, within the context of everyday conversation, speakers are rarely granted time to work out novel and complex verbal formulations, the recruitment of gesture as a form of expression economy is often resorted to as a solution.

Looking at how gestures are used from the point of view of how they are brought in to contribute to the meaning of the utterance, thus, not only shows us the variety of ways in which this medium can be employed, but it can also raise interesting questions about what leads to their use by speakers. Central to an understanding of this are factors such as the speaker's own linguistic skills and resources and skills in using gesture, the immediate demands of the interactive moment and the speaker's perception of the degree of fit or adequacy between what is to be expressed and the utterance created for that expression. For all of these things much further analysis is needed than has been provided hitherto.[4]

---

[4] For work quite independent of our own, and using a different methodology, which points to a similar conclusion, see Holler and Beattie (2002, 2003).

11   On pointing[1]

In the course of his guided tour of Northant, GB takes his little group of tourists into the church. He describes the interior of the building and draws attention to various features. In one part of his discourse he says (GB 3.09.07) "there is Gil Crestwood (.....) and there is Floyd Craddock."[2] It would be impossible for any member of the group to know what he was referring to, however, without also taking into consideration the fact that, as he says this, he extends his straight arm upwards, angled first in one direction, then in another, in each case with his hand shaped so that only his index finger is extended. With these gestures, in each case, he directs his audience's attention to the location of the two objects he has named which are, in this case, statues. He *points* to each statue in turn, as he refers to them, but only by doing so does he make the speech in his utterance intelligible. Without these pointing gestures the meaning of GB's "there" in each case could never be known. As we saw in Chapter 6, gestures of pointing, or deictic gestures, have been recognized as a separate class by almost all of the students of gesture we have reviewed and it has always been understood that such gestures can play a fundamental role in establishing how an utterance is to be understood. There are very few studies, however, which have examined the way in which pointing is done. In this chapter we study one aspect of this, looking at the hand shape a person uses when pointing (such as the index finger, the thumb, or the open hand) to see if there are systematic differences in how these different hand shapes are used. As we shall see, the context-of-use studies reported here suggest that differences in hand shape used in pointing are related to differences in the way the object being referred by the pointing gesture is being used by the speaker in the speaker's discourse.

Gestures understood as pointing are commonly done with the hands, but they may also be done with the head, by certain movements of the eyes, by protruding the lips (Sherzer 1972, Enfield, 2001), by a movement of the elbow, in some circumstances even with the foot (see de Jorio 2000, pp. 70-74 for a description of some different forms of pointing). They all have in common, however, a certain characteristic movement pattern in which the body part carrying out the pointing is moved in a well defined path, and the dynamics

---

[1] The work reported in this chapter was done in collaboration with Laura Versante. Analysis of pointing in a Neapolitan context has been previously described in Kendon and Versante (2003). An extended account which includes many of the examples from Northamptonshire described here may be found in Versante (1998).

[2] Fictional names have been substituted in this quotation.

of the movement are such that at least the final path of the movement is linear. Commonly, but not always, once the body part doing the pointing reaches its furthest extent, it is then held in position briefly. In pointing, except when a moving object is being followed, the movement by which the gesture is accomplished is thus a movement which appears to be aimed in a clearly defined direction as if toward some specific target. Eco (1976, p. 119) refers to this feature of pointing as 'movement toward' and we shall use this term here, also.

Pointing gestures are regarded as indicating an object, a location, or a direction, which is discovered by projecting a straight line from the furthest point of the body part that has been extended outward, into the space that extends beyond the speaker. This space may be treated in more than one way. It may be treated as the physical space that the participants share, in which case the object of the point is an actual object or location somewhere in the environment. This object or location may be something that is currently visible to all participants, or it may be an object or a location that exists somewhere in the real world, but cannot be seen, as when one points in the direction of objects that lie beyond the walls of one's house. On the other hand, the space into which the speaker points may be structured by the speaker's own actions. In such cases the speaker creates, through a combination of words and deictically inflected gestures, a way of regarding the space into which the pointing is done as a sort of invisible map (this can be a three-dimensional map). This may be a map in which the relative locations of characters and objects in a story are laid out ('narrational' space, see Haviland 1993) or it may be a map in which components of the speaker's discourse, such as contrasting logical positions, are assigned locations. It is as if these components are treated as physical objects that occupy positions in the space into which the speaker's gestures are directed (cf. McNeill, Cassell and Levy 1993 on 'abstract deixis').

There are a few studies which suggest that how a pointing gesture is done may make a difference to its meaning. Calbris (1990) drew attention to the possibility that using a head movement instead of a hand movement in pointing, or using the thumb instead of an index finger, may make a difference to the meaning of the pointing action. She suggests (1990, p. 128) that one designates another person with the forefinger "in order to command or accuse" but "[t]he hand, which constitutes a surface rather than a line, presents or offers. Its concrete designations are polite and not imperative..." The use of the head to designate something may appear "impolite" according to Calbris, and likewise the thumb, "probably because of the symbolic signification of rejection or offhandedness attached to the thumb, its use [in designating] is cavalier and offhanded, even rude and authoritative..." (ibid.). Much earlier, de Jorio, writing in 1832 (de Jorio 2000, pp. 73-74), had noted that indicating something with the eyes, often combined with an almost imperceptible movement of the head, was done when it was wished to keep the act of indication inconspicuous. He also noted that to point to someone or something to one's side or behind one with the thumb was also to express one's disparagement of what was being pointed to. Wilkins (2003) has described how, among the Arrentya, a central desert Australian Aboriginal group, adult pointers use a repertoire of several different hand shapes which are used in a consistently different manner. For example, a hand shape in which the middle two fingers are flexed to the palm, with index and little finger extended, is a hand shape used to indicate a route or a direction. On the other hand, a single extended index finger is used to indicate a single object, while a hand shape in which the fingers are spread and the palm held facing downwards, is used when indicating a multiplicity of objects. Kendon (1988b, p. 241) has described how, among the Warlpiri and Warumungu of the central desert of Australia, depending how far away the thing pointed at is deemed to be, the angle of the arm is altered, so that in pointing to things that are very far away the arm may be lifted almost vertically, and then thrust forward, whereas, when pointing to things close up, the angle of the arm is much closer to the horizontal, or angled toward the ground, if very close.

The present chapter reports a comparative study of hand shape use in pointing, as this has been observed in a selection from our collection of recordings. We describe seven different kinds of manual pointing, distinguished in terms of the shape of the hand in combination with the rotation position of the forearm. From a consideration of the discourse contexts in which we have observed them in use, we conclude that the form of pointing adopted by a speaker is systematically related to the way the object being referred to is presented in the speaker's discourse. That is, if the speaker points to an object because it is to be an example of something, or because it illustrates a concept, then the form of pointing adopted will be different from the form adopted when the speaker points to an object because it is being identified as something distinct from other objects. It is as if the form of pointing adopted provides information about how the speaker wishes the object being indicated to be regarded.

In attempting to delimit the field for this investigation, it was decided to concentrate on gestures that are entirely *specialized* for pointing. It often happens that a gesture occurs that certainly appears to point at something, but which, at the same time, also incorporates other functions. For example, one can combine with the pointing action components that seem to characterize the object pointed at. Gestures in which this combination was noted are not included in the analyses discussed in this chapter. However, before proceeding it will be useful to give examples of pointing in combination with other gestural functions.

Fig. 11.1   Example 45. Pointing combined with description. Customer at a fruit stall indicates the scales at the same time as she characterizes the movement of the scales' needle by rotating her index finger back and forth.

A woman at Vincenzo's fruit stall is buying bananas (Example 45, Fruttivendolo 00.05.11. Fig. 11.1). She protests when the fruit seller removes the bananas she has asked for from the scales, before the needle of the scales has stabilized. She calls out *"Huà scennënë nu' scennënë! Monello"* ('Hey! They [the scales] go down they're not going down! Cheat!') and as she does so she lifts up her arm, also straight, and directs it toward the scales with her index finger extended. Instead of simply holding her arm extended, however, she rotates her forearm back and forth three times at the same time.

Here, in directing her arm and extended index finger toward the scales she indicates them (and thus disambiguates what she refers to), but with the movements performed with her arm in this position she shows in gesture what she sees the needle of the scales to be doing. The extended index finger in this case, thus, appears to be not only an *indicating* finger, but it is also a 'body-model' (Ch. 9) for the needle of the scales, the movement of the hand displaying the type of movement the woman sees. Here the gesture both indicates an object (the needle of the scales) and provides a description of the activity of something (the movement of the needle).

In Example 46 GB, the tour guide, is talking about a building with a gable that slopes backwards (GB 2.29.57). In indicating the gable in question he directs his hand toward it. However, once his 'movement toward' is accomplished, he adds movement that appears to characterize the lean of the gable. Thus, as he says "You can see that that gable leans backwards" he raises his arm upward at a steep angle, looking at the gable in question at the same time. His hand is a flat or open hand, held with the palm facing away from him.

(...1.33...)You can SEE that that GAble leans BACKwards
|~~~~~~~~~~~~~~~**~~~*******~~********-_-_-_-_-
    P1   [1] P2   [2]   P3   [3]

Fig. 11.2   Example 46, GB 2.29.57. As GB says "leans backwards" he moves his hand from 'back' position, P3, to 'forward' position [3]. This is a repetition with greater amplitude of the movement from 'back' to 'forward' which he makes as he says "that gable" P2, [2]. The upward arm extension indicates the object he is discussing, and thus is deictic (the apex of the pointing movement is reached at [1]), the positional changes of the hand and the shape of the hand characterize the object. The gesture is not 'pure' pointing but is a descriptive gesture with a strong deictic inflection.

The movement of the arm has the characteristic linear 'movement toward' of a pointing gesture, but as he says "that gable leans backwards" he also twice flexes his wrist, as if to display the position of the gable relative to the roof. In this gesture, then, he at once indicates the gable but, also, incorporates into it a representational component (again using a form of 'body-modelling' for the flat or open hand characterizes the flat and extended surface of the gable he is referring to), showing what the angle of the gable in question is like (Fig. 11.2).

Functions other than representational ones can also be combined with deictic features. For example (Example 47), Giovanni, in the recording Bocce I (7.48.02), suggests that the breaking down of a door in the office of the club that had happened as part of what seemed a pointless burglary is a type of vandalism (Fig. 11.3). As he speaks he twice uses a gesture sequence in which

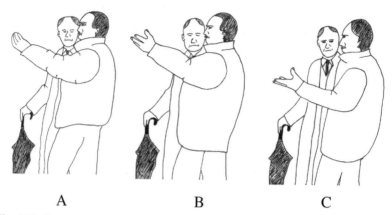

A   B   C

Fig. 11.3. Example 47 (Bocce I 07.48.02): A parsing or discourse structure marker gesture (*grappolo*–open hand) directionally inflected toward the location of the object the speaker is commenting on.

e allorë (.) s'adda ricërë ca è tipë vandaliscëmë
| ~~~~~~~~~~~~~~~~~~/***********/*****/
                    p1   [1]   [2]
and well   one must say that it is a type of vandalism

A. *Grappolo* hand lifted, directed left, as speaker states 'topic' (p1). Note speaker looks in the same direction as gesture, which is an additional clue to the deictic component this gesture has. B. Hand opens as speaker gives his 'comment' [1]. C. Opened hand lowered and speaker turns to look at interlocutor as he completes his phrase [2].

the fingers of the hand are drawn together to a 'finger-bunch' (or *grappolo*) form and then they are spread so the hand is 'open'. This is a gesture sequence commonly used to mark the 'topic/comment' components of a discourse and is, thus, a discourse structure marking or *parsing* gesture (to use the terminology proposed in Chapter 9).[3] Thus, he uses the 'finger bunch' as he says "*s'adda ricërë ca*" ('one must say that') and 'open hand' as he says "*è tipë vandaliscëmë*" ('it is a kind of vandalism'); 'finger bunch' again as he says "*ëëë vandaliscëmë*" ('uh vandalism') and 'open hand' as he says "*'ngoppa cca*" ('over here'). However, as he does so, his arm is extended well to his left, in the direction of the office where the vandalism he is talking about had occurred. Thus, at the same time as he uses a hand movement sequence that marks the topic/comment structure of the discourse, he adds, in his arm movement, a

[3] The gesture employed here is discussed in Chapter 12 as a member of the G-family, a gesture family in which the 'purse' hand shape or *grappolo* hand shape is employed. The form employed here, serving as a topic/comment marker in this case, is discussed as the third of four closely related gestural expressions that have been identified in this family.

'movement toward' which serves to make reference to the location mentioned by the locative expression " *'ngoppa cca*" ('over here').

The gestures described in these three examples certainly have a pointing or deictic function and, like pure pointing gestures, they exhibit the linear 'movement toward' which is characteristic of such gestures. However they have components that show that they are also participating in other kinds of gesture-functions. In general, gestures may be said to vary in the degree to which they show a deictic component. This component may be more or less strong or dominating. Gestures that are said to be pointing gestures are dominated by the deictic component almost to the exclusion of everything else. We may say of such gestures that they are *specialized* as pointing gestures. It is these gestures that we examine in the present chapter.

After comparing many examples of pointing gestures defined in this way we have noted that seven different hand–arm configurations may be employed. That is, there are seven different hand shape/forearm orientation combinations that are used in gestures judged to be specialized as pointing gestures. These are illustrated in Fig. 11.4. The seven hand positions are: Index Finger Extended Prone (palm down), Index Finger Extended Neutral (palm vertical), Thumb Extended (orientation of forearm is variable), Open Hand (i.e. all digits extended and adducted) Neutral (palm vertical), Open Hand Supine (palm up), Open Hand Oblique (forearm supination partial, palm of the hand faces obliquely upwards) and Open Hand Prone (palm faces downwards or away from speaker, depending upon flexion of the elbow or extension of the wrist). In Campania all of these hand positions have been observed in use in pointing, except for Open Hand Prone (palm down or away). In Northant all have been observed in pointing, except that, for the Index Finger Extended hand shape the position of the forearm (whether prone or neutral) is not significant. Let us now see how these different hand shapes are employed in pointing according to how the speaker, in the verbal component of the utterance, is using the object referred to by the point.

Index Finger Extended

When a speaker singles out an object which is to be attended to as a particular individual object, in pointing at it the Index Finger Extended is most likely to be used. Very characteristically, also, the speaker will use an explicitly deictic word, such as 'here', 'there', 'this', 'that' or '*qui*', '*là*', '*questo*', '*quello.*' For example, when Luigi says to his interlocutor (Example 48, Fig. 11.5A) "*quello era un nostromo*" ('that man used to be a boatswain'), indicating a specific

Fig. 11.4   Hand configurations used in pointing in Northant (Northamptonshire) and Campania. A. Index Finger Extended Neutral (palm vertical). B. Index Finger Extended Supine (palm down). C. Thumb. D. Open Hand Neutral (palm vertical). E. Open Hand Prone (palm up). F. Open Hand Oblique (palm oblique). G. Open Hand Prone (palm away). In Campania there seemed to be a consistent contrast in the use of the two Index Finger Extended forms which was not observed in Northant. Open Hand Oblique was not observed in Northant, Open Hand Prone (palm away) was not observed in use in Campania.

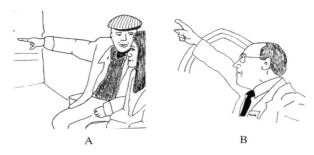

A   B

Fig. 11.5 Two examples of object individuating pointing with Index Finger Extended Prone (palm down).

individual, he holds his arm fully extended with Index Finger Extended in the direction of the individual. Likewise, when, in Northant, the guide GB draws his audience's attention to a statue in a church (Example 49, Fig. 11.5B), he says "There is Gil Crestwood." As he does so, he directs his fully extended arm with Index Finger Extended toward the statue. In these examples the object of reference is singled out to be attended to in itself and in these cases, also, the speaker uses deictic words such as 'that', there', '*quello*', '*là*', and the like.

In the Campanian material we found that speakers tended to point with Index Finger Extended Prone (palm down) whenever they individuated an object in this fashion, as just illustrated by Example 48 (Fig. 11.5A). However, if they distinguished an additional object which was to be placed in some sort of relationship with the first, or if they then went on to say something about the object individuated, or if the object indicated was a condition or cause of something else, then the tendency was to point to it with Index Finger Extended Neutral (palm vertical). In Example 50, a woman at a fruit stall buying lemons picks up some lemons and places them in the scale herself. She then touches the stall owner to attract his attention and when he turns toward her she points toward the scale with the lemons in it with Index Finger Extended Neutral, saying "*e guardë, mezzo kilo!*" ('Look, half a kilo!'). Here it was not the group of lemons in contrast to other objects that was at issue but the consequence of her action of placing the lemons in the scales. Likewise, in an example taken from the recording Commerciante (see Example 91, p. 251), in which Peppe is playing cards with three friends as he waits for customers to come to his stall, at a certain point one of the participants asks of the students filming the occasion: "*Che titolo avrà 'stu film?*" ('What title will this film have?'). Peppe suggests that the film is being made for a popular science television programme called *Il Mondo di Quark* and that it will be about animals on the way to extinction because, in Peppe's opinion, *commercianti* such as himself are a species on the way to extinction. Peppe says: "*Ma è ooo (...) va al Mondo di Quark. Gli animali in via d'estinzione*" ('But it is ooh, it's for *Mondo di Quark*. Animals on the way to extinction'). As he says "*Mondo di Quark*" he directs his right hand, Index Finger Extended Neutral (palm vertical) toward the camera. By pointing at the camera here he indicates the activity of recording. He does not single out the camera as an object to be individuated in contrast to other objects.

We illustrate this contrast in use between Index Finger Extended Palm Down and Index Finger Extended Palm Vertical by an example in which the two forms are used in the same discourse. As the focus of the discourse shifts from individuating an object (in this case a person) to making some comments about the object, so also the mode of index finger pointing changes. Thus Peppe (Example 51, Fig. 11.6), in Commerciante 00.09.33, indicates a certain individual to one of the filmers who have been talking with him, identifying this person as a city councilman. As he does so he points to him using Index Finger Extended Prone and says "*Quello è n'assessorë...*" ('that man is a city councilman...'). After a brief pause he resumes with a comment on this councilman. He points to him again, but this time using Index Finger Extended Neutral, at the same time he says: "*può darsi uno dei pochi assessori se-eee...onesti e seri*" ('maybe he is one of the few Councilmen ser- honest and serious').

Open hand in pointing

As mentioned already, we do not see consistent differences in use between Index Finger Extended Prone and Index Finger Extended Neutral in the Northamptonshire material. However, in both this material and the material from Campania we see a clear contrast in what is being done when the Open Hand is being used to point to something as compared to what is being done when the Index Finger Extended is being used. In all cases when the Open Hand (of any variety) is being used, in contrast to the use of the Index Finger Extended, the object being indicated is not itself the primary focus or topic of the discourse but is something that is linked to the topic, either as an exemplar of a class, as the location of some activity under discussion, because it is related to something that happened, or it is something that should be inspected or regarded in a certain way because this leads to the main topic. It is particularly interesting to note that whenever the index finger is used in pointing, the speaker also often employs a deictic word, whereas when the Open Hand is used, deictic words in the associated speech are less often observed.

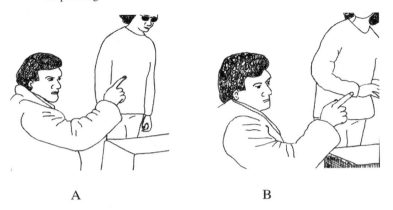

A   B

Fig. 11.6   Example 51. Pointing with Index Finger Extended Prone (palm down) and Index Finger Extended Neutral (palm vertical) in contrast. Peppe uses Index Finger Extended Prone when he identifies the city councilman (A) and Index Finger Extended Neutral when he again points in his direction and makes a comment about him.

Example 51 (Commerciante 00.09.33)

That fellow is a city councilman, it doesn't seem so, [but] he's a city councilman.
P: quello è n' assessore, non ci sembra, è n' assessore (.)
|~~~ **_____|
                [1]

maybe [he is] one of the few city councilmen ser- uh honest and serious
può darsi uno dei pochi assessori se - eee   onesti e seri (.)
|~~~*********************~~~|
                [2]

because he has never profited, but unfortunately he is the only one
pëcchè n' ha mai approfittato, però purtroppo è sulë issë

[1] Points with index-palm-down. [2] Points with index-palm-vertical.

Open Hand Neutral (palm vertical) and contrasts with Index Finger Extended

This contrast is well exemplified when we compare the following two cases, both from the Northant guided tour (Examples 52 and 53, Fig. 11.7). At GB 2.20.24, GB says: "Across the way there (3.43 sec) we have the school bookshop." As he says "across the way there" he directs his extended index finger toward the location of the bookshop (he completes his locution with "we have the school bookshop", which is not accompanied by any gesture, only after he changes his location and comes to stand almost in front of the bookshop. It is this that accounts for the three-and-a-half second pause in his speech). A little later on, moving his tourists to a different side of the street, he happens to find himself near one of his wife's favourite shops in the town, a shop called "Parry Irving". He now says (GB 2.23.30): "I'm going to do a little unsolicited testimonial, if you like. A little praise of Parry Irving." As he says "A little praise of Parry Irving" he extends his left arm forward and to his left toward the shop, not with an Index Finger Extended but with an Open Hand Neutral (palm vertical). Note that GB does not say "here is Parry Irving" or the like. His gesture allows the recipient to see what it is that is 'Parry Irving' but the form of the discourse here is not the individuation of the shop, pointing it out as something distinct from other shops, but the testimonial to it to be offered. Note that this utterance would be unanchored and thus have no apparent relevance, without the gesture.

Similar examples can be found in the material from Campania. For instance, Luigi is responding to his interviewer's inquiry as to where she might find experienced sailors to talk to (Example 54, Fig. 11.8). He says: *"vujë jatë là vicinë là niente so' tuttë"* ('You want to go close to there, they are all there'). As he says *"vujë jatë là vicinë"* ('You want to go close to there') he points with Index Finger Extended Palm Down. After two brief interventions, one by another sailor and one by the interviewer, Luigi returns to making reference to the location he indicated before as he says: *"nientedimenë so' tuttë marittëmë lo"* ('they actually are all sailors there') - but this time he points with Open Hand Neutral (palm vertical). Here, thus, when, in the first piece of discourse it is a precise location that is foregrounded, as it is when it is nominated as the location to which the interviewer should proceed, he uses Index Finger Extended Prone (palm down). Later, when he characterizes what is to be found in that location, and this now becomes the focus of what he is saying, the hand used again to point to the location now becomes Open Hand Neutral.

Open Hand Supine (palm up)

The example just described illustrates one of the uses of pointing with the Open Hand Supine. In this usage, the speaker acknowledges another as the source of something said or indicates that what the other has said is correct or that he is in agreement with it. We shall encounter other examples of this in Chapter 13 where we discuss the family of gestures in which the Open Hand Supine is used. The use of this hand shape in pointing, illustrated here, is one among several of its uses all of which, as we will see in Chapter 13, are united by the common semantic themes of presenting and being ready for receiving. In using the Open Hand Supine (palm up) in pointing, more generally, the speaker is typically pointing to some object as if it were being 'presented' to the interlocutor as something that should be looked at or inspected. In such

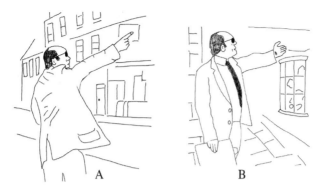

Fig. 11.7   Example 52 (GB 2.20.24) and Example 53 (GB 2.23.30). Contrast in use in pointing of Index Finger Extended and Open Hand. A: GB says "Across the way there (3.4) we have the school bookshop" and as he says "Across the way there" he points with Index Finger Palm Vertical toward the school bookshop (he names the bookshop after a 3.4 second pause, during which he moves to stand closer to it). B: GB says "I'm going to do a little unsolicited testimonial, if you like, a little praise of Parry Irving." As he says "a little praise of Parry Irving" he directs an Open Hand Palm Vertical toward the shop Parry Irving.

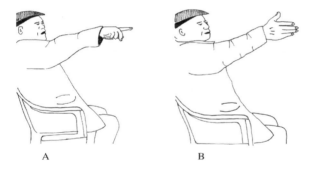

Fig. 11.8   Example 54 (Marinai 00.43.54): Contrast between Index Finger Extended Palm Vertical and Open Hand Palm Vertical. A. Speaker points with Index Finger Extended Palm Down as he says "*là vicinë*" in "*vujë jatë là vicinë là niente so' tuttë*" ('you want to go there close by there, they all are there'). B. Speaker points with Open Hand Palm Vertical as he says: "*nientedimenë so' tuttë marittëmë lo*" ('they actually all are sailors there').

cases the object is not just individuated as topic, nor is it indicated as the pretext or location associated with some other discourse focus. Rather the object is indicated as something that should be attended to and inspected in a particular way. This, as we shall see in Chapter 13, is but one kind of manifestation of the themes of 'presentation' and 'reception' that seems to unite all uses of the Open Hand Supine in which the hand is either placed in the space in front of the speaker or combined with a 'movement toward' some interlocutor or object.

Here are two examples. In Example 55, the card game (Commerciante II 00.08.14, Fig. 11.9), at one point the men make a joke about the fact that the two young women filming them have remained for such a long time. One of them says: *"No pëcchè hanno vistë Aniello nu bellë uaglionë!"* ('No because they have seen Aniello, a handsome fellow!'), and as he says this he directs his Open Hand Supine toward Aniello, as if presenting him for inspection. Likewise, from Northant, GB has been explaining how the rear of a certain building is as elegant as the façade that faces the street (GB 2.32.36, Example 56, Fig. 11.10). He walks his party of tourists round to the back of the building and, as it comes into view he says "and uhm, you see what I mean! It's uh very much similar" - extending his Open Hand Supine toward the building as he does so. A short while later, after having explained who the architect was and who was responsible for building the house, and after mentioning another structure that is at the bottom of the large garden that extends behind, he turns back to refer to the rear façade of the house and says, again with Open Hand Supine directed toward the building: "Uhm but you can see again the quality of the building, in this particular case."

A third example, Example 57 (Fig. 11.11), illustrates a further use of the Open Hand Supine in pointing and it also is another exemplification of the contrast between the use of Index Finger and Open Hand in pointing. In this Example (Bocce I 7.56.32), the participants are discussing a robbery that had taken place at the premises of the *bocce* club a day or so before. Part of what was at issue was a key that was missing to a door that had been locked after the robbery, suggesting that the robbers themselves possessed the key. Enzo says: *"Quando vennero a rubare la volta scorsa"* ('When they came to rob the last time') but Giovanni immediately intervenes, completing Enzo's turn with *"s'arrubbajënë purë 'a chiavë"* ('they stole the key'). Enzo immediately resumes speaking. He repeats what Giovanni just said: *"s'arrubbajënë purë 'a chiavë"* ('they stole the key') and immediately continues with *"chella chiavë llà"* ('that very key'). When he repeats Giovanni's words he directs an Open Hand Palm Up toward Giovanni. In this use of such a pointing gesture the source of something that the speaker is now saying is indicated or acknowledged. When he continues with *"chella chiavë llà"* ('that very key'),

Fig. 11.9   Example 55 (Commerciante 00.08.14). Vincenzo playfully suggests that the two attractive young women filming them have remained a long time in doing so because Aniello is such a handsome fellow. He says: "*No pëcchè hanno vistë Aniello nu bellë uaglionë!*" ('No because they have seen Aniello, a handsome fellow!'). He extends Open Hand Supine (palm up) toward Aniello, looking round at the film makers as he does so. He thus invites one to appreciate Aniello as a specimen of handsome manhood.

Fig. 11.10   Example 56 (GB 2.33.0). GB extends Open Hand Supine (palm up) toward a building that he invites his audience to look at for its architectural quality.

Uhm but uhm (...) you can SEE again the QUALity of the building in this particular case.

|～～～|***～～～***～～～**************|-.-.-.-.-.-.-.-.-.-.-.

      [1]   [2]   [3]

At [1] hand reaches the position shown in the figure and is held briefly. [2] and [3] are strokes in which the hand is moved downwards in association with the stressed syllables of "see" and "quality". After the second stroke the hand is held in position.

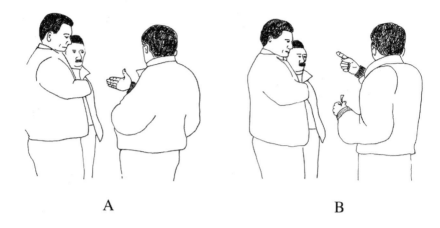

A   B

Fig. 11.11   Example 57 (Bocce I 7.56.32): Contrast between pointing with open hand palm up and index finger. A. Enzo extends open hand palm up toward Giovanni as he repeats Giovanni's completion of Enzo's phrase. B. Enzo directs index finger forward as he specifies a particular key as topic.

> E   quando vennero a rubare la volta scorsa...
>   when they came to steal   the last time...
>
> G   =s'arrubbajënë purë 'a chiavë
>   =they stole   also the key
>
> E   =s'arrubbajënë purë 'a chiavë chella chiavë llà
>   /********************/ /**********/
>   [A]   [B]
>   they stole   also the key that key there [that very key]

an utterance that specifies a particular object, Enzo points with an extended index finger. Here, then, as the speaker points to the source of something that he is saying he uses Open Hand (it is not Giovanni as a specific individual to be distinguished from others that is at issue for Enzo but Giovanni as the source of his current words). When the speaker specifies a particular object as distinct from others - "that very key" - he uses Index Finger Extended.

Open Hand Oblique

The Open Hand Oblique, when used as a form of pointing, at least in Campania, is often used when someone indicates an object when a comment is being made, either about the object itself or, in some cases, it seems, about the relationship between the interlocutor and the object. Commonly, the object indicated is a person, and the comment being made is negative. We describe three examples. Example 58 is from Commerciante I 00.04.25 (see Fig. 11.12A). Here Vincenzo directs an Open Hand Oblique towards Aniello while he first criticizes Peppe for looking at Aniello's cards and then criticizes Aniello for holding his cards so that another can see them. Immediately prior to Vincenzo's intervention the four players have been occupied by looking at the cards they have just been dealt. Suddenly Vincenzo looks at Peppe and tells him not to "look at the cards of this fellow" and as he does so he extends his right hand, Open Hand Oblique, toward Aniello who stands opposite him. The Open Hand Oblique here serves as pointing, and disambiguates the pronoun "this". At the same time, directing this hand to Aniello already conveys a critical attitude toward Aniello on the part of Vincenzo. This becomes clear when Vincenzo addresses Aniello directly, declaring that he has allowed others to see his cards.

Example 59 (Commerciante II 00:30:29, Fig. 11.12B) involves the same speaker. Salvatore, Peppe's partner in the card game (he sits opposite Peppe and usually cannot be seen in the video because Vincenzo is often in the way), asks Vincenzo what the score is. Vincenzo, who is of the opposite team, reproves him and tells him he should ask his *"cumpagnë"* ('partner'). He says: *"stattë zittë 'ddumantë u cumpagnë tuojë"* ('Be quiet, ask your partner!'). As he says "Be quiet" Vincenzo rapidly lifts an open hand upwards towards himself in what may be a gesture of throwing something over the shoulder which, in this context, when addressed to another, as here, can mean 'throw away what you are doing.' (Compare de Jorio 2000, p. 312.) As he says *"'ddumantë u cumpagnë tuojë"* ('ask your partner') he directs Open Hand Palm Oblique toward Peppe while looking toward Salvatore as he speaks. In this context Vincenzo's expression *"'u cumpagnë tuojë"* ('your partner') conveys a scornful attitude to Salvatore for it refers to Peppe only in his capacity as Salvatore's co-player in the opposing team. The Open Hand Oblique here indicates Peppe for Salvatore's benefit, the form here conveying a negative attitude toward Peppe on the part of Vincenzo.

Example 60 comes from Marinai 00.41.39 (see bottom left hand image in Fig. 11.4). This is at the beginning of the recording where two old sailors have been approached by the interviewer to see if they would be willing to talk about their life as mariners. They call to another that he should come over. They say he has much

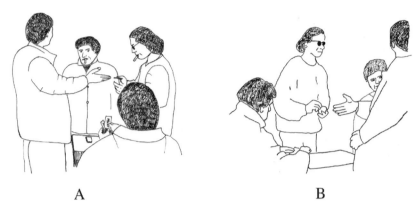

A   B

Fig. 11.12   Two instances of Open Hand Oblique. A: Example 58. B: Example 59.
For descriptions see text.

experience. However, he is a bit shy about talking about his life and Saverio makes fun of him and says Aniello will speak only if the interviewer pays him. Aniello says: *"vo i sordë vo truannë i sordë"* ('He wants money, he wants to find money'). In the present context this means that, according to Aniello, it is Saverio who wants money for the interview. As he says this, he addresses the interviewer and as he does so he directs his right hand, formed as Open Hand Oblique, towards Saverio.

In each of these examples the Open Hand Oblique is used as a way of indicating an object, in all cases another person, who is in some way the butt of a critical remark or a critical attitude. In each case, however, there is always a third participant in the interchange. That is to say, the critical remark or attitude is not only directed to the person being criticized but it is made in the hearing of others and, most commonly, the addressee of the utterance is another and not directly the object of the criticism. Thus, in the first example, although Vincenzo criticizes Aniello for letting his cards be visible, he does this indirectly by a remark directed to Peppe. Although, in the second example, Vincenzo addresses Salvatore, he simultaneously directs his gesture to Peppe, thus drawing Peppe in as a second addressee in the interchange. In the third example, the disparaging comment about Saverio is directed to the interviewer, while Aniello's Palm Oblique gesture is used to indicate whom he is disparaging. In these examples, thus, the Open Hand Palm Oblique, appears as a gesture that directs a third person to attend to the target of the criticism and thus plays a role in making that criticism public.

Open Hand Prone (palm away)

Here the open hand is sustained on a prone forearm but the wrist is extended so that the palm is oriented so that it faces away from the speaker, as may be seen in Fig. 11.4G (p. 206). This form, observed only in the material from Northamptonshire, is used when the speaker is referring to an object in virtue of its aspect of spatial extent, or when several objects are being considered together as an ensemble. For example, in GB 3.40.06 (Example 61) GB is drawing attention to some buildings, built by a boarding school in Northant, that were erected in 1909 but which have the look of seventeenth-century houses. They were built to be in the same style as a building of that era that they were to be next to, a seventeenth-century inn known as the Talbot. GB refers to the school's instructions to the architect: "But the school said they must be in sympathy with the range of buildings of the Talbot next door. He really worked at it and did a pretty good job." As he says "they must be in sympathy with the range of buildings of the Talbot next door" he extends his left arm horizontally towards the buildings, directing an Open Hand Prone (palm away) toward them. The arm is withdrawn at the end of the phrase, then extended again in the same manner as he says "He really..." and then retracted to a non-gesture position thereafter. His extended arm here serves to link his remarks to the buildings in question for which, in this context, their spatial extent is a salient feature (for another example see Example 113, pp. 270-271).

Likewise, in GB 2.08.21 (Example 62) GB is comparing an eighteenth-century building which is more recent than another one which is located elsewhere in the town (in fact it is the Talbot, just mentioned in the previous example). He says, referring to the building he is standing next to: "And this dates from only one generation after the Talbot, which we shall see at the end of the walk, which is just round the corner there." As he says "after the Talbot, which we shall see at the end of the walk" he lifts his hand, held open, palm down, and extends it twice away from him in the direction where the Talbot actually lies. Then, as he says "which is just round the corner there" he switches to an Index Finger Extended Palm Down, and directs this in the same direction. Here, in referring to the Talbot, which is to be considered as a building with architectural features, indicating its location nevertheless, he uses Open Hand Palm Down. When he refers to the specific location of the building, however, he switches to using an Index Finger Extended.

Again, at GB 3.49.58 (Example 63) GB, at the end of the tour, is telling his audience about other guided walks in the town. He says: "there's another one [i.e. tour] which takes us down the eastern end there, which is the School Chapel, the Jesus Church." As he says "which takes us down the eastern end there" he directs an extended index finger in a direction in front of him, thus indicating a specific location where the walk goes to. As he mentions the two buildings that stand in that location, each one in a slightly different place, he uses Open Hand Prone (palm away). What becomes the focus of the discourse at this moment is not the location that is to be individuated in contrast to other locations - this GB has already done - but the objects to be seen there, and here we see the use of the Open Hand Prone (palm away) (Fig. 11.13).

A   B   C

Fig. 11.13   Example 63 (GB 3.49.58). Contrast between Index Finger Extended and Open Hand Prone (palm away). Index finger used for a location - "eastern end there"; Open Hand Prone (palm, away) used when naming two places of interest to look at which are in the "eastern end".

there's another one which takes us down the eastern end there
|********************************|
[1] Index Finger Extended

which is (.) the School Chapel (. . .) the Jesus Church
|************************|~~~|*************|
[2] Open Hand Prone (palm away)   [3] Open Hand Prone (palm away)

Pointing with the thumb

In all of the examples of thumb-pointing we have examined, the objects pointed to are either to the side or to the rear of the speaker. Anatomy may play some role here. If you extend only the thumb, because it already projects upwards and, due to its curvature, it seems to project backwards, it may be somewhat awkward to compensate for this, as one would have to do, if one were to use the thumb to point forward. However, since we also can observe instances where an extended index finger is used to point to something that is to the side or behind the speaker, we cannot conclude that anatomy is the only factor involved.

One general circumstance in which the thumb is used to point with is when it is not important to establish the precise location or identity of what is pointed at. This may be because, among the participants, there is such shared knowledge of the environment that it is not necessary to indicate location or identity precisely. It may also be because the location or identity of the object referred to has been previously established. It is also clear from our examples that when the thumb is used in pointing in these circumstances the identity or location of the object pointed at is not the focus of the discourse.

The first example, Example 64, comes from Bocce I, 7.54.47 and is part of the burglary discussion. Here we see a contrast between the use of the index finger and the use of the thumb within the same interactional moment, which suggests how the thumb is used when the location of what is pointed at is known and where its location is no longer an issue in the discourse. Two speakers both make reference to the same object - a door - and both, as they do so, point in its direction. In the first reference, however, the first speaker, Enzo, states specifically which door in particular it is that is being discussed, and here he points in the direction of the door using Index Finger Extended Neutral (palm vertical) (Fig. 11.14A). His interlocutor, Giovanni, responds with a comment about the door (it is a comment about the way the door had been broken down) and here, as he refers to the door, he directs his thumb toward it (Fig. 11.14B). The example begins when Enzo enters the room with new information about a particular door. He says: *"'a masckaturë stevë apertë (.) quella porta che porta sul terrazzo"* ('The lock was open, that door that leads on to the terrace'). As he specifies which door he is talking about he points with his index finger. Giovanni then responds by saying that the door in question had been broken down from the inside (this is the mystery of the robbery: why was an unlocked door broken down by the robbers?). Here, the issue of which door it is, is now secondary. Enzo has already settled the matter. Now when Giovanni points in the direction of the door he does so with his thumb. When the discourse is focused on the question of which door it is, in pointing to it an index finger is used. When the discourse is focused on the state of the door and its identity is no longer in doubt, in pointing to it the thumb is used.

This example is similar to others that we have collected in which a speaker refers twice to the same location. When the location is first referred to, an index finger may be used, and commonly the speaker glances in the direction of what is being pointed at. For the second reference, if there is pointing, the thumb tends to be used, and the speaker does not glance in the direction of the object indicated. In these cases it is as if the thumb point is an anaphora for the index finger point.

As an illustration we cite two passages from Marinai 00.45.22 and Marinai 00.46.13 where we find Luigi explaining to the interviewer how he worked for years in an abattoir (Example 65). He describes how he used to work as a sailor, and then he explains that subsequently worked at the abattoir in Torre del Greco. As he explains this, he points behind him, in the direction of the abattoir, using his index finger to do so. Somewhat later in the same discussion the topic has now shifted to the pension he now receives. He says that nowadays he has enough money since he also has contributed to a pension scheme at the abattoir for thirty years. As he mentions the abattoir he again points to it, but this time he uses his thumb. Here, thus, when the focus of his discourse is the abattoir as a location for his work, introduced for the first time into his discourse, he uses his index finger to locate it in pointing. When the

A   B

Fig. 11.14   Example 64 (Bocce I. 7.54.47): Contrast in use of thumb and index finger in pointing. Enzo points with index finger as he specifies a particular door (A). Giovanni makes a comment about this same door, points to it using his thumb (B).

    the lock   was open   that door that leads on to the terrace
E: /'a mascëcaturë stevë apertë/ (1.0.) /quella porta che porta sul terrazzo/
                          |****|
                           [A]

   and therefore, professor, and therefore it's like and therefore
G: e allorë prufëssò/ e allorë / e cummë è allorë (0.6))

    listen to me,   that door there has been broken surely from inside
  statëmë a sentì/chella porta là è statë scecassatë sicurë a'intë/
             |**********|
            [B]

abattoir is mentioned incidentally because it is the source of his pension, he points to it using his thumb.

A further example (Example 66, Maranai 00.50.29, see Fig. 11.15) illustrates the observation that the thumb is used in pointing when it is not necessary to indicate the precise location of something. However, this example shows how speakers make choices about when to use the thumb and when not to. In this case a speaker first corrects his use of a pointing gesture from Thumb to Index Finger when he wishes to indicate something behind him that has a precise location, and then he reverts to the use of the Thumb again when he indicates something which does not require precise specification. Here the speaker, an old sailor from Torre del Greco, is explaining to his interlocutor about his three sons. One, he says, is in the army. As he says this he raises his thumb in a gesture of enumeration. The next son, he says, is working in a fish-shop,

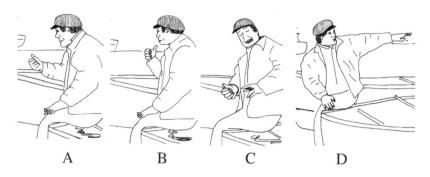

A   B   C   D

Fig. 11.15   Example 66 (Marinai 00.50.29): Contrast in the use of thumb and index finger in pointing. Saverio raises right hand thumb in an enumeration gesture as he mentions his first son [A]; directs right hand thumb backwards as he begins to point towards the fish-shop where his second son works [B]; in a pause in speech immediately after "*chella* - that" he reorganizes his posture [C]; points with left hand Index Finger Extended Palm Down as he refers again to the fish-shop where his second son works [D]. He turns back to I as he begins to speak of another son and with his right hand does a gesture for '*fazzoletti*' [E], and then points behind himself with thumb, [F], sustaining this gesture without speaking until I responds with a head nod. ([E] and [F] are not shown.)

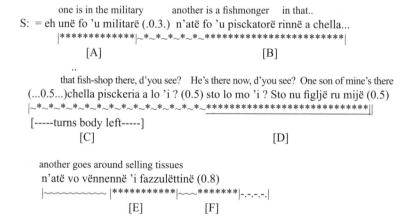

But what work do they do?   You have spoken of the sailor, what did you say?
I: Ma che lavoro fanno ?   Voi avete detto il marittimo che avete detto ?

      one is in the military   another is a fishmonger   in that..
S: = eh unë fo 'u militarë (.0.3.) n'atë fo 'u pisckatorë rinnë a chella...
    |*************|~*~*~*~*~********************|
         [A]   [B]

    ..
    that fish-shop there, d'you see?   He's there now, d'you see?   One son of mine's there
(...0.5...)chella pisckeria a lo 'i ? (0.5) sto lo mo 'i ? Sto nu figljë ru mijë (0.5)
|~*~*~*~*~*~*~*~*~*~*~********************************||
[-----turns body left-----]
     [C]   [D]

    another goes around selling tissues
    n'atë vo vënnennë 'i fazzulëttinë (0.8)
  |~~~~~~~~~|***********|~~*******|-.-.-.-.|
      [E]   [F]

which happens to be currently visible, but behind the speaker. As he begins his sentence referring to the second son he begins to direct his thumb behind him, in the direction of the fish-shop. What he says is: *"'n'atë fo u pisckatorë (.)rinë'a chella---chella pisckeria a lo 'i?"* ('Another is a fishmonger in that - that fish-shop, see?'). When he reaches the word *"chella"* ('that') in his sentence he breaks off, reorganizes his posture so that he can turn round and extend his arm with Index Finger Extended Prone (palm down) behind him toward the fish-shop he is specifying. It is as if the sentence he was using required an index finger point, not a thumb point. The interruption in speech and the restart do not stem from something wrong in speech production, they stem, rather, from the need to change the kind of gesture he is engaged in. Here we have an example of a 'self-repair' but the repair is to an error in the gesture being used rather than to an error in speech (see footnote 3, Chapter 8, p. 134). Then, when the speaker goes on to talk about his third son, who works as an ambulant vendor of paper tissues in the town that is situated behind him, he again uses his thumb to point behind him. Here, however, this is quite appropriate, insofar as an ambulant vendor is found in no particular location, but only in a general area.

This example demonstrates a contrast between the use of the index finger in pointing and the use of the thumb; it also proves that pointing to something behind one need not be done with the thumb, hence to use the thumb is to make a choice of a form of pointing that is also semantically appropriate.

Conclusion

Deixis refers to those linguistic features or expressions that relate utterances to the circumstances of space and time in which they occur. When the conditions which allow these expressions to function are discussed there is usually some reference to pointing, for it is recognized that, in a fundamental sense, it is only through some non-linguistic action or non-linguistic aspect of the situation, that the tie between an utterance and its spatial or temporal circumstance can ultimately be established (Bühler 1990, pp. 126-128) and the gesture of pointing is one of the most obvious ways in which this is done. In many circumstances, indeed, it cannot be done without.

Despite this, it is commonly assumed that the gesture of pointing itself does no more than establish this necessary tie between word and circumstance. It serves to indicate what the referent of a deictic word might be but it is not supposed that it makes any of the distinctions that deictic words can make, such as between gender and participation status (as in personal pronouns), singularity and plurality ('this' vs 'these'), or closeness and far-offness ('this' vs 'that' vs 'that yonder'), and so on. The idea that distinctions of this sort might also be made gesturally has hardly been explored.

Birdwhistell (1966), in his discussion of what he called 'kinesic markers', observed that directionally distinctive movements of the head or other body parts associated with stressed pronominals varied according to closeness and singularity and plurality. Eco (1976, p. 119) suggested that variations in what he called 'dynamic stress' in finger pointing gestures marked the difference between 'closeness' and 'distance'. Apart from these two discussions and the work of Wilkins (2003), Calbris (1990) and de Jorio (2000) we mentioned at the beginning of this chapter, it seems that the idea that the character of the pointing gesture itself might vary systematically in relation to semantic distinctions of various sorts has not been seriously examined.

This chapter has described an investigation that makes a start on such an examination. We distinguished seven different hand shape and hand shape/ forearm orientation configurations. Our observations have led us to say that the form of the pointing gesture is not a matter of idiosyncratic choice or variation unrelated to the other things the speaker is doing. It seems, rather, that the hand configuration a speaker uses in pointing is a patterned component of the utterance ensemble. It is as if the speaker uses a different form for the pointing gesture according to how the object being referred to is being used in the discourse.

In order to understand the relationship between the forms of pointing distinguished and the different semantic and discursive implications they appear to have, it will be useful to compare the forms in these gestures with those found in other, non-pointing gestures. For example, we observed that a semantic contrast is marked by whether the index finger is used in pointing or the open hand. In index finger pointing there is always present the idea of the singularity of the object being referred to, whereas in open hand pointing the object pointed to is being referred to in virtue of its status as a symbolic, conceptual or exemplary object. If we look at differences between non-pointing gestures that use the extended index finger and those that use an open hand there seem to be certain parallels. For example, there is a gesture of negation in which the hand, with the index finger only extended, held vertical with the palm of the hand facing outwards, is moved laterally away from the speaker's mid-line in a well-defined manner. This is used when something specific is being denied and contrasts with another gesture of negation, which has the same lateral movement, which uses the open hand with the palm facing away. This is used as an expression of refusal or as an expression that can be glossed with an expression such as *basta* ('it is enough'), thereby indicating that whatever has been in progress (for example the filling of a grocery order, food being served or consumed, or the like) one now wishes to stop. It seems that the index finger negation gesture negates a specific component within a transaction, but does not negate the entire transaction, whereas the open hand negation negates an entire transaction - something much more general. (Gestures using the Open Hand Prone (palm away or palm down), which often function as gestures of negation, are discussed in Chapter 13.)

In the same way we can compare the contrasts between the three different orientations of the open hand that we have described for pointing gestures with like contrasts found in certain non-pointing gestures. For example, the Open Hand Supine (palm up) is used in gestures in which one offers something or requests something or in which one expects to receive something (see Chapter 13; Müller 2004). As we suggested, from the contexts in which we have observed the Open Hand Supine (palm up) in use in pointing, it occurs in contexts where the speaker is indicating an object as if it is being presented to the interlocutors, as if it is being offered as something to be inspected or contemplated. Thus the use of this hand shape in pointing gestures is semantically linked to these other uses of the open hand with palm up orientation.

As we will see in Chapters 12 and 13, where we discuss so-called 'pragmatic' gestures, there may be something like a 'morpho-semantics' with parallels with what has already been described in sign languages (see Penny Boyes Braem 1981, Volterra 1987, Radutzky 1992). In these chapters we show it is possible to establish families of gestures based on shared kinesic features, and that the various gestures within each of these families also share certain semantic themes. We propose that these semantic themes derive from the fact that the various forms of gestures serving pragmatic functions are stylized and conventionalized versions of various manipulatory actions such as seizing, gripping, pushing away, offering or being open to receiving something. Perhaps gestures of pointing can also be interpreted in these terms. In pointing to an object (whether real or virtual), the actor acts directly in relation to the object. As we have seen, a specific object may be individuated, it may be referred to as an exemplar, it may be offered as an object for inspection. The different forms of pointing we have described in this chapter may be thought of as different kinds of actions that the actor may take in relation to the objects referred to. To this extent, thus, there is an overlap with what we shall find in the case of 'pragmatic' gestures. And it is in respect to gestures that derive from actions done directly upon or in relation to objects, rather than gestures that construct representations of objects, that we find there to be an emerging 'morpho-semantics'.

12 Gestures of 'precision grip': topic, comment and question markers

In the last three chapters we have explored the ways in which gesture can add to the propositional meaning of the utterance of which it is a part. However, as we stated in Chapter 9, speakers *also* use gestures as part of the way in which they 'do things' with utterances. A speaker always produces an utterance to *achieve* something. As a participant in a conversation I may complain, evaluate, disagree, refuse, plead, assert, maintain something in opposition, mock, attack, retreat, show deference, ignore, exhibit scepticism, give an honest answer, ask, and many other things. As has long been noted, gesture often plays an important part in carrying out such actions. Indeed, as we shall see, there are gestures that appear to be *specialized* as actions which, in their very performance, can constitute a particular move or 'speech act'.

As explained in Chapter 9, the functions gestures have as they contribute to or constitute the acts or moves accomplished by utterances are referred to as *pragmatic* functions. In the terminology proposed, gestures which show what sort of a move or speech act a speaker is engaging in are said to have *performative* functions. Gestures are said to have *modal* functions if they seem to operate on a given unit of verbal discourse and show how it is to be interpreted. Gestures may serve *parsing* functions when they contribute to the marking of various aspects of the structure of spoken discourse.

It must be made clear that this is a typology of functions, not of gestures. Any given gestural form may, according to context, function now in one way, now in another. For example, a gesture in which an open hand, held so the palm faces downward or obliquely away from the speaker and is moved laterally in a 'decisive' manner (see Chapter 13), may be done so that it is understood as an act of rejection or denial. In such a case we would say that it is a *performative*. However, it may also be used as a way of expressing an implied negative and, in some contexts, in virtue of this, it may serve as an intensifier for an evaluative statement. As such it would be seen as a *modal* gesture. But this same gesture is also used in contexts where it serves to indicate that the speaker using it has come to a finish in a line of argument. It may mark the point at which the speaker is ready to proceed to deal with something else. As such it might be seen as a *parsing* gesture.

In this chapter and the one to follow we shall describe some findings from context-of-use studies of several groupings or families of gestural forms which are employed pragmatically in these ways. Through a comparative study of the contexts in which the forms selected for study are found to be used, we attempt to formulate a description of their significance that will fit as many occasions of their use as possible. It is suggested that each of the gestural forms investigated has its own *semantic theme* - and this theme, being introduced as it is in different ways in different contexts, through the way it interacts with the (usually verbal) meaning of the spoken component of the utterance, contributes to the creation of a highly specific local meaning. Thus, to revert to the open hand palm down gesture mentioned above, as we show in Chapter 13, its semantic theme appears to be one that refers to the interruption or cutting off of some process or line of action that is in progress (or that could be in progress). When applied in specific contexts, however, it can be a gesture of *denial*, a gesture of *negation*, a gesture that commands the *interruption* of something, or a gesture of *evaluative intensification*.

These chapters do not attempt a comprehensive treatment of the pragmatic functions of gesture, nor do they describe all the different kinds of gestures that have been observed that fulfil these functions. Our aim, rather, is to illustrate a particular approach to the analysis and description of gesture, an approach that is well adapted, at least, to forms of gestural expression that are widely used within a given communication community. In this approach, a specific recurrent gestural form is taken as a starting point. Collections of video recordings are examined and examples of the recurrent form chosen for study are noted and then extracted as 'specimens' so that they may then be compared with one another in terms of the interactional and discourse contexts in which they are seen to occur. This approach has become much less cumbersome and expensive since the development of digital video which makes the assembly of large collections of specimens of gestures in use very easy. Through a comparative study of such collections, not only can we sort out the various versions of the form selected for study and so arrive at sub-groupings of these forms, we can also compare the contexts-of-use. From such comparisons we endeavour to arrive at what appear to be the semantic and pragmatic functions of the forms chosen for study.

The various pragmatic functions of gesture we have outlined have been recognized (and particularly valued) for a very long time. Thus, as will be recalled from Chapters 3 and 6, Quintilian recognized these functions for gesture many centuries ago when he remarked that we use our hands in speaking "to demand, promise, summon, dismiss, threaten, supplicate .... question or deny..." (XI, III.85–87). As we saw in those chapters, writers from the seventeenth and eighteenth centuries also recognized these functions, and some writers in our own era have, as well, although this has not often been an aspect of gesture function that has attracted much modern interest. Desmond Morris, however, has offered some insightful observations and these deserve some comment.

Morris (1977) distinguished what he called 'baton signals' which "beat time to the rhythm of spoken thoughts". According to Morris the role of these gestures is to "mark the points of emphasis in our speech". However, he observes that in making these gestures the hands may be posed in a variety of ways. He interprets each of the poses he has distinguished as a form of action and suggests that, by means of these hand poses, the speaker shows the kind of action he is engaging in as he speaks. For example, when a speaker uses what Morris distinguishes as the "Thumb and Forefinger Touch" he engages in a form of the precision grip and indicates, thereby, "that he wishes to express himself delicately and with great exactness. His hand emphasizes the fineness of the points he is stressing" (p. 58). On the other hand, the "Hand Extend, with the Palm Up" is "an imploring hand...Hand batons in this posture beg the listener to agree" (p. 59). Morris's taxonomy, although not fully systematized, is certainly interesting and his interpretations, although not backed by any systematic context-of-use studies, often appear quite plausible. His underlying idea, that we can account for these gestures as if they are derived from manipulative actions of various kinds, is also very interesting. We shall return to a discussion of this later. His presentation makes it clear that detailed systematic studies of the different hand poses used by speakers in gestures of this sort would be well worth while.

In the present chapter, and the one to follow, we describe four different gesture *families* and illustrate the uses of several of the members of these families. When we refer to *families* of gestures we refer to groupings of gestural expressions that have in common one or more kinesic or formational characteristics. We shall show that, within each family, the different forms that may be recognized in most cases are distinguished in terms of the different *movement patterns* that are employed. As we shall see, each family not only shares in a distinct set of kinesic features but each is also distinct in its semantic themes. The forms within these families, distinguished as they are kinesically, also tend to differ semantically although, within a given family, all forms share in a common semantic theme.

In this chapter we shall discuss two gesture families, both of which involve what Morris would refer to as precision grip actions. In one group all of the fingers are brought together so that their tips are in contact. In the other group, only the thumb and index finger are put into contact at their tips. In Chapter 13, we describe two other gesture families. In both the open hand is used, but in one family the open hand is always held with the palm facing away from the speaker, or downwards, while in the other family, the open hand is always held so that the palm faces upwards (or obliquely upwards).

There are certainly other gesture families. For example, there is a gesture family in which the open hand is held with the palm vertical. The movement patterns used in this family include 'placing' and 'chopping'. In one-handed versions members of this family appear to be used in contexts in which the speaker is setting up positions for (usually) abstract objects (such as different logical positions), establishing the starting points or end points of periods of time, or indicating movement through space along a specifed route. Two-handed versions, in which the two hands are held out, palms facing one another, appear to be used in contexts where the speaker is setting limits to something, such as setting up the boundaries for a topic to be discussed. An example of this type of gesture from this family was described in Chapter 8, Example 9. Another family that can also be identified, in all likelihood, is a family of gestures which use the extended index finger. Work on the identification and description of these (and other) possible gesture families has hardly begun, however.

We begin in this chapter with a family of gestures in which all members have in common a hand shape in which the hand is held with palm upwards with all the digits drawn together so that they are in contact with one another at their tips (Fig. 12.1). For this hand shape we shall use the Italian word *grappolo* ('bunch, cluster') and the gesture family which makes use of it we shall call the *G-family*. The *grappolo* hand shape has also been referred to as the 'purse hand' (Morris et al. 1979), or as the 'finger bunch' (Kendon 1995). As we shall see, the *grappolo* hand shape is involved in gestures which appear to mark the topic of a speaker's discourse but also in gestures which are employed when the speaker is asking certain kinds of questions or demanding an explanation or justification for something.[1]

A second gesture family will then be described. In this family the members have in common the use of a hand shape in which the tips of the thumb and index finger are placed in contact with one another, but held so that a roughly circular space is maintained between them. This hand shape was named the 'ring' by Morris et al. (1979). Accordingly, we shall refer to the gesture family that employs this hand shape as the *R-family*. Once again, we find that somewhat distinct forms can be differentiated according to the movement patterns employed. All of the gestural expressions in the R-family, however, are used in contexts in which the speaker is indicating that he means to be very precise about something, that what he is saying is 'exact' in some way, and that it demands special attention for this reason.

As already suggested, and following Morris (1977), both the gestures in the G-family and those in the R-family are thought of as being derived from

---

[1] The Italian word *grappolo* is appealing because it is used to refer to such things as a bunch of grapes or a swarm of bees when hanging as a cluster in a tree, clusters or bunches, that is, that often tend to have a conical shape also seen in the hand shape to which we are applying this term.

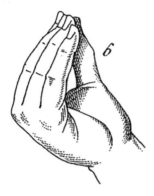

Fig. 12.1   The hand shape here termed the *grappolo* ('bunch') as depicted in Plate XXI in de Jorio (1832)

forms of hand action employed in the 'precision grip'. The 'grip' undertaken in forming the *grappolo* hand shape, however, is a different sort of 'grip' from the one undertaken in forming the 'ring' hand shape. We shall see that contexts of use of these two different 'grip' gestures are different and that their 'semantic themes' are different, accordingly.

The G-family: gestures using the *grappolo* or 'finger bunch'

The group of gestures found in this family all have in common the so-called 'purse hand' or 'finger bunch' - here to be termed the *grappolo* - in which the digits are all extended but flexed at the knuckles (the A joints) and drawn together so that they are in contact with one another at their tips. In all forms in this family, furthermore, the forearm tends to be maintained in a supine orientation so that the palm of the hand faces upwards. Four different, but closely related expressions using this hand shape will be described and discussed. They are distinguished in terms of how the hand is transformed, either into or out of the *grappolo* shape, and in terms of the movement pattern of the stroke. The expressions as we distinguish them are as follows: A. In the action of the gesture, the hand is *closed* to the *grappolo*. B. The hand, in *grappolo* pose, is oscillated upwards and inwards toward the speaker several times. C. The *grappolo* opens to a hand shape in which the fingers are extended. D. The *grappolo* hand is sustained in a vertical position and moved downwards vertically.

Fig. 12.2   Example 67. S closes his open hand (dotted line) to *grappolo* rotating it in towards himself as he says *"Tenë n'atu nummërë"* ('he had another number'). This action is repeated twice more in S's utterance, as shown in the transcription below.

Example 67   Bocce I 7.42.37.
~~~ preparation; *** hand as *grappolo*; <<< hand opens.

> he had another number, that was twenty-three, I don't know who he was telephoning
> tenë n'atu nummërë, chillë erë vintitrè nun saccië a chi telefonavë
> |~~~~**************|<<<<<<*********|<<<<<<<<<<<<*********|
> [1a]   [1b]   [2a]   [2b]   [3a]   [3b]

A. *The hand closes to the* grappolo *from a partially open pose.* Here the digits of the hand are drawn in to the *grappolo* shape and, at the same time, the hand is drawn in toward the speaker. The end position is such that the hand is held in the *grappolo* pose on a supine forearm, palm facing upwards, that is, and the hand is fairly close to the speaker's body. We see this action sequence employed when a speaker is nominating a topic for consideration, but in contexts where, in doing so, the speaker is trying to clarify or make more specific what is to be considered. It seems to be an action by which a speaker can bring a topic to the fore and emphasize that it is this that is to demand attention, or that it is this that is of immediate pertinence in the discussion.

For example, in Bocce I 7.42.37 (Example 67, Fig. 12.2) Sandro has explained to Giovanni that they are still waiting for Ninuccio because he has gone off to make a telephone call. Giovanni asks Sandro: *"Già tenë un 'nata?"* ('He already had another [number]?') to which Sandro replies *"Tenë n'atu nummërë, chillë erë ventitrè, nun saccië a chi telefonavë"* ('He had a number, that was twenty-three, I don't know who he is telephoning').

Sandro lifts his hand up and closes it to the *grappolo* as he says *"Tenë n'atu nummërë"* ('he had another number') [1a, 1b]; he opens his hand [2a] and closes it to a *grappolo* again as he says *"chillë erë vintitrè"* ('that was twenty-three') [2b]; and again opens it and closes it again to *grappolo* as he says *"nun saccië a chi telefonavë"* ('I don't know who he was telephoning') [3a, 3b]. Thus in relation to the two components of the topic specification, that the person being referred to had another number, and what this number was, the hand closes to *grappolo* and the hand is held still in this pose. Note that in association with the final part of the discourse, which is a kind of question, the *grappolo* is oscillated forward and back. As we shall see below, it is just this *oscillation* of the *grappolo* that is used when a question is being asked.

In Teatro 9.02.39 (Example 68), S, who is the leader of a small amateur theatre company which is meeting to discuss its next production, having reviewed various issues ends by saying *"Che altri problemi ci stannë?"* ('What other problems are there?'). D says *"Ma mi scusi, di questo teatro?"* ('But excuse me, of this theatre?') whereupon S responds *"Di questo"* ('Of this [theatre]'). As D asks for confirmation of what the other problems might be pertinent to, he closes his hand to the *grappolo*.

In these two cases, although each in a somewhat different way, the speaker establishes a topic which is to become the focus of attention: as a clarification for another's puzzlement (Example 67), or as a specification of something so that its pertinence can be established (Example 68). In each case, as what is established as the focus, the speaker closes the hand to form the *grappolo*. As we shall suggest below, the act of closing the hand to the *grappolo* is derived from the act of seizing something. In examples of the sort described here we may say that, with this gesture, the speaker 'seizes' the topic.

B. *The* grappolo *is held on a supine forearm and is moved upwards and sometimes somewhat toward the speaker several times.* The movement may be accomplished by action from elbow or by wrist flexion or by a combination. This is the gesture that has been described by Poggi (1983) and Kendon (1995b) under the name of the *mano a borsa* ('purse hand'). It is often depicted in vocabularies of Italian gestures as a gesture used for asking a question (see, for example, Munari 1963, Diadori 1990) and it was described by de Jorio (2000, p. 129). There are many variations in how it is performed, and these variations may serve to add overlays of meaning of various kinds. The common feature of all instances of this gesture, however, is that the *grappolo* is oscillated (usually in the vertical plane, but sometimes horizontally).

This gesture is used in contexts in which the speaker, confronted with something that undermines his expectations or his understanding, demands an explanation or a justification. It is used when a speaker asks a question about something because he is surprised, annoyed or puzzled by it, or when he is testing another's knowledge of something. It is not usually used when the speaker is simply requesting information.

In many cases this gesture is used on its own, however it is often combined with the gestural action described under A. That is to say, not infrequently one may see the closing of the hand to the *grappolo* being done and then, afterwards, the *grappolo* is sustained by the speaker and the oscillation is then added. We suggest that whereas, as we have said, the closing to the *grappolo* is a gesture that specifies something as pertinent, the addition of the vertical oscillation is the addition of an action that serves to make salient the pertinent object *for the other*. The oscillation in effect says: "Look well at this" - with the implication that the interlocutor is to say something relevant to the 'this' that is being held up before him.

Here are some examples taken from Bocce I. Enzo (Telefono: 7.33.24, Example 69) has just discovered that a telephone call must be made which he assumed had been made already. It is a telephone call that he himself cannot make because he has something else he has to do so he must find someone else to do it for him. So he says: "*A chi vacë a truvà ië mo a chest'orë?*" ('Who might I go to find for this now at this hour?') using the oscillating *grappolo* as he does so.

In Example 70 (Bocce I 7.44.52) Luigi comes to tell Enzo that the telephone number he had tried in order to reach someone on Bocce Club business was not correct. Enzo is puzzled by this because he thought he had given Luigi this number. Enzo asks Luigi: "*Ma chi 'o pigliajë 'o nummërë ri Cacciatori?*" ('But who got this number for the Hunters?') using the oscillating *grappolo* as he does so.

In Example 71 (Bocce I 7.49.28, Fig. 12.3), Sandro is puzzled because the robbers who entered the Bocce Club stole the telephone. Because it was a telephone rented from SIP (the Italian state telephone company), it could not be re-sold and so it seemed to be of no value to a robber. Using the oscillating *grappolo*, Sandro asks: "*Ma a chi servë chillu telefënë?*" ('But for whom is that telephone useful?'). Of interest in this example is the way in which Sandro begins his utterance with the oscillating *grappolo* (see [1] in the transcription for Example 71). This serves to draw the attention of Peppe and Giovanni. Note, also, that after he has finished speaking, he sustains his hand as Peppe makes his follow-up remark - in this case not a direct response to Sandro's rhetorical question, but a comment that seems to support the purport of Sandro's question: that it makes no sense for someone to steal a telephone (see [4] in the transcription for Example 71).

In Example 72 (Bocce I 7.48.21), Peppe asks Giovanni how he thinks the robber could have entered the building. Giovanni, as puzzled as Peppe, turns

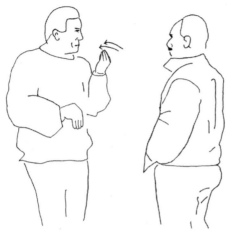

Fig. 12.3   Example 71. Sandro's oscillating *grappolo* as he asks "*A chi servë chillu telefënë?*" ('For whom is useful that telephone?').

Example 71 Bocce I 7.49.28.
*** *grappolo* moved inwards/outwards; **** *grappolo* held still, forearm vertical.

	But for who is that telephone useful?	For telephoning it costs a thousand lire odd
S:	Ma a chi servë chillu telefënë?	P: Pë telefoná costa spara millë lire?

~~~~****/******/****/*************************************|
     [1]   [2]   [3]   [4]

the question back to him as he says: "*Don Pe' ma dicitëmë vujë, ma unë che trasë cca dintë, ca vo 'i a rrubbà cca dintë. Che mariuolë è?*" ('Don Peppe, but you tell me, but someone that enters here in order to steal here inside. What [sort of] thief is he?').
As G begins the phrase that begins "*ma unë che trasë ccà dintë..*" ('but someone that enters here...') he lifts his arm and extends it to his right (which is in the direction of the location in the building where G believes the robber entered), the fingers of the hand extended and separated. He draws his arm inwards and, as he does so, closes to the *grappolo*. Here we have an example of topic specification associated with closing to *grappolo*, or Form A, as described above. Then, as he adds "*Che mariuolë è?*" ('What [sort of] thief is he?') he extends his hand, still in *grappolo* pose, in the direction of Peppe, and oscillates it.

C. *The* grappolo *is sustained, moved outward, and then the fingers open.* Here the initial hand shape is a closed form, the *grappolo*, and the main feature of the stroke is the *opening* of the hand, often combined with a forward or downward thrust. In many cases we see just *grappolo*-to-open, but quite often this is preceded by the hand closing, as described under A. This is the sequence of action described in Kendon (1995b) as the Finger Bunch.

This sequence of action is used when a speaker establishes a topic, then follows with something that comments on it, something that makes it more precise or completes it. The closure-to-*grappolo* is associated with topic nomination, the *grappolo*-to-open is associated with the comment, the part of the discourse that specifies the nominated topic or that completes it in some way.

Example 73 (SG 11.30.56) illustrates this. This is taken from a recording in which a woman is talking about what she thinks is of central importance for Neapolitans and what constitutes the main features of Neapolitan culture. She has been asked to indicate which parts of the city she considers to be 'true Napoli' and she replies by saying that it is constituted by the *centro storico* at its core, surrounded by certain other streets and *quartieri* that she mentions. She ends by saying:

Example 73. SG 11.30.56.
*** *Grappolo* hand; ooo Open hand

All this Quarter here,   The historic centre
D: Tutto questo quartiere qua. Il centro storico

This is true Naples, in effect, for me!
Questa è Napoli vera, in effetti per me!
|*******|ooooooooool
   [1]   [2]

As she says "*Questa è*" she presents both her hands in the *grappolo* form. As she says "*Napoli vera*" both hands open. Here, thus, in specifying as topic what she has just referred to (a certain area of the city) she closes her hands to the *grappolo*, as she comments on this - that it is "*Napoli vera*" ('true Naples') she opens her hands.

Again, the same speaker, later in the conversation (Example 74, SG 11.34.56), talks of the Neapolitan *presepe*, the arrangement of dolls representing the Holy Family surrounded by various *pastore* (shepherds) and other figures, often representing all aspects of Neapolitan life, which is typical in Naples in the Christmas season. D says "*Il presepe è l'essere napoletano*" ('the *presepe* is the Neapolitan being'). D is saying, that is, that the *presepe* is of central significance for Neapolitans. As she says "*Il presepe è*" she forms her hand in the *grappolo*, moving it downwards slightly. As she says "*l'essere napoletano*" she opens the *grappolo*.

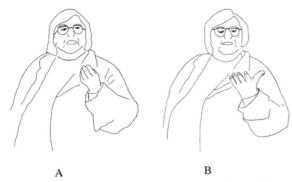

A   B

Fig. 12.4   Example 74. A. Speaker closes hand to *grappolo* as she says "*Il presepe è*" ('The *presepe* is'). B. Speaker opens hand as she says "*l'essere napoletano*" ('the Neapolitan being').

The level of structure in the spoken discourse to which this pattern of *grappolo*-to-open-hand can be related can vary considerably. In Example 75, in Iacone (Iacone I 030914) the speaker, P, is trying to explain the character of certain flowers (*papaveri* - poppies) to someone who has not recognized the name of them. He says "*i fiori rossi*" ('the red flowers'). As he says "*i fiori*" he lowers his hand in a rapid vertical movement forming the *grappolo* as he does so. As he says "*rossi*" the hand is opened. Here we have the nomination of a general class followed by a modifier. The nomination is associated with the *grappolo*, the modifier of the class is associated with the open hand.

In contrast, sometimes we see the pattern *grappolo*-to-open-hand organized so that it relates to much higher level discourse structures, such as premise-conclusion. In Example 76 (Artigiano 12.33.39), the speaker has been talking about the difficulties that young men face in Naples in finding work. He says, however, that the Neapolitan can always set up in the street with a box of fruit to sell if he wishes to go to the trouble.

Here, as the speaker states the possibility available to the Neapolitan, he uses the *grappolo* [1]. Then, as he refers to "who" - the subject of the possible action - he re-presents the *grappolo* [2], opening his hand at the end, as he refers to the condition that must be met if the selling of fruit is to be done [3].

Example 76. Artigiano 12.33.39.
***grappolo; ooo Open hand; <<< hand opens.

       The Neapolitan can put [down] still with a box of fruit, who wants to work
A: 'O napulitanë 'o può mettërë purë cu na sportë 'e fruttë, chi vo faticà
       |**|<<<<<looooool
           [1]   [2]   [3]

Examples of the kind we have presented here can easily be multiplied (see also Example 47, pp. 203-204). They illustrate a very general pattern, marking a fundamental structure in discourse: the establishment of a focus or topic followed by something that comments on it, qualifies it, or modifies it in some way. The *grappolo*-to-open-hand sequence, at least among Neapolitan speakers, is widely seen to pattern in this way.

The three forms we have distinguished within the G-family are all closely related, it is clear, and they may be seen performed in conjunction with one another as a single complex of action. Given the contexts in which we see these forms employed it seems appropriate to say that the action motif that all these share is that of holding on to something and making it prominent for the attention of the other. In form A it is the action of seizing this thing that is the central feature of the stroke of the gesture. In form B it is the oscillation of the *grappolo*, as if to make the thing seized prominent for the other's attention (when someone holds up an object to show it, it is common for the object to be moved back and forth rapidly) that is the salient feature. In form C, however, it is the thrusting or delivering of the object to the other that is made prominent.

De Jorio, who discussed the use of this hand shape as a gesture used when asking a question, suggests that the gesture is an action that proposes that the person being questioned bring together or summarize what he is trying to say. De Jorio writes: "... by uniting together in a single point all the fingers of the hand one is understood to be saying: 'Bring your ideas together, collect all your words together in one, or in brief, in one point, and tell me, what is it you wish to say?' In short: 'What are you talking about?'" (De Jorio 2000, p. 129). Somewhat similarly, in informal discussion with Neapolitans today it has been suggested that closing the hand to the *grappolo* is an action that is done when one extracts the 'essence' of something. That is, it is seen as a gesture that expresses the idea of pulling out what is essential from something. Some have also associated it with the idea of squeezing something to extract the juice of it. Such ideas are not far from the idea of topic specification that we have suggested here.

D. *The hand closes to the* grappolo, *held so that all the fingers point upwards and it is moved downwards vertically, the hand being sustained in the* grappolo *form throughout.* This fourth pattern of action in which the *grappolo* is involved seems to be a more specialized form. It is used just when the idea of the essence, core or heart of something is being expressed. Here are four examples:

In Example 77 (SG 11.35.26), as a concluding comment at the end of an extended discussion of the Neapolitan *presepe,* in which the speaker has talked about how the young people of Naples nowadays prefer the Christmas tree and

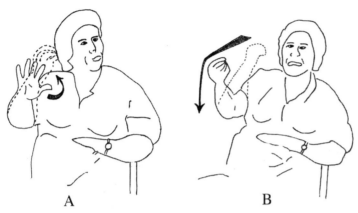

A   B

Fig. 12.5. Example 78. C closes open hand to *grappolo* (A), lowering her hand vertically as she does so, and saying "*Il proprio 'o cuorë 'e Napoli*" ('The true heart of Naples'). As she continues with "*è chesto ccà*" ('is this here') she moves her *grappolo* hand up and towards herself, and then forward and down (B). As she moves her hand forward and down she directs her gaze toward the location to which she moves her hand. The forward extension of the arm and the gaze to the hand's destination both suggest that the gesture here is 'inflected' with a deictic component.

do not seem to appreciate the *presepe*, D says: "*L'essenza di Natale è il presepe*" ('the essence of Christmas is the *presepe*'). Prior to beginning the verbal part of this utterance, she lifts her hand up, closes it to the *grappolo* and lowers it vertically, uttering "*L'essenza*" only at the end of this downward movement. As the word "*essenza*" is continued the hand is lifted up again and becomes fully open as she says "*di Natale*". As she says "*è presepe*" her hand closes again and it is dropped in relaxation to her side. The vertical lowering of the *grappolo* as the first element of the utterance provides the idea of "*essenza*" gesturally. The verbal expression that follows clarifies what "*essenza*" is being referred to.

In Example 78 (DSGA (I) 21.18, Fig. 12.5) C, who has been asked to explain what for her are the geographical boundaries of "true Naples", ends a fairly elaborate explanation by saying "*il proprio 'o corë 'e Napulë è chesto ccà*" ('the true heart of Naples is this here'). As she says "*Il proprio 'o corë*" she extends her arm forwards and lowers her hand vertically, drawing the fingers into the *grappolo* as she does so. In this action there is also a deictic component. The extreme forward extension of the arm is here a reference to the centre of an area she has just previously laid out, sketching out a sort of virtual map of the streets that she regards as bounding the heart of Naples.

In Example 79 (LB 11.57.15) the topic of the Neapolitan *presepe* has been raised and LB, who, with her husband, owns a shop where the terracotta figures used in the *presepe* are made, has just explained to M how her husband, who had intervened in the conversation from afar, had meant to say that the *presepe* as a representation of the city of Naples is beautiful but that the real people of Naples, this is another matter. M responds to LB's explanation by saying: "*Ho capito, questa è la sostanza*" ('I understand, this is the substance [of what he was saying]'). As he says "*questa*" he moves his hand downwards vertically, closing it to the *grappolo*.

Again, in Example 80 (LB 11.58.22), and again on the topic of the *presepe*, M asks LB if the art of the *presepe* is tied to "*un certo essere napolitani* " ('a certain being Neapolitan'). As he says "*essere napolitani* " he turns his hand, already in *grappolo* form, and sets it in a vertical position, moving it downwards vertically very slightly.

These examples would seem to confirm a rather specific use of the *grappolo*. Notice that, in these cases, the *grappolo* is no longer functioning pragmatically. It is not marking topic nomination, for example, or indicating a certain kind of illocutionary act. In these cases it is employed at the propositional level, giving expression to the idea of 'essence' or 'substance', 'core' or 'heart'. It is serving as a part of the referential content of the utterance, that is to say. Yet, as will be clear, such a usage is closely related to what is being expressed when the *grappolo* is used in a pragmatic way.

The R-family: gestures which use the 'ring' hand shape

The group of gestures we now consider, those belonging to the R-family, share in common that they all make use of the so-called 'ring' or R-hand shape. In this hand shape the tips of the index finger and thumb are brought into contact so that the two digits together outline a more or less circular space. See Fig. 12.6 (and see also Fig. 4.1, p. 47). This hand shape was termed the 'ring' by Morris et al. (1979) and we retain this term here. A number of writers have described gestures that employ this hand shape, including de Jorio ([1832] 2000), Efron (1972), Munari (1963), Morris et al. (1979) and Diadori (1990).

De Jorio (2000) describes seven different gestures in which the hand shape resulting from the tips of the index finger and thumb being brought into contact is used. These include gestures for love and affection (p. 83), obscene insult (p. 191), smelling something (p. 304), taking snuff - typically used as a gesture that suggests idleness or indifference (pp. 390–392), asking a question (p. 129), justice (pp. 233–234), and various expressions for perfection, correctness or exactness (pp. 321–322). In describing these gestures, he is careful to show how each differs from the other in terms of such features as movement, whether of the digits or of the arm as a whole, how the hand is oriented, or how it is positioned in relation to other parts of the body. And in some cases he is careful to point out that the exact shape of the space surrounded by the two digits is important.

Fig. 12.6   Two examples of the R-hand shape

From his account it is clear that the gestures that employ this 'ring' arrangement of the hand have very different derivations. In the case of love and affection he writes (p. 83) that the "index finger and thumb are brought together so that the papillae of their final joints make contact as if they are kissing each other." He points out that this gesture is to be distinguished from the one for extreme insult, for in that gesture "the extremities of these digits make contact in such a way that thumb and index finger together almost form a circle" (ibid.). The gesture in which a very similar hand shape is used in asking a question is distinguished from that for love and affection by the fact that "in denoting friendship the tips of the fingers are often joined and then separated, whereas when a question is being expressed they always remain combined and firm". Furthermore, "in questioning the fingers must always be turned upwards, whereas in dealing with friendship the gesture has the same meaning no matter what the direction of the fingers". Finally, in the gesture expressing a question the hand oscillates, whereas it remains still if friendship is referred to (see p. 129 and p. 134).

In the gesture used to express the idea of justice, on the other hand, the "thumb and index finger [are] joined at the tips, forming a cone, [and] the hand [is] turned downwards". How such a posture of the hand can come to express the idea of justice, de Jorio suggests, can be derived from the idea of "the balance as an emblem of justice... Accordingly, it can be understood why arranging the fingers of the hand in the same way as is commonly done when holding up a balance when weighing something, recalls the idea of justness, of rightness or correctness in general". (pp. 233–234). De Jorio goes on to add that "the word *giusto* 'just' can also be taken in a more extended sense, to denote 'optimum', 'perfect', 'exact', 'accomplished'. Hence these gestures can be used to express these meanings" (p. 234). He devotes another section to this in which he again describes the use of this digit arrangement for the expression of ideas such as perfection, exactness, and the like (see p. 321).

From the foregoing it will be seen that seemingly very similar hand shapes can come about in very different ways. The so-called 'ring' hand shape can be posed to refer to a shape (as in obscene insult, where it is the shape of a bodily orifice that is indicated), it can be created as a result of an action that portrays the actions of two individuals who come into intimate contact with one another (the repeated joining together of the papillae of the index finger and thumb in an expression for love or friendship), or it can be created as a result of action by which something is grasped and held on to, as in the case of the gestures for justice, perfection, exactness and related meanings (and also in the case of gestures for taking snuff or smelling something). Although de Jorio does not say so, this is probably also the origin of the hand shape used in asking a question where, in this case, the hand shape is employed in questions in which one is asking for some very precise or exact answer.

It is our view that it is the group of 'ring' hand shapes that is derived from holding something between the tips of the index finger and thumb, that constitute the R-family. We agree with Desmond Morris (see Morris 1977 and Morris et al. 1979) that we can distinguish a group of gestures that use the 'ring' hand shape, all of which are derived from the 'precision grip' - the use of the index finger and thumb to pick up and to hold onto something small. As we shall see, context-of-use studies of this hand shape, as used by speakers when not otherwise performing the more specialized gestures such as those described by de Jorio for friendship, obscene insult and the like, suggest that the semantic theme that they share is related to ideas of exactness, making something precise, or making prominent some specific fact or idea. Just as, with the *grappolo*, we suggested that the underlying motif involved in the formation of this hand shape is a motif of seizing or grasping something, so we believe this to be the case for gestures of the R-family where, however, the manner of grasping, and hence, by implication, the nature of the object grasped, is different. In the seizing action of the *grappolo* something is either being squeezed, an object of moderate or indifferent dimensions is being picked up, or small objects that are somewhat dispersed are being brought together (as in gathering a handful of something, for instance). In the seizing action of the R-hand shape, on the other hand, a very small object is being picked up, a specific item is being extracted or picked out from a crowd of different objects.

Our observations on the Ring hand shape in R-family gestures, when used in association with speech, have led us to distinguish three patterns of use:

A. The Ring is formed as the initial hand shape in a sequence in which the hand is subsequently 'opened'. This is similar to the pattern described under C in the previous section in which the *grappolo* opens to a kind of 'open' hand. This may be referred to as the R-to-Open sequence.

B. The speaker lifts up his hand and forms it into the Ring as he does so, thereafter 'presenting' or 'holding in place' his hand, as if to show the hand so posed to his interlocutor. We shall refer to this as the R-display.

C. The hand, formed in the Ring pose, is held so that the palm of the hand faces towards the speaker's mid-line (the forearm is in 'neutral' position), and the hand is then moved vertically downwards one or more times in coordination with points of stress in the vocal discourse. This we shall refer to as the R-vertical. In many cases a sequence of such emphatic movements is followed by the hand being opened in a pattern similar to that referred to under A.

The contexts of use of each of these patterns are somewhat different, with different implications for what appears to be being expressed. However, the semantic theme that seems to unite all of these usages is the theme of "making precise". That is to say, these gestures are used in conjunction with spoken expressions that either quote some exact fact or figure, or clarify an idea, a description, an observation or an opinion. However, when these R-gestures are used there is always the implication that 'making precise' or specifying something is being done against a background of an incomplete or inadequate understanding on the part of the speaker's interlocutor. It is as if the R-gestures are brought into play whenever, for the speaker, 'making precise' or clarification seems necessary or important in gaining the agreement, the conviction or the understanding of the interlocutor. Let us now turn to some examples.

A. R-to-open: the Ring as an initial hand shape in a 'closed–open' hand shape sequence. As we saw in our discussion of the *grappolo* the closed hand was often coordinated with the specification of a topic, the subject component of a sentence, or the nomination of an object class, while the opening of the hand was coordinated with the speaker's comment, the predicate component of a sentence, or the modifier of the object class. Where we see the ring instead of the *grappolo* in sequences otherwise similar, the speaker is often engaged in a discourse in which something quite specific is being mentioned, most typically in the context of an already established topic.

In our first example, Example 81 (Nap. Sott. 10.29.34), a guide is giving a background lecture on the ancient subterranean aqueducts below the city of Naples. He has stated that the system used to be managed by workers who actually spent most of their time inside the aqueducts. He says: "*Tutti questi acquedotti in sotteranea venivano gestiti da un operaio che lavorava quaggiù. Si chiamava il pozzaro*" ('All these aqueducts below ground used to be managed by a worker that used to work down here. He was called the *pozzaro*'). As he says "*Si chiamava*" ('he was called') he holds both hands forward, palm down, and flexes thumb and index finger so they are in contact at their tips. As he says "*il pozzaro*" ('the *pozzaro*') the index fingers extend, the hand is now open.

Similarly, the same speaker, in another part of his discourse (Example 82, Nap. Sott. 10.25.30), speaks of a huge tank hacked out of the rock which stored drinking water. He specifies how many cubic metres of water it could hold. As he commences the sentence in which he specifies how much water the pool could contain, he holds both his hands with the index finger and thumb in contact in the Ring pose [1], he then opens his hands [2], closing them briefly into the *grappolo* [3] and opening them once again over the final word "*potabile*" ('drinkable') - the modifier of "*acqua*" [4].

Example 82. Nap. Sott. 10.25.30
rrr 'ring' hand; ooo 'open' hand; ggg 'grappolo' hand

It's a huge pool
È una piscina enorme.

It was able to hold fifteen thousand cubic metres of drinking water
Poteva contenere quindici mila metri cubi di acqua potabile
|rrrrrrrrrrrrrrrrrrrrrrrrrrrrrrrrrrrr|ooooooooooo|ggggg|oooooo|

    [1]   [2]   [3]   [4]

Note, thus, how in both of these instances when the speaker focuses on a specific feature of what he is talking about - the exact name of the well-worker, the exact quantity the tank could contain - he uses the R–Open sequence.

B. R-display. The hand is raised and closed to the ring and then held up and sustained in position, as if to display it to the interlocutor. This is commonly seen when the speaker makes something clear or offers precise information or precise instructions, once again in a context in which this is in contrast to what has been presupposed hitherto. This 'display' use of the ring seems to be used when the speaker is counterposing something to what he or his interlocutor has previously said. The Ring–open hand sequences described above occur in expository discourse, rather than in countering responses.

The R-display used when giving precise instructions is seen in Example 83 (LB 11.57.22). Here M has turned to ask LB about Neapolitan cooking and he asks her to give a recipe. Notice how, in the extract in this example, the speaker first asks if LB can give a "typically Neapolitan recipe". He then goes on to explain more precisely what he wants her to do. It is here, with this latter part of the discourse that he holds up his hand in the Ring hand shape, or uses the R-display:

As he says "*descrive cioè*" ('describe that is') he uses the R-display [1]. When he continues with "*dall'a alla zeta*" ('from A to Z') he moves the hand, still with

Fig. 12.7   Example 85. D, asked what constitutes true Naples, replies "*Il centro storico, il centro storico, almeno per me*" ('The historic centre, the historic centre, at least for me'). As she says "*il centro storico*" the first time (left figure) she tilts her head backwards and directs a spread open hand behind, as if indicating its location (the traditional centre, the so-called *corpo di Napoli*, is behind where she is standing). When she repeats "*il centro storico*" she displays the Ring-hand shape (right figure), making it precisely clear what for her is true Napoli.

Ring pose, laterally [2]. Here he now combines, thus, the 'making precise' of the Ring with a movement that suggests a sequence or range that he wants the explanation to cover.

Example 83. LB 11.57.22 *** 'ring' hand

> On cooking, can you give us a recipe typically Neapolitan
> Sulla cucina, ci può dare una ricetta tipicamente napoletana
>
> describe [it] that is from A to Z, for four persons.
> descrive cioè dall'a alla zeta, per quattro persone.
> |***********|***********|
>   [1]   [2]

In the next example (Example 85 SG 11.30.40, Fig. 12.7) we see the R-display being used where the speaker is specifying her own particular opinion on something. In this example, the speaker has been asked to say what, for her, constitutes the true city of Naples and she replies immediately that it is that part of the city known as the *centro storico*, the historic centre. As she does so, she indicates both with a backward head movement and with a backwardly directed open hand, the direction in which lies the true centre of the *centro storico*. This is a *piazzetta* where a statue sometimes referred to as the *Corpo di Napoli* ('Body of Naples') is to be found. Her interlocutor does not immediately reply, whereupon she repeats the phrase "*centro storico*", but in this repetition she uses the R-display and does not make any deictic movement with her head. The force of the R-display here seems to be to express the idea: "precisely the *centro storico*". She follows this by saying "*Almeno per me*" ('At least for me'), pressing both her open hands, palms inwards, to her chest as she does so.

In this example, thus, it seems that the speaker repeats her opinion as a way of making it clear and shows, in her following phrase, that this is *her* view. Again, it seems, the R-display is used here as a specific viewpoint is indicated in contrast to other possible views. We might add in passing that this is another example of how speakers, in repeating a verbal construction, may yet deploy different gestures in relation to it and thus create different meanings in consequence. This example may be added to those described and discussed at the end of Chapter 8.

Example 86 (DSGA II 31.14) illustrates another context in which we see the R-display in use. C has been talking about how loyal Neapolitans can be to one another. M comments that when a Neapolitan declares his friendship he will always maintain his friendship. C replies: *"Però majë, majë, ch'he fattë chella fëtënzjë, si scarutë ro corë"* ('But if ever ever you do him wrong, you are banished from his heart'). Here, as she says *"ch'he fattë chella fëtënzjë"* ('you do him wrong') she holds up her hand with the R-hand shape. Thus, when she gives the precise conditions that would destroy a friendship, she uses the R-display.

The R-display may also be used when the speaker is quoting something precisely. This example is also taken from DSGA (Example 87, DSGA II. 00.34.33). The conversation has turned to the presence of criminals in Naples. M has asked C if there are thieves and criminals in Naples. She replies that indeed there are, whereupon M says *"Come stannë a tuttë parte"* ('As there are everywhere'). C then says: *" 'O sapitë 'o dittë antichë?"* ('Do you know the old saying?' and then she asks: *"Lo posso dire?"* ('Can I say it?'). M replies *"Sì, sì, sì"* whereupon C quotes it: *" 'O rittë antichë ricë: arò nun cë stannë 'e campanë nun cë stannë 'e puttanë"* ('The saying says: Where there are no bells [i.e churches], there there are no prostitutes' - i.e. more generally, evil-doers). As she quotes the very words of the proverb she uses the R-display. It is interesting to note that when she first mentions the proverb, asking if M knows of it, she lifts her hand in the R-display. This exemplifies the use of the R-display in asking a question, and it is to be noted that the question, just as de Jorio had suggested (see de Jorio 2000, pp. 129, 406 and Plate II. See also Fig. 4.1, p. 47), is a question that has a quite specific focus. In this case it is as if C says "Do you know just this old saying I refer to?"

One final example further illustrates the use of the R-display in a question, again in a manner similar to that described by de Jorio. This example, Example 88, is taken from the recording Iacone (Iacone I 030914), in which the discussion has turned to how it was in Naples during the Second World War. It has been mentioned that when people did not have enough to eat they would go into the streets and collect weeds from the sides of the roads. These weeds included poppies which, if you ate these, because of the opium they contained, would make you sleepy. In the moment for this example P uses the word *"papagni"* which is the Neapolitan word for *papaveri* ('poppies'). As soon as he uses this word, he asks his interlocutor (who is perhaps forty years younger than the speaker), M, if she knows what *papagni* refers to. He says *"Sai papagni che sono"* ('You know what *papagni* are?'). M replies *"Papagni? Non lo so."* ('*Papagni?* I don't know'). Here she repeats the word P has mentioned, as if to confirm that she has heard it correctly. As she repeats it, she raises her hand with the R-hand shape. Here the R-display adds to what she is saying. It is as if, with R-display, she says: "Is it precisely this that I utter as I use the R-display, precisely this word, that you are asking me about?"

C. The R-vertical: The hand, posed in the Ring shape, held so the palm of the hand is vertical - the rotation of the forearm is neutral - is moved downward or forward in one or more well-defined baton-like movements. This we see when a speaker is making a specific point, giving a specific piece of information on which he is insistent and which, once again, is counterposed to what has been presupposed. As we have noted, this is often performed as part of a sequence in which the speaker ends by opening the hand.

Gesture sequences of this type are seen where a speaker is making clear an opinion or a position which is explicitly or implicitly in contrast to some other opinion or position. This may be illustrated by Example 89 (SG 11.34.41), in which a woman is being engaged in conversation about the characteristics of *napolitanità*. The topic is the Neapolitan *presepe* and the speaker has stated that the young people of today in Naples no longer appreciate the *presepe* but prefer the Christmas tree instead. She explains, however, that for her, if there is no *presepe* there is no Christmas.

Example 89, SG 11.34.41 ^^^^ 'ring' hand moved up; vvvv 'ring' hand moved down; ooo 'open' hand; o͟o͟o͟ open hand held

For me Christmas without *presepe* is not Christmas
Per me Natale senza presepe non è Natale.
|^^^^^vvvvv|^^^^^vvvvvv|oooooooooooo|
  [1]   [2]   [3]

At my house the *presepe* one must set up
A casa mia il presepe si deve mettere(-- --)
|vvvvvv^^^vvvvv|oooooooooooo͟o͟o͟o͟o͟o͟o͟o͟
   [4]   [5]

I set it up on the eighth of December
Io lo metto l'otto dicembre (-- --)
|~~vvvv^^^vv^^^|oooooo͟o͟o͟o͟o͟o͟o͟
  [6]   [7]

As will be seen in the extract from her discourse transcribed here, in which we have indicated the Ring–open hand sequences, in each case the premise of each of her assertions is accompanied by the Ring, the consequence or conclusion is accompanied by the Open hand. Thus she raises (^) and lowers (v) her hand in the Ring-hand shape in segments [1], [2], [4] and [6], and moves her open hand (oo) laterally with a short hold at the end of each stroke (oo) in segments [3], [5] and [7]. The pattern is again similar to the *grappolo–*open hand sequence we described above, but here the speaker is clarifying or making precise her own position, which is in contrast to that of the young people she has referred to.

In a second example, Example 90 (CPIV 14.37), a woman is talking about difficulties she has had with a colleague at a school where she teaches. She has explained how this difficult colleague has, without her permission, moved some papers from a place where she had put them. She then quotes what she said to her colleague (or perhaps what she would like to have said to her) when, on a Monday morning, she arrived to find the papers displaced. She says: "*Scusami, dove mi hai messo i fogli che erano lì?*" ('Excuse me, where have you put for me the papers that were there?'). She then follows this by stating that she has a right to keep the things she is responsible for wherever she likes. It is not for her colleague to move them around. She says: "*La mia roba, la tengo dove voglio e come voglio. E tu non hai il diritto di toccarla!*" ('My stuff, I keep it where I want and as I want! And you do not have the right to touch it!'). Here she accompanies the premise of her question ([1] in Extract I) or the premises of her assertion of her rights ([1] and [3] in Extract II) with

Example 90 CP IV 14.37
*v*v R-hand moved downward repeatedly; 000 R-hand opened.
Extract I

> Excuse me, where have you put for me the papers that were there?
> Scusami, dove mi hai messo i fogli che erano lì?
> |*v*v*v*v*v*v*v*v*v*v|000000000000000|
>   [1]   [2]

Extract II

> My stuff, I keep it where I want and as I want
> La mia roba, la tengo dove voglio e come voglio
> |*v*v*v*v*v*v*v*v*v*v*V|0000000|
>   [1]   [2]

> And you do not have the right to touch it!
> E tu non hai il diritto di toccarla!
> |*v*v*v*v*v*v*v*v|000000000|
>   [3]   [4]

a succession of downward movements of the hand in the Ring pose, opening her hand as she comes to the concluding part of each one of her sentences ([2] in Extract I and [2] and [4] in Extract II).

It is perhaps appropriate to suggest here that a ritualized version of this 'assertive' use of the Ring-hand could be the explanation for the gestural expression quoted by Efron (1972, p. 213, No. 77) as a gesture of 'warning'. To raise the hand, posed in the ring, and move it back and forth in the direction of someone is to threaten or warn them. It may sometimes be seen in use by mothers or others with care of small children. It may be interpreted as a use of the "making precise" gesture (as we might call the R-hand using gestures collectively) - for what it expresses is: "You pay precise attention to me and do what I say, otherwise..."

The foregoing series of examples exemplifies some of the contexts in which the R-hand is used and, as will be seen, what is common to them is that something is being singled out, something is being made precise, something specific is being stated, but always in a context in which such making precise, such specificity is called for as a move of needed clarification. Similar examples and a similar interpretation were given in Kendon (1995b). As we have also commented, this interpretation is also shared by Morris (1977 - see also Morris et al. 1979, pp. 102-103) and, by implication, by de Jorio. Also in agreement with Morris, we are inclined to interpret the gestures in the R-family as all being derived from a species of precision grip. The wider implications of this view of this gesture as a kind of 'ritualization' of a form of manipulatory action, which we have also applied to the interpretation of gestures in the G-family, will receive some further discussion at the end of the next chapter, after we have completed our survey of the pragmatic gestures that we have selected for study.

13 Two gesture families of the open hand

In this chapter we continue our exploration of gestures with pragmatic functions with a consideration of two further gesture families: the Open Hand Prone (OHP) family and the Open Hand Supine (OHS) family. In both of these families the hand shape is 'open'. That is, the hand is held with all digits extended and more or less adducted (they are not 'spread'). In the Open Hand Prone family (informally the 'palm down' family) the forearm is always in a prone position so that the palm of the hand faces either toward the ground or away from the speaker, depending upon how the elbow is bent. In the Open Hand Supine family (informally the 'palm up' family), in contrast, the forearm is always supine, so that the palm of the hand faces upwards. Within each family different gestural expressions are distinguished in terms of the movement employed in the expression.

In terms of contexts of use, the two families are quite different. Gestures of the Open Hand Prone or 'palm down' family are used in contexts where something is being denied, negated, interrupted or stopped, whether explicitly or by implication. Open Hand Supine (or 'palm up') family gestures, on the other hand, are used in contexts where the speaker is offering, giving or showing something or requesting the reception of something. It also includes gestures in which, very often, both hands, sustained in the Open Hand Supine pose, are moved away from one another, as if being withdrawn from the space immediately in front of the speaker. The semantic theme of these gestures is that of the withdrawal of action or of non-intervention.

Although many of the examples in this chapter are drawn, once again, from Neapolitan material, Open Hand Prone gestures and Open Hand Supine gestures are very widely used, and in much the same way, well beyond the confines of southern Italy. Among Neapolitans, however, there is a precision of articulation which seems to be less apparent among speakers of English, whether in Britain or the United States.

The Open Hand Prone ('palm down') family

A context-of-use study of Open Hand Prone gestures suggests that they all share the semantic theme of stopping or interrupting a line of action that is

248

in progress. By 'line of action' we mean any project that someone might be engaged in, whether this involves physical action, communicative action (such as saying something), or mental activity, such as pursuing a train of thought or assuming a certain mental attitude toward something. Some of the gestures within this family have been described by others. For example, in the section titled *Negativa, No* of his treatise on Neapolitan gesture of 1832, Andrea de Jorio describes several different hand gestures of this kind. Thus he writes (de Jorio 2000, p. 291): "Simply to extend the arm in a relaxed way, with the hand opposed to whatever is rejected, indicates 'no'. If the arm is further extended and the fingers of the hand are spread forcefully, a 'no' of greater resolution is expressed; if both arms are extended in this manner, one expresses one's horror at what has been proposed or at what one sees". De Jorio writes that negation may also be expressed by an "open hand raised and oscillated from left to right" and he describes a similar gesture of "greater emphasis" that may be done with the "palm turned toward what is to be denied or rejected, with the index finger extended and a little separated from the other fingers, and then wagged back and forth". In another manual gesture of negation the hands are "lifted naturally towards the shoulders, with the palms opposed to whatever is denied or rejected". In the section *Fermare* ('Stop, Halt') he describes a gesture in which the "arm extended with the palm raised vertically, [is] turned toward the person on whom it is wished to impose a halt" (ibid., p. 210).

We also find depictions of several of these gestures, as well as others which are similar, in the "Short Dictionary of Southern Italian Descriptive and Symbolic Gestures Drawn by Professor Stuyvesant Van Veen" that is to be found as an appendix to the 1972 edition of David Efron's *Gesture, Race and Culture* (Efron 1972). Figure 13.1 presents a selection from this "Dictionary" which shows all of those examples listed which share the kinesic features of the OHP family. That is, those which include an 'open hand' oriented so that the palm of the hand faces either forward or downward, and in which the movement is either forward, away from the actor, downward or lateral and horizontal. As will be clear from the glosses that Efron provided, with one exception, these are related to meanings of stopping, halting, or rejecting something, or cutting something off. The exception is No. 52, which is glossed as "Very good" but also as "Unapproachable". As we shall see, OHP gestures are also found in contexts where a speaker gives an extreme positive evaluation of something. As we argue later, extreme positive evaluations often imply a denial of alternatives, and the use of OHP gestures in such contexts gives expression to this. Efron's own gloss of "Unapproachable" for No. 52 is in line with this analysis.

In terms of kinesic organization, the gestures in the Open Hand Prone family fall into two groups: those in which the forearm is vertical or the wrist is extended, so that the palm of the hand faces directly away from the speaker

Fig. 13.1   Gestures of the Open Hand Prone (palm down or away) family extracted from 'A Short Dictionary of Southern Italian Descriptive and Symbolic Gestures Drawn by Professor Stuyvesant Van Veen' published as an appendix in Efron (1972). The glosses for the gestures provided by Efron are as follows: 3. Command, Imperiousness, Stop, Salutation. 81. Stop, Attention, Quiet, Wait. 51, 114, 115. Rejection. 41. Surprise. 23. Rejection. 52. Very good, Unapproachable. 84, 83. Go slowly, Take it easy, Be calm, Wait, Listen! 142. Through, separation. 45. Finished, Through.

(*Vertical Palm* OHP gestures, called here VP gestures), and those in which the palm of the hand is held so that it faces either obliquely away or directly downwards (*Horizontal Palm* OHP gestures, called here ZP gestures).

Open Hand Prone ('vertical palm' VP) gestures

These are used in contexts where the speaker indicates an intention to halt his or her current line of action, a wish that what is being done jointly be halted, or a wish that what is being done by the interlocutor should be halted. This is illustrated with the following four examples.

In Example 91 (Commerciante 33.16) Peppe makes a suggestion in jest for the name of the film he imagines will be made from the video tape the students are making of him and his friends. He suggests that it is a film about animal species that are becoming extinct. According to him, the small-time street vendor, such as himself, is a species that is becoming extinct. He suggests that the film being made will be used in a well-known television programme called *Il Mondo di Quark*. He says: "*Va va al Mondo di Quark. Gli animali in via d'estinz- (0.75 sec) Ecco! Scrivete ëëë 'la specie in via di estinzione'*" ('It goes it goes to *Il Mondo di Quark*. Animals on the way to extinct- (0.75 sec). Here you are! You write eeh "A species on the way to extinction"').

As he says "*al Mondo di Quark*" he directs an index finger (palm neutral) toward the camera. Then he says "*Gli animali in via d'estinz-*". This is the first proposal he makes for a title of the film. As he says this, he moves his right hand, open hand palm away, in an upward and rightward motion, probably a version of a 'horizontal palm' or ZP gesture that expresses the idea of something being pushed to one side or being erased. He does not complete the word "*estinzione*", however, but breaks off his speech. Then follows a pause of three-quarters of a second. His speech resumes with "*Ecco!*" and thereupon he proposes a slightly different title for the film and, at the same time, he uses a gesture that suggests how the title will be written up on the screen. The self-interruption in speech and the pause that follows mark the fact that there is to be a revision in his formulation of the film title. At the moment of the self-interruption, and during the pause that follows, he holds both his hands up in a two-handed VP gesture and by so doing he shows that he is interrupting himself, he shows that he is halting his current line of action, his current utterance, that is (see Fig. 13.2). When he resumes speaking he announces that he has a new formulation with "*Ecco*" and he then proceeds to re-state the title of the film together with a gesture that suggests the way the title will be written up on the screen.

Thus in this example we see how the speaker inserts a VP gesture to signal the moment of self-interruption, which allows him to reorganize his formulation of his proposal.

Fig. 13.2   Example 91. Peppe's two-handed Vertical Palm OHP gesture performed in a pause following a self-interruption.

In Example 92 (CPIII 00.10.40, see Fig. 13.3), we see this gesture being used as a speaker tells about how he interrupted himself in some project he had been engaged on in the past. This Example is taken from a recording made at a family dinner party. A has been asked by his wife why he did not bring more white wine - evidently the company is running short. He explains that he would have had to have transferred such wine into bottles from a demijohn in order to bring it, but as he had already changed into his good clothes before he realized he needed to do this, he decided not to try:

Example 92 CPIII 00.10.40. **Palm Away with lateral movement (both hands). hwhw: palms of hands brush one another. This is a gesture used when referring to something that is finished, abandoned, given up. Here it could be glossed as 'I give up.' Note it completes A's sentence.

> No, you know why, now I tell you seriously
> No, sai perché, mo' te lo dico serio.
>
> I had to begin the fifty litre demijohn,
> Avia inizià la damigiana di cinquanta litri
>
>   and I was already changed/And then I said
> (...0.36...) e m'ero già cambiato/E allora aggio rittë
> |*******| |hwhw|

Note that, in this example, as in Example 91, the VP gesture is inserted in a pause. The speaker, recounting a past process, reaches the point in his narration where he tells us what he has realized he has to do - to start transferring wine from a new demijohn - and it is at this point that he interrupts his project. At this point, then, he does a VP gesture that announces the interruption - and *then* he explains why: that he had already changed his clothes.

In Example 93 (DSGA 26.44), a VP gesture is used as a person explains how she limits herself in the use of a certain ingredient in cooking a bolognese *sugo* (Fig. 13.4). She says she makes this with just a little tomato extract. Note, however, how she adds the word *"veramente"* ('truly') which emphasizes that the 'little' tomato extract she uses is to be taken literally. In other words she restrains herself in the use of this ingredient.

Example 93. DSGA 26.44. **VP (one hand), ++ Head shake

I put either some little tomatoes or a little tomato purée, truly
C: ci metto o dei pomodorini o un po' di passata, veramente
                    |*******************|
                    <++++>

Note that she uses the VP gesture when, in her discourse, she says she just uses a little *passata* and that she here uses a head shake, as well (just as she says *"passata"*). The VP gesture suggests the self-imposed limit beyond which she does not go. Its use adds to the meaning of what the speaker is saying here. Together with the head shake, it gives expression to the negative that is implied by what she utters verbally.

VP gestures may also be used when a speaker indicates that it is the interlocutor who should interrupt or suspend a current line of action. In Example 94 (from Commerciante) one of the card-players, Peppe, has claimed his team has won an aperitif. At the same time as Vincenzo shakes his head to deny Peppe's claim, he uses a VP gesture (Fig. 13.5). He uses this gesture again as he repeats his explanation that Peppe's team has not yet won an aperitif.

Example 94. Commerciante 36.34. **VP (one hand), ++ Head shake

        ooh one aperitif   gone   now let's go for the second
    P: uu un aperitivo è andato (.) mooo andiamo per il secondo

        a San Bitter
    T: = un San Bitter

            we're still at the first aperitif   we are
    V: (.............) stammë sempë 'u primmë aperitivë stammë
        |*******| |*******|
        <++++++++>

Vincenzo's use of a head shake at the same time as he uses a VP gesture in his initial (and gestured-only) response, suggests a double response: with the head shake Vincenzo says 'no' and with the VP he says 'stop what you are thinking'. The use of the VP coincidentally with *"aperitivë"* serves to add the

Fig. 13.3   Example 92. The two-handed VP gesture that A inserts in a pause in speech immediately after he had explained that he would have had to start decanting wine from a fifty-litre demijohn and which announces his interruption of this project.

Fig. 13.4   Example 93. One-handed VP gesture as C indicates that she is restrained about how much tomato purée she uses when making a *sugo* for a *bolognese*.

Fig. 13.5   Example 94. Vincenzo's VP gesture as he advises Peppe that he has not yet won enough points to earn an aperitif.

idea that we are still stopped at the first aperitif, we are not yet going beyond it. Note that, if this interpretation is accepted, this example is a nice illustration of how kinesic expressions can be used to create multiple meaning layers simultaneously.

VP gestures, as we have suggested, serve to propose that a line of action be suspended or interrupted because it is the actor who wills it. A consideration of the examples collected suggests that, in the performance of this gesture, where the hand is placed, relative to the speaker's body, indicates whose line of action is to be stopped. If the hand is placed close to the speaker's own body a stop to *his own* line of action is being announced. If it is placed a little in front of the speaker's body, it is proposed that the line of action shared by speaker and interlocutor be interrupted. If the hand is moved forward toward the interlocutor, then the speaker proposes that the *interlocutor* stop whatever he is doing or saying.

Open Hand Prone (or 'horizontal palm' ZP) gestures

In the gestures discussed here, referred to as ZP gestures, the open hand is held so that the palm faces horizontally downwards or at an oblique angle, depending upon the degree of flexion of the elbow. In all cases the hand is moved in a rapid horizontal lateral movement, away from the midline of the speaker's body. These gestures may be performed with one hand or with two. The contexts in which these gestures are used can all be interpreted as involving a reference to some line of action that is being suspended, interrupted or cut off. In contrast to the VP gestures, however, this interruption in the line of action is due to external circumstances and is not something that the speaker controls or seeks to control.

The contexts in which we have observed ZP gestures in use include the following. (1) When a person states that something they were trying to do or something they had embarked upon was stopped or interrupted by something or someone else, or when a situation is described which renders some project or its continuation impossible. The ZP gesture may be used in such contexts, whether the speaker uses negative or positive terms to characterize the situation. (2) When reference is made to circumstances in which no further action is necessary, as when a statement is made that is deemed complete or sufficient, requiring no further inquiry or comment. (3) When statements are made which are universal, for which no exception is possible. (4) When an extreme assessment is made, whether positive or negative.

In the case of the first type of context mentioned, the ZP gesture may be thought of as a kinesic parallel to the denial, interruption or negation expressed verbally. In the other cases, however, the ZP makes kinesically explicit the denial, interruption or negation that is *implied* by what is in the words.

When making a statement that is deemed sufficient or complete, there is an implication that *no* further comment or action is necessary. When a universal statement is made, the implication is that there can be no exceptions. When an extreme positive assessment is made a negative is again implied, for to assert that something is the best it can possibly be is to imply that there is nothing else as good. In each of these cases the negative implied by the verbal expression is made explicit with the ZP gesture.

We now illustrate these uses with examples and discuss further the interpretations just provided.

(1) Reference to circumstances that render the execution or continuation of some action or project impossible. In Example 95 (Bocce Telefono 7.33, Fig. 13.6), U explains to E how he has tried a certain telephone number but no one replied, and as he says this he uses a version of the ZP gesture. The conversation, which takes place at a Bocce (indoor bowls) club, occurs in the context of an attempt by Bocce Club officials to contact an office regarding inter-town competitions. The lack of any response to the telephone call interrupts this project.

It is interesting to note, in this example, that the ZP gesture is done in relation to "*risponnë*" ('they responded') rather than in association with either "*nun*" ('not') or "*niscunë*" ('no one').[1]

Example 95. Telefono (Bocce) 7.33. **ZP (one hand) .

    Professor, I dialled sixteen   and no one replied
U: Prufessë, ho fatto seidici e nun risponnë niscunë

                |******|

In Example 96 (OMARKET Cheese), an example from England, a woman selling cheeses at a market stall explains to a customer who wants to buy a particular kind of brie that she only has small portions of the kind he wants. She explains that after those are sold that kind of brie will be finished. She says: "Uhm now I haven't got any of the big portions, but there's those small those small ones, the same brie, they're ninety-nine each, and then it's the finish of that particular brie." As she says "the finish", she moves her two open hands, palms down, away from one another horizontally and holds them in position thereafter until the end of the phrase. She uses a two-handed version of the ZP gesture, that is. To say something is 'finished' is to say that any attempt to get

---

[1] Kendon (2002) observes that when a head shake is used in conjunction with a spoken phrase containing a negative particle, it often coincides with the word or phrase that the negative particle modifies, rather than with the negative particle itself.

Fig. 13.6. Example 95. U uses a ZP gesture as he says "*risponnë*" ('responded') when he says he had tried a certain telephone number "*e nun risponnë niscunë*" ('and not responded no one'). The shape of the hand seen in this example, in which the thumb and little finger are extended separately from the other digits, is a variant of the ZP gesture. Frequently seen in the Neapolitan region, it is possibly an emphatic form.

more of it will be thwarted. A potential line of action - in this case acquiring this kind of brie - will thus be interrupted.

In explaining the situation regarding her brie, the woman could have said "there will be no more of that brie" - that is, she could have used an explicitly *negative* expression. As it is, there is, in the woman's statement, an *implied* negative. It is this implied negative that receives explicit expression in the ZP gesture. The speaker also uses a head shake as she says "of that" and this reinforces this interpretation. This is not unlike what we saw in Example 93 (p. 254) where the speaker, when saying she uses "*un po' di passata veramente*" ('a little *passata*, truly'), implies that she does *not* use much - and this implication, made explicit in her VP gesture, is *also* indicated by the use of a head shake, just as she says "*passata*".

A further example illustrating how a ZP gesture may be used in contexts where a state of affairs that could be described with a negative expression is described with a positive term is seen in Example 97 (Iacone I, 050503). This is taken from the recording Iacone, where the speaker, P, is recalling the journey to Rome that he and his young wife made, years ago, when they were first married. He recalls how they went to the Vatican to receive a blessing from the Pope but when they had finished this they could not remember the way back to their hotel. He suggested that they find something to eat first, and then find the hotel, but his wife wanted to find the hotel first. In consequence, because they were lost and it took them a long time to find the hotel, they got quite hungry. P says it was "*na giornatë proprio digiunë*" ('a day of true fasting'). As he says "*proprio digiunë*" ('true fasting') he uses a ZP gesture. He could have said something like *"una giornata senza mangiare"* ('a day without eating') in which case the ZP gesture would have paralleled the negative expressed by *"senza"* ('without') but here he uses a positive term *"digiuno"* ('fasting') but uses a ZP gesture at the same time. The ZP gesture that he uses has the very abstract meaning we have attributed to it, but its use here in conjunction with the expression *"proprio digiunë"* ('true fasting') makes a direct reference to the prevention, interruption or impossibility of something. In this context it seems to make the whole expression more vivid.

(2) *Reference to circumstances which render unnecessary further action, inquiry or comment.* In Example 98 (DSGA I 00.17.30), Salvatore has been asked by Massimo (who serves as a conversational stimulant for this recording) how you can tell someone is a Neapolitan if you see them in the street. Salvatore says you can see it immediately. As he says this he uses a ZP gesture. In this case, to say, as Salvatore does, that one can recognize a Neapolitan at once, implies that it is not necessary to engage in any further scrutiny or inquiry. The ZP gesture here makes manifest this implication.

Example 98. DSGA I 00.17. 30. **ZP gesture (one hand).

One sees at once
S: Si vede subito
     |***********|

When you see the people in the middle of the street, they are Neapolitan, it's clear.
Quando virë la gente in mezzo alla strada, sono napuletan, è chiaro.
                                            |************|

In Example 99 (DSGA I 21.09) Concetta has been asked by Massimo to describe what, for her, constitutes 'true Naples'. In her reply she lists the streets that, in her opinion, form the boundary of the true 'heart' of the city. This she summarizes by saying that just in this part (where she lives) is Naples, with the implication that other places are not true Naples. She says: *"Proprio questa qua è Napoli"* ('Just this here is Naples'). As she says *"è Napoli"* ('is Naples'), she uses a ZP gesture which, in our interpretation, indicates that any other proposal about Naples that might be thought of is rendered unnecessary or unacceptable.

(3) *Universal statements which exclude all other possibilities.* In Example 100 (DSGA 23.05), C talks about the people from Naples who live in the north. She says that these people cook in the Neapolitan fashion. She claims that all southerners in the north cook in this fashion with the implication that there are no exceptions. She says: *"...però o' meridionale che sta là cucinë napoletanë"*

Fig. 13.7   Example 99. C uses a horizontal ZP gesture as she says *"è Napoli"* in *"Proprio questa qua è Napoli"* ('Just this here is Naples'). Another example of the possibly emphatic form of the ZP gesture.

('but the southerner that stays there [i.e. in the north], cooks Neapolitan'). As she says *"cucinë napoletanë"* ('cooks Neapolitan'), she uses a ZP gesture (in this case with a repeated horizontal lateral movement, rapid and with restricted amplitude), at the same time, shaking her head.

In Examples 98, 99 and 100, in each case, in what the speaker says in words a negative is implied. In the case where one can "see immediately" someone is a Neapolitan, the implication is that it is *not* necessary to look further. In the case where it is asserted that "this here" is Naples, it is implied that what lies beyond "here" is *not* Naples. And if it is asserted that the southerner who lives in the north cooks in a Neapolitan manner, the implication is that such a person cooks in *no* other manner. As we noted in this last example, the speaker also uses a head shake as she makes this assertion. This reinforces the interpretation that there is an implied negative in what the speaker says here.

(4) *Positive assessments.* A ZP gesture (and also, in some cases, an associated head shake) may also be used when making a positive assessment. Some writers have sought to account for this apparently paradoxical usage by suggesting that in such contexts these gestures now serve as intensifiers and must be treated differently from the other cases.[2] We agree that they are intensifiers but argue that they are so just because they express an implied negative. A positive assessment that carries with it the implication that nothing else is as good as the evaluated object is an intensified evaluation. If I use a ZP gesture or a head shake, or both together, when I make a positive evaluation of something, my gestures intensify my evaluation. By using them, I bring in the implication that there are no others of the class of objects I am referring to that can be similar in value.

[2] M. H. Goodwin (1980) and McClave (2000) suggest this in regard to the head shake.

This point is supported by the fact that positive assessments are sometimes made using an explicit negative. For example, if I have seen a sunset that was overwhelming in its beauty, I might say "It was the most extraordinary sunset I have ever seen" but I might equally well say "I have never seen a sunset as extraordinary" and I might also say "You have no idea how extraordinary it was" or "You cannot imagine how beautiful it was." As people use expressions of this type, they may use a ZP gesture or a head shake, and sometimes both. We see this in the following two examples.

In Example 101 (Portiere F 04.32), an elderly Neapolitan is talking about what it used to be like in Naples during the war. He participated, he says, in the Neapolitan resistance to the German occupation of the city at the end of the Second World War. He then goes on to say that, later, he spent time in Germany and he found that the Germans were very kind to him, so kind, indeed, that it is not possible to conceive of greater kindness. And as he expresses this idea he uses a ZP gesture and a head shake:

Example 101. Portiere F. 04.32. **ZP gesture (one hand); ++Head shake.

> and the actions that I have had from the Germans, one cannot imagine,
> PF: e le azione che ho avuto dai tedeschi, non può immaginare,
> |***************|
>   <++++++>
>
> these [actions] I have not had from the Neapolitans
> quelle che non ho avuto, dai napolitani

The form of verbal expression used by PF, in this case, as will be seen, though it makes an extreme positive assessment is, nevertheless, a negative expression.

This use of a negative gestural expression as an intensifier in positive evaluations can also be seen in certain uses of the head shake. For instance, in an example described in Kendon (2002, Example VII.4, p. 174), a speaker is giving an account of her recent trip to China and Japan. She describes the gardens she has seen in Japan. Here, like PF in Example 101, the speaker uses a negative expression to give an extreme positive assessment, making explicit the claim that is made in such cases that there is *no match* for what has been experienced.

Example VII.4. Texas Th. 03.28.24. +++ Head shake

> S: The gardens. I mean it was every leaf was entering into its maturity just so.
>   I just went "Ahh!"
>   I never saw anything more beautiful in my life.
>   <+++++++++++++>

In the cases just given, the negative gestures, whether head shake or ZP gesture or both, match the verbal expression. Where the verbal expression is positive and yet we see a head shake or a ZP gesture (or both), such gestures serve as intensifiers, but they do so, as we have suggested, just because they give expression to the negative that is always implied in positive assessments. Thus, when the same speaker, S (Kendon 2002, Example VII.3, pp. 173-174), in another part of her account of her travels, tells of a school for artistic children that she visited in China she says:

Example VII.3. Texas Th. 00.31.10. +++ Head shake

S: And the children are given this by the government so that they can excel.
    The children were charming.
    <+++++++++++++++++++>

She shakes her head as she makes this positive statement about the children. The head shake here refers to the implication that there could not have been any children more charming.

To return to ZP gestures, we likewise see them with positively expressed positive assessments where they serve in just the same way, as the following two examples illustrate. Example 102 is taken from another of our Neapolitan conversations, this time from LB in which a woman who runs a shop selling figurines for the Neapolitan *presepe* (Christmas crib) talks about the characteristics of Naples. The speaker is asked about Neapolitan cooking. Immediately LB, the speaker, intervenes to say: "*La cucina napoletana è (...) è la più bella cucina*" ('Neapolitan cooking is (...) is the finest cooking'). As she says this she uses a two-handed ZP gesture. Notice that she performs the gesture twice.

Example 102. LB 11.56.32. **Two-handed ZP gesture.

	Neapolitan cooking is	it is the finest cooking
LB	la cucina napoletana è (.........) è la più bella cucina	
	<************>~~~<****>	

In Example 103, this time from a recording of a conversation among young women undergraduates in the eastern United States, S has been describing a class that she enjoys. She declares "I absolutely adore it!" As she says "absolutely" she moves her left hand laterally in a (rather ill-defined) version of a ZP gesture.

Example 103. ES (Schwarz) I: 8.00.17. **ZP gesture (one hand).

S: The class is fascinating 'cos it's
        Like I've decided that that's what I wanna do
        And I (...) absolutely adore it
                |********|

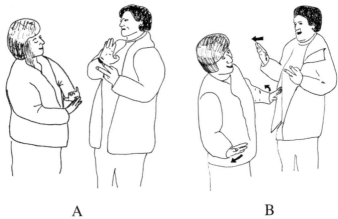

A   B

Fig.13.8   Example 102. A shows the start, B shows the completion of the stroke of the first of two gesture-phrases of LB. Note that M performs the same ZP gesture simultaneously (but with one hand only). His left hand maintains a "two" shape because he had just listed two things to discuss, of which one was Neapolitan cooking, the other the *presepe*. LB interrupts him with her remark about Neapolitan cooking and thus, for M, the *presepe* still remains on the agenda.

Concluding comments on Open Hand Prone gestures

Our comparative study of the discourse contexts in which we observe the use of Open Hand Prone gestures (both Vertical Palm or VP gestures and Horizontal Palm or ZP gestures) has led us to the interpretation that all the members of this family share in the expression of a common semantic theme, that of interrupting, suspending or stopping a line of action - 'line of action' here being understood to mean any kind of project that someone might be engaged in, whether a line of physical action, communicative action (such as saying something), or of mental activity, such as following a line of thought or assuming a certain mental attitude toward something. The gestures we have been concerned with in this section all appear to mark 'stopping' in some way.

One group of these gestures, the Vertical Palm or VP group, we interpreted as an indication of the actor's intent to stop a line of action, whether this be the actor's own, the line jointly engaged in with others, or that of the interlocutor. In this group of gestures it is as if the speaker uses the flat surface of the hand to establish a barrier to stop something in progress, to push back or to stop something that is advancing toward him, to push something away, or to keep something from rising up before him.

Horizontal Palm or ZP gestures, in contrast, those in which the 'open' hand, oriented so that the palm tends to face downwards, is moved laterally, horizontally, rapidly ('decisively', one might say), away from the mid-line of the actor's body, perhaps derive from the action of cutting something through, knocking something away or sweeping away irregularities on a surface, as in rubbing out any marks or traces of something (Calbris 2003 includes this gesture in her analysis of 'cutting' gestures). We suggest that what the actor is doing with these gestures is showing that something in progress is interrupted, that some process is cut off. However, in the ZP gesture, it is not the intent or wish to interrupt the actor's own line of action or that of another that is signalled. Rather, the gesture shows that some line of action *is interrupted*. So whereas in VP gestures the actor engages in a schematic act of stopping something or holding something back, in ZP gestures the actor uses an action to *represent* some event or circumstance of which he is not the author. These two kinds of gestures, thus, would seem to be quite different, semiotically. Vertical Palm gestures constitute actions that the actor wilfully performs. Horizontal Palm gestures are actions that *describe* something that has happened, is happening or could happen.

Can we regard Open Hand Prone gestures as gestures of *negation*? We have suggested that, in all the situations in which we see these gestures being used, there is the implication that there is a line of action to be stopped or that will be or would be stopped. But to stop something or to describe something that is being stopped is not, in itself, an act of negation. However, if I claim something and you stop my claim, the relationship created between the two acts constitutes *denial*. Likewise, if an assertion is made about a state of affairs and, at the same time, treating that assertion like an object, I knock it to one side, then the assertion can be said to be negated. These gestures, then, come to serve as negations if there is something presupposed in relation to which they act. In everyday situations of conversation, spoken language provides what is to be presupposed and the gestures act *on* these presuppositions.

These gestures may be regarded as *operator* gestures (and may be included in the broader group of *modal* pragmatic gestures, accordingly), just as the spoken language particles of 'no' and 'never' and the like are verbal operators. Spoken language negative particles have the specific function of acting to negate or deny something, and their operations are limited to whatever is expressed in the words in the constructions in which they occur. On the other hand, the Open Hand Prone gestures we have been discussing (and also the head shakes that so often accompany them, as described in Kendon 2002), although they can be used like verbal negative particles, they can also be used to draw into a current utterance the dialogic context that the utterance implies. Thus when Concetta (in Example 99, p. 258) says *"Proprio questa qua è*

Napoli" ('Just this here is Naples') and employs a ZP gesture as she says *"è Napoli"* she *adds* a reference to ideas that might not be in accord with this and simultaneously blocks them or stops them. Or when LB, in Example 102 (p. 261) declares that *"la cucina napoletana è la più bella cucina"* ('Neapolitan cooking is the most beautiful cooking') and uses a two-handed ZP gesture as she does so, she *adds* a reference to the idea that some cuisine might be better than that of Naples which, simultaneously, she cuts off or interrupts. We maintain that the head shake in Example VI.3 (quoted from Kendon 2002) functions in a similar fashion.

In such cases the OHP gestures (and/or head shakes) are not serving as operators on the words they are associated with. Were they to do so, they would contradict what is being asserted. Rather, it is as if they conjure up counter responses that might be evoked by what is said, and then operate in relation to *that*. They enrich the utterances of which they are a part, by making reference to the *dialogue* that any assertion implies. They simultaneously evoke this dialogue and make a move within it.

The Open Hand Supine (OHS) or 'palm up' family of gestures[3]

We turn now to the second 'open hand' family to be discussed in this chapter, the Open Hand Supine or 'palm up' family, in which the open hand is maintained on a supine forearm, so that the palm of the hand faces upwards.

The gestures of this family are very widely used, and various versions of them have been described by others from Quintilian down to the present day. Müller (2004) reviews many of these descriptions and shows that the various meanings that have been attributed to Open Hand Supine gestures (which she calls gestures of the Palm Up Open Hand) have in common the idea that it is a gesture of offering or giving, or a gesture of showing readiness to receive something. Müller suggests that it is derived from the action of extending the open hand with the palm oriented upwards as is done when some object is being offered to another, shown to another or when an object is requested from another. It is supposed that the gesture continues to mean 'giving' or 'expecting to receive something' even when it is used in contexts where physical objects are not involved. As a consequence, it serves to define whatever might be the content of the utterance of which the gesture is a part as being something being 'given' or as something being 'asked for'. Expressions such as "let me offer an idea" or "let me give an example" or "give me an explanation" are in common use. Open Hand Supine gestures perhaps provide kinesic parallels to such uses.

In the gestures in this family that are accountable in terms of the themes of 'offering' and 'receiving', the Open Hand Supine may be extended into

---

[3] Maria Graziano collaborated in the work reported in this section. See Graziano (2003).

the space immediately in front of the speaker, as if it is being presented or displayed there. It may also be directed toward the interlocutor, as when, for example, the speaker requests something or offers something. It may also be used in indicating objects in the external environment. Examples of this were discussed in Chapter 11. As was explained there, when pointing with the Open Hand Supine, the speaker seems to 'present for inspection' or to 'display' the object pointed at, rather than merely to individuate it. A gesture in which the Open Hand Supine is 'presented' or 'displayed' but which is not moved as if to indicate something will be called a *Palm Presentation (PP) gesture*. A gesture in which the Open Hand Supine is directed toward something (whether to another person or an object) will be called a *Palm Addressed (PA) gesture*. Together we may refer informally to these two kinds of gesture as 'palm presenting' gestures.

These contrast with a third kind within the Open Hand Supine family in which the open hand with palm up is moved laterally and often somewhat backwards, as well. Both hands are often employed (PP gestures are usually one handed, and PA gestures perhaps always so) and the effect of the lateral and backwards movement is that the hands, moving away from one another, withdraw from the speaker's central and frontal space. A gesture with these characteristics will be referred to as a *PL gesture*. There is a tendency for gestures of this kind to be combined with a raising of the shoulders in a 'shrug' and a certain range of characteristic facial expressions (see Fig. 13.12, Example 126 for an example). The more extensive and conspicuous these extra-manual components are, the more intense the expression conveyed by the PL gesture may be said to be.

The semantic theme of PL gestures is that of '*withdrawal*' rather than that of 'offering' or 'presentation'. The lateral and backward movement of the hands appears to indicate that whatever has been presented is being withdrawn from, as if it is being let stand or abandoned. As we shall see, PL gestures are found in contexts where the speaker displays either an unwillingness to intervene with respect to something, or an inability to do so. For example, we see the PL gesture in use when a speaker asks a question for which there can be no answer, when a response is being given to a situation which cannot be helped or for which no solution can be offered, or when something is being expressed that is 'obvious', that is to say, something that is redundant and about which nothing further can be said.

Palm Presentation (PP) gestures

As already described, in PP gestures the speaker extends the Open Hand Supine into immediate frontal space. Commonly, this is achieved through a wrist extension, often combined with a slight lowering of the hand, and followed by a hold.

The PP gesture is typically used in association with passages in the verbal discourse which serve as an introduction to something the speaker is about to say, or serve as an explanation, comment or clarification of something the speaker has just said. We illustrate this with examples of PP gestures in use in the following contexts: (1) passages in which the speaker supplies an explanation for a term or a phrase just used; (2) when the speaker is expounding the premises or conditions for understanding something; (3) when the circumstances that provide the setting for a narrative are being described; (4) when a conclusion or a summary with regard to something that has just been said is being given.

(1) *Explaining the meaning of a term or a phrase.* In the recording GB (Example 104, GB Cobthorne 00.51.13), GB is talking about the name of the town he will give a tour of. He explains that the name could derive from the name of an ancient tribe that settled in the area of the town. He says: "Uhm 'undela' is one of the phrases or words that's used and that cou- can mean 'undivided'. Now it could be that there was a tribe called Undela, meaning an undivided tribe." All of the first part of his discourse is without manual gestures, but as he says "meaning an undivided tribe" he extends his right hand in a PP gesture.

Similarly, in Example 105, from Schwarz (Schwarz I 031503), a recording of a group of young women who are talking about the courses they are taking at their university, one of them states that she is taking a course in neuropsychology. She is asked to explain this. She says "What it is, is like studying how the brain functions" and as she says "functions" she uses a PP gesture. She goes on to explain that one way to study how the brain functions is to "study people who've got problems with parts of their brain". She continues: "So there's like one type of problem where uhm, it's called 'neglect', people just neglect half of the world." As she gives the name of the problem, saying "it's called 'neglect'", she uses a PP gesture.

In Example 106 (GB 2:20:40) GB, the tour guide, has just drawn the attention of his tourists to a bookshop known as "the School Bookshop". He continues with the following: "Now that's one of the best bookshops in Northamptonshire. Why? Because to a large extent they've got a captive audience, if you like. They've got the staff of the school, they've got the pupils." With this last phrase he explains what he means by a "captive audience" and as he does so he uses a PP gesture.

(2) *Expounding the premises or conditions for understanding something.* In Example 107 (Iacone II 073000), Signora Iacone is explaining how her mother did not want her to marry the man she had chosen because he was not a farmer, he did not cultivate land. As she explained it, "*pëcchè 'o campagnuolë nun së morë maj 'e fammë*" ('because the farmer never dies of hunger'). This seemed

important at the time, just after the Second World War when, in the area around Naples, there were great food shortages and only those who had land to cultivate did not suffer from hunger. In this discourse, in association with the phrase quoted in which C gives her mother's reason for preferring a farmer as her daughter's husband, she uses the PP gesture.

Again, in Example 108 (Schwarz I 031503), the same speaker as in Example 105 continues to talk about the course in neuropsychology she is following. She gives an account of a particular neuropathological problem known as 'neglect'. She explains that when people develop this problem they refuse to admit there is anything wrong with them. In Example 108 she tells a story as a specific illustration of the problem. Her speech and pertinent PP gestures are shown in the following transcription:

Example 108 Schwarz I 031503. ** PP; >*> OHS moved right to a new location.

So there's this woman, she's in the doctor's office
|~~~~~~************|>*>*>*>*>***********|
　　　　　[6]　　　　　　　　　　[7]

and she can't, she doesn't recognize half of her body.

She's neglecting half of her body and the doctor walks over an' picks up her arm

and says "Whose arm is this?" and she goes "Well, that's your arm"

and he's an Indian doctor
|~~~~~***********|
　　　　[8]

In this example it will be seen how the speaker employs a PP gesture as she sets up the conditions for the narrative ([6] and [7]) and then, again, when she explains that the doctor was an "Indian doctor" [8]. This is also a condition for understanding the story. That the patient refused to recognize her own arm even when the skin colour of the doctor who picked up her arm was clearly different from hers, makes the phenomenon even more remarkable.

(3) *Giving an account of circumstances that provide the setting for a narrative.* In Example 109, again from the recording Iacone, C is telling a story about how she and her husband got lost in Rome when they went there for the first time on their *viaggio di nozze* (honeymoon). They went to the Vatican to receive a blessing from the Pope, but then when it came time for them to leave for their hotel they did not know which way to go. In setting the stage for the description of this moment, C lists the succession of things they did that day, and for each item in the list she uses a PP gesture. In the extract shown in the

transcript, she uses a single-handed PP in segment [1], in [2] and [3] it is two handed, and in [4], [5] and [6] the PP gestures continue to be two handed, but now are displaced to the left, to the centre, and to the left again. Each item on the list is thus marked by a new PP, further differentiated by contrasts in the space used for the strokes. At the end of the list, when she says "*Quann ascett'm ro' Papa, ch' strad' eram piglia?*" ('When we came out from the Pope, what road were we to take?') she uses a vertically oscillated G-family gesture (form B from this group), followed by a head shake combined with leaning forward and looking straight at her interlocutor.

Example 109 IAC I 052809. ** P-P; gg G, form B; ++ Head shake; ??? Untranscribable

> all the roads lead to Rome.   And we started to walk.
> C: tuttë 'e stradë portanë a Romë. Cë mëttettëmë 'ncamminë
>
> And we walked, we went to the Pope,   to mass, the blessing
> E cammënajëmë, jettëmë addo Papa, 'a messë, 'a benerizionë,
> |**************|********************|*******|***********|
>   [1]   [2]   [3]   [4]
>   1 hand   2 hands   2 hands 2 hands left
>
> [??????]   and received the parchment
> [???????] e cë rettë 'a pergamenë
> |*******|*****************|
>   [5]   [6]
>
> When we came out from the Pope, what road were we to take?
> Quannë ascettëmë ro' Papa, chë stradë eramë pigliá?
>
> |gggggggggggggggggggggggggg|+++++++++++++++++++|

Quite similar to this usage is the usage of the PP gesture that may be seen when a speaker gives examples that provide the details of something that is being described. Thus in Example 110 from the recording Crick, SC, who has worked as a caterer, is discussing how she first became interested in food. She says that when she was a young girl she worked as a waitress in the dining room of one of the residential houses of the famous old public school that dominated the town where she grew up. She recalls being very impressed with a great Christmas dinner, and it was this great feast that first aroused her interest in food.

In the passage in which she describes the feast there is an introductory and concluding passage, but there is also a passage in which she lists the items that made up the menu of the dinner. This list serves as an explanation for the statement "And we had the complete Christmas dinner." It is just in association with the list of items that illustrates what might be meant by this that the speaker uses PP gestures, one stroke for each item on the list.

Example 110 Crick I 053102 'Turkey' ** PP gesture (two hands).

And we had the complete Christmas dinner uhm

(...1.7...) turkey and all the trimmings and all this sort of thing
|~~~~********|
   [1]

And then the Christmas pudding (..0.43..) and then came the mince pies
~~~~~~~~~~*************|-.-.-.-.-.-.~~~~~~~**************|
    [3]   [4]

(..0.56..) and bowls of oranges and sweets and nuts
~~~~~~~~*****************|~~~*****|~~~~***|
     [5]   [6]   [7]

An' I'd never seen any and the table was decorated beautifully

In a similar example, Example 111, from Iacone (Iacone I 011503), there is a part of the discussion in which conditions during the Second World War are being recalled. Signora Iacone and Signore Iacone had been describing in general terms how they were afraid during the bombardments, but they became habituated and were able to escape from immediate fear so long as they remained in the underground shelters where they had to stay for many hours. One of her young interlocutors, M, asks what people used to do in those shelters. In her reply Signora Iacone lists some of the different activities. Here the list provides concrete detail and elaborates the more general description of what people did during the bombardments. Each item on the list of activities she provides is accompanied by a PP gesture, each positioned differently in the speaker's immediate gesture space:

Example 111 Iacone I 011503. *** PP; idid Index finger extended palm neutral

But then what did you do under there, madam?
M : E ma po' ch' faciv'n' là sott' signo'?

The fear, one prayed, some sang, some played games, some laughed, according to the person, let's say.
C : 'A paura, si pregava, chi cantavë, chi pazziavë, ch rirevë, secondo i soggetë diciamo
|~~*********|*************|**********|*******|idididididididididid|
   [1]   [2]   [3]   [4]   [5]

In strokes [1] to [3] C lowers her right hand, open with palm up, in each of three different locations on her lap. In [4] both hands open with palm up are extended toward her interlocutor. In [5] she directs her hand forward with index finger extended. This is perhaps an 'abstract point' in which the idea of pointing to different persons is expressed. In this example, thus, we see that as each different activity of the people in the bomb shelter is listed it receives its own P-gesture stroke, each one performed in a different position in space.

(4) *Giving a conclusion or summary for something just said, or making a comment on it.* In Example 112 (GB School Bookshop 00.25.28), GB has been describing several buildings that may be seen in the market square of Northant. The last building in this succession of descriptions, each one of which has been accompanied by a pointing gesture of some kind (in most cases the Open Hand Palm Away form - see Chapter 11) is a bank, which has a rather elaborated nineteenth-century façade that sets it apart from the other buildings which still retain the simpler appearance of buildings from earlier centuries. He directs his left hand, formed as Open Hand Palm Away and sustained on a fully extended arm, toward the bank, which is some distance away to his left. As he extends his hand in this fashion he begins his discourse and he sustains his Open Hand Palm Away pointing gesture throughout, until he ends with a final comment in which he draws a comparison between the bank and "everything else in this beautiful little town". As he makes this final comment he orients more completely toward the group of tourists and switches from his left hand to his right hand, now using a PP gesture with three distinct strokes, in each of which the OHS hand is lowered and held (each lowering separated by a preparatory lift of the hand). The placement of the PP strokes is shown in the transcript (only PP gestures are shown). See also Fig. 13.9.

Example 112. GB School Bookshop 00.25.28. ~~~ preparation; *** PP (held); -.-. recovery.

You've got a glorious rich uh victoriana for the National Westminster Bank.

And that's quality of its of its type.

Uhm I'm not normally a great enthusiast for victoriana

but I I have to confess that that has quality to it

and it it stands up to the uh scrutiny

that everything else calls for in this beautiful little town.

|~~~~~~~~~~~***~~~~~*****~~~~************-.-.-.|

   [1]   [2]   [3]

In Example 113 (GB School Bookshop 01.50.29), also taken from the recording GB, GB has been discussing aspects of the structure of the house now occupied by the bookshop. He ends by drawing the attention of his group to the fact that on the wall that projects above the lower building that is attached to it one can see an unfinished surface of rough stones. He says that that "indicates that before the Rose and Crown was there, there was a different building there earlier". Then he concludes with "Now that's the kind

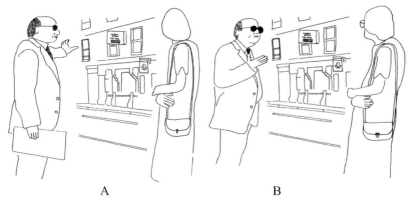

A   B

Fig. 13.9   Example 112. GB directs Open Hand Prone (palm away) toward the façade of
a building he is praising (A). Then he addresses an Open Hand Supine (palm up) toward
his audience as he offers a general comment (B). See transcript for Example 112.

of thing that uhm you can speculate a grea- about a great deal." Throughout
this concluding comment he uses the PP.

The examples given illustrate some of the commoner contexts of use in
which the PP gesture is used. In all of the instances described here, it will
be noted that while the speaker uses a PP gesture, in the verbal component
something is being said which, if it is to be interpreted properly, must be
applied to the main topic of the discourse. Thus, the PP is used when a term
or a phrase is being explained which makes for better comprehension of the
discourse in which the term or phrase is used. It is used when the speaker
gives conditions necessary for understanding a narrative or an explanation,
and it is used when the speaker comments on something previously said. The
PP gesture, thus, seems to be used to mark passages in the verbal discourse in
which some other aspect of the speaker's discourse is now the topic. That is
to say, it is associated with stretches of talk which stand in a *meta-discursive*
relationship to the rest of the speaker's discourse.

Palm Addressed (PA) gestures

We have already noted that the Open Hand Supine may be used in pointing.
As we said in Chapter 11, when the Open Hand Supine is used when pointing
to some object, it is as if the speaker 'presents' the object to the interlocutor as
something to be looked at or inspected for some quality to which the speaker
wishes to draw attention. When the Open Hand Supine is directed toward the
speaker's interlocutor, or to another participant, as we saw, for instance, in
Example 56 (pp. 212, 213), this is often done in contexts where the speaker

is acknowledging another as a source of something said or indicates that what another has said is correct. In addition to this, however, as will now be illustrated, the Open Hand Supine may be directed toward another as if the hand is being placed to offer something, or to receive something. For example, we see it used in conjunction with verbal expressions using the verb 'to give' or we see it used as if to indicate that one expects or hopes to receive something specific from the other to whom it is directed, such as some information, an explanation or a justification for something or, indeed, some physical object.

Thus, in Example 114 from the recording Commerciante (Commerciante III 004258), one of the students filming the card-players asks if they are bothering them by filming them. Peppe replies *"No, no assolutamente, mi dispiace che non vi possiamo dare più grande soddisfazione"* ('No, no, absolutely, I am sorry we can't give you greater satisfaction'). As he says *"non vi possiamo dare più grande soddisfazione"* ('we can't give you greater satisfaction') he directs his right hand as an Open Hand Supine toward his interlocutor in a clear version of the PA gesture, here directly associated with the verb *dare* ('to give').

Example 115 shows how the PA may be used to make explicit the expectation of receiving something. This example is also taken from Commerciante (Commerciante IV 00.50.36). Here Peppe asks his opponent, whose turn it is to play, if he has one of the 'money' cards (the players are using Neapolitan playing cards as they play the game of *tre sette*). As he says *"ma në tienë rënarë?"* ('but you have one of the money?' - i.e. one of the cards on which coins are represented) he places his Open Hand Supine on the table beside the pile of cards already played. By doing this he shows an expectation that the pile will receive the next card in play.

Example 116 (Iacone I 032913) illustrates the use of the PA in a context where the speaker is acknowledging something another has just said. This is similar to Example 56 in Chapter 11. The conversation is concerned with the period immediately after World War II when many people in Naples and the surrounding district had very little to eat and they used to eat weeds gathered from the sides of the roads. These weeds included poppies, which had a soporific effect because of the opium they contained. M has just been told that people also used to eat poppies. Upon hearing this she says: *"E se li mangiavanë? E chillë dice ca so' velenosi!"* ('And they used to eat them? It's said that they are poisonous!'). Immediately she says this, her interlocutor, P, says *"L'oppio! Eee së 'e mangiavënë, së 'e mangiavënë!"* ('Opium! Eee they used to be eaten, they used to be eaten!'). As he says *"L'oppio!"* ('Opium!') he directs an Open Hand Supine towards his interlocutor, in this way acknowledging that she is right in what she said when she said they were poisonous (see Fig. 13.10). Note how, at the same time, he names the poison in question. Two moves are performed simultaneously here: P at once shows that he has understood what M has

Fig. 13.10   Example 116. P directs Open Hand Supine (palm up) or PA towards M as he acknowledges that she understands correctly that poppies are poisonous, adding that they contain opium as he does so.

said and shows that she is correct in what she has said. At the same time, he supplies information, he specifies just why the poppies are poisonous.

The PA gesture is also used when something specific is indicated that the speaker desires to obtain from the interlocutor. This is the 'question' context of use of this gesture. In Example 117, from Iacone, P, the husband, has explained that he and his wife have just completed forty-six years of marriage but that this was preceded by a thirteen-year engagement. M expresses great surprise at this and turns to C, P's wife, saying "*Oo oo è questa che voglio sapere*" ('Oh ho! It is this that I would like to hear about!'). As she says "*questa*" ('this') she extends her Open Hand Supine forward toward C, indicating at once the long engagement, which is associated with C, as well as her request to receive something from C about it.

Discussion of the 'palm presenting' (PP and PA) gestures.

Both PP and PA gestures can be interpreted as gestures of 'offering', 'presenting' or being 'ready to receive', as Morris (1977) and Müller (2004) have suggested. In several of the examples described in this chapter and also in Chapter 11, the *motif* of 'offering' or 'presenting' often seems to be almost explicitly present. Thus, when the speaker points to something using the PA this is often combined with a phrase that suggests that the speaker is inviting a certain regard toward the object being indicated, as if the speaker is putting the object 'on offer' for contemplation. And in the cases where the Open Hand Supine is directed toward the interlocutor to indicate that something they just said is the source of what the current speaker is just now saying (as in Example 54, p. 211) or that what the interlocutor just said is correct (as in Example 116, p. 273), or that it is something that the interlocutor just said that provokes the speaker's question (Example 117, p. 273), it is as if what the interlocutor just said is being 'handed back' to the interlocutor or, in the last case, as if the speaker is holding the hand out ready to receive just some specific thing from the interlocutor.

In many other examples, however, when it is 'presented' rather than combined with the 'movement toward' of pointing, the Open Hand Supine is used in contexts in which the verbal discourse framed by the PP is discourse that has a *meta*-status in relation to the discourse focus. How can we understand the functioning of the Open Hand Supine in these cases? If it serves to indicate the *meta*-status of what the speaker is saying, how does it do so?

If we say that the Open Hand Supine gesture may be best understood as being derived from the action of offering something to another or showing a readiness to receive something, we say that the placing of the Open Hand Supine before the interlocutor serves as an *invitation* to take something or to give something. Now an object involved in a transaction of giving or receiving is an object that has a transitional status. It cannot be used for anything until the transaction of giving or receiving has been completed. We suggest that the PP gesture could work as a marker for the meta-discursive nature of the speaker's verbal discourse because it shows that the speaker is inviting the interlocutor to regard what is being said as having a transitional status in respect to the rest of the discourse (or in respect to the focus of the discourse that is shared by all of the participants). That is to say, the content of the verbal discourse that is framed by the PP gesture is being made available as something that can be given or taken, but is not *yet* in current use. What the speaker says while using the PP proposes how what is being said is to be used or may be used, but the discourse framed by the PP has the transitional status of discourse not yet in actual use.

Thus, a speaker's explanation of the meaning of a term (see Examples 104–106, p. 266) makes it possible to use that term in subsequent discourse, but the term itself is not in use while the explanation is being given. In the same way, when a speaker describes a series of circumstances which must be appreciated before the narrative that is to be given can be fully understood (as in Example 109, p. 268), while the circumstances are being described they are not yet in use. Their use comes only after the description has been completed. And again, when a speaker comments on something just said (as in examples 111 and 112, pp. 269-270), the speaker is suggesting how what has been said is to be interpreted, but as the comment is being made this interpretation is not yet in actual application. Hence the comments, as they are being made, have a transitional status and we suggest that it is this that the PP gesture indicates.

We may say, thus, that in using the Open Hand Supine in presenting or pointing, the 'invitation' or 'offer/receive' force of this gesture is being exploited to frame the spoken discourse and to show that the spoken discourse so framed has the transitional status that an object has when it is involved in the transaction of giving/receiving.

Open Hand Supine with lateral movement: PL gestures

In gestures in this group the movement of the hand or hands is lateral, away from the speaker's mid-line. Sometimes this movement is extended so that the hand or hands move backwards, almost until they are positioned behind the speaker's vertical median. In many cases the movement begins with an outward rotation of the forearm so that one's impression is that of the hand or hands 'opening' as they move apart from one another.

Gestures of this type, here called PL gestures, we have observed in use in the following contexts. (1) When the speaker expresses unwillingness or inability to intervene in respect to something. (2) When the speaker admits, accepts or claims that something is 'obvious', about which nothing further need be said. (3) When the speaker asks a question but has no expectation that an answer will be or can be forthcoming from anyone else. (4) When the speaker displays being open to suggestions or shows that something that has been suggested is a possibility which the speaker neither denies nor accepts. In such cases the gesture is a way of saying that something 'could be so' but without making any commitment to any position with regard to it. (5) When the speaker indicates that the other is free to do something, as when the other is invited to enter a shop, to make themselves comfortable in a restaurant, or in other situations where the speaker shows being available to serve the other.

In all such cases the lateral movement of the Open Hand Supine indicates that the speaker is *not* going to take any action with regard to whatever may be the focus of the moment. By this gesture the speaker shows inability or unwillingness to act, inability or unwillingness to offer any suggestions or solutions, to provide meaning or an appropriate interpretation of something. In the case of invitations the speaker shows that the other will be left free to do whatever they please without intervention by the speaker. The movement *motif* of gestures in this group is that of removing the hands from the arena of action. In this way the speaker displays *non-intervention*. This is the semantic theme of gestures in this PL group.

(1) *Unwillingness or inability to intervene in a situation.* Here the consequences of something just described are regarded as inevitable, or the circumstances leave no options for alternative possible courses of action. In such cases intervention is impossible. The speaker can do nothing about what is being described or, perhaps, the persons in the circumstances described are regarded

as being left with no possibility of doing anything. Thus, in Example 118, from Iacone (Iacone I 024327) the discussion is concerned with using weeds as a source of food during the food shortages in Naples in the Second World War. C has just explained how her family had a piece of land where they could grow vegetables, but that others did not have this. She refers to one family who used to go out and collect weeds from the roadsides. She ends her account by saying *"Facevë l'erbë"* ('they used to collect weeds') and follows this with a conspicuous PL gesture. Indeed, this family had no alternative, and the PL gesture indicates this. In this case the speaker, by using the PL gesture, shows her view that the family referred to had no alternative but to collect weeds.

Again, in Example 119 (Schwarz I 094127), taken from a recording of a conversation among young women undergraduates, the speaker is explaining why she feels unable to get on with her work as she should. She has explained that she has done all her homework and cannot go on with more, even though she feels she should do so. As she says "I can't do anything about that" she performs a PL with wide amplitude (see [1] in the transcript), and another one as she quotes what she will say to her professor when she will ask him what she is supposed to write about. Note that in both cases there is a pause in the speech immediately following the phrase during which the PL gesture begins. The spread hands are held still during this pause in the first instance while in the second instance they are returned rapidly and in an active manner to a rest position in what seems to be a marked action of 'dropping' the hands. They do not merely relax. Further note that, in the second example, in which the speaker acts out what she will say to her professor, she quotes how she will greet him (and this is when she does the PL gesture) and then specifies her question. In both cases the gesture is used as a visible declaration of the speaker's inability to act - that she can't do anything about a certain situation or that she cannot act without instructions from her professor. The pause that follows the speech associated with the gesture seems to be a pause that allows for the gesture's impact to be felt, before the speaker specifies the problem she faces.

Example 119. Schwarz I 094127. oo Open Hand Supine (PL)

But it's like, I have a sociology test coming up in two in three days
I'm studying with a friend tomorrow night and the night after
So like I can't do anything about that (-- -- -)
|~~~~~oooooo<u>ooooooooooooooooooooooooooo</u>o|
                    [1]
I've a paper coming up but I don't have anywhere to start
So I'm going to talk to my professor and say
"Hey like Dude (-- -- --) what's my topic?
     |~~oooooooo-.-.-|
          [2]
Y'know tell me where to look and what to do and I'll do it!"

A PL gesture can also be used by itself, serving as a comment on something others have been saying. Thus in Example 120 (Bocce I 7.45.59), when the puzzling robbery is being discussed, P has just re-stated the fact that the door of the office had been broken down and that this he does not understand. Here, S's response to P's utterance is to say "*Ma*" ('But'). This is then followed by a PL. Here S, by virtue of the PL, displays his unwillingness to enter into any comment on what P has said, his unwillingness to offer any suggestion that might relieve him of his puzzlement.

Example 120. Bocce I 7.45.5. oo Open hand palm up

But this fact that this open door, they broke the door, I haven't understood
P: Ma stu fattë ca chesta porta aperta, scassënë 'a porta nun aggio capitë

But
S: Ma (-- -- -)
l~~ooooooool

(2) *Something is declared 'obvious'. There is nothing further that can be added.* In Example 121 (Iacone I 030419) the use of weeds as a source of food is being discussed. It had been mentioned that poppies were among the weeds consumed. The speaker referred to them as *papagni* which is a Neapolitan term used by older speakers of Neapolitan, although not in much use by younger speakers. P asks his young interlocutor M if she knows what *papagni* are. M says she does not know. P begins to describe the flower but his wife, C, intervenes to give the Italian name. P immediately repeats the name, "*papaveri*" and, as he does so, moves his palm-up-open-hand laterally. Here he is repeating what his wife has just said and to this, of course, there is nothing further to add. And, indeed, M certainly knows the word "*papaveri*".

In Example 122 (Portici Stanze) one of the girls describes her aquarium. She describes the arrangement of the gravel and the rocks, the algae and the perforated tube that delivers the air. All this part of her discourse is accompanied by fairly complex descriptive gestures which serve to complete her descriptions (see Example 41, p.193). She ends her description by saying "*e ci sono i pesci d'entro*" ('and there are fish in it'). As she says this she performs a two-hand PL gesture. The statement that there are fish in the aquarium is not newsworthy. Indeed, it is 'obvious', especially as, at the beginning of her discourse, she had stated that she had "*sei pesci*" ('six fish'). This statement is added here, perhaps to bring the description to completion. The PL gesture that accompanies it here marks this statement as "obvious". Perhaps it could be glossed with the expression *ovviamente* ('obviously') or *naturalmente* ('of course'). The gesture thus serves as a comment on the speaker's own speech.

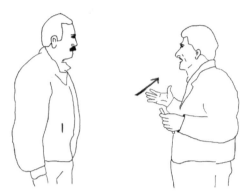

Fig. 13.11   Example 123. Enzo performs a PL gesture as he asks: *"Ma come s'è trovata chiusa chella porta se la chiave non c'era più?"* ('But how was that door found locked if the key wasn't there any more?).

(3) *The speaker asks a rhetorical question, a question for which no answer is expected.* In Example 123 (Bocce I 7.43.08. See Fig. 13.11), again from a passage in which the robbery at the Bocce Club is being discussed, G has just suggested that the door to the office had been broken down by the thief simply as a distraction. E responds by saying: *"Eh ma come s'è trovata chiusa chella porta se la chiave non c'era più? Eeee che è stata sempë apertë!"* ('But how was that door found locked if the key wasn't there any more? Eeee the door had always been unlocked!').

In this passage E is raising a question to which, for him, there is no answer. It is in relation to this that we see the PL being used. As he ends both of his phrases he ends with a two-handed PL which, as we interpret it, has the force here of showing that the speaker himself has nothing he can do about the topic of the question. The lateral movement of the hands here has the significance of 'letting stand' the issue of the locked door with no key available. It is left for others to deal with, if they can. Further, the force of the unanswerable question is maintained with the second part of this two-part discourse where he uses the PL as he makes the assertion *"che è stata sempë apertë!"* ('it had always been unlocked!').

The PL gesture can also appear as a 'tag' to a spoken utterance, showing that, for the speaker, what has just been said raises questions that cannot be answered. Thus, in Example 124 from Bocce I, again from a passage in which the robbery is being discussed (Bocce I 7.54.35), Peppe re-states the situation, that the door to the office was open, and yet the thief breaks down the door, and then he moves his open hand palm up hand laterally, a PL gesture which, as we interpret it, shows that, for the speaker (and so, by implication, for others), no intervention is possible in respect to what has been stated.

Example 124 Bocce I 7.54.35. ** Hand with index finger extended;
nn Open hand palm down; pl open hand palm up moved laterally.

Now you take something there in there.
Mo tu piglia na cosë cca ddinta cca.
|~*~*~*~*~*~*~*~****-.-.-.-.-.-|
     [1]   [2]

Now that was all open, thus he [i.e. the thief] breaks the door there
Mo chillë ha apertë tuttë cosë mo va a scassà 'a portë llà
|~~~~~~~~nnnnnnn-.-.-.|~~~~~~~***************/plplplpl
    [3]   [4]   [5]

Finally, in Example 125 (GB 014200) GB, the tour guide, wants to refer
to a general characteristic of the town to be toured. He says: "What is the
main feature of Northant? And the answer has to be: limestone, beautiful
limestone." As he asks the question "What is the main feature of Northant?"
he moves his right Open Hand Supine laterally in a clear, if brief version of
the PL. As he goes on to supply the answer to his own question, he twice
lowers his hand in a PP gesture. In the first part of this discourse, thus, he
introduces the topic of the "main feature" but does this by way of a question
to which he expects no answer. His use of the PL here serves to mark what he
says as a rhetorical question. GB's use of PP as he then goes on to supply the
answer is a good example of how this gesture is used to frame the discourse
that 'presents' the feature that he is referring to.

(4) *The speaker responds to a proposal by neither accepting it nor rejecting
it.* In Example 126 (Portici Stanze 024800, Fig. 13.12) G tells of a pet
tortoise that she once had, that died. She explains that the tortoise used
to go underneath a wash-tub and it got wet with the water that fell below
when her mother washed the clothes. One of her interlocutors, M, suggests
that the tortoise drowned. G replies with a two-handed PL gesture, and
then continues to explain that the water was falling on the ground where
the tortoise was. R, another member of the group, makes the suggestion
"It drank the water." G turns briefly to R and nods and then turns back to
look at M who suggests that it was because the water was full of soap that
the tortoise died. G's response to this is again to offer a two-handed PL
gesture, and then she simply concludes "*è morta*" ('it is dead'). Note that
in these cases the PL gesture is not accompanied by any articulate speech
- in each case G utters a breathy and partly vocalized exhalation, an
expression which is typically associated with this use of the PL gesture.

    In this example it will be seen, thus, that G twice responds to the
suggestions made by others with a two-handed PL, but she does not
actually accept these suggestions. Her PL gestures here show that she
allows these suggestions as possibilities, neither accepted nor rejected.

Fig. 13.12   Example 126. G performs a PL gesture as she responds to the suggestion that her tortoise died because it drank soapy water. The gesture is used to indicate that the suggestion is neither accepted nor rejected. Note the forward position of the head, open mouth and the lowered eyes. These features are characteristic non-manual components that are often part of this gesture.

Once again we see the *motif* of non-intervention, withdrawal from the arena of action being given expression.

(5) *Invitations*. Finally, the PL gesture may be used as a way of suggesting that the speaker is leaving the situation referred to open for any relevant action by others. In this way, it may be used as a gesture of invitation. Example 127 illustrates this, but it also illustrates how the PL gesture provides the invitation as an 'overlay' to the verbal component of the utterance, a further example of how gestures of this sort can provide levels of meaning beyond or besides those provided by the verbal component. The Example comes from the GB recording (GB Cobthorne 00.40.06) and is found at the beginning of GB's discourse, when he is explaining that he is a Blue Badge Guide. That is, that he is a guide who belongs to a particular organization of tour guides who has had a specific training related to the places where he gives guided tours. His verbal discourse and associated PL gestures are given in the transcript. He hopes that the tourists he is addressing will "use Blue Badge Guides in the future" if they have not encountered them before. The PL gestures associated with "if you've not had experience of us before" and with "use" in "use Blue Badge Guides in the future" here have the force of letting stand without intervention the idea of the "Blue Badge Guide" as something available for use. The PL leaves this idea available for others to take up and in this way it shows the speaker is offering an invitation.

Notice that in this example, the invitation appears as a consequence of the PL gesture. It is only implied by the verbal discourse.

Example 127 GB Cobthorne 00:40:06.

lll P-L; ~~~ preparation; -.-.-. recovery.

uhm Blue Badge Guides are available almost everywhere in the country these days

an' I hope uh if you've not had experience of us before

|~~~~~~~~~~lllllllllllllllllllllllllllllllllllllll-.-.-.-.-.-.|

[1]

you'll enjoy this afternoon,

and uhm use Blue Badge Guides in the future

llllllll

[2]

The nature of gestures with 'pragmatic' functions

In this and the preceding chapter we have presented a series of examples to illustrate some of the ways in which speakers use gestural expressions from four different 'gesture families'. A gesture family is a group of gestures that have in common certain kinesic features. For the families we distinguished here the kinesic features were hand shape and hand orientation. Within a given gesture family different gestural forms are distinguished according to the movement pattern employed in performing them. A comparative study of the contexts of use of the different gestural expressions within a family shows that there is a different semantic theme for each family. The semantic themes noted for the four families discussed in Chapters 12 and 13, are, for the G-family, the theme of 'topic seizing'; for the R-family, 'making precise' or 'making specific'; for the Open Hand Prone ('palm down') family, 'halting, interrupting or indicating the interruption of a line of action'; and, for the Open Hand Supine ('palm up') family, variations on the themes of 'presentation' or 'offering' and 'reception' for the PP and PA versions, and variations on the idea of 'letting stand' ('withdrawing from') something that has been presented or offered in the conversational arena, for the PL versions.

The gestures described in these chapters contribute to the significance of the utterance of which they are a part in several different ways. They can show the kind of *move* being undertaken by a turn at talk, indicating, for example, that it is a question, a denial, or an offer. In these cases the gestures have what we called *performatve* functions. On other occasions, however, by 'topicalizing' with a G-family gesture, or 'making precise' with an R-family gesture, the speaker may 'mark up' some feature of the discourse structure, and in such cases the gestures are said to have *parsing* functions. Yet again, we described gestures that *operate on* the verbal component of the utterance. We saw this with gestures of the Open Hand Prone family which can function in ways similar to negative particles, but which can also serve as intensifiers. They can transform an evaluative statement into a superlative one. In such cases we say the gestures have *modal* functions.

The ways in which these gestures achieve these results is partly by combining with the verbal or contextual meanings of the utterance, but also, at least in some cases (as in the 'intensifying' functions of ZP gestures and head shakes), as was explained in more detail above, these gestures achieve their effects by reaching beyond the bounds of the current utterance to operate in relation to the implied *dialogue* within which the utterance is embedded. In other cases, as we saw in some of the examples we gave in presenting gestures in the Open Hand Supine or 'palm up' family, the gesture served as an additional move, adding a layer of meaning beyond the meaning in the verbal component. Thus, in example 116 (p. 272) the PA gesture serves to confirm the speaker's agreement with his interlocutor at the same time as he verbally provides an additional piece of information. In example 123 (p. 278), as E repeats the assertion that the door was "always open" his PL gesture adds the unanswerable problem about this that he is raising. In Example 127 (p. 280) the PL gesture provides the invitation that is otherwise only implicit in the verbal discourse.

There seems little reason to doubt that the gestural expressions in the four families considered here are forms which are not created anew each time they are used but are widely shared within a given communication community and used consistently by different individuals. It is notable that, among members of the Neapolitan communities from which we have drawn many of our observations, the gestural expressions considered are often very well articulated, being easily recognized and distinct one from another. This suggests that they have undergone some considerable degree of conventionalization. In the case of some of them, most notably those gestures within the G-family, these seem to be rather specific to southern Italian culture. Others of the gestural expressions studied in these chapters appear to have a wider geographical distribution. Indeed, gestures that are recognizably of the Open Hand Prone and of the Open Hand Supine families are found in use in other parts of continental Europe, Great Britain and the United States. Whether they are even more widespread is a matter that remains to be investigated, however.

If so-called 'pragmatic' gestures appear conventionalized, this perhaps is not very surprising. Whereas what may comprise the substantive content of any utterance is without limits, and whereas how aspects of this content may be expressed gesturally may be a highly variable matter, the kinds of speech acts that there are, the types of organizational structures in turn-taking, and the ways in which discourse may be structured, are much more limited. If any aspect of conversational gesture is to become stylized, we might expect those aspects that function pragmatically would become stylized first.

In the introduction to Chapter 12 we briefly discussed Desmond Morris's suggestion that gestures of the type we have been discussing can be understood as being derived from various patterns of action based on the manipulation of objects. Following Morris, we suggested that both the G-family and the R-family gestures can be understood as ritualized forms of 'precision grip' actions. From the comparative analyses of contexts-of-use of these gestures it does seem that the semantic theme that unites both of them can be understood as a theme of 'seizing' and 'holding on'.

Open Hand gestures of the Prone and Supine families can also be seen to be derived from physical actions by which some material aspect of the environment is acted on or altered. Thus Vertical Palm (VP) gestures can be seen as derived from actions of creating a barrier against the advance of something, or pushing or sweeping something away. Horizontal Palm (ZP) gestures can be seen as derived from actions of cutting something through or of sweeping something aside or clearing off a surface (cf. Calbris 2003). Open Hand Supine gestures of the PP and PA groups may be seen as using the open hand as a flat surface on which to present something or to show that one expects to receive something. PL gestures, finally, may be seen as having the action motif of withdrawing the hands from any activity with regard to the object presented. With the PL gesture the speaker 'lets stand' the discourse object, pulling the hands away from it and thereby declaring that there will be no intervention in respect to it on his part.

More generally, we may conclude with Müller (2004), who in turn refers to Streeck (1994) in which a similar view is expressed, that pragmatic gestures are gestures in which it is the objects or foci of discourse that become objects of manipulation. It is as if these objects are picked up, shown, presented, held, placed, allowed to fall, are withdrawn from, and so forth. Such actions, taken in respect to discourse objects, display the terms in which they are being dealt with by the speaker, and exhibit frameworks for the stances toward these objects that the interlocutors are, at the same time, invited to assume.

14   Gesture without speech: the emergence of kinesic codes

We turn now to a consideration of gesture when it is used as the *sole* means of utterance. This occurs in a wide range of circumstances, whenever, for whatever reason, speech cannot be used. Depending upon the nature of these circumstances, a more or less well established *kinesic code* may come to be elaborated. In some cases such a code becomes sufficiently non-specialized in its use and sufficiently well established as a social institution for it to merit the term 'language'. Languages fashioned exclusively from the kinesic medium are generally termed 'sign languages'.

It is useful to distinguish between *primary* sign languages and *alternate* sign languages. *Primary sign languages* are sign languages that develop in communities of deaf people. These may have, at best, only an *indirect* relationship with the spoken language or languages in use in the society within which the deaf community in question is found. *Alternate sign languages*, on the other hand, are those highly elaborate kinesic codes that are found in some speaker-hearer communities, such as certain groups among the Aborigines of Australia or among the Plains Indians of North America. Here the relationship between the sign language and the spoken languages in use may be direct and, in some cases, the structure of the sign language may even constitute a kinesic representation of aspects of spoken language structure. Alternate sign languages will be discussed in a later section of this chapter. See also Kendon (1988b).

Most work that has been done on sign languages has been done on primary sign languages. As we saw in Chapters 3 and 4, primary sign languages attracted the attention of philosophers in the eighteenth century and were one of the main objects of interest for two of the most prominent students of gesture from the nineteenth century, Edward Tylor and Wilhelm Wundt. As we described in Chapter 5, from the end of the nineteenth century interest in sign language (and gesture in general) declined and was not to revive until the middle decades of the twentieth century. Since then, however, a large body of work has been undertaken which has shown beyond question that primary sign languages have structural and functional properties that are so similar to those found in spoken languages that they are amenable to treatment with the same arsenal of analytic methods and theoretical interpretations that is employed in the study of spoken languages. As a consequence, in the hierarchy of values

284

that governs attitudes and policies toward communication codes, kinesic codes regarded as primary sign languages now have the same status as spoken languages do, and their study is now a recognized branch of linguistics.[1]

Speaker-hearers may also use gestures, either in collaboration with speech or in alternation with it, that have structural properties similar to those established for the vocabularies of signs in sign languages. For example, as we noted in Chapter 10, there are some gestures that have 'narrow' glosses and some of these can be used, and occasionally are used, independently of speech as if they are an alternative to a spoken expression, or they may be used in alternation with speech, as a part of 'mixed syntax' (Slama-Cazacu 1976). These narrow gloss gestures include those that are commonly referred to as 'emblems' or 'quotable gestures'. Where extensive vocabularies of such gestures exist (see Chapter 16), analyses have shown that items within these vocabularies contrast in terms of such features as hand shape, place of articulation and movement, so that it is possible to speak of a 'phonology' for such gestures, much as is done for signs in sign languages (Sparhawk 1978, Poggi 2002).

A similar kind of analysis also seems possible for pragmatic gestures (those which function as performatives, modals and parsers). As we saw in Chapters 12 and 13, these gestures can be grouped as families in formational terms, different members of such families being differentiated in terms of different combinations of such components as hand shape, hand orientation and movement pattern. On the other hand, gestures that collaborate with speech in the exposition of specific content, such as gestures which function to suggest the size or shape of something, that show spatial relationships between entities or which serve as static or dynamic process diagrams, or which indicate path, manner and direction of movement (such as were illustrated in Chapters 9 and 10), do not appear to be amenable to an analysis in terms of a system of contrasting formational features, at least not in the same way.

To show that a structural analysis of this sort can be carried out for some aspects of gesture as used by speakers reminds us that the cluster of features in terms of which a system is identified as a language includes features that are found in systems that are usually not considered linguistic in any strict sense of that term. It also supports the idea that these properties arise in relation to the way in which the communicative actions in question are employed. It seems that the more gesture is used for the communicative tasks for which speech is used, the more it will develop properties that are linguistic in character. On this

---

[1] It is quite beyond the scope of the present book to review modern research on primary sign languages. For an excellent recent survey, see Emmorey (2002). For one history of the struggle to have sign languages accepted as languages in their own right, see Maher (1996).

view, the sign languages that are today the objects of linguistic inquiry are the products of cultural evolutionary processes which occur whenever gesture is adapted to wider and ever more unspecialized utterance uses. These processes are examined further in what is to follow here.

Autonomy in gesture and transformation of structure

A number of experimental demonstrations show what happens when speakers have only gesture at their disposal (Bloom 1979, see McNeill 1992, pp. 65-72; Dufour 1992, Singleton, Goldin-Meadow and McNeill 1995, Goldin-Meadow, McNeill and Singleton 1996). In the Bloom and Dufour studies speakers were asked, using gesture alone, to tell another person a well-known fairy story. It was found that people very rapidly improvised a small vocabulary of gestures with stable meanings which they used in constructions whose organization appeared to owe little to the syntax of their own spoken language. In the Singleton studies people were asked to describe in gesture alone and then in both speech and gesture, a brief scene with moving objects, presented in a short movie. These movies showed scenes such as a circle moving diagonally across the screen or a toy mouse jumping over a toy bed.[2] Half of the scenes presented showed simply one object in motion, half of them showed an object moving in relation to another stationary object.

In the condition where the subjects were permitted to use both gesture and speech to describe these scenes, they used gesture most often to depict movement or action. Gestures used that depicted the character of the objects were rare and used only when the objects in the film could not be easily identified. Occasionally, in doing a gesture for an action or movement, subjects used a hand shape that represented an aspect of the moving object. For example, in describing how a circle moved diagonally upwards across the screen some subjects made a 'circle' shape with their thumb and index finger and moved their hand with this hand shape diagonally upwards.

When the subjects had to describe the scenes using gestures alone, in most cases they invented gestures that named the objects observed in the scene and they were more likely to use a hand shape that represented an aspect of the moving object in the movement or action gesture. Not very surprisingly, the subjects produced gestures in strings, creating gesture sentences. In these sentences, the objects in the scene were referred to first, the gesture depicting

---

[2] These movies were made by Ted Supalla to form stimuli in his Verbs of Motion Production (VMP) test used in his studies of the structure of verbs of motion in American Sign Language (see Supalla 1982).

the action being given last. Where there was a stationary object with an object moving in relation to it, the stationary object was referred to first.[3] The features that appeared in the gesturings of the subjects in the gesture-only condition of this experiment - nominating gestures that combined with action gestures in *sequential* structures - are features that are found whenever gesture is used as the sole means of utterance. They are two of the most basic features of any communication system, including spoken languages, in which actor and action or agent and patient are to be represented symbolically and are not to be inferred wholly from context. Goldin-Meadow (1982) has referred to these as among the 'resilient' properties of language. Whenever such a communication system is established - in whatever medium - these properties will always be found.

Structure in the gestures of 'isolated' deaf

Goldin-Meadow and colleagues, over a long period of time, have studied a number of profoundly deaf children who, born to hearing parents, have been brought up with oral methods of training only (representative publications include Feldman, Goldin-Meadow and Gleitman 1978; Goldin-Meadow 1979, 1982, 1993; Goldin-Meadow and Mylander 1990; see also Goldin-Meadow 2003a). Over a period of about three years, these children (ten in the sample on which most of the reports have been based) were video taped in play sessions with their hearing mother or another hearing adult every two to four months. The children ranged in age between one and a half and four years at the beginning of the data collection to two and a half to six years by the end of it.

It was found that these children all created a repertoire of gestures which, according to Goldin-Meadow's analyses, in their organization and use have the 'resilient' features just mentioned, despite the fact that, in her view, these children in her sample did not have, in their input from others, a communication system with a consistent linguistic structure. For Goldin-Meadow this means that children, regardless of the kind of input they receive,

[3] It is interesting that the order of gestures used by the subjects when using gesture only is the same as the order of signs that deaf users of ASL use when they describe these same scenes in sign. That is, signers also tend to sign the action depicted in the scene last. It has also been reported that deaf signers who are either 'home signers' or members of small, isolated signing communities, when signing about items related by action of some kind, likewise sign the action last. See Yau (1985) for an 'isolated' deaf woman in Canada, Kendon (1980b) for a deaf signer from the New Guinea Highlands and Macleod (1973) for an isolated deaf man from Yorkshire in England. When one is confined to the gestural medium, when it is necessary to express the idea of two or more things as being related in some way, the things to be related must first be made present to the recipient, and so signed first, before their relationship can be shown. Yau believes this preferred ordering of signs reflects a fundamental principle of cognitive organization.

will create communication systems with certain properties also found in languages (whether spoken or signed).

The children commonly employed their gestures in strings and analyses of them suggested that they were making sentences comparable to the early sentences of children acquiring spoken language. The sentences were found to have a 'predicate structure' - for instance, a pointing gesture nominating a topic was commonly followed by a characterizing gesture that predicated something of the topic. Elements in these gesture sentences showed a consistent order. For example, considering the gestures produced in terms of the thematic roles they occupied in the gesture sentences, the tendency was to follow the orders PATIENT–ACT (that is, 'affected entity' followed by 'action that causes the affect', as in 'cheese'+ 'eat' in referring to a mouse who ate cheese), PATIENT–RECIPIENT (e.g. 'hat'+ 'cowboy' in referring to a toy cowboy who should have a hat put on him), or ACT–RECIPIENT (e.g. 'move-to' + 'table' in referring to something that should be moved to a table).

It was further found that many of the gestures referred to as 'characterizing' (in contrast to 'pointing' gestures) could be regarded as being made up from a system of hand shape and motion morphemes. For example, one child consistently used a 'fist' hand shape when referring to handling a long object, an 'O' hand shape (tips of fingers arched over to be in contact with the thumb) when referring to the handling of any small object, and a 'C' hand shape (fingers extended, held together, but curved, thumb opposed) when referring to the handling of a large object. These various hand shapes were combined with three different movement patterns (short-arc, to and fro arc and circular motion) to produce consistently different meanings.

Goldin-Meadow concludes that these deaf children have created a system of gestures which "serve as elements in gesture strings (forming a simple syntax) and are themselves composed of recombineable elements (forming a simple morphology)" (Goldin-Meadow 1993, p. 81). Great emphasis is placed by Goldin-Meadow and her colleagues upon the apparent self-created character of these gesture systems. It is stressed that the mothers of these children, although they use gesture in communicating with them, do not use gesture sentences and do not show the kind of consistency in hand shape use that the children do. It is claimed that the structured character of the children's systems is not derived from anything offered in the systems employed by their caretakers. It is to be noted, however, that Goldin-Meadow mentions that these children use a number of conventionalized gestures for characterizing actions (as in the gestures for 'give' and 'break') as well as a number of 'modulator' gestures (such as gestures for negation, affirmation and doubt), and these they must have learned from others.

Further studies of the character of the interactions between deaf children reared without access to sign language and their mothers and the other people in their daily environment could be very useful. Even if the mothers of these children do not, as Goldin-Meadow describes (Goldin-Meadow and Mylander 1984, 1990), employ in reciprocation a system of gesturing that matches that of the children, they yet must constantly provide evidence to the child that he is understood and this, in itself, would contribute in an important way to the processes by which his own kinesic code comes to be shaped. Some indication of this process is provided in a study by Da Cunha Pereira and De Lemos (1994) who describe how "the mother shows her acceptance of the child's form and meaning of a gesture by repeating, translating or mirroring the child's gesture" (p. 182). Although it is clear from Goldin-Meadow's studies that the deaf children she observed devised a systematic gesture system, even though they were not taught one, the process by which this happened remains to be fully understood.

Other studies of deaf persons who have elaborated complex gesture systems without contact with other deaf or with other users of sign language (so-called 'isolated' deaf) are studies of adults who were deaf at birth or from very early childhood. In these cases the individuals had, over a long period of time, developed systems of gesture which at least permitted them to communicate their basic needs. These studies include Kuschel (1973, 1974) who studied Kagobai, the only deaf individual on the Polynesian Outlier Island of Rennel and Yau (1985, 1992) who has studied cases from China, Japan and from the Cree nation in Canada. It is clear that in all these cases there is an extensive involvement of others, but it is not always clear from these reports how far the system of gestures developed by the 'isolated' individual is used by others. In the case of Mrs. Pettikwi (of the Cree Nation), reported by Yau, the signs she had evidently created were also used by her children. Mr. Kwok (of China), also reported by Yau, had learned his signs from his mother, who was also deaf.

The systems developed by these individuals, though quite elaborate, in some cases (Kuschel describes 217 signs) nevertheless show certain restrictions. The evidence suggests that it is the relative isolation of these persons from contact with other signers that is one of the conditions that restricts their elaboration. This is a point that Washabaugh (1986) has emphaiszed. He studied sign usage on Providence Island in the Caribbean, where there was an unusually high proportion of people born deaf. He found that the gesture systems used by these deaf showed a high degree of lexical variation and utterances were usually comprehensible only in the immediate contexts of their production. A community-wide, stable sign language had not developed. Deaf individuals lived, even into late adulthood, as dependants within their parental families where, for the most part, they were the only deaf. Within each family with deaf members, a highly local sign system had developed and because the deaf did not interact much among themselves (there was no school for the deaf, for example) there was little opportunity for a sign system to develop that was shared more widely in the island's society.

Washabaugh observes that the deaf in these families were looked upon as defective and were regarded as being in need of the same kind of anticipatory care and scaffolding that tends to be offered to children. His suggestion is that, because of this, even though adult, they had little *incentive* to develop a linguistic system beyond that which would serve in the contexts in which they lived. He argues that, for a linguistic system to develop fully, there must be a shared sense of community among the sign language users and that, to some extent at least, there must be a sense of identity *as* members of a community, as opposed to always being outsiders.

Emergence and growth of primary sign languages

Once a community of signers is established that extends beyond the single family, it becomes possible for gesturing to be developed into a widely shared system which progresses toward having increasingly the characteristics that will attract the label 'language'. Cases where these conditions are met are reported by Groce (1985) for Martha's Vineyard, Johnson (1991) for a Mayan community in Mexico and Kendon (1980b) for the Enga Province of Papua New Guinea, among others. The best documented example, however, is to be found in the work of Kegl and her colleagues (Kegl, Senghas and Coppola 1999; Morford and Kegl 2000) who, over the course of more than a decade, have followed the emergence of what is referred to as Nicaraguan Sign Language, whose history began in 1980.

Before that date, the deaf in Nicaragua lived with their families, typically widely separated from one another. In each of these families locally elaborated sign systems (so-called 'homesign' systems) were used but the social conditions needed to maintain the social network necessary for the maintenance of a sign language shared by the wider community did not exist. This only came into existence when, in 1980, the first special education school for the deaf was opened in Managua and deaf people of varying ages bringing with them their highly variable and idiosyncratic homesign systems came together into communities for the first time.

As these deaf people interacted among themselves using their own homesign systems, they developed together a shared system, which Kegl and colleagues call *Lenguaje de Señas Nicaragüense* or LSN. They characterize this as a "peer-group pidgin or jargon between the homesign substrates"

(Kegl et al. 1999, p. 180). Over time, LSN became stabilized and became the basis for the emergence of *Idioma de Señas Nicaragüense* or ISN, which Kegl and colleagues (p. 181) describe as a "full-blown" sign language. ISN, which emerged quite rapidly, was created first by the youngest children, those between the ages of six and seven years, who came to the school after LSN had been established. According to Kegl and colleagues the youngest children, in learning LSN as they encountered it among those already at the school, re-fashioned it. In doing so they reorganized it semantically and grammatically. It became more systematic and less context dependent. By 1987 younger signers, using ISN, began to enter a vocational school and to participate in adult activities, such as the local Deaf Association. By 1993 signers had developed a sufficient awareness of their own language that attempts were started to standardize it and to teach it explicitly to deaf people living in more remote areas of the country.

Kegl's work provides one of the most detailed accounts of the differences between different levels of organization within kinesic codes used by deaf people and it provides some valuable indications as to how forms used in loosely organized and context dependent systems can become stabilized and standardized as they are incorporated into systems that have structural characteristics of language. The work makes clear that even if, as Kegl herself would argue, the linguistic features that come to be established as young children rework the contact homesign systems into a more sophisticated form are shaped by structuring tendencies inherent as part of a 'language module', this can only come about if an already existing widely shared system, such as LSN, is already available, and that within groups of peers the various systems in use have reciprocal influence, so that one system develops in common. In 'isolated' families, on the other hand, in which only one or two deaf children are to be found, or where there is a single deaf parent, as Washabaugh's observations also suggested, the communication between the hearing and deaf tends to be asymmetric. It is only when there is a *reciprocity* in the communication systems used that we see the emergence of fully autonomous systems which have characteristics that invite us to refer to them as 'languages'.

Kinesic codes in speaking communities

Kinesic codes of varying degrees of complexity have developed at various times and places in communities of speaker-hearers for use in circumstances where speech either cannot be used for environmental reasons, or may not be used for ritual reasons. A comparative study of these kinesic codes reveals the way in which these systems are elaborated in response to their circumstances of use. The more *generalized* these circumstances are, the more complex these systems become. In addition, it is interesting to see the extent to which such systems created in the gestural medium make use of the resources of the spoken languages to which, in these cases (in contrast to systems elaborated by deaf people), their creators have full access.

Here we provide a brief comparative discussion of five of these *alternate* kinesic codes (as we shall call them). We shall begin with an example of a highly specialized kinesic code which Barakat (1969) would call a 'technical system'. The example is the system of hand signals used to guide the driver of a crane, as described by Brun (1969). Systems like this have also been described in use in broadcast studios, at race tracks, and in stock exchanges. They are adapted to convey a limited range of specific information and are structurally quite simple. We then discuss a gesture system developed in a sawmill in British Columbia, as described by Meissner and Philpott (1975). This had its origins in a technical system but circumstances allowed it some elaboration so that it could be used for purposes well beyond the original ones. We then turn to a gesture system in use in a Cistercian monastery in the United States, drawing on the work of Barakat (1975). This system is one of the monastic sign languages which were established to allow essential communication in religious orders where the use of speech was avoided for religious reasons (Rijnberk 1954, Umiker-Sebeok and Sebeok 1987, Kendon 1990b). We conclude with brief accounts of two systems from tribal societies which show a very high degree of generalizability and, correspondingly, a very high degree of complexity. These are the so-called Plains Sign Language of the Plains Indians of North America (Mallery 1881, West 1960, Farnell 1995), and the alternate sign languages in use among various groups of Aborigines in central Australia (Kendon 1988b).

Crane driver guider gestures

Cranes can raise or lower their loads, swivel to the left or to the right, raise or lower their derrick, move forward or back, halt or start moving. The gestures used by crane driver guiders cover these possibilities and no more. In the system considered here (taken from Brun 1969) there are five contrasting pairs of signals which involve distinct arm movements combined with distinct hand shapes which serve to instruct the crane in its possible movements; there is a sixth pair of signals for 'normal stop' and 'emergency stop'; and there is one signal, used to refer to the actual handling of the load, that involves a changing hand shape, which is used only in combination with another signal. According to which signal it is combined with, its meaning is different. Analysis of this system reveals the following points:

Fig. 14.1   Crane driver guider signals. Reproduced from Brun (1969), p. 92.

(1) Each signal, when compared with the other appears as a distinct combination of a limited set of elements: six hand shapes, two arm movements, two arm positions, and two combinations of two arms or single arms. These elements can only combine in certain ways: for example to use the hand shape with only index finger extended in the Jib Up/Jib Down pair would be incorrect. There is, thus, a repertoire of signal formation elements, 'sublexical' elements, with rules of combination thereof.

(2) Some compound signals occur, but there are restrictions. For example, to use the Clench/Unclench hand signal in combination with anything else besides Hoist or Stop would be incorrect.

(3) Combinations of 'sub-lexical' elements and combinations of whole signs are achieved simultaneously, not through sequences of signals.

(4) If we consider how signal form relates to signal meaning, we may see that the direction of movement of the signals that tell the crane to swivel left or right, move forward or back, and so on, correspond, in direction, to those movements. There is, thus, a form–meaning correspondence that is one of analogy and here the system shows iconicity. Despite this, however, these movements are discretely contrasted. Intermediate forms are not possible. Furthermore, the different hand shapes that are used in each of the signals in the set appear to serve partly to keep the signals distinct and do not have any corresponding relation to the meaning of the signal. To this extent the system is categorial and its units have an arbitrary relationship with their referents.

The features of the system we have just outlined are features that are found in other kinesic codes, including full-fledged sign languages. This notwithstanding, most would not wish to claim that the crane signal system is a language. Perhaps the most important reason why not is that it is strictly limited to the set of messages needed for guiding the crane and, even within this domain, novel utterances are not possible. This system, thus, is semantically specialized and closed or non-productive. Further, the system is asymmetrical for the guider gives the crane driver instructions as to how to move the crane and the crane driver responds by moving the crane accordingly. He cannot 'talk back' to the guider in the same 'language' that the guider himself can use.

In line with what the studies reviewed in the previous section suggested, we may suspect that this lack of reciprocity is an important feature that prevents the system of signals from opening out, for it prevents the two parties to the system from entering into and developing modifications to it while they are using it.

Sawmill system

As soon as we examine situations in which reciprocity of gestures is possible we observe an increase in complexity of the system. It is as if reciprocation itself induces a demand for more messages, and the system expands accordingly. This is suggested when we examine the kinesic code that developed in a sawmill in British Columbia described by Meissner and Philpott (1975).

Within the sawmill they studied, pairs of workers cooperated continuously in carrying out the various operations. For example, the man who controlled the movement of the log past the saw and the man who controlled the position of the log on the carriage that moves it back and forth - the sawyer and setter, respectively - had to cooperate to ensure that the log is cut into boards correctly; as must the trimmer and the man involved in bark removal. This cooperation was mediated by hand signals, for noise level and the distance between workers was such that the use of spoken messages was impossible. The workers, furthermore, were fixed in their positions during work and thus there was no possibility of anyone going over to another to speak to him.

Meissner and Philpott report that although the main use of the sign system was for technical messages, it had expanded to permit exchanges on a variety of topics unrelated to work. This nontechnical elaboration was especially favoured between men who were bound to interact frequently as a result of how they were positioned, who had worked together for a long time, who were similar in status and background and who were, in the words of one sawyer whom Meissner and Philpott interviewed, "willing to make a bit of a fool of themselves" (ibid., p. 298). Despite this expansion, the sign language remained restricted to a range of topics which, beyond the technicalities of the job, included discussions of time of day, special times such as coffee time, lunch time and quitting time - and such topics as beer, sex, wives and girlfriends. In its non-technical uses it had a playful, joking character. Furthermore, it was used only in the work-setting of the sawmill. It was not used elsewhere, as in the cafeteria or in settings away from the sawmill.

At the core of the system was a set of *number signs*, used primarily to indicate distances by which logs must be moved or by which saws must be adjusted, and a set of lexical signs which referred to the main pieces of equipment and their operation. The number signs were one-handed, involving various combinations of finger extensions and hand positions. The signs for equipment or technical operations had a basis in depiction or pantomime, but were quite stylized and reduced in form.

This system of number signs and technical signs was extended in certain ways. Supervisors and workers who serviced the equipment were referred to by number signs because they could be called for by means of specified numbers of blasts on the steam whistle. Two blasts meant Engineer, for instance, and five meant Foreman. Accordingly, in sign, the sign TWO meant Engineer and the sign FIVE meant Foreman. Again, the sign for 'knot against block'- used in one of the circumstances when a log gets jammed - was also used to mean 'wood knot' in general and also, by the rebus principle, it was used to mean the English word 'not'. Likewise, the sign for Carriage Dogs, the apparatus that grasps the logs in the carriage, was also used for the concept 'get' or 'grab'.

Additional signs were added, however, to make possible the exchange of an even broader range of messages. There were signs for kin types - mother, brother, father, uncle, etc.; signs for categories of person and occupational role; signs for verbs, such as 'walk', 'run', 'read', 'write', and the like; and a number of signs that served as adjectives and adverbs, including adverbs of time, many signs for qualities and feelings, and signs for sizes and shapes. There was one grammatical sign that marked an utterance as a question. Altogether, Meissner and Philpott describe over 130 signs.

The signs were derived in a variety of ways. The number signs were from displays of different numbers of fingers, although there were some special features to this. Some of the number signs, those for numbers above ten and for fractions, were derived by a 'layered' inflection of the sign, reminiscent of morphological devices in primary sign languages. Other processes of sign derivation included, among signs for objects, forms derived from abbreviated pantomimes for associated operations - as in the sign for 'car' which derived from pantomiming holding a steering wheel; forms derived from depicting the shape of the object, or forms in which the hand models the shape of something - as in the sign for 'gang saw', a saw which has multiple blades. This was signed, accordingly, with spread fingers. Verb signs were based largely on pantomimes of actions. Adjectival signs included several examples of metaphorical extension, as in the sign SMOOTH done by stroking the cheek or the signs for GOOD and BAD which were both done in relation to the stomach to indicate states of well-being or physical illness. As already mentioned, a few signs are derived via the rebus principle, as in 'knot against block' being used to mean 'not' or squeezing the biceps to sign 'weak' as a way of signing 'week'.

There were some compound signs. Some of these were signs which define a class of object followed by a sign that gives the species, as in MONEY plus HOUSE for 'bank', WOMAN plus BROTHER for 'sister'. Other compounds were calques from English, such as 'newspaper' signed as NEW plus PAPER, or 'knocked up' - meaning 'pregnant' - signed as KNOCK plus UP.

Despite these vocabulary expansions, the sawmill sign language remained relatively restricted. Many of the sign sequences described are fixed collocations. They were not formed according to any general rule that could be used to generate new combinations. It was also found that it was not possible to introduce topics of reference that were not already covered in the sign language.

These limitations can be understood in terms of the communication conditions. These ensured that only brief exchanges could ever be possible. For example, the extensive exchanges that took place between the head sawyer and the setter always had to be brief, because the setter was riding back and forth on a carriage and was opposite the sawyer only intermittently (about five times a minute). In addition, of course, there was the continual need to pay attention to the operation of the equipment that the task demanded. Furthermore, the conditions that favoured the use of this sign language prevailed for only part of each working day. Thus anybody who needed to engage in longer exchanges or exchanges covering other topics could do so in the cafeteria, after work at the pub, and the like. To some degree, the sign language was bound up with being on the job and its elaboration was a way in which the men could play with one another as they worked. Communication beyond the technical requirements of the job itself, on the one hand, and beyond the domain of on-the-job playing, on the other, could be delayed until later. This would be another reason why the sign language did not develop further.

Monastic sign languages

Several monastic orders, founded as long ago as the fourth century, follow a rule of silence. Ideally, the members of these orders devote all their time to contemplation, and communication with others, especially by speech, is a distraction. In the monasteries of these orders, silence is enjoined from an early hour in the evening until an early hour the next morning, and it is also required during mealtimes, and at all times in certain parts of the monastery. When speech is permitted, it should be kept to a minimum and confined to decorous subjects. However, it was recognized that within these restricted periods some communication could be necessary and, accordingly, a number of gestures were permitted. The first lists of permitted gestures were drawn up in the tenth century, and it is from these lists of official signs, revised from time to time, that present-day monastic sign languages partly derive. 'Unofficial' signs also evolved. These make possible richer communication during periods of silence than the official signs permit but their use is frowned upon and may sometimes incur punishment. Notwithstanding this, each monastery evolved its own version of sign language, with the result that visiting Brothers often found that they could not use sign language to communicate easily, beyond the minimum permitted by the official signs of the order. Lists of monastic signs and discussions of these sign languages may be found in Rijnberk (1954), Umiker-Sebeok and Sebeok (1987) and Kendon (1990b).

Barakat (1975) has published a study of the sign language in use at St. Joseph's Abbey, in Spencer, Massachusetts, and this appears to be the only contemporary study of a monastic sign language. All other discussions are based on written lists. Barakat describes over 1200 signs, discusses their derivation and the syntax employed. The signs described include the official list of 324 basic signs, 208 derived signs, formed from the basic signs by compounding, 292 additional, officially sanctioned signs special to St. Joseph's Abbey and, finally, 627 signs from the unofficial vocabulary of so-called 'original' or 'useless' signs elaborated at St. Joseph's Abbey. This is an open set, including many short-lived inventions. In addition, there is an unofficial set of signs for each of the twenty-six letters of the alphabet, and a set of numeral signs.

Many of the signs in the official lists have pantomimic origins, although some were purely arbitrary from the beginning. In the unofficial list, on the other hand, there are many signs that are attempts at a phonetic representation of a word. Forty-seven of the basic signs in the sanctioned list are compounds in which one sign stands for a general class of object and another specifies it. For example, to sign 'cabbage' one first clasps one's head with two hands, and then makes the sign VEGETABLE. In addition, there are compounds which are made up of two or more basic signs in which the referent is analysed into component concepts. Thus, in the St. Joseph's Abbey's list 'snow' is signed as WHITE+RAIN, 'storeroom' is signed as HIDE+HOUSE.

In the list of 'original' signs (i.e unofficial signs) the large majority are compounds and many of them are compounds of three or more signs. Many are apparently made up on the spur of the moment and they may or may not gain currency among the monks. Examples include 'Easter' signed as GOD+UP+DAY, 'grounds keeper' signed as RELIGIOUS (i.e. monk) + CHARGE + FLOWER, and 'Noah', reported to be signed as OLD + SAINT + ARRANGE + BIG + BOAT + TIME + BIG + WATER + FILL + COME.

Other compounds in the 'original' list arise from an attempt to create a sequence of gestures that represent the spoken sound of a word. Where an English word can be analysed into component words, or into parts that sound somewhat like English words, if signs already exist for these parts, then a compound will be formed from them. Thus, 'hurricane' may be signed as HURRY + CANE, or 'cookie' may be signed as COOK + KEY. Where this cannot be done, then letter signs will be used. However, letter signs are not used for spelling the word intended but as representations of speech sounds, generally as sounds that stand for syllables that cannot otherwise be equated with words for which a sign can be found. For example, 'pumpernickel' may be signed as PUMP + R + FIVE + CENTS, 'Ohio' may be signed as O + HIGH + O.

So far as syntax is concerned, although, in St. Joseph's Abbey, English syntax clearly played an important part in influencing how the monks structured their sentences, since there are no signs in their system to match the copulative, no pronominals, and no system of sign affixes by which, say, tense might be conveyed, various strategies of expression were employed which often led the monks to produce sequences that were very different from English. From Barakat's account one has the strong impression that a consistent productive system of syntax had not become established.

It is clear, nevertheless, that the monastic sign language described by Barakat is a good deal more complex than the sawmill sign language. This reflects the fact that it is used for a far greater range of topics and in a much wider range of interactive circumstances than the sawmill system. In the sawmill, as we saw, the workers were in fixed positions, most of their time given over to the management of special equipment in relation to the operation of which much communication had to be devoted. Such extra signing as there was, was not only highly restricted in topic, it was also restricted in terms of complexity of utterance, because of the time available and, also, because of the highly restricted circumstances in which exchange was possible.

For the monks, on the other hand, the sign language must be able to be used in a much wider set of interactional circumstances and a wider range of topics will be covered, accordingly. Nevertheless, there appear to be definite limits to the development of Cistercian sign language. First of all, apart from the use of signs in the official list, which deliberately permit only the most basic kinds of communications, the unofficial aspect of the language is under constant restraint because it is looked upon with official disapproval. Second, speech is used at formal interviews with authorities in the monastery, when serious theological issues are discussed, and there are also certain times of the day when the use of speech is possible. The limitations of the existing system could, thus, be overcome by using speech, if interaction was postponed to a later time. One might expect that, in consequence, during times of Silence the monks would avoid topics requiring expansion or elaboration of the language beyond what was needed during times of Silence.

In both the sawmill case and the Cistercian sign language case, then, we have examples of gesture systems that have been developed to a certain degree of complexity which is sufficient for the communicative routines for which they are needed, but where, since its use is almost always confined to specific contexts - and in the case of Cistercian sign language is restrained from further development by the general monastic restraint on all forms of communication - there appears to be no incentive for its further development and strategies of productive expression appear not to have been much developed.

Sign language among the North American Plains Indians

The Plains Indians of North America used an elaborate sign language which attracted the attention of several nineteenth-century authors, most notably Garrick Mallery (1880), who described many of the signs employed (see Chapter 4 and also Clark 1885, Seton 1918, Tomkins 1926, Umiker-Sebeok and Sebeok 1978). An attempt was made, in 1960, to undertake a detailed linguistic description of one form of this language. This work was carried out by La Mont West. It remains in the form of an unpublished Ph.D. thesis. Nevertheless it is the only detailed study we have (West 1960). Additional historical and ethnographic information may be found in Taylor (1978). Information on the current status of sign language in one Plains Indian group -

the Assiniboine - and some analysis of it (following a rather different approach from that of West) may be found in Farnell (1995).

Plains Indian sign language probably was at its zenith of development by the first half of the nineteenth century. Its origins are unclear, but there is reason to think that it spread into the Plains, brought there first in the seventeenth century, after Indians living in what is now the southwest United States and northern Mexico, who already used signs, acquired the horse from the Spanish and began to move into the Plains as they followed the buffalo. When they did so they encountered numerous other groups of Indians, some settled, some mobile hunters. These groups spoke quite different languages, and one of the functions that the Indians' sign language came to have was that of inter-tribal communication. It is uncertain whether this was its original function, as some have suggested, or whether it was developed originally for some other purpose, most probably a ritual use, and then adapted as a rapid means of linguistic communication among groups who spoke mutually unintelligible languages.

By all accounts it was a rich sign language, having a large vocabulary. As with other sign languages, many of the signs appear to be accounted for as derivations from visual representations of concrete objects or of actions. However, a high degree of formalization had occurred to such an extent that La Mont West, in his thesis, was able to proceed quite far in demonstrating duality of patterning in sign structure, much in the same way as has also been demonstrated for primary sign languages (as, originally, by Stokoe 1960).

According to both Garrick Mallery and West, there appears to have been a rather extensive development of compound signs. These included compounds of the Genus–Species type (such as we have already alluded to in monastic sign languages), and also compounds of the coordinate type, in which something is referred to by a string, sometimes quite lengthy, of signs for the attributes of something, a strategy also described by Barakat for the monastic sign language he studied. West gives an example of the skunk being referred to with a string of signs including signs for SMALL ANIMAL + PLUMED TAIL + STRIPED BACK + ODOR + BAD + EGG + SMASH.

According to West, the sign language he analysed showed little relationship to any of the spoken languages used by the groups that made use of it. He suggests that because these spoken languages are so different from one another, the sign language evolved as an autonomous system, independent of any specific spoken language. West's account of modes of syntactic expression is very reminiscent of what, later, came to be described for primary sign languages. The structured use of space and movement in establishing grammatical relationships within discourse, which is such a conspicuous feature of primary sign languages, was also found in the system West analysed. West describes 'layered' inflection, much as has been found in primary sign languages, as well as use of space for pronominal reference and for the expression of prepositional relationships. Of all the alternate sign languages that have been described, Plains Sign Language (as West called it) appears to share most features with a primary sign language. Evidently, because it was used as a means of communication between groups who spoke radically different languages, it developed in relation to none of them, and it was able to develop in its own fashion, following strategies of expression that seem most natural in the kinesic medium. This is in contrast to what we noted for the monastic sign language, already described. It is also in contrast to what has been found for the central Australian sign languages, to be described next.

Central Australian Aboriginal sign languages

Among the Aborigines of central Australia complex alternate sign languages have developed which permit communication in virtually all circumstances of daily life and about any topic (Kendon 1988b). These sign languages have developed as an alternative to speech, which is needed since there are taboos on the use of speech that must be observed by people when in certain ritual states. Thus, among the Warlpiri, for instance, or the Warumungu, it is the custom for women to observe more or less prolonged periods of speech taboo when in mourning. During these periods they use a sign language instead. During periods of speech taboo, women may participate in most aspects of everyday social life, so their sign language is not in any way specialized in terms of circumstance of use or topic. Furthermore, it may be used by those who know it, not only during periods of ritual silence, but at any other time when it is convenient to do so. It is used as an alternative to shouting over long distances, it may be used when people wish to be quiet, as in hunting, when people wish to communicate without being overheard, and it is also used when tired or ill. It can also function as a 'respect' language, in that it will be used rather than speech to refer to sacred matters. In any community of Aborigines in this part of Australia, at any time there will be several women using sign language out of ritual necessity. However, it is also in common use in other contexts. For the group of older women who share knowledge of this sign language it is in frequent, if not constant, use.[4]

These sign languages are quite rich - for example, for Warlpiri sign language well over 1500 lexical items have been recorded, and there are undoubtedly many more. An analysis of the formational features of the signs collected shows that systematic use is made of some 35 contrasting hand shapes, 18 body locations of articulation, and 23 movement patterns. Most signs are

[4] Among the Warlpiri, the Warumungu and other groups of the North Central Desert, sign language is little used by men, who regard it as the preserve of women. In other parts of Australia, however, such as the Western Desert, Arnhem Land and Cape York, sign languages are also used by men.

adequately performed with one hand, although there are quite a number of two-handed signs as well, both those in which the hands act symmetrically and those in which they act asymmetrically. A comparison of the formational features of Warlpiri sign language with a primary sign language such as ASL showed that the general principles that govern manual sign formation in these two quite unrelated languages are the same in each case. Many signs in Warlpiri sign language can be seen to be derived from visual representations of concrete objects or actions. Visual iconicity plays as strong a role in Warlpiri sign language as it does in any sign language that has been examined, although, again, we also find that signs are very highly evolved so that they no more rely upon any pantomimic character that they may have to convey their meaning than is found to be the case in other well developed sign languages, such as ASL.

Particularly interesting is the way in which Warlpiri sign language and the other central Australian sign languages are related to spoken language. It was found that there is an extensive relationship between the morphological structure of words and the structure of signs. For example, reduplication is a widespread word-formation process in Warlpiri. It operates as a form of pluralization, as in, say *kurdu* 'child' but *kurdukurdu* 'children' or *karnta* 'woman' but *karntakarnta* 'women'. It can also operate as a way of creating new words. Thus we have *wanta* 'sun', but *wantawanta* 'red ant' or *walya* 'ground' but *walyawalya* 'brown'. In the sign language the signs for the reduplicate expressions are, correspondingly, reduplicates of signs for the things referred to by the unreduplicate expressions, so the sign for 'brown' is WALYA + WALYA where the sign for 'ground' is WALYA; or the sign for 'red ant' is WANTA + WANTA where the sign for 'sun' is WANTA, and so on.

We find the same thing in respect to compounds. Just as in English there are words like 'housewife' which are compounds of the separate words 'house' and 'wife', so in the spoken languages dealt with here there are compound forms. The signs for the things referred to by these compounds are very often compound signs in which the separate parts are also the signs for the things referred to by the separate words that make up the compound. Thus, in Warumungu, the sign for 'scorpion' is a combination of the sign for 'mouth' followed by the sign for 'crab'. This corresponds directly to the spoken language word for 'scorpion' which is *jalangartarta*, a compound of *jala* 'mouth' and *ngartarta* 'crab'. In Warlpiri, in contrast, a scorpion is known as *kanaparnta* which is composed of *kana* 'digging stick' and *-parnta*, a suffix that means 'possessing'. Thus, in Warlpiri, 'scorpion' is 'digging stick-possessing' - the creature with the digging stick. In Warlpiri sign language 'scorpion' is referred to with a sign for 'digging stick' followed by a sign for the possessive suffix.

It is to be noted that the spoken language meaning units that the sign language represents are *content* units. In these languages, grammatical relations are signalled by morphology and word order has no grammatical significance. The morphemes that signal grammatical relationships are not represented in sign, however. One might expect that, as a result, in signing, sign order would be used to signal grammatical relationships. However, comparisons of sign order in signed narrative with word order in spoken narrative suggest that this is not so. Evidently, in signing the signer leaves the assignment of grammatical role to constituents in signed sentences up to the recipient..

Tense, also, receives no representation in sign. Once again, it is as if the signer takes it for granted that her recipient will assign tense to any utterance she produces. When a time frame must be specified a temporal adverb sign is used and this is placed at the beginning of the utterance.

The detail with which signs match the structure of the spoken forms depends upon the skill and knowledge of the signer. Some signers are very much better than others. The really good ones make use of signs that refer to suffixes (endings) in the spoken language and approach fairly closely a manual rendition of the morpheme sequences of the spoken language. It is as if, as the sign language develops, it converges ever more closely upon a form of which it could truly be said that it is a representation of the morpheme-meaning units of the spoken language (Kendon 1984).

Spoken forms, use and complexity in alternate sign languages

Two points emerge from this comparative review. First of all, the way in which, and the extent to which a kinesic code developed among spoken language users is related to the spoken language is quite variable. What sort of relationship obtains depends upon the complexity of the system and the purposes for which it has been developed but also upon the structure of the spoken language of its users. Secondly, there is a clear relationship between the specialization of the system and its complexity. The more generalized its use, the more complex the system is found to be. By comparing these systems in terms both of their complexity and their circumstances and manner of use, we gain some ideas as to what the social conditions are that encourage or discourage the elaboration of a kinesic code.

Relationship with spoken language

The simplest system we considered, the crane system, is not related to spoken language in any way. The signs it uses may be related to established gestures in other domains - such as beckoning and holding the palm of the hand forward and raised to mean 'stop'. To this extent it may prove to be to some extent a modification of interactive regulatory gestures within the wider culture beyond that of interaction with cranes, but it has nothing to do with spoken language.

The sawmill system does show some relationship to English, the spoken language of its users. The relationship is sporadic, however, and varied, and it seems to apply only at the level of sign formation. The short utterances that Meissner and Philpott provide do not suggest a strong conformity to English syntax. Indeed, there is some evidence that certain syntactic devices observed in primary sign languages are to be found here. So far as sign formation is concerned, although most signs have depictive or pantomimic origins, in a few cases, as with some of the number signs, certain inflectional processes were applied to create new lexical meanings. A few signs are extended in their meanings because of a phonological resemblance between the English word used to gloss them, as with the signs for 'weak' and 'week', and there are a few signs that map on to English syllables, as with the sign for 'newspaper'. There was one sign, the sign for TV, which was a form of spelling.

The Cistercian sign language showed rather more extensive relationships with English (the language of the users of the version studied by Barakat), although it did so only in regard to the 'unofficial' part of the system. The 'offical' part of the system appears to be an autonomous set of signs, either pantomimic or, in some cases, formed from compounds that express a kind of conceptual analysis of the meaning. This is not surprising. The 'official' system has been in existence for several centuries and was created at a time when Latin was widely used in spoken communication. In the 'unofficial' part of the system, similar kinds of relationship between signs and English words were noted, as were found in the sawmill system, but this aspect of sign formation was rather more developed. There was an extensive use of devices to represent the *syllables* of English words, either by finding signs for things that, in English, would be homophonous with the syllables (as in the example of COOK + KEY for 'cookie') or by using letter signs. These are not used to spell words, so much as to suggest sound values, hence conveying the word in its spoken form.

The most thoroughgoing relationship between an alternate sign language and spoken language was found in the Australian Aboriginal example. Here signs are established that represent the morphemes of the spoken language and the way in which signed utterances are constructed appears to be as a kind of transcription from the spoken form. What is represented in this sign language are the *semantic units* that the morphemes express, not their surface form, for there are no sign representations of syllables or other phonological features. This is probably related to the fact that these societies traditionally had no writing systems. It is interesting that it was found that it was the more proficient signers who mapped their signing on to the morphology of the spoken language most closely (Kendon 1984). This might suggest that as an alternate sign system elaborates, the spoken language comes to structure it more thoroughly.

Plains Indian Sign Language, in contrast, did not, as far as we know, map on to any particular spoken language. There are two possible reasons for this: first of all, the sign language appears to have been used as a lingua franca among groups of people whose languages were very different from one another. Second, however, whereas Warlpiri has a highly agglutinative morphology, so in this case it is relatively easy to set up a sign to morpheme correspondence, many Plains Indian spoken languages have a highly fusional morphology. Establishing a sign to morpheme correspondence would be much more difficult, perhaps not possible. The morphological structure of the spoken language, thus, may influence the extent to which an alternate sign language may reflect spoken language structures.

Circumstances of use and system complexity

In the simplest system, the crane driver system, the lack of symmetry between the guider's code and that of the crane driver probably has prevented this system from elaborating beyond its initial technical functions. In contrast, in the sawmill system where there is symmetry in the communication systems used as well as reciprocity in interactional circumstances, we saw a considerable degree of elaboration. The fact that, in the sawmill, the men were in visual contact with one another for quite long periods probably serves as the initial condition for the extension of the technical system. The extension was relatively limited, however, because other features of the situation, such as the need to pay attention to technical operations and, in some cases, as between the sawyer and the setter, the brevity of the moments when exchanges were possible. In addition, the sign language was not needed (and so not used) beyond the confines of the sawmill.

The monastic sign language, likewise, is limited in its development and again the scope for its use is also limited. All communication in the monastery is discouraged and signs were originally permitted only for the most minimal of purposes and there is a constant ideological restraint on its use. Like the sawmill language, although for other reasons, the occasions of use of the monkish sign language and the communicative purposes which it serves are quite restricted. In both cases, however, it is important to bear in mind that these sign languages are restricted in *when* they are used. For the sawmill workers, the sign language was used only in the sawmill. For the monks, signing was used only when and where silence was enforced. In other circumstances speech could be employed (although this, too, was limited). Plains Indian sign language, on the other hand, by all accounts, was used in a wide range of interactive circumstances, as is the case for the Australian Aboriginal sign languages considered. Accordingly, these sign languages have developed as highly elaborate, flexible systems of communication that can be used as full substitutes for speech in almost all circumstances. The factors important for the elaboration of a kinesic code are, thus, the presence of reciprocity in communication and the scope of the circumstances in which use of the system is demanded and permitted.

Conclusion

More generally, the review undertaken in this chapter suggests that there is no clear boundary that divides something we wish to call a 'language' from systems that do not seem to merit that term. As we saw, people for whom speech is not available (for any of a number of different reasons), yet who find themselves needing to engage in utterance, are quite able to employ the kinesic medium effectively in ways that are well adapted to the functions required. In certain circumstances the kinesic codes employed are progessively elaborated until they become systems which have all the functional features of a spoken language. However, along the way, as we might say, we can observe systems that are, in various ways, intermediate. This approach suggests, thus, that there are continuities between gestural expressions improvised on the spot by speakers who find themselves, for a moment, in circumstances where they cannot use speech, and the gestural expressions found in complex sign languages.

15 'Gesture' and 'sign' on common ground

In this chapter we examine some of the properties that have been described for primary sign languages and draw comparisons with forms of expression that occur in gesture, when used by speakers. We consider three topics: first, how a 'phonological structure' may emerge from iconic forms of expression, second, the use of space in the expression of relationships between discourse elements and third, the nature of 'classifiers', as this has been described in primary sign languages. We suggest that there are parallels in the way speakers use depictive gestures and the way signers use 'classifiers'. We conclude that forms of expression in gesture have much in common with certain forms of expression in primary sign languages. That is, there is common ground between 'gesture' and 'sign'.

Iconicity, sign formation and the emergence of 'phonology'

If the gestural medium is to be used as the sole means of linguistic expression it is obvious that gestures that can serve as referents to objects and actions must be created. This scarcely needs demonstration, and, indeed, as we saw, from the experiments by Bloom and Dufour and by Singleton and colleagues, described in Chapter 14, as soon as speakers were required to use only gesture to describe something, they immediately created a lexicon of gestural forms which they used in gesture sentences with considerable consistency.

But how are gestural expressions that can function lexically created? One way in which one can attempt to convey a referential meaning for another is to show the other an example of what one means. This may be done either by presenting the object in question or by pointing to it, or, if it is an action of some kind, by actually performing the action. This might be called *reference by real ostension*. However, if the object referred to is not to hand, or not within sight, or if the requisite circumstances for the action are not present, one may nevertheless attempt to create a representation of the object or action in question. One might draw a picture of it, one might sketch it, model it by body posturing, imitate its sound (if it has one), or pantomime a pattern of action characteristic of it or associated with it. To follow these strategies is to engage in what may be called *reference by virtual ostension*. This is what a speaker does when a so-called iconic gesture is used. For example, when, as described in Chapter 9, M, speaking of his father's cheeses, said "They came in crates about as long as that" and used his two hands in such a way as to show something of the shape and size of the crates in question, he evoked or *enabled*, as we said, a virtual object which his deictic pronominal "that" referred to.

Where only gesture is available for utterance, however, the actions by which an image that is evoked or enabled may become established as the means by which the referent is referred to. Actions that, at first, were employed to evoke an image of something in lieu of the real thing now become actions that are symbolic of the idea of that thing. For example, Carolyn Scroggs (1981) describes the utterance strategies of a nine-year-old deaf boy who had had no training in sign language. The boy tells a story involving a motorcycle. When he first introduces 'motorcycle' into his discourse he gives an elaborate pantomime of mounting the cycle, starting it, revving it up, using hand motions to indicate the twisting of the throttle on the handlebar. In subsequent references to the motorcycle, however, just this hand motion was used. Thus a hand action derived from a pantomime of twisting the throttle came to serve as a symbol for the concept of 'motorcycle'. In other words, the boy first created *representations* in gesture of the things he wished to refer to, and then he used *elements* from these representations as signs for these things.

In this case, these signs were not stable forms, and they were not shared by others. They very quickly can become so, however. Tervoort (1961), who also worked with deaf children who had no formal sign language instruction, gives an instance in which an elaborate modelling of the facial appearance of a new teacher at the school, who had very well developed dimples, came to be established as a way of referring to this teacher. Quite rapidly, however, the sign was reduced until it was performed simply by a certain pointing movement toward the cheek. The elaborate description, thus, was stripped of its complexity and was reduced to a single movement and now served as the name for the teacher in question.

A consideration of the changes that complex depictions undergo as they become signs suggests that there are certain quite regular processes that are involved. Two-handed forms tend to become one-handed; there is a tendency for movement patterns to become simplified to one- or two-phrase movements; and there is a tendency for the hand movements to be performed within a relatively restricted, centralized space, typically immediately in front of the person's upper chest. Furthermore, it is important to note, in the transformation from elaborate depiction or enactment to a reduced sign-like gesture, features from the original enactment are only retained if they remain in contrast with features of other gestures in the system.

These processes have been described many times in the primary sign language literature (see, for example, Klima and Bellugi 1979, Chapters 1 and 3; Bellugi and Newkirk 1981; Kyle and Woll 1985) and they may also be seen at work in the alternate sign languages of central Aboriginal Australia (Kendon 1988b) and in a local sign language from a valley in the Enga Province of Papua New Guinea (Kendon 1980b, Part II).

From these accounts, three points emerge. First, an element from an elaborate pantomime or descriptive movement sequence gets selected for repeated use and comes to serve as a label for a concept. Second, as a result of economy of action, the element becomes simplified to such a degree that its image-like or iconic character is no longer apparent. It turns into an arbitrary form as it comes to be shaped by the requirement that it be a distinctive form within a system of other forms. Further, however, as it undergoes this process, it is freed of any requirement that it be a 'picture' of something. However, it is this that frees it, also, to take on a highly general meaning. It thus becomes available for recombination with other forms and so may come to participate in compound signs or sentences.

Thus, elaborate presentations of visual descriptions through gestural action, or the elaborate acting out of action patterns characteristic of particular activities which serve as evocations of the objects or actions that the person wishes to refer to can quite rapidly become transformed into highly simplified forms that serve as symbols for these referents. They come to be transformed into the functional equivalent of words and, like words, they can be combined in sequences to create units of discourse-constructed meaning or sentences. In this way, the visual representations and enactments for which the kinesic medium is so well adapted are transcended and a system of symbols that can operate in a quite abstract way is established.

Discourse construction considerations

If discourse is to be carried out in the kinesic medium, two or more separate expressions must be conjoined so that they become components of a construction. If there are consistent ways in which this is done we may speak of a syntax. That is, we may speak of rules and devices by which the relationships between the elements in a construction are established. In alternate sign languages, as we saw in Chapter 14, the spoken language of their users has an important influence on this although, as we also saw, the nature and extent of this influence is not a simple matter. In primary sign languages, on the other hand, where spoken language can have, at best, only an indirect influence, syntactic devices follow principles that exploit extensively the properties of the kinesic medium.

In the kinesic medium it is possible to structure expressions spatially as well as sequentially. Further, because the bodily instruments that any kinesic code makes use of - the two hands, the head, the face, the eyes, the torso, and so forth - are spatially distributed, and because, to a degree, they can be moved differentially in relation to one another, a kind of orchestration of bodily instruments is possible. That is, more than one thing can be signified kinesically at the same time. Furthermore, it is also possible to use some bodily expressions in such a way that they frame or bracket together expressions by other parts of the body. Thus, facial gestures, such as eyebrow movements or positionings, movements of the mouth, head postures and sustainments and changes in gaze direction can, and do, serve as important means by which relationships between successive expressions, such as those produced by the hands, can be linked together in various ways. For example, marking a discourse sequence as subordinate to some other sequence in which it may be embedded may be accomplished through the use of head positions, gaze direction changes and facial gestures of various kinds.

In sign language these possibilities are exploited extensively with the result that syntactic structures can be observed that are very different from anything that can be observed in a spoken language, which cannot use the three dimensions of space. These differences, which appear so striking if we compare a primary sign language with a spoken language, appear less so if we compare discourse in sign with the gesture–speech ensembles commonly encountered in everyday spoken interaction. There are strategies of expression that speakers employ when organizing the gestural components of their utterances that have much in common with strategies of expression in sign language discourse. Here we outline features of the syntactic use of space and the use of 'classifiers' in sign language and describe examples of gesture use by speakers that seem very similar.

Space

It has long been noted how, in sign language, the deployment of signs so as to establish spatial relationships between them plays a central role in establishing grammatical relationships between elements in a discourse. There are many verbs in American Sign Language, for example, that are performed so that they require a path of movement and an orientation that exhibits the agent and the goal of the action all within one phrase of action. For example, in signing the phrase "I see you" a signer can move the hand shaped for the sign SEE (a hand shape in which just the index finger and middle finger are extended and separated - the 'V' hand shape) in such a way that the tips of the extended fingers of the hand are directed toward the interlocutor. It is enough that the sign itself moves from self toward the interlocutor to establish who is related to whom in the act of seeing. To say "You see me" the SEE sign would start out oriented and directed toward the interlocutor and end up by being oriented and directed to the signer. To refer to third persons, the SEE sign can be moved toward or away from locations diagonally between the parties to the conversation. If the signer wanted to say "They look at each other" it would be possible for both hands to be used, each with the hand shape for SEE, each oriented toward the other, each hand moved alternately toward the other.

As Liddell (2000) has recently argued, such spatial inflections of verb signs constitute cases in which the verb sign is combined with an act of pointing. As he shows, signers will direct verb signs of this sort in relation to actually present persons and objects, if these are the topics of discourse. If the persons and objects are not actually present then the signer establishes locations in the immediate signing space which stand in for the arguments of the discourse and the verb signs are then combined with pointings in relation to these locations. Depending upon what the signer is saying, the signer may establish locations in space as tokens for the presence of these absent objects. At other times, however, what Liddell calls *surrogates* may be established. For example, if a signer wants to say something about looking at something on the roof of a house, he could so organize his posture and gaze, and extend his hand formed for SEE as if he were attending to something high up and some distance away. He would behave as if there was a surrogate house present. Liddell argues that previous attempts to deal with the way in which, in signed discourse, locations are set up and signs are directed in relation to them, as if we may speak of these locations as morphemes affixed to the verb signs, do not work. This is because signers do not make use of discretely defined and arbitrarily established locations in inflecting their signs directionally. Rather, if the persons and objects that are the arguments of their discourse are present in current physical space, they direct their signs in relation to their actual locations. If they are not present, then signers can set up a virtual spatial representation of the situation and they then inflect their signs in relation to these locations as if they were pointing at them.

This kind of spatial inflection of signs has its parallel in the spatial inflection of gestures. Examples have been described in previous chapters. Thus it will be recalled how, in Example 46 (p. 203, see Fig. 11.2) GB, referring to a gable on a building that had been displaced, says "You can see that that gable leans backwards" and, as he does so, he extends a flat hand, palm facing forward, upward in the direction of the gable he is talking about and moves his hand from a 'back' position to a 'forward' position as he does so. He does here a gesture that, with the hand shape, represents the wide flat character of the gable, and, with the movement, indicates that it has changed position but, at the same time, he inflects this gesture so that it incorporates, deictically, a reference to the very gable he is talking about.

And just as signers may set up, in Liddell's terms, surrogates for things that are not present and deictically inflect their signs in relation to these, gesturers do so in just the same way. Thus we may recall, from Chapter 10, Example 37 (See Fig. 10.9, p. 189) in which the speaker UB is talking about the salacious phrases the boys write on the backs of the seats of the buses he drives, right in front of the girls. As he says "*e il ragazzo a fianco, il fidanzato di una ragazza che continua a designare e pennellare*" ('and the boy in the next seat, the boyfriend of a girl, that continues to draw and paint'), he leans over to his left, extending his left hand forward as he does so and acts as if holding a brush. He thus gestures holding a brush or pen and positions this as if it is directed toward a surface in front of the man he is sitting next to. He continues with "*e loro guardano*" ('and they [i.e. the girls] watch') and as he says this he rapidly points first to the man he is sitting next to and then to the space in front of him where he had been enacting 'painting'. As he names in words the activities of drawing and looking, in gesture he acts as if there is the back of a bus seat in front of him and he treats the man sitting next to him as if he were his seat mate on the bus. In this way, through gesture, UB adds much specific detail to what is conveyed in the words of his utterance. This is exactly parallel to the way in which signers can add detail to what they say with lexical signs by inflecting their verb signs in relation to surrogates in their surrounding signing space.

Speakers may also use gestures to establish spatial locations in gesture-space which serve as tokens, in Liddell's sense, either for persons or objects being talked about, or for abstract entities. For example, things or individuals referred to in a discourse may be assigned locations in gesture-space by a consistent pattern of spatial inflection of gestures that the speaker is using in relation to what he is talking about. Pointings or directionally inflected movements may be used to differentiate separate locations for the referents of a discourse. Keeping the referents spatially separated by means of gesture is a way of keeping them conceptually separate.

Examples have been described by Haviland in his account of narration in Guugur Yimithirr speakers in Queensland (Haviland 1993, 2000) and by Marianne Gullberg in her comparative accounts of the use of gesture in narrations by speakers speaking their own language or a language they are learning (Gullberg 1998: 139ff. See Fig. 15.1, p. 313). These examples are directly comparable with what has been described for sign language. Poizner,

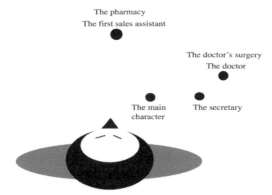

Fig. 15.1   Diagram of the locations in 'gesture space' that speakers in Gullberg's study used when referring in gesture to the various characters and locations as they retold a cartoon story (Redrawn from Gullberg 1998: 141).

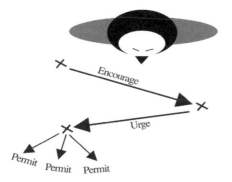

Fig. 15.2   An illustration of how different agents and patients of a multiclausal sentence can be given different locations in 'signing space'. A signer signed a sentence translated as 'John encouraged him to urge her to permit each of them to take up the class.' This was signed as JOHN followed by the sign ENCOURAGE which is moved as indicated by the labelled arrow. This established that John's encouragement is directed to another. The sign URGE now follows, moved now to a new location. From this new location the signer signs PERMIT with a succession of separate directional movements. This is described as an 'exhaustive' inflection and renders the idea of a finite number of individuals as the objects of the verb 'permit'. This sequence was then followed by the signs TAKE-UP and CLASS. Redrawn from Poizner, Klima and Bellugi (1990, page 19).

Klima and Bellugi (1987, p. 19) exemplify this with a signed sentence in which the signer says "John encouraged him to urge her to permit each of them to take the class." It will be seen (Fig. 15.2) how the path of movement of the signs ENCOURAGE, URGE and PERMIT have distinctive spatial origins and terminations, which correspond, in this case, to the locations established as referents for the people referred to in this sentence .

Example 128 from the film ISP 00161 also illustrates this. In this film several psychiatrists and psychiatrists-in-training are discussing a case. In response to something one of the participants has just said, the psychiatrist who is presenting the case attempts to clarify what he takes to be a misunderstanding. He explains that sometimes the patient believes she has acted one way, but that her mother has told her that she has acted another way. The two principals in this discourse, the patient and her mother, are gesturally referred to by movements that appear to establish two different locations, one for each. The discourse and how gestures relate to speech in this example are given in the transcript below. See also Fig. 15.3. As the speaker says "She feels that this is not the case at times" he thrusts his hand forward slightly over "she" and wags it back and forth in association with "this is not the case" using a 'negation' movement. He then says "it's mother that has told her that she's been this way". As he says "mother" he thrusts his hand to his left, establishing a location in the left side of his gesture space. He then says "and she's kind of accepting it". As he says "and she's" he moves his hand back again into the space previously moved to over the first "she". He then continues with the patient as topic, explaining that he does not think the patient believes her mother. During this part of the utterance he moves his hand down vertically in the space to his right.

Example 128 (ISP 001 61)

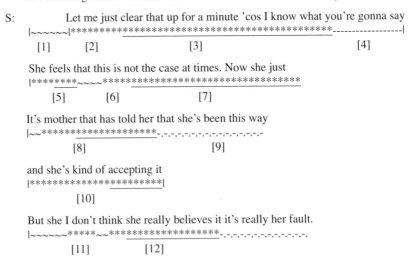

A: I'm wondering uh what she says in effect is that/ she has gotten uh her brother to
    do something sexual with her/ she hasn't said what it is/ but she says

S: Let me just clear that up for a minute 'cos I know what you're gonna say
    |~~~~~~|***------------------|
    [1]   [2]   [3]   [4]

    She feels that this is not the case at times. Now she just
    |********~~~~~************************************
     [5]   [6]   [7]

    It's mother that has told her that she's been this way
    |~~********************-.-.-.-.-.-.-.-.-.-.-.-.-.-
      [8]   [9]

    and she's kind of accepting it
    |*********************|
          [10]

    But she I don't think she really believes it it's really her fault.
    |~~~~~~*****~~****************-.-.-.-.-.-.-.-.-.-.
       [11]   [12]

V   Let me just clear that up for a minute
      'cos I know what you're gonna say

W   She feels that this is not the   **X**   It's mother that has told
      case at times, now she just-   her that she's been this way

Y   And she's kind of accepting it   **Z**   But she I don't think
                                                     she really believes it

Fig. 15.3   Example 128 (ISP001 61). Illustrations and explanations for the accompanying transcript. During A's utterance ("I'm wondering" etc.) S lights D's cigarette (D is to the right of S, and not shown), then his own, and shifts posture to orient toward A and as A says "but she says" S lifts his left hand, which is holding a folder of papers [1] and thrusts it forwards in the direction of A [2] and sustains this position [3]. This position of S is shown in V. W: S now embarks on his account of what he thinks is the patient's point of view. As he says "she feels" he moves his right hand vertically downwards [5], and this is then followed by a restricted amplitude 'back and forth' movement over "this is" [6]. The movement here is a feature that expresses the negative in the account S gives of the patient's feelings. X: As S then says "It's mother ..." he turns his head toward his left and then moves his hand rapidly toward the left side of his gesture space [8] where he holds it until the end of his phrase, the hand relaxing somewhat over the last part [9]. Y: He now returns to the patient as topic ("and she's kind of accepting it") and with this he moves his hand back into the right side of his gesture space [10], where the hand now moves up and down vertically as he finishes with his comment, shown in Z, that he does not think the patient really believes what her mother tells her [11], [12].

Sign language classifiers

An important feature of American Sign Language and, indeed, of any primary sign language, as far as we now know, is the role of so-called 'classifiers'. These are forms that are conventionalized to stand in for various classes of objects which can be moved freely or positioned in space in various ways as a way of describing the activity, shape or fate of something without having to use an extended string of lexical signs. When a signer wishes to talk about some object, such as a person, a small animal, a car and so forth, and wants to say something about what the person or animal did, or what happened to the car, instead of using a specific sign for the object in question, a hand shaped in a certain way can be used to *represent* or *stand in for* the person, animal or object. This can then be moved around in space or positioned in space relative to the other hand or in relation to previously assigned positions in the signer's sign-space. These movements and positionings function as statements about the action, fate or spatial position of the object the hand shape is used to refer to. Because different hand shapes are used consistently for different classes of objects, some writers have referred to these forms as 'classifiers' arguing that they are analogous to classifiers that are used in certain spoken languages to mark nouns as belonging to different classes (see Allan 1977). Serious doubts have been expressed about the validity of this analogy, and other terms have been proposed (see Schembri 2003). None of these other terms have gained much acceptance, as yet, so it seems simpler to continue to use the term 'classifier'. However, this does not mean, necessarily, that we consider these expressions to have much in common with what have been called classifiers in spoken languages.

As an illustration, consider the signing of the sentence 'A cat is sitting on the fence.' (See Liddell 1980, pp. 93-96.) This may be done, in ASL, using classifiers, in such a way that the relationship between the cat and the fence is displayed directly as a spatial relationship. In signing this the signer first uses a lexical sign for 'fence'. This is a two-handed sign in which the hands begin in contact with one another, fingers partially spread, palms facing the signer. The hands then may be moved apart in a horizontal manner. In this example, the sign for 'fence' is immediately followed by the sign for 'cat'. In this sign the right hand, held so the tips of the index finger and thumb are in contact, is brought into contact with the cheek. While the signer does this, the left hand remains in the position it used for the sign 'fence' and this hand position, so maintained, now comes to serve as a sustained reference to the object 'fence'. Immediately after signing 'cat' the signer now moves the hand downwards, away from the face, shaping the hand in doing so, so that the index and second finger are now bent at the second and third joints. This 'bent fingers' hand

Fig.15.4 A signer signs the sentence "A cat is on the fence." She first gives the lexical sign FENCE. This is followed with the lexical sign CAT while leaving her other hand in place with a vertically oriented partially spread hand which serves as a classifier for 'fence'. Finally, her left hand assumes the 'bent V' hand shape used as a classifier for a 'small legged creature'. This hand now stands for 'cat' and it is placed on top of the other hand which still maintains the classifier for 'fence'. In this way the spatial relationship of fence and cat are displayed directly through the relative spatial positionings of the classifiers. From Liddell (1980, p. 93).

shape is a hand shape routinely used in ASL as a 'stand in' for 'small animal'. In this context it serves to refer to 'cat'. This 'bent fingers' hand is now moved so that it is positioned on top of the left hand which, as we saw, was earlier designated as a referent for 'fence'. In this way the signer shows directly that the cat is on the fence. It will be seen that, according to the way the 'small animal' classifier is positioned and oriented in relation to the classifier that has been assigned the meaning of 'fence', the signer may make a variety of statements about the cat in relation to the fence. He can show the cat beside the fence and, by moving the small animal classifier from one side of the fence classifier to the other he can say 'the cat jumped over the fence'.[1]

In American Sign Language, according to Emmorey (2002), there are four kinds of classifiers. These she calls *Whole entity, Handling instrument,*

[1] Liddell (2003) suggests that what is referred to by Emmorey and others as a classifier which is then regarded as being combined with one or more movement morphemes is better understood in terms of the idea that it is a 'depicting verb' which combines lexically encoded meaning with depiction, that is, gradient, or analogue representation. Thus in the cat-on-fence example, the 'bent v' is a lexical item meaning 'small animal' and its movement, which is a component integral to it, depicts its action. It may be considered to be a verb, that is, with the meaning ANIMAL-BE-AT+location – in this case the location is the fence-surface. Liddell, thus, has re-framed the account of these phenomena to bring it into line with his view of ASL as a language in which gradient or analogue representation is integrated into its grammar. This analysis does not affect the point being made here which is that, to use Liddell's now current terminology, signers' use of depicting verbs seems reminiscent of the way speakers use certain depictive gestures in some contexts.

Limb and *Extension and Surface* classifiers. A *Whole entity* classifier stands for an entire object and within this class there are a variety of hand shapes that are used consistently for different kinds of whole entities. Thus a hand shape in which the thumb, index and middle fingers are extended and spread is commonly used when the entity is a vehicle, an upright extended index finger is used to refer to a person, the 'bent fingers' shape is used for a small animal, as we just saw. A *Handling instrument* classifier is a form used to refer to an agent handling an instrument of some kind, such as a knife, a pen, and the like. A *Limb* classifier refers to a limb, such as a paw, an arm or a foot. In *Extension and Surface* classifiers a hand shape is used to refer to the depth or width of an object (extension classifier), or it may be used to refer to the surface of an object, or whether the object is long and thin or narrow or broad, and so forth.

In use these classifiers are combined with a movement pattern of some sort, and it is this combination that serves as the complex that says something about the object referred to with the classifier. According to Emmorey four different movement patterns may be distinguished (she calls them 'movement morphemes'). These are: a movement which *positions* the entity referred to by the classifier (in the example given above, moving the 'small animal' classifier on top of the 'fence' classifier would be an example of such a *positioning* movement); a movement which shows the *path* of movement - moving the 'small animal' classifier over the 'fence' classifier might show the path of movement of the cat as it jumped over the fence. This can be combined with further movement modifications to show the *manner* of movement, as when a vehicle classifier is moved upwards in a back and forth manner to show that a car weaved back and forth as it climbed a hill. Finally, there are so-called *extension* movements. These are 'tracing' movements that show the size or shape of something. Included here are movements which show the arrangement of an unspecified number of objects in a given space, such as a row of books on a bookshelf.

All this may recall for the reader what was said in Chapter 9. There we showed how a speaker, when using gesture to indicate the size and shape of an object, to show how that object is positioned, to trace the shape of something, to show how an object is handled as a way of referring to that object, and so forth, makes use of a restricted range of hand shapes and movement patterns that constitutes a repertoire of *representation techniques*. These techniques have much in common with what has been described for classifiers and their associated 'movement morphemes'. In American Sign Language there is a high degree of consistency in how the various hand shapes for the different classifiers are used, and how the movement patterns are carried out when they are employed. However, this seems to be but a regularization of techniques that are widely used by speakers when using gesture for depictive purposes. We need further work on the forms employed in depictive gestures, however we strongly suspect that speakers are rather consistent in how they use hand shapes to depict long narrow objects in contrast to long fat objects, large round objects as compared to small round objects, broad flat surfaces in contrast to thin edges, and the like. We further expect that it will be shown that the forms of movement employed by speakers in using gestures for object depiction will contrast in consistent ways depending, for example, upon whether the movement is to establish the position of an object (as in M showing how the cheeses were arranged in the crate, or as in G showing how the big rocks were placed in her aquarium - in Example 41, p. 193), to sketch the shape of an object, to show a surface, to show a path of movement, and the like (see Calbris 1990, Müller 1998).

As we showed in Chapter 9, the depictive gestures receive their interpretation by being combined with the verbal discourse. M, for example, used a very particular form of hand shape and positioning that is commonly used when a speaker is specifying the size and shape of some entity, but what entity it is, is not determinable from the gesture by itself. The entity it stands for must be assigned to it by other means - in the case of spoken discourse this is generally done through speech. It is notable, however, that this parallels very closely what is observed in sign language when classifiers are used. We saw this in the first example we gave, where the bent fingers classifier is designated as 'cat' by the prior use of the lexical sign for 'cat'.

Let us illustrate the parallels between classifier use in sign language and depictive gesture use in spoken discourse with two further examples, one from a signed discourse described in Emmorey (2002), the other from an extract from Crick III which we have already partly described in Chapter 8. The extract from the signed discourse used here is from a lecture in sign about hanging pictures. Selected frames from a film of this discourse, with explanation, are given in Figure 15.5. The signer first uses a lexical sign PICTURE. He follows this with a classifier in which he uses both hands, index fingers extended, to outline a rectangular shape. Note that this is done in front of his face in such a way that the rectangular shape is oriented vertically as if it is before the signer's eyes. This, it seems clear, is a way of showing that he means to refer to 'picture' as a rectangular entity oriented in a particular way and in a particular sort of relation with an observer. This is then followed by a series of signs which are glossed as meaning that people are walking back and forth and slamming doors. The signer again gives the lexical sign PICTURE which he then follows with an action in which two 'L' hands are lifted up, again at the 'in front of face' position that recalls the position in which the rectangular shape was drawn, and these hands are so positioned as to suggest

A. Topic: PICTURE   B. Cl: Oblong shape

C. Adv: SOMETIMES   D. Cl: People walk back   E. Cl: Doors slamming
                      and forth

F. Topic: PICTURE   G. Cl: Picture-shift

H. Cl: Adjust-picture

Fig. 15.5   A signer explains how you can adjust a picture that has become crooked as a result of vibrations from people walking back and forth and slamming doors. A. Signs PICTURE. This establishes the topic. B. The 'Size-Shape Classifier' that follows shows the orientation of a picture in relation to a person, as it might be if it is hanging on a wall. C. Signs SOMETIMES. D. A classifier to show 'walking back and forth'. E. A classifier to show 'slamming doors'. F. PICTURE. Re-establishes topic and 'nominates' the classifier that follows. G. Classifier to show picture now askew on the wall. H. Classifier to suggest action by which an askew picture may be readjusted. Adapted from Emmorey (2002, p. 75), based on a discourse in *Pursuit of ASL: Interesting Facts Using Classifiers* (Interpreting Consolidated 1998).

a rectangular entity before the signer's eyes, but now askew. The combination of the lexical sign PICTURE and the classifier that follows is translated to mean 'picture shifts'. The final element in this discourse is two fisted hands which suggest 'grasping' something, these are again held in front of the face, and they are moved, one down slightly, one up. This refers to the action of adjusting the picture that has been made askew by the vibrations from passing people and door-slamming.

In this example it will be seen that the signer signs PICTURE and follows this with an action that provides us with the idea of a rectangular object with no depth (this is interpreted as 'picture' because of the lexical sign that immediately preceded it) oriented vertically in front of the face of the signer - but not right up close to him: in other words he gives us a highly schematic representation of a picture hanging on a wall. The subsequent references to what happens to the picture (that it shifts position and that it can be readjusted) could not be understood without this initial representation. The later classifiers are intelligible, thus, because they 'feed off' the first one.

The sequence taken from Crick III, with which this signed discourse may be compared, has already been partially described in Chapter 8 (see Example 15 and Fig. 8.12, p. 148). M, speaking of his father who was a grocer, describes how, at Christmas time, he would have sent down from London a huge Christmas cake, ready iced and decorated. Customers could come in and buy pieces of this cake by weight. He explains this as follows: "He used to have sent down from London, a Christmas cake, and it was this sort of size, and they'd cut it off in bits and you'd go in and say: 'Can I have a pound and a half?' and he'd cut you off a pound and a half." The gestures M uses as he says this are given in Fig. 15.6. As he states the topic of his discourse, "Christmas cake", he remains in a posture in which he leans with his hands pressed against the table in front of him (Fig. 15.6 A). Then he says "and it was (1.02) this sort of (0.4) size." As we described in Chapter 8, as he says this, during the pauses in his speech, he draws with his extended index fingers a large square shape, as if to suggest a large square-shaped object set horizontally on the table in front of him (Fig. 15.6 B). It will be noted that the sequence of events here is extremely similar to the sequence noted in the picture-hanging sequence just described. In that sequence the signer first uses a lexical sign to specify 'picture' and follows this with a classifier oriented to show how the rectangular-shaped object was arranged vertically, as if on a wall. In the same way, M here first names the object, "Christmas cake" and follows this with a size-shape-orientation specifying gesture, giving us an image of a large square object on the table in front of him. It will be seen that M's 'sketch' to show the size and relative position of the cake serves just the same role in his discourse as does the signer's classifier which provided a sketch of the size and relative

A

In me father's shop,
he used to have sent down from London,
a Christmas cake...

B

and it was (1.02) this sort of (0.4) size

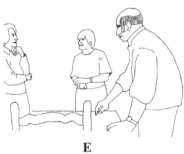

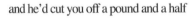

C

and he'd cut it off in bits

D

and you'd go in and say:
"Can I have a pound and a half?"

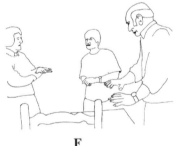

E

and he'd cut you off a pound and a half

F

A: And that was ready iced, was it?
M: Decorated. the lot!

Fig. 15.6   M explains the Chrstmas cake and how customers could buy pieces of it.
For an explanation see text.

position of the picture. Just as the signer says, lexically, 'picture' before he does the classifier, so M says "Christmas cake" before he does his gesture. His size-shape-position specifier gesture is thus assigned its 'pro' status in just the same way as the signer assigns the 'pro' status of the classifier that follows the sign 'picture'.

As we saw in the account of the picture-hanging sequence, the signer later uses two other classifiers, first to show the position of the picture on the wall after it has become askew and second to show what you can do - take hold of the picture and set it straight. And, as we saw, these subsequent classifiers are only intelligible because of the initial classifier which refers us to the idea of a rectangular picture hanging on the wall. In just the same way, the gestures that M uses in the rest of his discourse about the Christmas cake depend, for their intelligibility, upon the initial size-shape-orientation specifying gesture that he did at the beginning. Thus he continues: "And he'd cut it off in bits and you'd go in and say 'Can I have a pound and a half?' and he'd cut you off a pound and a half." As he says "and he'd cut it off in bits" he lowers his hand, now a palm-vertical open hand, in a 'cutting action' and he does this in one corner of the space he had previously designated as the space on the table where the large cake had been placed (Fig. 15.6 C). In gesture, thus, he uses something that is quite analogous to a 'handling classifier' and through the movement he shows just where and how the grocer would cut off a piece of the cake. This 'cutting' gesture, however, would not be fully intelligible were it not for the previously established size and position of the cake that was done through the first 'sketch' gesture. The 'cutting' gesture thus derives its intelligibility in just the same way as the 'picture skewed' classifier derives its intelligibility from the previously established idea of a picture hanging on a wall, itself established by the sequence of the lexical sign PICTURE followed by the 'rectangular flat-shaped vertically oriented' object classifier in the picture-hanging sequence.

As M then says "and you'd go in and say: 'Can I have a pound and a half?'" he extends a palm-up open hand toward A (Fig. 15.6 D). By this form of pointing gesture he suggests the role of customer for his interlocutor, A (compare Examples 55, 56, and 57 in Chapter 11 and the deictically inflected Open Hand Supine gestures described in Chapter 13). Then he says "and he'd cut you off a pound and half". As he says this he returns to the space on the table in front of him, where before he had located the cake in the gesture depicted in Fig. 15.6 B. By drawing out an area with his index finger on the surface of the table he indicates a corner of the cake that the grocer might cut off. His sketching gesture (which is just like an 'extension classifier') here suggests the size of a pound-and-a-half portion (Fig. 15.6 E). Here, again, this gesture gains its intelligibility from what had been established by the first size-shape-orientation specifier gesture at the beginning of the sequence. And again it is quite similar to the way in which the final 'adjust' classifier in the picture-hanging sequence gains its intelligibility from the initial size-shape-orientation classifier that the signer provided after he had specified the topic of his discourse.

The parallels between the way M uses his depictive and enactive gestures in this sequence, the way they are assigned meaning, and the role they play in adding details to his discourse, and the way the classifiers function in the picture-hanging sequence are striking. This suggests that the strategies a speaker uses in deploying depictive gestures in his discourse may be quite similar to those followed by signers when they use classifiers. As we undertake more detailed and systematic studies of just how speakers employ gesture we may expect to find many parallels with what happens in sign language. This should be neither surprising nor embarrassing. Speakers' uses of kinesic actions and signers' uses of kinesic actions are cut from the same cloth. Where kinesic action cannot be or is not conjoined with speech then it will be put to additional uses - a lexicon will have to be created, for example - but we are still dealing with something that is in the same *family* of communication systems.

'Sign' and 'gesture'

Some writers have raised the question "Do signers gesture?" as if a sharp distinction can be drawn between 'gesture' and 'sign'. Emmorey (2002) sets up a list of features in terms of which she contrasts 'gesture' with 'sign' and suggests that these two modes of expression are quite different from one another. She shows, nevertheless, with two or three illustrative sequences, how signers may insert 'gestures' into their discourse. This indicates that, just as users of spoken language may find limitations in this medium which induce them to employ gestural expressions, so users of sign language may find similar limitations in that medium, and, in much the same way, on occasion move from sign to gesture to overcome them.

A somewhat different approach to the question of the relationship between 'sign' and 'gesture' has been taken by Scott Liddell. As we saw above, he has shown that, at least in respect to the way in which signers inflect signs spatially, a scalar, 'analogical' and, therefore, 'non-morphological' component is regularly employed as an integral part of expression in sign language (Liddell 2000, 2003). For Liddell the analytic tools taken over from the structural analysis of spoken languages cannot be used to account for everything that happens in sign language, as some have tried to make them do. Thus it could be said that 'gestural expression' is found fully integrated in signing.

However, as indeed the comparison with the picture-hanging sequence and M's discourse about the cake in his father's shop suggests, when speakers use gesture they may also use strategies that are found in use by signers. Furthermore, in any discourse, whether signed or spoken, there are always to be found features of the performance that do not fully admit of being accounted for in strictly linguistic terms. As Bolinger pointed out many years ago, in a paper we have already had occasion to cite (Bolinger 1946), the boundary between what is linguistic, and what seems not to be, is hard to establish in any non-arbitrary way. To a degree it is determined by what seems convenient from the point of view of the particular tools of analysis that we currently wish to make use of.

The present chapter (and also the previous one) has been written in this spirit. We have not tried to decide on the boundary between 'sign' and 'gesture'. Rather, we have sought to show that when people employ the kinesic medium to express themselves, depending upon what other media of expression are also available, so the way the kinesic medium is shaped and structured will vary. If a spoken language is being used, for example, kinesic expressions may be brought in at certain points in relation to spoken discourse to enrich descriptions in various ways, but the kinesic expressions employed for these purposes, as we have seen, do not have a semantic autonomy in respect to spoken language. There is good reason for this: they would not work as they do if they did. On the other hand, some kinesic expressions used by speakers do have a certain autonomy in respect to spoken expression and these, as we saw, develop a vocabulary of forms and acquire structural features that admit of analogies with phonology in spoken languages much as can be shown for kinesic systems that are used by non-speakers - sign languages, that is to say.

To adapt something that Leila Monaghan (2002) has written, languages, whether signed or spoken, may be seen as islands of order within larger seas of sound and movement. As we speak or sign we constantly mix in with our discourse all manner of expressive devices, some more, some less well-patterned. Signers use words and syntactic constructions, but they also modulate the performance of their signs in various ways, employ 'classifiers' and pull in kinesic expressions of all kinds, some from the kinesic vocabulary shared by the wider community, some improvised. Speakers act similarly. They use words and syntactic constructions, but they also use intonation patterns, voicings and vocalizations. And when they use gesture they reach out for strategies of expression that are also found in sign languages.

16   Gesture, culture and the communication economy

As we saw in Chapter 3, the idea that gesture could serve as a universal language was widely entertained in the seventeenth century. Both Bonifacio and Bulwer believed that it was a natural form of expression that could be understood universally and Bonifacio, explicitly, hoped that his book *L'Arte dei Cenni* might contribute to the re-establishment of gesture as a common mode of communication and thus return mankind to the state it was in before it strayed from its God-given existence, when communication was unimpeded by the difficulties created by different spoken languages. The idea that gesture could form the basis of a universal language continued during the eighteenth century. However, despite the efforts of Abbé de l'Epée, his pupil Sicard, and others, it was soon realized that a gesture language, like any other, would diversify with use and was not inherently superior as a basis for a universal language.

Nevertheless, the idea that gesture is a universal form of expression that does not need to be learned to be understood has remained a very persistent one. At the same time, it has also always been recognized that there are differences from one nation to the next, from one culture to the next or from one stratum of society to the next, in how gesture is used and differences in the specific gestures employed in different cultures has long been noted. How may these two views, seemingly contradictory, be reconciled?

Tylor, and other writers in the nineteenth century, tended to use the expression 'the gesture language' as if there was one universally recognized system. Mallery, in his study of Plains Indian Sign Language, although he understood that there were many local dialects, also believed that gestural expression was fundamentally the same everywhere. Some modern writers have shown similar tendencies. Gordon Hewes, for example, who revived the idea that the first form of language must have been gestural (Hewes 1973), gathered together a great many accounts of first contacts between European explorers and local tribes in North America, the Pacific and elsewhere. He quotes numerous examples from the diaries of travellers that describe how gesture was successfully employed as a means of communication in these first contacts. In his view, this showed the potentially universal character of this medium and thus its suitability as the medium for the first form of language (Hewes 1974). In recent years, notwithstanding the great emphasis placed on the diversity of primary sign languages, many indications have been noted that suggest that, syntactically, these differ from one another far less than spoken languages do. Furthermore, when people from different Deaf communities using different sign languages that are not mutually intelligible meet, as happens at international conventions of the Deaf, a mutually intelligible mode of communication is established very quickly in a way that cannot happen if spoken languages are used (Jordan and Battison 1976; Supalla and Webb 1995).

There are grounds, thus, for thinking that there are aspects of gestural expression that are universal. On the other hand, the view that the uses and significance of gesture are not universal but differ markedly from one culture to another has also been widely maintained. Especially in American anthropology, between the period that extends from the end of the first decade to the end of the fifth decade of the twentieth century, starting with Boas, the doctrine that differences in behaviour and personality from one culture to another are entirely or mainly the consequences of cultural tradition dominated. Accordingly, differences in gesture use from one group to the next were seen as a consequence of differences in cultural tradition. This was clearly expressed by Edward Sapir (1951[1927]) and elaborated in a widely cited article by Weston La Barre (1947). Inspired in particular by the article by Sapir, Ray Birdwhistell developed his project for a kinesics which, as we saw (in Chapter 5), was to be patterned methodologically after the model for structural linguistics developed in the tradition of Bloomfield by George Trager and others. It was assumed that there would be divergent kinesic codes, just as there are divergent languages.

By the middle of the fifth decade of the twentieth century, however, the pendulum began to swing the other way. In 1957 Chomsky published his *Syntactic Structures* which initiated the search for universal grammatical forms. By 1969 Ekman and his colleagues had begun to publish their work on facial expression showing that Darwin was right and that there *are* universals in human facial expression. And the steady advance of animal behaviour studies and developments in genetics led to the emergence of sociobiology and to attempts to develop a human ethology. This, too, revived interest in the possibility that there are, after all, universal forms of human expression (Eibl-Eibesfeldt 1989, Morris 1977). Specifically, in gesture studies, while there had been a number of publications that listed vocabularies of gestures in which the emphasis definitely seemed to be upon the idea that there are cultural differences, at the same time, as gesture attracted the interest of psychologists, cognitive scientists and psycholinguists, its spontaneous, natural character came to be emphasized. An assumption implicit in much of this work is that what these studies reveal about the nature of gesture is universal and to be found in all humans, regardless of culture.

In previous chapters in this book, we have had occasion to suggest that people have to learn how to employ gesture in appropriate ways and that the ways in which it is used are governed by social convention. From time to time we have drawn attention to differences between Neapolitan gestural practice and the gestural practice of English speakers which are surely attributable to differences in social tradition. We have noted, too, the way in which specialized 'narrow gloss' forms are used and that these forms are often quite specific to a given culture. There is, thus, an aspect of gestural practice that is clearly shaped by culture. How gesture is used, furthermore, and what forms it takes and how prominent a role it plays in face-to-face interaction also seems to be something that varies from one culture to another. This is the theme taken up in the present chapter.

Gestural practices as cultural tradition: evidence from historical studies

Dilwyn Knox (1990, 1996) has noted that already by the late medieval period and early Renaissance, various writers had commented that gestural practices differed widely from one part of Europe to another. "Gesture in late medieval and Renaissance Europe" he writes (1990, p.13) "was...a Babel of vernaculars..." One of the most persistent observations appears to be that in southern Europe, among Italians in particular, gesture was regarded as being especially prominent. Knox mentions a work from Prague from the very early Renaissance dealing with rhetorical delivery in which it is noted that the Italians are well known for their lively use of gesture. Burke (1992) has drawn attention to writers from the late sixteenth to the early eighteenth centuries who have commented on various aspects of gestural differences in Europe. In particular, the evident expressive immobility of the ruling Spanish dignitaries in Italy is noted, which was seen to be in marked contrast to the liveliness of the French as well as the Italians. Burke notes that from the mid-sixteenth century onward there was a growing interest in gesture and this he links to the reforms of gesture which were part of the moral discipline of the Counter-Reformation. At that time there appeared a growing sense of the inappropriateness of extensive bodily expressiveness for both the priesthood and the laity and a number of manuals of conduct from the fifteenth century onward can be cited that recommend restraint and moderation. Especially in the north of Europe, with the rise of Protestantism, flamboyance in bodily expression seems to have been disapproved of. Perhaps it is for this reason (Burke suggests) that the tendency for the prominent use of gesture in Italy came under notice.

One interesting expression of this is to be found in Henri Estienne's *Deux dialogues de nouveau langage françois italianizé et autrement desguizé*, published in Paris in 1578. In this work Estienne, a Calvinist, complains that the upper strata of French society had begun to adopt Italian idioms and manners which had been brought to French court circles following the presence of Catherine de' Medici and her retinue in the court of Henri II.[1] Efron (1972) provides a brief account of this. He writes (p. 53) that the satirical dialogues that Estienne wrote which criticized the French upper classes for becoming too 'Italian' in their manners "are especially interesting in that [they indicate] that the French courtiers, and apparently also the Frenchmen of other social strata, of the preceding period, considered gesticulation an impolite and 'vulgar' form of behavior. The habit of upper class Frenchmen of Catherine's time to use gestural movement in conversation is resentfully ascribed by Estienne to the strong influence exerted in Paris by the forms of social demeanor of the Italian courtiers of the niece of Clement VII."

Observations of this kind not only seem to confirm the commonly accepted idea that there are national or cultural differences in gestural use, but they also suggest that these may change according to fashion. As Efron shows, if Catherine de' Medici and her retinue made a certain 'Italian' style of gestural expression popular in court circles, in French society, somewhat later, a rather different style came into vogue. This was the style of the *honnête homme* whose conduct was to be governed by *raison* and who should always be calm and in control. This ideal also derived from Italy, from the Italian works on courtesy by Castiglione, Guazzo and della Casa, which came to be very widely read at this time. According to Efron, the fashion for calmness and graceful self-control arose as a part of a process of social domestication that came about as a rising middle class began to dominate and the nobility began to lose its political power. However, towards the middle of the eighteenth century, in the decades that preceded the Revolution, fashion changed again and calm, reasonable conduct gave way to a much more emotional style of conduct - the *honnête homme* was replaced by the *âme sensible* or 'sensitive soul' and displays of feeling and vigorous gesturing came to be much more acceptable.

Historical studies such as these (See also Elias 1994 [1939], Schmitt 1990, Hibbitts 1992) are sufficient to show that bodily expression and gesture use are subject to social regulation, however they are insufficient for a full understanding of just which aspects of gesture are subject to it. For this the only solution, as Efron himself well realized, is direct comparative observations of persons of different social and cultural backgrounds. We have

---

[1] Catherine de' Medici (1519-1589), daughter of Lorenzo de' Medici (Duke of Urbino) and niece of Pope Clement VII, married Henri II, King of France in 1533 and was influential in court circles for about forty years.

already referred to Efron's work of this nature in Chapter 4 where we observed that it still remains the most thorough attempt so far to specify through observation the nature of cultural differences in gestural conduct. As such, and notwithstanding the fact that it has been very widely quoted, it deserves a further examination here.

Efron's "comparative experimental study"

At the suggestion of Franz Boas, David Efron undertook a comparative study of gestural action among different ethnic groups in New York City. He gathered material in the Jewish and Italian communities in Manhattan where he was able to find large numbers of recent immigrants still using their own languages. He also gathered material among assimilated members of these two ethnic groups in the hope of being able to show what changes, if any, had come about in the use of gesture as people became assimilated to American culture. He describes his study as "a tentative investigation of some of the spatio-temporal and 'linguistic' aspects of the gestural behavior of Eastern Jews and Southern Italians in New York City, living under similar as well as different environmental conditions" (Efron 1972, p. 65).

Efron gathered his material according to four different methods. He undertook field observations, making notes as best he could. He undertook what he called "rough counting" by which he meant that he made quantitative observations in the field in respect to specific parameters, such as counting the number of times he observed gesticulators extend their hands beyond a certain point, and the like. He filmed people in conversational situations of all kinds. As we noted in Chapter 5, Efron is one of the first to use film in inquiries of this sort. Finally, he gained the cooperation of an artist, Stuyvesant Van Veen, who, independently, made numerous sketches of people in conversation, also making extensive notes on what he observed.[2]

His study was based on a very large amount of material. He shot about 5000 feet of film, a third of which he analysed in detail, and he collected 2000 sketches from 600 individuals, as well as material gathered through note taking in the field. In all he states that he based his analyses on studies of 850 "traditional" Jews, 700 "traditional" Italians, 600 "assimilated" Jews and 400 "assimilated" Italians.[3] The quantitative findings that he presents, given in all cases as simple counts with no statistical analyses, are based on somewhat

---

[2] Stuyvesant Van Veen (1910-1988) taught art at City College, New York, and was well known in the late 1930s as a painter of murals reflecting the liberal ideals of the New Deal.
[3] This adds up to 2550 subjects. Efron states on p. 67 that he studied in all 2810 individuals. The discrepancy is not explained.

smaller samples than these figures suggest, although these are still large by comparison with the numbers of individuals studied in most observational studies today.

In analysing his material he pursued three different lines of inquiry. First, he undertook a very careful kinetic or kinesiological analysis, examining the radii of gesturing, the plane in which gesturing tended to be performed, what body parts were employed and how they were differentiated, and what he called the tempo of the action of gesture. Second, he analysed gesturing from what he called an "interlocutional" point of view - that is, he looked at how participants in conversations gestured in relation to one another, the spatial arrangements they employed (he called this the "geography of conversation"), and whether and how they engaged in physical contact in conversation. Third, he analysed gesturing from a "linguistic" point of view, that is, he attempted to analyse the different ways in which gestures are related to the content of the utterances with which they are associated.

Efron found marked differences between the 'traditional' Italians and the 'traditional' Jews with respect to all three of these aspects. He also found, however, that the assimilated Italians and the assimilated Jews differed far less and that, indeed, they used patterns of conduct that were similar to those observable in the Anglo-Saxon community. Efron's work has been taken as a conclusive demonstration that differences in gestural conduct such as he showed between the unassimilated Jews and Italians are due to cultural influences and not to biological or racial factors.

This conclusion was important in Efron's day, when explanations in racial rather than cultural terms were widespread. Today, however, now that a cultural view is generally accepted, the differences that Efron demonstrated between the two groups he studied need to be examined from the point of view of what they might imply about how cultural factors may influence the use of gesture. Efron himself made no attempt to explore this question. As he put it (p. 160), "the question as to what specific factor may have been operative in patterning each of the gestural characteristics described above goes beyond the scope of this book and calls for a separate, and probably very difficult, inquiry". However, the kinds of differences he described suggest some hypotheses about how cultures may differ in how gesture is used as a communicative resource.

The differences Efron found between the traditional Jews and the traditional Italians were the following. From a kinetic point of view he found that, in the gesturing of the Jewish population he observed, most of the movements of the forelimbs were made from the elbow, the upper arm generally being kept close to the body, whereas among Italians the tendency was for the whole arm to be employed, the upper arm often being lifted up, the gestural movements

Efron (1972), Fig. 7, p. 164. Ghetto Jew: confined gestural radius; palm at angle to forearm.

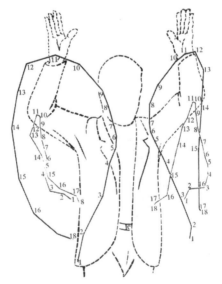

Efron (1972), Fig. 37, p. 177. An example of a tracing from a film showing the wide gestural radius and movement of the arms from the shoulder typical of 'traditional' Italian gesturing.

Fig. 16.1   Two illustrations from Efron (1972) showing the kinesic contrasts he describes between 'Ghetto' Jews and 'traditional' Italians.

pivoting from the shoulder rather than the elbow. The form of movement was different, too. In Jewish gesturing the movement patterns were intricate and angular. When reproduced on paper they presented the appearance of an "intricate embroidery" (p. 73), whereas among Italians the movement patterns appeared more "rounded'. In Jewish gesturing the movements of the forearms and hands were mainly in the frontal plane, directed toward the interlocutor, whereas Italians tended to make their gestures more widely to the side. In Jewish gesturing he found much differentiation in how the parts of the arms and hands are moved. Among the Italians, in contrast, the arm tended to be moved as a whole and there was little differential finger movement. In Jewish gesturing frequently only one arm would be used at a time or, if both were used, there tended to be an asymmetry in their employment or, at times, gesturing begun with one arm would be continued with another. Among the Italians, on the other hand, both arms were often involved in a symmetrical fashion. Finally, Efron noted that among Jewish speakers head movements were often a conspicuous and important part of gesturing, whereas among the Italians the head seemed to be much less often involved. Figure 16.1 shows two of Efron's illustrations which present these differences.

With regard to the "interlocutional" aspects, Efron notes that 'traditional' Jews tended to form very closely spaced conversational knots, conversationalists quite often would seize hold of the clothing of the other as they talked, and commonly directed their gesturings directly at their interlocutors. Among the Italians, on the other hand, conversational spacing was much larger, simultaneous gesticulation was rare and speakers rarely touched one another.

The differences Efron describes with regard to what he called the "linguistic" aspect are the most interesting. He found that among the Jewish subjects, gesturing was predominantly "logical" or "discursive". Thus he writes (p. 98): "the 'traditional' Eastern Jew very seldom displays physiographic or symbolic gestures". He continues: "...the 'traditional' Jew very rarely employs his arm in the guise of a pencil, to depict the 'things' he is referring to, but uses it often as a pointer, to link one proposition to another, or to trace the itinerary of a logical journey; or else as a baton, to beat the tempo of his mental locomotion". This is in marked contrast to the traditional Italians who use gesture mainly as a form of illustration of what they are saying and who also make use of a considerable vocabulary of symbolic gestures. Efron writes (p. 121): "The gestures of the Italian appear to be related more to the objective content of the discourse than to its logical trajectory." Again (p. 122), "If the movements of the 'traditional' Jew have been likened to gestural 'charts' outlining the logical itineraries of the corresponding ideational processes, those of the 'traditional' Italian may be said to be something like gestural 'slides', illustrating the very things referred to by the accompanying words". Efron notes (ibid.), furthermore, that the descriptive gestures used by the Italians can be "conveniently used as the exclusive means of communication". He continues (p. 123) "...we have been able to draw a more or less exhaustive inventory of the 'bundle of pictures' that a 'traditional' Southern Italian usually carries in his hands. This gestural vocabulary comprehends no less than 151 manual 'words', implying more or less definite meaningful associations". This listing of a gesture vocabulary that was possible for the Italians was not possible, according to Efron, for the traditional Jews that he observed.

These differences are striking. While no one has undertaken another study like that of Efron's that might confirm his findings so far as East European Jews are concerned, his observations on the character of Southern Italian gesturing seem to accord well with what has been written about it by other, earlier observers. Writers such as Galiani (1789), de Jorio (1819), Wiesman (1832) and Mayer (1948 [1840]) have all commented on the propensity of the Neapolitans to use gesture extensively and have noted that they often used it as an exclusive means of communication. More recently, the apparently large vocabulary of gestural forms in common use among Italians in the Neapolitan area and elsewhere has been noted quite often, as may be seen, for example, from Barzini (1964), Gadeau (1983), Carpitella (1981), Paura and Sorge (1998). See also Kendon (1995b, 2004).

The differences between the Southern Italian use of gesture and the use made of it by the East European Jews, as described by Efron, suggests that in these two cultures gesture had a different value as a communicative instrument. It is as if the resources of gesture as a medium of expression are being relied upon for somewhat different purposes in the two cultures. What might be the reasons for this? Why should there have developed, among the Italians, a set of gestural forms so stable and conventional and with meanings so well established that it was possible, among them, for gestures often to be used as a sole means of communication, whereas among the Jewish people gesture evidently was not used in this way? Among the Jewish people gesturing was observed to be extensive and conspicuous in conversation but the communicative role it appeared to play seems to have been different.

Later in this chapter we offer a hypothesis, taking Naples as an example, concerning the way in which the micro-ecology of everyday social life could favour the elaboration of gestural communication. Before coming to this, however, we will deal with two lines of inquiry that, in part, have been prompted by Efron's work. The first concerns the study of 'emblems' and the second concerns comparative studies of how co-speech gesturing may vary according to the language spoken.

'Emblems' or 'quotable gestures'

Efron himself recognized a kind of gesture that he called "symbolic" or "emblematic" and this he defined as a gesture "representing either a visual or a logical object by means of a pictorial or non-pictorial form which has no morphological relationship to the thing represented" (Efron 1972, p. 96). As noted in Chapter 6, Ekman and Friesen (1969) re-worked Efron's classification of gestures and proposed the term 'emblem' to refer to any gesture that had become established as a vocabulary item with a shared meaning, which could be used in place of words. Such 'emblems' included Efron's "symbolic or emblematic gestures" but they also included any gestures that Efron might have called "descriptive" provided they had an established form and a shared meaning.

Besides the terms used by Efron and Ekman and Friesen, just mentioned, gestures of this type have been variously referred to as "semiotic gestures" (Barakat 1969), "formal pantomimic gestures" (Wiener et al. 1972), or "symbolic gestures" (Poggi and Caldognetto 1998; Poggi, 2003) or "autonomous gestures" (Kendon 1983). More recently, I proposed the term "quotable gesture" (Kendon 1992) to refer to any gesture that makes its way into an explicit list or vocabulary. This was intended as a definition that would reflect a user's viewpoint and avoid the difficulties involved in trying to decide whether or not a gesture met the formal criteria proposed in the other definitions (for an attempt to establish a theoretically coherent definition see Hanna 1998).

There are many questions to be explored with regard to gestures that are quotable. We may ask: what functions do they fulfil? What is gained by using a gesture when a verbal expression exists that has an apparently similar meaning? What semantic domains do quotable gestures cover? Are they specialized in their meanings in some way? Do they fall into different groups according to their meanings and use? Within what sections of a community are they used and known? Given that it is known that communities differ in their vocabularies of such forms, how do they differ? Are some much more widespread than others? Let us now look at such work as has been done that might bear on some of these questions.

Comparative studies of quotable gestures

Everyone agrees that quotable gestures differ from one society to another. Several books have been published that show how there are different gestures for the same meaning in different cultures and it has often been suggested that teachers of foreign languages should consider gesture, not only so that students may learn to 'move' the language they are learning, as well as to speak it, but also so that misunderstandings arising from wrong gestural usage are avoided (see Wylie 1977, Monahan 1983, Diadori 1990). Despite this, there appear to be only two systematic comparative studies. Creider (1977) reports a study comparing gesture vocabularies in four adjacent East African societies. Morris et al. (1979) report a large-scale attempt to compare knowledge of twenty different gestural forms in forty different locations in Europe, distributed from the north (Britain and Scandinavia) to the south (Spain, Italy, Greece and Turkey).

The East African societies studied by Creider were the Luo, the Kipsigis, the Gusii and the Samburu. The Luo and Kipsigis are geographically contiguous and speak related Nilotic languages. The Gusii, also geographically contiguous with the other two, speak a Bantu language. The Samburu speak a Nilotic language, but are located to the north of the other two Nilotic-speaking groups, and are separated from them by the territories of two other groups. Creider collected vocabularies of quotable gestures in all these societies (seventy-one gestures in all) and these he compared with one another and also with gestures listed in Saitz and Cervenka (1972), which contains a gesture vocabulary for North America and one for Columbia.

Creider found that the four East African societies shared the same gestures to a high degree (79 per cent of the gestures listed were found in two or more of the four societies, 68 per cent found in three or more). The Bantu-speaking Gusii have as many gestures in common with the Nilotic-speaking groups as the Nilotic- speaking groups have with each other, except that the Gusii do not make use of fourteen specialized counting gestures that the other groups make use of. However Creider found that there was quite a large number of gestures in the African groups that were also found in the two American gesture vocabularies he consulted: 17 (or 24 per cent) of the African gestures coincided with gestures found in the North American list and 22 (31 per cent) coincided with gestures found in the Columbian list. Most of these gestures that coincided transcontinentally, however, were also gestures that were found in all four of the East African societies and most of these turn out to be gestures that are found very widely elsewhere. For example, Creider finds that Columbians, East Africans and North Americans all use a head shake for negation; a shoulder shrug is glossed as 'don't know' in all groups; a flat hand placed with palm against the cheek and the head tilted slightly to one side is glossed in all groups as referring to sleep; a flat hand held forward on extended arm and positioned a short distance above the ground is glossed as referring to the height of a small child; and gestures used to beckon someone or to instruct them to come to a halt were found to be the same in both the African and American groups.

These findings remind us that we may expect that any comparison involving groups geographically and culturally very different from one another may reveal at least a small set of gestures with very wide distributions. It seems that gestures that deal with negation and affirmation, certain interpersonal regulatory gestures, gestures of pointing and gestures depicting the size, shape and height of things, may all be found to be similar from one very different part of the world to another. Some of these widespread gestures may be understood as being derived as ritualizations of certain basic moves of approach, giving attention, and seeking or offering manual contact with the persons or things approached and attended to, and the converse of these. That is, moves of avoidance, withdrawing attention, and of rejecting or pushing away persons or objects. Various authors have offered suggestions along these lines for the head gestures of affirmation and negation (e.g. Spitz 1957; but see Jakobsen 1972), for pointing (Wundt 1973; Werner and Kaplan 1952), for shoulder gestures (Givens 1977) and for size-shape specifying gestures (Wundt 1973). Further development of these suggestions and for a better understanding of how even seemingly universal gestures may, nevertheless, have local variations, will require comparative studies that are a good deal more attentive to the exact ways in which such gestures are performed and to their contexts of use, than has hitherto been the case. The specialized counting gestures Creider reports in use among the Nilotic-speaking groups but not among the Bantu-speaking Gusii suggest, however, that some locally elaborated gestures may be tied to the local spoken language. On the other hand, Creider also found a number of gestures not found outside East Africa, which were shared throughout the region. Culturally specific quotable gestures need not be closely tied to specific spoken forms, but may spread over language boundaries within regions that are otherwise culturally similar.

This last phenomenon is also to be seen in the study of Morris et al. (1979). These investigators selected twenty hand shapes that represented twenty "symbolic" gestures (i.e. gestures that are not obviously iconic) and they then attempted to map the uses and meanings of these gestures in different locations in Europe. Forty locations were chosen, from Britain and Scandinavia in the north to Spain, Italy, Greece and Turkey, in the south. At each of these locations thirty adult males, selected in the street at random, were shown a set of drawings depicting twenty different gestural forms and, for each one of them, they were asked if they knew whether the gesture was used locally and, if so, what they knew it to be used to mean. The responses, recorded in the informant's own words, were subsequently grouped into more generic meaning categories, and the occurrence of forms and their generic meanings was then mapped for the entire region. The findings from this were rich (Kendon 1981 provides an extended critical discussion). Here the main points will be summarized.

Of the twenty forms studied, only two were acknowledged to occur by more than half their informants in all forty locations. Five other gestures were found to be quite widespread, but there were fourteen gestures that were found to be local in their occurrence. Evidently cultural areas within Western Europe differ quite markedly in the repertoires of gestures of this sort that they make use of. Nevertheless Europe has regions of gestural usage that are not defined by national or language boundaries. Thus Britain and Scandinavia were found to be quite similar, and markedly different from Italy and Spain, which have much in common. Italy and Spain, in turn, were found to be more similar to one another than Greece and Turkey, which also have much in common. Many of the gestures studied, thus, were found to extend beyond the boundaries of a national or language grouping, just as Creider found to be the case in East Africa. Regions of Europe also differed in the number of gestures recognized, many more being recognized in the south than in the north of Europe. This fits with the popular view that those parts of Europe with a Latin influence have a much richer repertoire of quotable gestures than those parts which do not have this influence.

Morris and colleagues take the view that many of the gestures studied originated separately in different locations and whatever range of use they were found to have came about through diffusion. Some gestures were found to have remained restricted in their region of use because they have become identified with a national characteristic of an adjacent group and rejected for this reason. Thus the finger-tips kiss, widely used in France and Italy as a positive comment on something, is not used in England because it is seen as too undesirably 'French' or too 'Italianate'. On the other hand, some gestures may become attached to a cause or a social movement and can become very widespread for this reason. A notable modern example is the V for Victory gesture that was deliberately established by Winston Churchill in the Second World War (Schuler 1944) which underwent a number of transformations of use eventually becoming a gesture associated with the Civil Rights and Peace movements in the United States as well as Europe. More generally, however, a gesture may be limited in its spread if another gesture, having the same function, is already in use in a given area. A gesture may also be limited in its spread if it is formationally similar to another in an adjacent area, but cannot be modified so that it can be differentiated from it.

Morris and colleagues explore the histories of many of the gestures they discuss and show that many of them are very old. They report a study of the geographical distribution of two kinds of head gesture used in negation in Italy. The so-called 'head-toss' (in which the head is thrown back, the eyes closed and the tongue clucked against the roof of the mouth) and the head-shake. The head-toss, also used in Greece and Turkey, is found in those regions of Italy that were once the regions settled by the Greeks in the sixth century BC. It is not found in the more northerly parts of Italy that were never part of

Magna Graecia (see also Collett and Contarello 1982 and Rohlfs 1959). This interesting finding suggests, as do a number of other observations reported by these investigators, that certain gestural expressions may be remarkably stable over very long periods of time. In this, gestural expressions seem to differ from verbal expressions. Further, Morris et al.'s historical studies also suggest that gestural forms do not derive from previous gestural forms, as words derive from earlier words. Gestures, once established, may alter and expand in their meanings, but they do not alter their forms, at least not in the way that words do.

Quotable gestures in use

These comparative studies of quotable gestures raise interesting questions regarding their diffusion and historical persistence. However, few studies have asked what the processes are that lead to the emergence of such gestural forms. For an understanding of this, detailed context-of-use studies are needed. Two studies have been published that have made a start in this direction (Sherzer 1991, Brookes 2001). Before discussing these, however, a brief summary will be given of a comparative study of the published glosses of quotable gestures. Crude though this approach may be, it suggests that quotable gestures tend to arise only in relation to certain semantic domains. This observation in turn may suggest clues as to what leads to their emergence or persistence.

In 1981 I compared six lists from five different countries in terms of the categories of meaning that were suggested by the glosses given for the gestures listed (Kendon 1981) and found that the great majority of these (between 60 and 80 per cent) were accounted for by three broad categories: interpersonal control (gestures with meanings such as 'stop!', 'be quiet!', 'I'm warning you!'), announcement of one's current state or condition ('I'm amazed!', 'I'm broke!', 'I'm hungry'), and evaluative descriptions of the actions or appearances of another ('he's crazy', 'pretty girl!', 'he's dangerous'). Similar analyses by Washabaugh (1986) for a community on Providence Island and by Payrató (1993) for a collection of Catalan quotable gestures yielded similar results. In all such lists gestures that are given a purely nominal gloss are relatively rare. There are gestures such as Sparhawk's 'bracelet' (Sparhawk 1978, p. 72), or a gesture such as the very well known one from Italy for 'money' (see de Jorio 2000:181 or Diadori 1990: 64), or 'scissors' (de Jorio 2000:392), but not many of these are listed and when they are their gloss usually implies a context which suggests that they are used as an expression for some request or activity. Thus the 'money' gesture is used when asking for money, the 'scissors' gesture when saying that someone is a gossip, and so forth. Evidently, when people give the meanings of these gestures they give them meanings that suggest that they are almost always used as complete interactional moves and not as lexical forms that can be used in a sentence.[4]

In Chapters 12 and 13 we saw, through context-of-use studies, how certain stable gestural forms with what we called 'pragmatic' functions are used. The forms studied included some which are found in gesture-lists. They appear to have emerged as ways of treating certain recurrent features of discourse in interaction, including topic specification, refusal, negation, and offering and asking. That gestural expressions are used to treat these kinds of moments may be explained in part by the fact that such moments transcend any particular form of verbal expression, they can be indicated and treated apart from speaking as well as simultaneously with it and can serve, thus, as modulators of or as operators upon whatever spoken discourse may be involved.

From the analyses presented in Chapters 12 and 13 it was found that, for each of the gestural forms studied, a unifying, abstract semantic theme could be established which, through its intersection with a particular context, came to have a specific meaning. This can be compared with the approach of Sherzer who has shown, both for a lip-pointing gesture as used among the Cuna of San Blas (Sherzer 1972) and for the thumbs-up gesture as this is used in urban Brazil (Sherzer 1991), that an 'inherent' or 'paradigmatic' meaning links all of the uses of these gestures together, but that these gestures also have a diversity of 'syntagmatic' meanings. Just as we showed in the cases of the gestures studied in Chapters 12 and 13, so in the cases of the gestures studied by Sherzer, the meaning that any specific use of one of these gestures has is a consequence of an intersection between the paradigmatic meaning and the place it has in the specific interactional syntagma in which it occurs.

In his study of the thumbs-up gesture in urban Brazil Sherzer (1991) showed that it has two basic meanings around which all its specific meanings are built. These are: a meaning of 'good' or 'positive' and an interactional meaning by which the user of the gesture indicates that the social obligation he or she is under in a given interactional context has been (or will be or is being) met. Sherzer gives seven different contexts in which the thumbs-up gesture is used. These are (1) to indicate that something is good (as when a fellow jazz musician gives the gesture after a colleague has just done an exceptional solo), (2) as a positive response to a question (a passenger boarding a bus asks the driver if the bus goes to a certain place, the driver responds with thumbs-up), (3) to demonstrate that one has grasped the point of something (a waiter asks

---

[4] In Chapter 10 we described the use of a number of what we called narrow gloss gestures, including the Italian gesture for 'money'. We saw how, when these are used in conjunction with speech they are often used as if they are a gestural rendition of the spoken word. In these cases the gesture is used as a part of a sentence and its meaning may be just that which the word has with which it co-occurs. We saw, however, that even in cases of apparent complete redundancy, the gesture could have other roles, such as enhancing the attention of addressees or, perhaps, serving as a presentation in physical form of the concept referred to by both word and gesture.

a customer to remind him of what he ordered, makes the thumbs-up when the customer tells him), (4) to acknowledge a remedy another has offered (as when A tells B she has left her car lights on, B says "thank you" and then does thumbs-up), (5) used as a mutual greeting (a bus driver does the thumbs-up to another bus driver through the window of his bus, when both buses are stopped at a red light), (6) as an acknowledgement that one knows one has reached a certain step in an interactional sequence (a bus driver gives the thumbs-up to a passenger after he has told him he will announce when the bus reaches a certain destination), (7) as a request to do something (a customer uses the thumbs-up to a waiter when he enters a restaurant as a way of asking if a certain table is free for him). In each of these situations a specific meaning could be given to the thumbs-up but in each there is a meaning of 'positiveness'. However, in addition, the gesture is a move in a sequence, either simultaneously serving as a comment and a move that completes an expected move in an interactional sequence, or serving as a separate acknowledgement of the expected move.

Sherzer summarizes his observations by saying that the thumbs-up serves as a marker which displays or signals points reached in interactional routines including greeting, leave-taking, showing one is attentive, acknowledging another's action, and showing understanding. These are universal points in the structure of any interaction which always receive some kind of marking. The thumbs-up in the Brazilian urban settings Sherzer has described is the form that has been adopted when a marker is needed, as it is when people are in 'passing' relationships rather than in some on-going interchange. This is one of the contexts which seems to favour the use of gesture. Sherzer suggests that the thumbs-up may have become established in urban Brazilian use because it is an easy way to maintain harmonious, positive relations in a social situation which, because of vast socio-economic differences, is often fraught with potential conflict. He quotes a Brazilian ethnographer, Roberto Da Matta who suggests that "the gesture has the power of disarming disagreement. [The thumbs-up gesture is] really a 'peace' gesture, above all, in dense and politically congested Brazilian urban areas" (Da Matta, personal communication to Sherzer, quoted in Sherzer 1991, p. 196).

A similar analysis, but of a very different gesture, has been reported by Brookes (2001). She has undertaken ethnographic studies of gesture use among male African youth in the black townships near Johannesburg, South Africa. In this society gesture plays a prominent role in everyday interaction, especially in the fluid society of male youth who, according to Brookes, with limited education and few employment prospects, spend much time in street corner gatherings, clubs and bars, where one's survival depends upon one's ability to negotiate often complex and delicate relationships with a wide range of others and where one's ability to recognize the intentions, status and role

Fig. 16.2   The *clever* gesture as depicted in Brookes (2001).

of others in these settings depends upon one's skill in the reading of and the appropriate self-management of dress, gesture, modes of talking and bodily movements. Brookes writes: "Negotiation of boundaries and status within and across male groupings involves skilful use of both language and gesture often in exaggerated narratives of sexual conquest and male daring" (Brookes 2001, p. 168).

Accordingly, it is of great importance to be 'clever' - that is, to be streetwise, highly alert, to be quick in sizing up situations and knowing with rapidity how best to deal with them. Brookes analyses a widely used gesture that is often used to express this idea. The gesture, which she names the *clever* gesture, is performed as follows: the hand posed so that only the index and little fingers are extended, is directed so that, with the palm facing downwards, the finger tips are directed toward the eyes, the hand being moved in a sideways diagonal direction across the face, sometimes in a side-to-side fashion (Fig. 16.2). According to Brookes' analysis, the paradigmatic meaning of this gesture makes reference to 'seeing'. There are some variations in how it is performed. The amplitude of the lateral movement across the face can be restricted or exaggerated and when it is used as a gesture of greeting or recognition of another, the hand may be directed toward the person greeted rather than towards the gesturer's own eyes.

The gesture is used in many different contexts. It is used to indicate to another that he should be on the look-out (as when the gesture was done to the driver of a minibus which was being towed by another car who had not seen in time that the car driver had slowed up). It can be used to indicate to another that the gesturer wishes to meet with him (as if to say "I want to see you"). It is used in greeting, especially in situations where one is acknowledging that the others being greeted are recognized as being part of one's own group. To use the gesture in this way is to acknowledge that 'we are streetwise, we are *clever*'. The gesture is also used to comment on the character of another person (to say of another that he is 'street-wise' for instance) or to comment on the character of something someone just did (as when saying to another that something he did was 'clever' or 'smart'). In all of these uses there is a reference to the act of 'seeing' but, according to the interactional context in which the gesture is used, and also to how it is modified in its performance, numerous other meanings can be built up from this basic meaning.

In both of these studies a gesture that is symbolic of a concept that is of special importance in the conduct of everyday interaction in the prevailing culture comes to be employed as a way of making reference to that concept at important points in the ritual of everyday interaction. As a consequence, it comes to a be a way of greeting, comment, warning and the like. But why does a *gesture* get selected to fulfil these functions? A brief consideration of the properties of gesture as a medium of expression, taken together with what we know about the ecologies of everyday interaction in urban Brazil and in the Black townships of Johannesburg can suggest an answer.

First, a gestured utterance can be executed more quickly than a spoken utterance. The thumbs-up gesture or the *clever* gesture, placed in context, can convey something quite complex. Yet it can do this by a single action, and this can be of great value where the encounters are fleeting, as they often are in the circumstances considered in these studies.

Second, gesture is silent which means that it can be used in conversational situations at the same time as speech is being used. It makes it possible to use a gesture to communicate something to others who may be beyond the boundaries of the current interaction, or one can rapidly communicate one's comment to another as a 'side exchange' (Goffman 1963) within a spoken encounter without interrupting the flow of talk.

Third, gesture is also visible, and this means that it can be used over distances greater than speech allows. It is clear from the examples given both by Sherzer and by Brookes that many of the exchanges in which the thumbs-up or the *clever* gesture is used are *distance* exchanges. For instance, a young man can use the *clever* gesture to warn his brother to "watch out" (knowing that his enemies are lurking to beat him up) as he sees him pass on the other side of the street, or one bus driver can signal with the thumbs-up gesture to another in another bus as a way of greeting him or thanking him for some traffic courtesy. Spoken expressions in such circumstances would be of no use.

Fourth, for its production and reception gesture does not seem to require the kinds of organization of mutual orientation that spoken exchanges do. An exchange of spoken utterances requires that the participants orient to one another and that they jointly disattend other things that may be going on at the same time (Goffman 1961, 1974; Kendon 1990a, Ch. 8). Gesturally mediated interactions may be less demanding in this respect. This is why, in the crowded public settings of Brazilian cities described by Sherzer, or the "bustling streets" of the black townships described by Brookes, the exchange of comments, greetings, acknowledgements, warnings and the like in settings where one is very likely to encounter others whom one knows and must acknowledge in some way, gesture comes to be selected for the fleeting in-passing interactions that are so common.

In short, it will be seen how a gesture such as the thumbs-up or the *clever* gesture, which can gather to itself semantic themes that are important in the cultures where they are used, can come to be selected for frequent and diverse use, given the ecological circumstances of daily interaction, because of the properties of the gestural medium.

The two studies just reviewed provide excellent models for the kinds of context-of-use studies that are needed if we are to arrive at a serious understanding of what the factors are that lead to the emergence of quotable gestures within a community and what contributes to the way in which certain gestural expressions and the underlying concepts that they express get selected. We shall return to these themes in the final section of this chapter when we come to discuss factors that may have contributed to the development of high gesture use in the Neapolitan context.

Comparative studies of gesture in relation to language structure

When speakers gesture at the same time as they speak, there are, broadly, two different questions to be explored. We may examine how gesture phrases are organized in relation to speech phrases - this we undertook at some length in Chapters 7 and 8 - or we may examine how what is expressed in gesture is related to what is expressed in speech. This we discussed from Chapter 9 onwards. In what we have presented so far, we have relied upon examples from English speakers and speakers of Italian and Neapolitan but we have not sought to discuss whether there might be differences in how gesture is employed in relation to speech according to which group of speakers we are dealing with. However, as we have seen from our review of Efron's work, there may well be differences in how speakers belonging to different ethnic groups and speaking different languages employ the two modalities in relation to one another. As we saw, among Italian speakers, if Efron is right, gesture is often used in relation to the referential content of the utterances, whereas among the Jewish Yiddish speakers he studied it serves mainly to provide kinetic diagrams of the logical structure of the discourse.

Differences of this sort may be attributable to differences in the role gesture plays in what may be called (modified after Hymes 1974) the 'communication economy' of these two cultures. This idea we discuss in the last section of this chapter. There is also the possibility that structural differences in spoken languages may have consequences for differences in how gesture is employed. A few studies have been published which suggest that this may be so, and any attempt to account for why one cultural group uses gesture differently from another must include this possibility.

The studies to be reviewed here have all followed a methodology that McNeill (1992) developed. A person is shown a film, usually an animated cartoon, and they are then asked to re-tell the story of the film to another person who, purportedly, has not themselves seen the film. This method has the great advantage that speakers' descriptions, including, of course, their use of gesture, if any, can be compared in respect to the same scenes in the film. Using this approach McNeill (1992), McNeill and Duncan (2000) and Kita and Özyürek (2003) have published studies in which descriptions of two or three scenes from the same cartoon are compared between speakers of different languages. The languages compared in these studies have been English (all North American), Spanish, and Mandarin (McNeill and Duncan) and English, Japanese and Turkish (Kita and Özyürek). The question investigated is whether the grammatical structures and semantic categories provided by a specific language influence how speakers of that language use gesture when speaking.

In the work of McNeill and his associates that follows this line of inquiry much use has been made of the typologies suggested by Leonard Talmy (Talmy 1985). Talmy has compared languages in terms of how the semantic components of a 'motion event' (i.e. something moves from one place to another, how it does so, and the path it takes through space) are packaged linguistically. He has suggested that a distinction can be made between languages in which the motion verbs in a language can incorporate information about the path of movement and languages in which path information is conveyed by verb 'satellites' (particles and prepositions) instead (so-called 'verb-framed' and 'satellite-framed' languages, respectively. See Talmy 1991). Talmy further points out that languages differ in whether verbs of motion incorporate manner of motion or whether manner of motion must be expressed by a more complex construction, such as an adverbial phrase.

In comparing speakers of languages that differ in these ways, the question has been: do these speakers also differ in how they use gesture, when they use it in describing a motion event? If they are speaking a language in which manner is often incorporated in the verb but in which path requires a separate element (as in English), will they use gesture differently from those who are speaking a language in which path is often incorporated into the verb, while manner requires a separate element (as in Spanish)?

McNeill and Duncan (2000) compared English speakers and Spanish speakers as they describe scenes from an animated film (a Sylvester and Tweetie Bird cartoon). In one scene Sylvester, the cat, is pushed rapidly down a drain pipe from the top of a building by a bowling ball, which he swallows, and when he comes out of the drain pipe he has the shape of a large ball and he rolls rapidly across the street and into a bowling alley opposite. In English, in describing such an event, one can very readily encode, in the motion verb, the *manner* of Sylvester's motion. One can say, for instance, "he rolls across the street". In Spanish, on the other hand, Sylvester's movement from one place to another and the manner in which he moved is more likely to be expressed using a more complex construction.

McNeill and Duncan found that speakers of English describing this scene always use a verb that incorporates the manner of Sylvester's movement. When gesture accompanies this, sometimes the gesture displays the manner of motion, but in other cases it may just show the path. Whether manner is shown in the gesture, or only path, will depend upon which aspect of the scene being described is salient for the speaker. In Spanish, in contrast, where more syntactic work is often required of a speaker if manner is to be built in to a motion event description, gestures that appear to indicate *both* path *and* manner of motion at the same time are frequently used and often expressions of manner are added, where none was given in the spoken language. It is as if the Spanish speakers are more likely to call upon gesture to enrich certain aspects of their descriptions because to do this verbally requires more work than it does in English.

Kita and Özyürek (2003) undertook a similar study in which they compared English, Japanese and Turkish speakers as they described another scene from the same cartoon. In this scene Sylvester moves from one side of a street to another by hanging on to the end of a rope and swinging across. In English, speakers can use the verb 'swing' in describing this scene. For example, a speaker could say: "He swings himself on a rope across the street from one building to another." It is suggested that the English verb 'swing', when used in such a context, incorporates the idea of an arc-like path of movement. In Japanese and Turkish, on the other hand, no verb is available that is the equivalent of the verb 'swing' which incorporates an arc-like movement path. It was observed that all of the fourteen gesture-using English speakers used an arc-like gesture, whereas five of the seventeen Turkish speakers and five of the fifteen Japanese speakers used only a horizontal gesture as part of their description. The remaining people in these two latter groups (twelve and ten, respectively) used arc gestures, in some cases using straight gestures as well.

It is regarded as significant that, whereas all of the English speakers used an arc-like gesture, several of the speakers in both the Japanese and the Turkish groups used only a horizontal gesture. According to Kita and Özyürek, this means that because, in Turkish and Japanese the arc-like path is not a part of the verb used to refer to the transit of the character from one tall building to the other, this path is less likely to be present in how the event is described linguistically, and so is less likely to be represented in any associated gesture. It is as if the semantic features of the categories provided by the language being used can have an influence on the way what is being described is recollected and this, in turn, influences what is displayed in gesture.

Kita and Özyürek also compared descriptions of the event in which the cartoon character, now round like a ball because he had swallowed one, rolled down a street, as was explained above. In English it would be possible to describe the motion of the cartoon character with a single clause: "He rolled down the street." Here motion and its manner are incorporated in the verb "rolled" and the path is expressed with the prepositional phrase "down the street." In Turkish and in Japanese, in contrast, speakers are much more likely to describe this event using two clauses, one to express the manner of motion, another to describe the motion's path. Comparisons of the descriptions showed this to be the case. Accordingly, for those speakers who used gestures in describing this scene, whereas the English speakers used a single gesture, the Japanese and Turkish speakers used two separate gestures, one with each clause.

A further way in which linguistic structure may influence gesture use is suggested by McNeill and Duncan's (2000) comparison of English and Mandarin Chinese speakers, when describing scenes from the Sylvester and Tweetie Bird cartoon. Speakers of Mandarin Chinese, which has a large lexicon of motion verbs that also incorporate manner, do not use gesture in motion event descriptions as a way of adding an expression of manner not mentioned in the verb. However, Mandarin speakers differ from English speakers in how they time a gesture within a phrase. English speakers perform a gesture depicting manner of action or path of action in close association with the lexical verb that is also used (compare Example 6 in Chapter 8). Mandarin speakers, in contrast, are likely to place a gesture that depicts an action at the head of the phrase even though, in words, only the topic of the sentence has been announced. In the example given a speaker says "*lao tai-taina-ge da bang hao-xiang gei to da-xia*", literally translated as 'old lady hold big stick, seem cause him hit down' (free translation: 'The old lady apparently knocked him down with a big stick'). As the speaker says *bang hao* ('big stick') she performs a 'knock-down' gesture, while no gesture is used when she gets to the verb. According to McNeill and Duncan, following Li and Thompson

(1976), in Mandarin topic is placed at the head of a unit of discourse, in this way limiting the range of things to which subsequent predications can apply. Evidently this tendency in Mandarin affects the placement of gesture as well. McNeill and Duncan write (p. 152): "It is as if the gesture shifts forward in the surface speech stream in the direction of the utterance-initial position characteristic of topic statements in Chinese speech."

The studies reviewed suggest that grammatical and lexical differences between languages may play a role in structuring the way a speaker organizes associated gestures. There seem to be at least four ways in which they may do so:(1) Where it takes more syntactic work in one language as compared to another to describe a scene, gesture may be used as a supplement to spoken description in the former case (McNeill and Duncan: Spanish speakers tended to use more manner gestures than English speakers). (2) The semantic features of something that a lexical expression such as a verb may encode may influence what features are brought out in a description of it. If gesture is a part of that description, gesture will be influenced accordingly (Kita and Özyürek: Turkish, Japanese and English comparisons). (3) Speakers of languages differing in the number of separate constructions needed to describe a given motion event may differ in the number of separate gesture phrases they also use (Kita and Özyürek: Turkish, Japanese and English comparisons). (4) Differences in how topic is structured in discourse may give rise to differences in where, in relation to the discourse, a pertinent gesture phrase is placed (McNeill and Duncan: Mandarin–English contrasts).

The suggestion that lexical and grammatical differences between languages may have consequences for how speakers of those languages use gesture is certainly interesting, but the work done hitherto shows that this is not a simple matter. Further studies in which the precise way in which speakers of these different languages use gestures would be useful. For example, as we saw, Kita and Özyürek report that many of the speakers of Turkish and Japanese, where the verb available for describing the transit of the cartoon cat did not incorporate a reference to an arc-like path, nevertheless used arc-shaped gestures in addition to horizontal gestures. It would be most interesting to know how these types of gestures were deployed in relation to the spoken discourse. For example, were arc-shaped gestures ever used simultaneously with the verb phrase employed to describe the cat's transit or were they only used either in alternation with speech or in association with other kinds of verbal expressions?

Ecology, cultural values and gesture: a hypothesis for Naples

The studies summarized above, together with the findings from Efron which we have also presented, suggest that there are differences from one language community to another in how gesture is employed in relation to speech. These studies confirm and, to a degree, refine the popular observation that people in different cultures gesture differently. However, it remains unclear how far these differences may be due to differences in the *languages* spoken or how far they may be due to wider differences in customs relating to the conduct of interaction, and the like. We need more comparative studies to explore this issue, and these studies must be more attentive not only to language differences but also to differences in culture and social class within any culture, and to differences in discourse situations. Few of the studies described so far have taken factors of this sort into consideration in an explicit way. For example, it is quite possible that the fact that Efron did not find his Jewish speakers using much in the way of gestures that expressed aspects of the content of talk, although they used gesture extensively as a way of marking out the logical structure of their discourse, might reflect the fact that Efron's sample was overweighted with conversations in settings where Talmudic, abstract and logically disputatious discussions prevailed.

Probably the best established culturally distinct gestural 'profile' is the one that has been described for the Neapolitan. Efron's description of a gestural practice in which gesturing is conspicuous, elaborate, and in which a considerable vocabulary of widely shared forms of expression is used, many of which are quotable, and which can make possible the use of gesture as an autonomous mode of communication in certain circumstances, seems well confirmed by the accounts of many others who have written about Neapolitans (see above).

Comparative studies that I have carried out, in which Neapolitan gesturing is compared to gesturing in speakers in central England, also confirm many aspects of this profile. In one such study (Kendon 2004), two stretches of semi-public continuous discourse were analysed for the way in which gesture phrases and speech phrases were organized in relation to one another. One stretch was a discourse by an Englishman, the other by a Neapolitan, both in their upper middle age. The Englishman was a guide giving a guided tour of a small town in Northamptonshire, the Neapolitan was the concierge of a building in Naples and was speaking at length about how it used to be in Naples when he was a youth.

In terms of numbers of speech phrases and numbers of gesture phrases the two passages were very similar. However, there were marked differences in how the gesture phrases were placed in relation to speech phrases, the amplitude of the gestural movements, the range and complexity of hand shapes employed, the detail with which aspects of content were represented in gesture, and in how gesture was used to mark aspects of discourse structure or the type of speech acts being performed in the discourse. In contrast to the English speaker, the Neapolitan showed greater complexity in his gesturing. His gestural actions employed greater amplitude in movement and used a wider range of locations than those of the Englishman. The Neapolitan also used a great variety of hand shapes. He employed fourteen distinct hand shapes in the course of his two-minute discourse, where the Englishman employed only one. The way in which the gesturing relates to the speech shows that not only does the Neapolitan speaker present aspects of the content of what he is saying in gesture in much greater detail, he also tends to mark out aspects of discourse structure or to provide gestured versions of 'speech act' types in a way that the English speaker did not. The Neapolitan was observed to use gestures that serve to 'present' what he is saying to his interlocutor. Through gesture, thus, although also in other ways, the Neapolitan seems to make a much more direct appeal to his interlocutors. It is as if he does not take his audience for granted, but repeatedly turns to them and addresses actions to them that invite, and indeed expect, a response.

The features of gesturing in the Neapolitan this comparison revealed fit the gesturing of many other Neapolitan speakers. They are consonant with the observations of Efron on the gesturing of southern Italians (it will be recalled that most of the Italians he observed had emigrated from the Neapolitan area). We may take it, thus, that these characteristics are well verified.

Let us now turn to the question as to why such a 'profile' of gesture use should prevail in Naples. What sort of considerations should we turn to if we are to try to explain why gesturing among Neapolitans should have these characteristics? We suggest that, if cultural differences in gestural practice are to be understood, gesture must be seen as a component in an ensemble of communication practices that is shaped by the communicative requirements of a culture. We may speak of a 'communication economy' and note that such economies will vary in the weight and role that gesture may be assigned therein.

The notion of a 'communication economy' we have borrowed from Dell Hymes. He writes (Hymes 1974, p. 4) of the "communicative economy" of a community, as a way of referring to "[t]he boundaries of the community within which communication is possible; the boundaries of the situations within which communication occurs; the means and purposes and patterns of selection, their structure and hierarchy". Our idea is similar to Hymes' but it also considers how the different modalities of communication are employed, how they are related to one another and how they 'trade off', one in relation to the other, according to the circumstances of communication. This is patterned within a given culture and cultures can differ in the nature of this patterning. What follows is an attempt to sketch an account for the case of Naples. However it is suggested that the approach taken here has a much broader relevance.

A first point to be noted is that the style of gesturing described for Neapolitans has the effect of enhancing the visibility of the speaker. Thus the amplitude of the movements employed and the tendency for many gestures to be enacted above the speaker's waist, often at the level of the shoulders or above, tend to make gestures directly noticeable to an interlocutor. Indeed, a striking feature of Neapolitan gesturing is the way in which a speaker may reach toward his interlocutor, sometimes bringing his hands very close to the other, even making physical contact with him (here our observations differ from those of Efron).

All of this has the consequence of enhancing the vividness of the speaker and of compelling the attention of others. This has long been noted as being a characteristic of Neapolitan expression. Writing in 1789, Ferdinando Galiani (1970, p. 34) describes how the Neapolitan "assists himself with gestures, with signs and movements. Every member of his body, every part of him is in movement and would wish to give expression." And a little later (p. 35) he adds how this performance "shakes" and "thrills" the onlookers. In 1832 we find Andrea de Jorio writing in a similar vein. After explaining how, in expressing himself, the Neapolitan will leave no rhetorical technique untried, he continues by saying how "[a] gesture is carried out with all parts of the body. [The speaker] magnifies it in various ways in a most tasteful manner, and to give it greater force he repeats it; he uses other, similar gestures, grafting one upon the other and blending them together. He interrupts his gestures, he begins them again, he decorates them with countless interpositions so that he produces a kind of rapture in the spectator, who becomes so amazed by such a plethora and vivacity of gestures that, although he does not know what draws his attention the most, he is not only persuaded, but he comes to share in the very feelings of the gesturer himself" (de Jorio 2000, p. 93).

However, it is not only the speaker's interlocutor who has his attention drawn by this performance for it often appears to be for the benefit of an audience of bystanders as well. Many commentators on Neapolitan life have suggested that the expressive style of the inhabitants of that city is theatrical. It is as if, whatever one may be doing, when in public, one is always engaged in a show or a performance that is to be witnessed and judged by a wider audience than that which is constituted by one's immediate interlocutor.

Perhaps this derives from the public character of everyday life in Naples. In this city there was, for many centuries, little space for expansion and most people inhabited buildings that were several storeys high, many of them set very close together. Naples had attracted a large population, and had grown extensively, especially in the latter half of the eighteenth century, to become one of the most densely inhabited cities in Europe (Ghirelli 1992, p. 121). But the benign climate made it possible for people to spend much time out of doors and in consequence this, combined with the crowded conditions inside, meant that much life was lived in the street. As a result, there was an intermixing of domestic and occupational life. An artisan, a tailor, a shoemaker, carrying on his trade on the street in front of his *basso*, also carries on much of his domestic life there. And this he will do in full view of the crowds that may gather around nearby food-stalls, around the ambulant sellers of lemonade or *acqua sulfurea*, around the purveyors of medicinal remedies, the puppet shows, the jugglers and the public story-tellers, to say nothing of religious processions and the incessant traffic of carriages, omnibuses, horseback riders and pedestrians that passed up and down on any of the larger thoroughfares.

Accounts of daily life in Naples from the early nineteenth century include Mayer (1948 [1840]), De Bourchard (1854/1866) and Lombardi (1988 [1847]). A typical description of Neapolitan street life, brief enough to quote here, is given in the following passage, cited in a guidebook for Naples from the writings of Lord Broughton. He writes: "The rumble of carts and carriages of every description, which, with the greatest velocity and frightful shouts, cut through the crowds of people every moment, the running, struggling, pushing, and fighting, form the most extraordinary picture that can be seen in Europe. ... [C]oachmen, cartmen, muleteers, and pedestrians, all [contribute] to the incessant din; some swearing, some screaming, some singing, some holding forth on the new opera, others on the last lottery, and all talking even more with their hands than with their tongues. Amidst this throng of passengers everything which can be done under the open canopy of heaven is going forward in this busy street. The shoemaker, the tailor, and the joiner are all there at work; the writer sits at his desk, and his employers stand beside him, dictating with the utmost gravity the secrets of their hearts, which they are unable themselves to indite. A decrepit old woman is screaming out a hymn as a penance, whilst her voice is drowned in that of a quack doctor recommending his wares. Jugglers play their tricks, gamblers shout out the number of the game they are playing, females are stuffing mattresses, cleaning vegetables, plucking poultry, and scouring pans, all in the open way."[5]

In such circumstances, where several different behaviour settings (the term is from Barker and Wright 1954) occupy the same physical domain at the same time, individuals must compete with one another for attention. Further, because they are likely to participate in more than one behaviour setting at a time, they must be

[5] Quoted in *Cook's Tourist's Handbook for Southern Italy and Rome*. London: Thomas Cook and Son, 1884, p.188 and attributed to Lord Broughton.

able to monitor multiple sources of information simultaneously. It is suggested that this could have been one of the factors that encouraged gesture to become elaborated as a form of communication.

Perhaps it is not surprising, therefore, to find that gesture among Neapolitans also included an elaborate substantive vocabulary which permitted conversations in gesture, allowing exchanges over distances too great for the voice, or in the noisy circumstances that so often prevailed. C. A. Mayer, a German resident of Naples in the 1830s, who wrote a valuable account of many aspects of everyday life, describes several circumstances in which gestures were used in this manner. Thus housewives living on upper storeys accomplished transactions with street vendors "half in words, half in signs" as they exchanged money and goods by means of a basket lowered to the street on a rope (Mayer 1948 [1840], p. 19). Most of the houses were provided with balconies where people often sat to enjoy the fresh air and to watch the spectacle of street life below. Mayer notes (ibid.) that they also watched each other: people on opposite balconies could see one another as if they were on a stage. He remarks how often he enjoyed the conversations that take place between balconies, carried on by "quiet words, gestures and looks". He adds that in much of the city "it is not possible to make oneself understood in words, because of the noise; therefore the coachman, and his boy who walks behind, speak a mute language with their acquaintances along the street; also the neighbours, from window to window, from balcony to balcony, from roof to roof carry on among themselves marvellous conversations with the head and hands" (op. cit., pp. 74–75).[6]

The need to make oneself a heightened object of attention in conversation, because of competition from other sources, and the interest one has in commanding attention from bystanders, could encourage the use of gesture as display. The noise of the street, or the inconvenience and difficulty of visiting one's neighbours when they could so easily be seen from one window, balcony or roof to the next, perhaps encouraged the use of gesture as an autonomous means of conversation. Further, however, given the very public nature of everyday life, given that much of domestic life took place on the street among so much else, private exchanges between people could be very difficult. Here again, gesture is useful. Since it is silent it is well suited to surreptitious communication. Thus Mayer (ibid., p. 80) describes an elaborate conversation between a lover and his sweetheart which, so he claims, was characteristic: the lover comes to the courtyard and attracts his sweetheart's attention. She

---

[6] Compare, among others, Andrea de Jorio, who wrote in the 1819 edition of his guide to Naples (de Jorio 1819, p. 108) that "the language of our common people [*popolo basso*] is double, with both words and gestures. This second language is together full of both grace and philosophy. It is surprising to see two persons, at a distance from one another and in the chaos of the more populated streets of Naples, speaking together and understanding each other well" (trans. AK).

tells him, in gesture, that visitors are present. Through gesture they agree on a time for him to return, and through gesture they exchange expressions of their passion for one another.

There is a further consideration to be borne in mind, however. In 'traditional' Naples (that is Naples as it was more or less until the Second World War and still is to a considerable degree even today, at least within the *centro storico*), within neighbourhoods or *Quartieri* within the city, the people living there were largely connected by extensive kinship networks. Whereas in 'modern' cities typically people live in anonymous relationships outside their families, in Naples this was not so. There were close networks of actual or quasi kin relationships and within each micro-neighbourhood it was as if people were living together as overlapping extended families. This meant that people did not define their relationships with one another through interaction, they already always were in certain relationships with one another. Accordingly, occasions of co-presence, which, in any case, were almost continuous, became loci for individuating performances. Where relationships are fixed through kinship or a kin-like permanence, and not fashioned through interaction, communication conduct can become to a considerable degree a matter of display - an assertion of individual identity. The 'display' that gesturing makes possible is thus not only an adaptation to the necessity of competing for attention. It is also part of showing off who one is, what sort of a 'character' one aspires to play in the drama of everyday life. The common observation that writers have often remarked on – the 'theatricality' of everyday life in Naples – has already been mentioned. It seems that in this city conduct in co-presence is often dramatized and the elaborate use of gesture is undoubtedly a part of this dramatization.

If we are to understand why there are cultural differences in the way in which an expressive modality such as gesture is used, in the first place we should look to what such a modality affords its users as a means of communication, and consider in detail the circumstances of its use. We must look at the ecological circumstances of daily interaction. In the second place, however, we must also take into consideration the prevailing norms by which conduct in co-presence is governed. And in a city such as Naples this means that we cannot ignore its cultural and social history. What I have outlined here is no more than a beginning, but I suggest that an investigation of a communicative style in both historical and ecological perspectives may lead to a better understanding of how cultural differences in communication are sustained. This, in turn, should contribute to the view that modes of communication develop adaptively, their features becoming adjusted as the communicative tasks require change.

17   The status of gesture

What is the status of gesture? On the one hand it has been valued as a component of self-presentation and public performance, even cultivated as an art. On the other hand, it has been looked upon as something to be avoided, its use betraying a lack of proper self-control or an inadequate command of spoken language. At times it has been deemed worthy of scholarly attention and analysis, being viewed as a phenomenon of theoretical and philosophical importance for the light its study might throw on the nature of language, symbolic processes and expression. At other times scholars have paid it scant attention, it being dismissed as a superficial ephemera of no importance.

As we saw from our historical survey of interest in gesture in the West (Chapters 3-6), at least since the time of Quintilian, nearly 2000 years ago, gesture has been recognized as a component of human utterance. Quintilian saw it as a natural companion of speech, however he believed that it should be refined and shaped in accordance with rules and principles that would ensure that it would be an effective part of the rhetorician's art. Gestures were seen as enriching and elaborating the audience's experience of the orator's speech, and if not performed correctly and with proper decorum they could have seriously negative consequences. Accordingly, it was important to shape the use of gestures so that they would contribute to ensuring that the speech of which they were a part would have the maximum effect. Clearly, for Quintilian, gestures were important and consequential.

Although, as we then saw, emphasis upon Delivery in rhetoric, which included a consideration of gesture, appears largely to have disappeared during the medieval period, following the rediscovery of certain of Cicero's works on rhetoric at the end of the fourteenth century, and the discovery of the complete text of Quintilian's treatise at the beginning of the fifteenth century, as well as certain changes in religious and political life, Delivery once again became important, and by the early seventeenth century treatises devoted to gesture began to appear. As we saw, by the eighteenth century something like an art of gesture had become established. Bodily expression appears to have been carefully cultivated among educated people, it being clearly recognized that it played an important part in the effectiveness with which one presented oneself not only in public declamation but also in the *salon*.

However, at the same time that gesture was cultivated as an art, its 'natural' character was never forgotten and indeed, as we saw, the early treatises of the seventeenth century were written in part to defend the idea that gesture was the 'natural' and 'universal' language of humans. As Knox (1990) has suggested, this probably came to be widespread following the growing awareness in Europe of 'savage' peoples in other parts of the world, especially the New World. It was reported how European travellers were able to enter into communication with these strange humans using gesture and this reinforced the idea of it as a natural and universal human language, an idea that had had currency at least since Quintilian.

Early in the eighteenth century the question of the natural origin of human language began to be debated and a number of thinkers, from Vico onwards, proposed that gesture could have been the first form of human language. Some, indeed, supposed that gesture could form the basis of a new universal language (the search for a universal language had been widely pursued, at least since the beginning of the seventeenth century) although this idea, as we saw, did not persist for very long. Nevertheless, gesture was recognized as being of considerable philosophical interest. Its seeming 'naturalness' and the apparent fact that gesture was used as a means of expression and communication by all human beings, suggested that its study could provide insight into questions about the natural origins of language, the nature of symbolic expression and the relationship between thought and expression.

As we move into the nineteenth century, interest in gesture persists. However, at the same time, in this period, the idea of an autonomous science of language became established and this, eventually, was one of the factors that contributed to the marginalization of gesture as a focus of scholarly interest. We may note here, for example, the development of the comparative method in the historical study of languages which showed an apparent lawfulness in how languages changed over time, which seemed quite independent of any specific human agency. This was important for the notion that language was a system with its own laws that merited, therefore, a discipline of its own. By the mid-nineteenth century the science of *linguistics* had been named, a science which was to seek to establish the structural properties of languages as if they were autonomous systems. By the turn into the twentieth century, especially under the influence of De Saussure and his followers, the idea of 'language' as a self-operating machine had firmly taken hold (Harris 1987). Gesture lost its place as something which students of language could be interested in, for gesture, manifestly, does not appear as a part of the linguistic system as this came to be defined as an object of study.

More generally, interest in gesture declined because it came to seem less and less pertinent in public life. For example, in the mid-nineteenth century, at least in England, there appears to have been a change in the style of public expression. A sober, non-moving style of public speaking came to be adopted and this would have meant a decline in gesture use, but it must also have greatly strengthened the reliance upon what could be written down of what someone said as being the true record (Efron 1972).

Not unconnected to this is the fact that it is in the nineteenth century that the culture of the *printed word* finally came to prevail. Although the consequences of the technology of printing for European culture had begun to be apparent from an early stage after its introduction (McLuan 1982, Eisenstein 1979), it was the development of mass-printing technologies in the nineteenth century that led to it becoming dominant. In the eighteenth century, European society still had a strong *oral* component. With the wide diffusion of cheaper printed materials, with the growth of bureaucracy that ensued as nation states emerged and for which the use of written language and printing was essential, with the concomitant spread of universal compulsory education which gave rise to an ever growing proportion of the population who could use the written and, therefore, the printed word, who needed to use it and who desired to use it, by the middle of the nineteenth century European society appears to have finally shifted into being a predominantly *text-based* society.

Language in its written form, perhaps, above all, in its printed form, came finally to be fixed as the true form of expression, certainly as the form of expression that had the greatest prestige, and it set the standard for expression for anyone who claimed to be or wished to become a member of the educated classes. To the extent that language as a form of human communication was taken as an object for academic analysis, such other modes of expression as gesture were, increasingly, ignored.

Thus it was that, in the middle of the last century, when audio-visual recording technology became sufficiently widespread for scholars to begin to use it as a tool to examine the activities of persons engaged in communication with one another, for example in the context of psychotherapeutic conversations, there was much amazement and wonder at the seemingly new discovery that people did not only pronounce words, they also moved their bodies about and did a number of other things that could never be captured by writing down only what they said but which, nevertheless, seemed of great importance for the communication that seemed to be going on. As we saw, it was this wonder and amazement that gave rise to the idea of 'nonverbal communication' - an idea that could only have arisen in the context of an ideology that had insisted that it was the *words as they could be written* that constituted the basis of communication.

In this atmosphere 'gesture' now reappeared to view. In the eighteenth century, as we have seen, gesture was recognized as an interesting and common component of speaking, it was seen as something that should be cultivated, and it was also seen as something that, being natural to humans, might also carry important clues about the nature and origin of human expression. Nevertheless, it was not regarded as something odd or puzzling. Yet it seems to have appeared as odd or puzzling to observers in the middle decades of the twentieth century, shortly after it had been 'rediscovered'. A number of the early students of gesture and 'nonverbal communication' wrote as if they had never before observed that humans used gesture. Now that they had noticed that they did, they could not understand it. It seemed like a mystery, demanding an explanation. For example, one well-known investigator of the period and his colleague wrote that gestures produced when speaking "are an intriguing phenomenon because all normal adults do them to some degree when talking". Yet, say these writers, such gestures "have no obvious communicative function" for in conversation "between normal adults... the message is carried in the verbal mode".

Despite this, it seems highly likely that, even to those most puzzled by gesture, and certainly to just about everybody else, gestures, as encountered in everyday life, were no more mysterious than they had ever been. So transparent are they, indeed, that often they are not even noticed. It was the ability that audio-visual recording technology provided for us that made it possible to 'look back' at gesture, to contemplate it as an 'object', that created for many a sense of puzzlement. This was because the theoretical model of communication implicitly employed by almost all students of the topic at the time was a model that regarded communication as a sequential, alternating exchange of well-formed spoken sentences, much as we are led to believe it to be by those two gentlemen, A and B, who have so long been found on page 27 of the *Cours de linguistique générale* (Harris 1987, pp. 163ff). Partly as a consequence of this it appears that even with the recent revival of interest in gesture it often has not been studied for its own sake. It has been seen as a new 'window' on the mind or it has been seen as somehow a 'help' to speaking or thinking. Thus it is studied for what it might reveal about inner processes, and rather less often as an integral part of a human's expression, studied for its own merits and for the part it plays in communication and expression.

As we noted in Chapter 5, the idea that gesturing is something that has significance mainly for the processes by which *verbal* expression is attained, and not as a component of the speaker's final utterance, remains under discussion. In this book, especially in the light of the examples of gesture use presented in Chapters 7-13, we have maintained the view that when speakers produce gesture they do so as a partnered component of the utterance, planned for and produced by the same guiding programme of production that serves for verbal expression. As our survey has suggested, the way in which speakers use gesture in conversation is variable, and intimately dependent upon what the overall communicative aims of the speaker appear to be. It appears that gestures produced in relation to speech are an integral component of the communicative act of the speaker. Regardless of whether and how they contribute to the interpretation of the communicative act by others, they must be seen as part of the speaker's final product, and not as symptoms of some struggle to attain verbal expression. If gestures help to make clear our own thoughts, they do so in much the same ways as words do. Any utterance is always addressed to another, even if that other happens to be only oneself. (Cf. p. 82, note 3). Utterances, however expressed, are the means by which thinking progresses, because this is always a dialogic process, even if the dialogue is within one body and not between more than one. Gestures can certainly be a part of this process, but are so just as words can be a part of it.

In describing gesture use in conversation, we have drawn a broad distinction between those uses of gesture which appear to contribute to the referential or propositional content of the utterance (this includes both depictive and indicative gestures), and those uses which we called 'pragmatic', in which gesture appears to serve to indicate the type of 'act' or 'move' the speaker is engaged in, how the speaker regards the utterance, or how the discourse is to be structured.

With regard to gestures that are deemed to contribute to the referential content of utterances we saw that speakers employ various *techniques of representation* which appear to be quite general and in widespread use. From what we saw of these techniques, we suggested that such gesturings are best understood as actions by which the speaker constructs or manipulates virtual objects or, in some cases, acts out some pattern of action that could be attributed to such an object. The speaker draws, sculpts, models and acts out to *enable* virtual objects to appear for others. They succeed in this because these acts are intelligible for others *as* acts of sculpting, depicting, modelling and the like. The question remains as to how it is that these actions can be understood by others for what they are. It seems that others directly perceive them as purposeful constructive actions. How this is so is little understood, although the recent work on so-called mirror neurons, as has been noted by more than one writer, could suggest a neurophysiological mechanism by which movements of this sort do become intelligible (Rizzolatti and Arbib 1998, Young 2002) .

We saw further, in connection with the study of pointing presented in Chapter 11, that the different ways in which the hands are employed when a speaker indicates an object, can also be understood in terms of how the speaker displays for others the different ways in which the objects indicated by such pointing gestures are to be used in the discourse, and so how they are to be understood by others. We saw, for example, how in pointing different hand shapes can be used which variously 'single out', 'present' or 'offer' the object referred to. When we came to a consideration of 'pragmatic' gestures we again saw that it seemed appropriate to view them as having been derived from manipulatory action of various kinds. We followed Desmond Morris' general suggestion here and interpreted the G and R families as 'gestures of the precision grip'. The Open Hand Prone family of gestures was interpreted as being derived from the actions of using the hand to push something away (for the vertical or VP gestures) or in a cutting through or sweeping away action (for the ZP or horizontal OHP gestures). The Open Hand Supine group were interpreted as derived from the action of offering or presenting or being ready to receive for the PP and PA groups. The PL group, rather different, was interpreted as being derived from a display of removing the hands from the field of action as a way of showing an intention not to intervene.

When speakers use gestures, thus, whether these are depictive, indicative or 'pragmatic', they are engaging in actions on, or in relation to, objects and spaces in a virtual environment (cf. Kita 2000). The actions of gesture are derived from the uses of the body, mainly the hands, in making things, arranging things, operating things, acting on things or on other actors. We have seen, however, that these gestural actions can be employed as an integral component of utterances and they are deployed in various, but always coherent ways, in relation to what is being expressed in the spoken component of the utterance.

The very intimate way in which gesture is integrated with speech could suggest that speech itself is intimately linked to manipulatory activity. It is hardly necessary to be reminded of the fact that one of the most outstanding features of the human species is its capacity to modify and restructure its own environment and to fabricate all manner of objects for an extraordinarily wide range of purposes. The human species is the fabricating species, or *Homo faber*, as Henri Bergson long ago proposed. We suggest that the intimate reciprocal deployment of speech and gesture in the utterance supports the view that language, also, is best understood as being rooted in this fabricating activity.

Any elaboration of a view of language (in the broad sense) as a form of constructive and manipulatory activity, and how this view might be integrated into a general view of how language arose and evolved is well beyond the scope of our present enterprise which, in any case, has lasted long enough and must now be brought to a close as rapidly as possible. It is our hope, however, that what has been presented in this book will further encourage the growth in the attention being paid to gesture that has been witnessed in recent years. We believe that gesture deserves this attention even though, in our daily experience and use of it, it seems evanescent and, as long as it is combined with speech it contributes to the comprehension by others of what is said in a variable and sporadic manner and is rarely recalled on its own when we recount what another has said to us. For this reason alone there is a temptation to ignore it or not to take it seriously. Yet, as we have seen, when speakers use it, they use it as an integral part of the activity of utterance production, and in everyday co-present interaction it can often have an important role to play in the communicative process, even if only a momentary one. For a truly inclusive view of human language, gesture must be taken into account. Once we do so we may come to see that language cannot be properly understood if it is regarded only as a system of abstract symbols governed by quasi-mathematical rules of operation that are *sui generis* and remote from practical action. Language must be seen, rather, as embedded within, and as a part of, the action systems by which the environment and objects within it are manipulated, modified, organized and created. Despite the complexity of elaboration and despite the apparent detachment from practical action of spoken language, gesture's intimate tie with it teaches us that, after all, when humans put forth their thoughts in utterances this is, at bottom, but an aspect of *fabrication,* which is so fundamental a characteristic of our species.

Appendix I   Transcription conventions for speech and gestural action

The transcriptions used as part of the descriptions of the examples given throughout the book are meant to contain just enough information to make the explanations of the examples clear. For speech, we have used standard orthography. For the transcription of gesture we have followed a highly simplified method which, we hope, is immediately readable, showing in the transcriptions only those aspects of gestural action that are directly pertinent for the account being offered. Other gestures in the examples are often not shown, therefore, and interesting and important aspects such as postural changes, bodily and facial orientation and direction of gaze are indicated in the transcripts only if they are relevant to the immediate purpose for which the example is being used. To follow any other practice we felt would overload the transcriptions to the point that most readers would find it too much work to follow them.

The following conventions have been used in most of the transcripts. When there are particular features of an example that need to be brought out, conventions not listed here may have been followed. In these exceptional cases the conventions are explained in a key accompanying the transcription.

Speech is transcribed using conventional orthography. Tone unit boundaries are shown by /. Where tone units are numbered a number in round brackets is placed above the line of text at the beginning of the tone unit. When deemed appropriate, tonic syllables are indicated in small capitals. Pauses in speech are indicated by dots placed in round brackets within the line of text. Where appropriate the length of the pause is given in tenths of a second.

The speakers in the material recorded in the Provinces of Naples and Salerno use both various forms of Neapolitan and regionalized forms of Italian. In transcribing Neapolitan we have mainly followed the orthographic recommendations of D'Ascoli (1993) except that we have used 'ë' to indicate where the vowel is atonal or indistinct, as commonly happens in final position (see De Blasi and Imperatore 1998 and Iandolo 2001). Apostrophes are used to indicate environments where certain word segments are dropped. Translations into English from both Neapolitan and Italian are fairly literal. We have not thought it necessary to supply an interlinear.

Gestural action is shown by symbol sequences placed below the line of speech in such a way as to show how it is perfomed in relation to speech. These symbols, which generally only indicate the phases of gestural action, are aligned as closely as possible with speech, however since we have used ordinary orthography it has not been possible to show the relationship according to actual timing. Generally, alignment is to the nearest syllable.

| indicates gesture phrase boundaries.

The phases of gesture phrases are marked as follows:

Preparation (P): ~~~~~

Where preparation and stroke cannot
be sharply distinguished (PS): ~*~*~

Holds within the preparation phase: _____

Stroke (S): ****
Strokes, when numbered, are numbered S1, S2 etc.

Different phases of stroke action separated by /: ***/***
These phases may numbered S1a, S1b, etc.

Gesturing body part held in position at end of stroke (post-stroke hold): **** . Any Hold may be labelled H.

Right hand: rh
Left hand: lh
Head: hd

No attempt has been made to notate the content of gestural action. We have relied on verbal descriptions or drawings to explain the nature of the gestural expressions. Sometimes, however, within a succession of strokes, it is useful to indicate different hand shapes. For example, in Chapters 12 and 13 we deal with gestures that involve sequences in which one hand shape changes to another. In such cases the different hand shapes are indicated by lower case letters. A key showing the significance of these is given with the transcript itself. Generally, the following have been used:

pppp: stroke action involving the Open Hand Supine (palm-up) configuration (see Chapter 13). An 'open hand' is a hand shape in which all digits are more or less fully extended, but not spread.

gggg: stroke action involving the 'bunch' or '*grappolo*' hand shape (see Chapter 12). This is a hand shape in which the fingers are flexed so that their tips are in contact with one another.

rrrrr: stroke action involving the 'ring' hand shape (see Chapter 12). This is a hand shape in which the index finger is flexed so that its tip is in contact with the tip of the thumb.

oooo: indicates an 'open' hand (digits extended) following either a 'grappolo' hand shape or a 'ring' hand shape (see Chapter 13).

nnnn: indicates stroke action using open hand, forearm prone (Open Hand Prone family. See Chapter 13).

Where the stroke action symbols are underlined, this indicates that the acting body part is 'held'. Usually this indicates a 'post-stroke hold'.

Head shake: <+++>

Gesture phrases and their component phases may be numbered or lettered for convenience of reference in description and discussion in the text. Square brackets are used to enclose these numbers or letters, which are placed immediately below the relevant segment of gestural action.

Where appropriate, the different levels of gesture phrase and gesture unit organization are shown by brackets, thus |_____| placed below the line indicating gestural action. Gesture phrases are numbered with Arabic numerals, gesture units are numbered with Roman numerals.

fgp: forearm gesture phrase

hgp: head gesture phrase

fgu: forearm gesture unit

hgu: head gesture unit.

Appendix II: The recordings

The occasions recorded in the video tapes used in the analyses reported in this book were made in ordinary settings of people talking together, in most cases while they were in pursuit of their own purposes. They include occasions such as meals, committee meetings, a casual card game, interactions between customers and vendors at market stalls, semi-public presentations by tour guides, and informal conversations. We have also used recordings in which the participants told about their childhood and youth, discussed the state of the city they live in, or talked about what they considered to be important aspects of their own local culture.

All of the recordings from Campania, Italy, all of those from Northamptonshire, England, and certain recordings from the eastern United States of America were made by myself or by students under my direction, for the purpose of collecting material for the study of communication conduct in face-to-face interaction. They were made openly, with the full knowledge and consent of the participants. In most cases it was explained to the participants that we wanted to make the recordings as a documentation of aspects of everyday life. Some of the material made in Northamptonshire was made for the benefit of a local historical society or as a documentation of the activities of a small local museum. Some of the material from Naples comes from conversations about the character of Naples and its inhabitants. A number of recordings from the United States were not made under my direction, but were made by other scholars of social interaction with similar aims. Details of their origin are explained below.

With one exception, when 16 mm film was used, the recordings were made using VHS, 8 mm, Hi8 and Mini DV video formats. Analysis equipment has included VHS and 8 mm video players with slow motion playback facilities. In more recent years all of the material has been transferred to digital format and analysed using technology developed by Apple Computer.

Campania, Italy

Telefono (Bocce), Bocce I, Bocce II. These recordings were made in 1991 by Kendon in a small town not far from Salerno. They were made at a Bocce (Indoor Bowls) Club and include about thirty minutes of informal conversation and about forty-five minutes of a committee meeting. Topics included a robbery that had taken place at the Club's premises the day before and various administrative problems of the club, such as problems with finding a correct telephone number and, in the Committee Meeting, a variety of topics having to do with the Club's business. The speech transcription and Italian translation of this material were originally made by Maria De Simone of Salerno and have been revised by Carmen Pacifico of the Province of Salerno.

AVIS. Recording made by Kendon in 1991, with assistance from Prof. Pina Boggi Cavallo, in a small town near Salerno of a group of volunteers gathered at the headquarters of a local chapter of the *Associazione Volontari Italiani del Sangue* (Italian Voluntary Association for Blood, an organization that promotes blood donations and undertakes voluntary medical assistance, ambulance service, etc.). Discussion ranged from problems to do with the best ways to promote blood donations to the unruly behaviour of today's youth. Speech transcription by Maria De Simone of Salerno.

Commerciante. A recording of four men playing cards and chatting behind a stall in the market in the piazzetta of Torre del Greco, a town on the Bay of Naples. One of the players is the proprietor of the stall. The recording was made in 1996 by Laura Versante, Rosaria D'Alisa and Mario Cimmino. The speech transcription and Italian translation were made by Laura Versante.

Marinai. A recording made in 1996 of conversations among old sailors and fishermen at the harbour at Torre del Greco. Recorded by Laura Versante and Mario Cimmino. The speech transcription and Italian translation were made by Laura Versante.

Fruttivendolo. Made in the *piazzetta* of Torre del Greco. A recording of the activities of customers and the proprietor of a fruit-stall. Speech transcription and Italian translation by Laura Versante.

Portiere F. Made in Naples by Chiara Afeltra in 1996. A custodian of a residential building and his wife talk at length about their past in Naples or offer opinions on the state of the city. Speech transcription and Italian translation by Chiara Afeltra.

Piccolo Teatro. Made in Naples by Chiara Afeltra in 1996. A discussion between two residents of an apartment in Naples about how it was during the Second World War. Speech transcription and Italian translation by Chiara Afeltra.

DSGA. Made in Naples in 1999 by Teresa Stanzione and Massimo Serrillo. In this recording an artisan engaged in making materials for the *presepe* and his wife talk with Serrillo about what it is to be a Neapolitan and how Neapolitans differ from other Italians and they also describe various Neapolitan recipes. The recording is nearly an hour in length and is very rich in Neapolitan expressions. Speech transcription and Italian translation by Teresa Stanzione.

Napoli Sotterranea. A video of a guide giving a pre-tour lecture about ancient subterranean aqueducts in Naples. Made in Naples by Adam Kendon in May 1998. Speech transcribed by Cinzia Capone.

LB, ARTIGIANO and *SG*. Made in Naples in 1999 by Adam Kendon, Teresa Stanzione and Massimo Serrillo. In these recordings, each one lasting about twenty minutes, Massimo Serrillo engages in conversations with residents of the *Centro Storico* of Naples about what it is to be a Neapolitan and what is important for Neapolitans today. The speech in all of these recordings has been transcribed by Teresa Stanzione.

Pasqua and *CPIII 'Vino'* were recorded in the spring of 2000 by Carmen Pacifico. These recordings, which in total last about an hour, were made at a family *pranzo* (midday dinner) in Salerno. The speech has been transcribed by Carmen Pacifico.

IAC (Iacone). Recorded in June 2001 by Adam Kendon and Maria Graziano in Portici, a small town near Naples. In this recording an elderly couple, in their own apartment, discuss their youth and marriage, their experience of the Second World War and other matters with two young friends. There is also a good deal of talk about mutual acquaintances. The four participants in the film have known each other for many years. Speech transcription and Italian translation by Maria Graziano of Portici.

Portici. Recorded in May 2001 by Adam Kendon and Maria Graziano. A group of girls between the ages of 7 and 13 years who are members of a youth group attached to a church talk about their homes, their pets, things they like to cook and their favourite cartoons with two adult leaders. The speech was transcribed by Maria Graziano of Portici.

Northamptonshire, England

The recordings made in Northamptonshire were all made in a small historic market town in Northamptonshire, here called 'Northant', and they were all made by Adam Kendon and the speech has been transcribed by him.

GB. A recording of a guided tour of the town by a semi-professional guide. His discourse is spontaneous and informative. The recording lasts about two hours. It was made in August 1997.

OMUS. A recording of a meeting of the management committee of the local museum. The recording is about two hours in length and was made in August 1997.

OCC. A recording of a meeting of the committee of the local Cricket Club, again about two hours in length. Recorded in August 1997.

OMARKET (cheeses). A recording made in August 1997 of customers and proprietors at a stall selling cheeses and related products at Northant Market.

Crick. A recording made in March 2000 of a conversation of two older native residents of Northant in which they talked about their childhood and youth in the town with a member of the local Historical Society. This recording forms part of the Oral Archive of the Historical Society.

OMUSACT. A recording of an 'activity day' for children at the local museum in Northant. This was recorded in August 2000. This recording forms part of the archive of the museum.

Recordings made in the USA

ISP 001 61. A film made at Eastern Pennsylvania Psychiatric Institute, Project on Human Communication, in 1961. It was made by Jaques Van Vlack and Ray L. Birdwhistell as part of a series of training films for psychiatrists called Teaching Psychotherapy. In this film two psychiatrists, a social worker and psychiatrists in training discuss a case that is presented by one of the psychiatrists.

Pollack. A recording made in about 1981 at Connecticut College, New London, Connecticut of people recounting well-known stories. The recording was made as an exercise by a student for a class taught by Kendon.

Preceptor II and *Preceptor VII* are from a series of recordings of discussions between a medical intern and supervising physician made at the Hospital of the University Pennsylvania under the direction of Jack Ende and Frederick Erickson in 1999. These recordings were made for a study of the nature of the preceptor–intern interaction as part of a project for the study of medical education. The excerpts are used with the permission of Dr. Jack Ende.

Texas Th. is a recording made at a house party in Austin, Texas by Leslie Jarman, in about 1995. The excerpts are used with the permission of Leslie Jarman.

Chinese Dinner. A videotape made under the supervision of Charles Goodwin in about 1970 of two couples eating a take-out Chinese dinner in the home of one of the couples. I am grateful to Charles Goodwin for making this video tape and the transcription of it available.

ES (Schwarz). A videotape made in the autumn of 2001 by a student who participated in a seminar on gesture taught by Adam Kendon at the University of Pennsylvania in Philadelphia. The recording is of four women undergraduates chatting together about their courses, films they have seen and other matters.

TP-1-2000. A video of a family and guests having lunch or chatting in the living room in Takoma Park, Maryland. Recorded by Adam Kendon in the spring of 2000.

References

Adams, Florence Adelaide F. 1897. *Gesture and Pantomimic Action*. Fourth Edition. New York: Werner.

Aldrete, Gregory S. 1999. *Gestures and Acclamations in Ancient Rome*. Baltimore: The Johns Hopkins University Press.

Alibali, Martha, Sotaro Kita and A. J. Young. 2000. Gesture and the process of speech production: we think, therefore we gesture. *Language and Cognitive Processes*, 15:593–613.

Allan, K. 1977. Classifiers. *Language*, 53:285–311.

Allport, G. W. and Phillip E. Vernon 1933. *Studies in Expressive Movements*. New York: Macmillan.

Amira, Karl von 1905. Die Handgebärden in den Bilderhandschriften des Sacsenspiegels. In *Sitzungsberiche der Akademie der Wisseschaften zu München*, 23 (2):161–263.

Angenot, M. 1973. Les traités de l'éloquence du corps. *Semiotica*, 8:60–82.

Armstrong, David F., William C. Stokoe and Sherman E. Wilcox 1995. *Gesture and the Nature of Language*. Cambridge: Cambridge University Press.

Austin, Gilbert 1966 [1802]. *Chironomia or, a Treatise on Rhetorical Delivery*. London: T. Cadell and W. Davis. Edited with a Critical Introduction by Mary Margaret Robb and Lester Thonssen. Carbondale and Edwardville: Southern Illinois University Press.

Bacon, Albert M. 1875. *A Manual of Gestures in Oratory*. Chicago: S. C. Griggs & Co.

Barakat, Robert A. 1969. Gesture systems. *Keystone Folklore Quarterly*, 14:105–121.

Barakat, Robert A. 1975. *Cistercian Sign Language. A Study in Nonverbal Communication*. Kalamazoo, Michigan: Cistercian Publications.

Barker, Roger G. and Herbert F. Wright 1954. *Midwest and its Children*. Evanston, Illinois: Row, Peterson and Company.

Barnett, Dene 1987. *The Art of Gesture: The Practices and Principles of 18th Century Acting*. Heidelberg: C. Winter.

Bartinieff, Irmgard with Dori Lewis 1980. *Body Movement: Coping with the Environment*. New York: Gordon and Breach Science Publishers.

Barzini, Luigi 1964. *The Italians*. London: Hamish Hamilton.

Bassili, John N. 1978. Facial motion in the perception of faces and of emotional expression. *Journal of Experimental Psychology: Human Perception and Performance*, 4:373–379.

Bates, Elizabeth 1979. *The Emergence of Symbols*. New York: Academic Press.

Bateson, Gregory 1936. *Naven*. Cambridge: Cambridge University Press.

Bateson, Gregory 1955. A theory of play and fantasy. *Approaches to the Study of Human Personality*. Washington, D.C.: American Psychiatric Association, Psychiatric Research Reports, No. 2, pp. 39-51.

Bateson, Gregory 1958. Language and psychotherapy: Frieda Fromm-Reichmann's last project. *Psychiatry,* 21:96–100.

Bateson, Gregory 1968. Redundancy and coding. In *Animal Communication: Techniques of Study and Results of Research,* Thomas A. Sebeok, ed. Bloomington: Indiana University Press, pp. 614–626.

Bateson, Gregory and Margaret Mead 1942. *Balinese Character: A Photographic Analysis.* Special Publications of the New York Academy of Sciences, Vol. II. Wilbur G. Valentine, ed. New York: New York Academy of Sciences.

Bateson, Gregory, Don D. Jackson, Jay Haley and John H. Weakland 1956. Toward a theory of schizophrenia. *Behavioral Science,* 1:251–264.

Bavelas, Janet Beavin, Nicole Chovil, Douglas A. Lawrie, and Allan Wade 1992. Interactive gestures. *Discourse Processes,* 15:469–489.

Baxandall, Michael 1988. *Painting and Experience in Fifteenth Century Italy.* Oxford: Oxford University Press.

Beattie, Geoffrey and Jane Coughlan 1998. Do iconic gestures have a functional role in lexical access? An experimental study of the effects of repeating a verbal message on gesture production. *Semiotica,* 119:221–249.

Beattie, Geoffrey and Jane Coughlan 1999. An experimental investigation of the role of iconic gestures in lexical access using the tip-of-the-tongue phenomenon. *British Journal of Psychology,* 19:35–56.

Beattie, Geoffrey, and Heather Shovelton 1999a. Do iconic hand gestures really contribute anything to the semantic information conveyed by speech? An experimental investigation. *Semiotica,* 123:1–30.

Beattie, Geoffrey, and Heather Shovelton 1999b. Mapping the range of information contained in the iconic hand gestures that accompany spontaneous speech. *Journal of Language and Social Psychology,* 18:438–462.

Beattie, Geoffrey and Heather Shovelton 2001. An experimental investigation of the role of different types of iconic gesture in communication: a semantic feature approach. *Gesture,* 1:129–149.

Bellugi, Ursula 1981. The acquisition of a spatial language. In *The Development of Language and Language Researchers: Essays in Honor of Roger Brown,* F. S. Kessel, ed. Hillsdale, New Jersey: Lawrence Erlbaum, pp. 153–185.

Bellugi, Ursula, and Don Newkirk 1981. Formal devices for creating new signs in American Sign Language. *Sign Language Studies,* 30:1–35.

Benzoni, Gino 1970. Bonifacio, Giovanni. In *Dizionario Biografico degli Italiani.* Rome: Enciclopedia Italiana Treccani.

Birdwhistell, R. L. 1952. *Introduction to Kinesics: An Annotation System for Analysis of Body Motion and Gesture.* Louisville, Kentucky: University of Louisville.

Birdwhistell, R. L. 1966. Some relationships between American kinesics and spoken American English. In *Communication and Culture,* A. G. Smith, ed. New York: Holt, Rinehart and Winston, pp. 182–189.

Birdwhistell, Ray L. 1970 *Kinesics and Context: Essays in Body Motion Communication.* Barton Jones, ed. Philadelphia: University of Pennsylvania Press.

Blake R. 1993 Cats perceive biological motion. *Psychological Science,* 4:54–57.

Bloom, Ralph 1979. Language creation in the manual modality: a preliminary investigation. 9 August 1979. Student paper, Department of Psychology, University of Chicago.

Bloomfield, Leonard 1983 [1914]. *Introduction to the Study of Language*. New York: Henry Holt. New edition edited with an Introduction by Joseph Kess. Amsterdam: John Benjamins.

Bloomfield, Leonard 1933. *Language*. New York: Henry Holt.

Bolinger, Dwight 1946. Some thoughts on 'yep' and 'nope'. *American Speech*, 21:90–95.

Boring, Edward G. 1957. *A History of Experimental Psychology*. New York: Appleton Century.

Boyes-Braem, Penny 1981. Features of the hand shape in American Sign Language. Dissertation submittted in partial satisfaction of the requirements for the degree of Doctor of Philosophy, Department of Psychology, University of California, Berkeley, California.

Bronowski, Jacob, and Ursula Bellugi 1970. Language, name, and concept. *Science*, 168:669–673.

Brookes, Heather J. 2001. *O clever* 'He's streetwise'. When gestures become quotable: the case of the *clever* gesture. *Gesture*, 1:167–184.

Brown, Roger 1973. *A First Language: The Early Stages*. Cambridge, Massachusetts: Harvard University Press.

Brun, Theodore 1969. *The International Dictionary of Sign Language*. London: Wolfe Publishing Ltd.

Bruner, Jerome 1975. The ontogenesis of speech acts. *Journal of Child Language*, 2:1-19.

Bruner, Jerome and Tagiuri, Renato 1954. The perception of people. In Gardner Lindzey, ed. *Handbook of Social Psychology*, Volume II. *Special Fields and Applications*. New York: Addison-Wesley, pp. 634-654.

Bucci, Wilma and Freedman, Norbert 1978. Language and hand: the dimension of referential competence. *Journal of Personality*, 46:594-622.

Bühler, Karl 1990. *Theory of Language. The Representational Function of Language*. A translation by Donald Fraser Goodwin of *Sprachtheorie* (1934). Amsterdam and Philadelphia: John Benjamins.

Bullowa, Margaret, ed. 1979. *Before Speech: The Beginnings of Interpersonal Communication*. Cambridge: Cambridge University Press.

Bulwer, John 1974 [1644]. *Chirologia or the Natural Language of the Hand, etc. [and] Chironomia or the Art of Manual Rhetoric, etc.* London: Henry Twyford. Edited with an Introduction by James W. Cleary. Carbondale and Edwardville, Illinois: Southern Illinois University Press.

Burke, Peter 1992. The language of gesture in early modern Italy. In *A Cultural History of Gesture,* Jan Bremmer, and Herman Roodenburg, eds. Ithaca, New York: Cornell University Press, pp. 71–83.

Butterworth, Brian and Geoffrey Beattie 1978. Gesture and silence as indicators of planning in speech. In *Recent Advances in the Psychology of Language: Formal and Experimental Approaches*, R. Campbell and P. Smith, eds. New York: Plenum Press, pp. 347-360.

Butterworth, Brian and Uri Hadar 1989. Gesture, speech and computation stages: a reply to McNeill. *Psychological Review*, 96:168-172.

Calbris, Genevieve 1990. *The Semiotics of French Gesture*. Bloomington: Indiana University Press.

Calbris, Genevieve 2002. From cutting an object to a clear cut analysis. Gesture as the representation of a preconceptual schema linking concrete actions to abstract notions. *Gesture*, 3:19-46.

Carabelli, Giancarlo 1996. Veneri e Priapi. *Culti di fertilità e mitologie falliche tra Napoli e Londra nell'età dell'Illuminismo.* Lecce: Argo.

Carpitella, Diego 1976. Cinesica 1: Napoli. [16 mm film]. Rome: Istituto di Luce.

Carpitella, Diego 1981. Cinesica 1: Napoli. Il linguaggio del corpo e le tradizioni popolari: codici democinesici e ricerca cinematografica. *La Ricerca Folklorica*, 37:61–70.

Cassell, Justine, and David McNeill 1990. Gesture and ground. In *Proceedings of the 16th Annual Meeting of the Berkeley Linguistics Society: General Session*, K. Hall, J.-P. Koenig, M. Meachum, and S. Reinman, eds. Berkeley, California: Berkeley Linguistics Society, pp. 57–68.

Cavé, Christian, Isabelle Guaïtella and Serge Santi, eds. 2001. *Oralité et Gestualité. Interactions et comportements multimodaux dans la communication.* Actes du colloque ORAGE 2001, Aix-en-Provence, 18–22 juin 2001. Paris: L'Harmattan.

Chomsky, Noam 1967. The formal nature of language. In *The Biological Basis of Language* by Eric Lenneberg. New York: John Wiley & Sons, pp. 397–442.

Clark, Katerina and Michael Holquist 1984. *Mikhail Bakhtin.* Cambridge, MA: The Bellknap Press of Harvard University Press.

Clark, William Philo 1885. *The Indian Sign Language, with brief explanatory notes, etc.* Philadelphia: L. R. Hamersly.

Cleary, James W. 1959. John Bulwer: Renaissance communicationist. *Quarterly Journal of Speech*, 45:391–398.

Cocchiara, Giuseppe 1959. *Popolo e letteratura in Italia.* Torino: Einaudi.

Cocchiara, Giuseppe 1981. *Storia del folklore in Italia.* Palermo: Sellerio.

Collett, Peter, and Alberta Contarello 1987. Gesti di assenso e di dissenso. In *Comunicazione e gestualità*, Pio Enrico Ricci-Bitti, ed. Milan: Franco Angeli, pp. 69–85.

Condillac, Etienne Bonnot de 1971. *An Essay on the Origin of Human Knowledge (1756).* Facsimile Reproduction of the Translation of Thomas Nugent, edited and with an Introduction by Robert G. Weyant. Delmar, New York: Scholars' Facsimiles and Reprints.

Condon, William C. and Richard Ogston 1966. Sound film analysis of normal and pathological behavior patterns. *Journal of Nervous and Mental Disease*, 143: 338–347.

Condon, William C. and Richard Ogston 1967. A segmentation of behavior. *Journal of Psychiatric Research*, 5:221-235.

Conley, Thomas M. 1990. *Rhetoric in the European Tradition.* Chicago and London: Chicago University Press.

Creider, Chet A. 1977. Towards a description of East African gestures. *Sign Language Studies*, 14:1–20.

Critchley, MacDonald 1939. *The Language of Gesture.* London: Edward Arnold.

Critchley, MacDonald 1975. *The Silent Language.* London: Butterworths.

Crowder, E. M. 1996. Gestures at work in sense-making science talk. *Journal of the Learning Sciences*, 5:173-208.

Crystal, David 1969. *Prosodic Systems and Intonation in English*. Cambridge: Cambridge University Press.

Crystal, David and Derek Davy 1969. *Investigating English Style*. London: Longmans Green and Co.

Da Cunha Pereira, M. C. and C. De Lemos 1990. Gesture in hearing mother–deaf child interaction. In *From Gesture to Language in Hearing and Deaf Children*, Virginia Volterra and Carol J. Erting, eds. Berlin: Springer-Verlag, pp. 178–186.

Danesi, Marcel 1993. *Vico, Metaphor and the Origin of Language*. Bloomington: Indiana University Press.

Darwin, Charles 1871. *The Descent of Man*. London: John Murray.

Darwin, Charles 1872. *The Expression of the Emotions in Man and Animals*. London: John Murray.

D'Ascoli, Francesco 1993. *Nuovo vocabolario dialettale napoletano*. Naples: Adriano Gallina Editore.

Davis, Martha 1972. *Understanding Body Movement: An Annotated Bibliography*. New York: Arno Press.

Davis, Martha and Janet Skupien. 1982. *Body Movement and Nonverbal Communication: An Annotated Bibliography, 1971-1981*. Bloomington: Indiana University Press.

De Blasi, Nicola and Luigi Imperatore 1998. *Il napoletano parlato e scritto*. Naples: Fausto Fiorentino.

De Bourcard, Francesco, ed. 1857-1860. *Usi e costumi di Napoli e contorni*. Volume I (1857), Volume II (1860). Naples: Gaetano Nobile.

De Jorio, Andrea 1819. *Indicazione del più rimarcabile in Napoli e contorni*. Naples: Simoniana.

De Jorio, Andrea 1832. *La mimica degli antichi investigata nel gestire napoletano*. Naples: Fibreno.

De Jorio, Andrea 2000. *Gesture in Naples and Gesture in Classical Antiquity*. A translation of *La mimica degli antichi investigata nel gestire napoletano* (1832), and with an Introduction and Notes, by Adam Kendon. Bloomington: Indiana University Press.

Dell, Cicely 1970. *A Primer for Movement Description. Using Effort-Shape and Supplementary Concepts*. New York: Dance Notation Bureau, Inc.

De Ruiter, Jan Peter 1998. *Gesture and Speech Production*. MPI Series in Psycholinguistics, No. 6. Nijmegen: Max Planck Insitute for Psycholinguistics.

De Ruiter, Jan Peter 2000. The production of gesture and speech. In David McNeill, ed. *Language and Gesture*. Cambridge: Cambridge University Press, pp. 284-311.

Diadori, Pierangela 1990. *Senza Parole. 100 Gesti degli Italiani*. Rome: Bonacci.

Diderot, Denis 1916 [1751]. Letter on deaf mutes. In *Diderot's Early Philosophical Works*, translated and edited by Margaret Jourdain. Chicago: Open Court Publishing Co., pp. 158 -225.

Dittrich, Winand H., Tom Troscianko, Stephen E. G. Lee, and Dawn Morgan 1996. Perception of emotion from dynamic point light displays represented in dance. *Perception*, 25:727–738.

Dobozy, Maria 1999. *The Saxon Mirror: A* Sachsenspiegel *of the Fourteenth Century.* Philadelphia: University of Pennsylvania Press.

Dufour, Robert 1992. The use of gestures for communicative purposes: can gestures become grammatical? Doctoral Dissertation, Department of Psychology, University of Illinois, Champaign, Illinois.

Dumas, Alexandre 1999 [1843]. *Il Corricolo.* Introduzione e note di Gino Doria. Naples: Colonnese Editore.

Dutsch, Dorota 2002. Towards a grammar of gesture: an analysis of Quintilian's *Institutio Oratoria* 11:85–124. *Gesture*, 2:265–287.

Eco, Umberto 1976. *A Theory of Semiotics.* Bloomington: Indiana University Press.

Efron, D. 1941. *Gesture and Environment.* New York: King's Crown Press.

Efron, D. 1972. *Gesture, Race and Culture.* Preface by Paul Ekman. [Reissue of Efron 1941] The Hague: Mouton and Co.

Eibl-Eibesfeldt, Irenäus 1989. *Human Ethology.* New York: Aldine de Guyter.

Eisenstein, Elizabeth L. 1979. *The Printing Press as an Agent of Change.* Cambridge: Cambridge University Press.

Ekman, Paul 1976. Movements with precise meanings. *Journal of Communication*, 26: 14–26.

Ekman, Paul, ed. 1982. *Emotion in the Human Face.* Second Edition. Cambridge: Cambridge University Press.

Ekman, Paul 1985. *Telling Lies: Clues to Deceit in the Marketplace, Politics and Marriage.* New York: Norton.

Ekman, Paul and Friesen, W. 1969. The repertoire of nonverbal behavior: categories, origins, usage and coding. *Semiotica*, 1:49–98.

Ekman, Paul and Wallace Friesen 1972. Hand movements. *Journal of Communication*, 22:353–374.

Ekman, Paul, and Wallace Friesen 1982. Felt, false and miserable smiles. *Journal of Nonverbal Behavior*, 6:238–252.

Elias, Norbert 1994. *The Civilizing Process.* Translation by Edmund Jephcott of *Über den Prozess der Zivilisation.* 2 vols. Basel: Haus zum Falken, 1939. Oxford: Basil Blackwell.

Emmorey, Karen 2002. *Language. Cognition and the Brain. Insights from Sign Language Research.* Mahwah, New Jersey: Lawrence Erlbaum.

Emmorey, Karen and S. Casey 2001. Gesture, thought and spatial language. *Gesture*, 1:35-50.

Enfield, Nicholas K. 2001. 'Lip-pointing': with a discussion of form and function with reference to data from Laos. *Gesture*, 1:185–212.

Engel, Johann Jakob 1785-86. *Ideen zu einer Mimik.* Berlin: Auf Kosten des Verfassers und in Commission bei August Mylius.

Engel, Johann Jakob 1820. *Lettere intorno all mimica.* Versione dal tedesco di G. Rasori. Aggiuntovi i capitoli sei sull'arte rappresentative di L. Riccodoni. Milano: Batelli e Fanfani.

Facchini, M. 1983. An historical reconstruction of the events leading to the Congress of Milan in 1880. In *SLR '83: Sign Language Research.* William C. Stokoe, and Virginia Volterra, eds. Roma: Istituto di Psicologia del Consiglio Nazionale delle Ricerche, Silver Spring, Maryland: Linstok Press, pp. 356–362.

Farnell, Brenda 1990. Plains Indian Sign-Talk: action and discourse among the Nakota (Assiniboine) people of Montana. Doctoral Dissertation, Department of Anthropology, Indiana University, Bloomington, Indiana.

Farnell, Brenda 1995. *Do You See What I Mean?* Austin, Texas: University of Texas Press.

Feldman, Alan 1959. *Mannerisms of Speech and Gesture in Everyday Life.* New York: International Universities Press.

Feldman, H., S. Goldin-Meadow, and L. Gleitman 1978. Beyond Herodotus: the creation of language by linguistically deprived deaf children. In *Action, Symbol and Gesture: The Emergence of Language*, A. Lock, ed. New York: Academic Press, pp. 351-414.

Fox, R., and C. McDaniel 1982. The perception of biological motion by human infants. *Science*, 218:486–487.

Freeberg, Ernest 2001. *The Education of Laura Bridgman.* Cambridge, Mass.: Harvard University Press.

Freedman, Norbert 1972. The analysis of movement behavior during the clinical interview. In *Studies in Dyadic Communication*, Aaron W. Siegman and Benjamin Pope, eds. New York: Pergamon Press, pp. 153–175.

Freedman, Norbert 1977. Hands, words and mind: on the structuralization of body movements during discourse and the capacity for verbal representation. In *Communicative Structures and Psychic Structures: A Psychoanalytic Approach*, Norbert Freedman, and Stanley Grand, eds. New York and London: Plenum Press, pp. 109–132.

Freedman, Norbert, Jacques Van Meel, Felix Barroso and Wilma Bucci 1986. On the development of communicative competence. *Semiotica*, 62:77-105.

Friedman, Lynn A., ed. 1977. *On the Other Hand: New Perspectives on American Sign Language.* New York: Academic Press.

Friesen, Wallace, Paul Ekman and Harald Walbott 1979. Measuring hand movements. *Journal of Nonverbal Behavior,* 4:97–112.

Gadeau, Pierre 1983. La civilisation incarnée. Synthèse d'une approche de la culture gestuelle italienne. *Geste et Image*, 3:19–36.

Gadeau, Pierre 1986. Regard sur les classiques: Andrea De Jorio. *Geste et Image*, 6/7: 215–225.

Galiani, Ferdinando 1970 [1789]. *Del dialetto napoletano.* Edited from the text of the 1789 edition by Enrico Malato. Rome: Bulzoni.

Gardner, R. Allen and Beatrice T. Gardner 1969. Teaching sign language to a chimpanzee. *Science,* 165 (3894, 15 August), 664–672.

Gardner, R. Allen and Beatrice T. Gardner 1971. Two-way communication with an infant chimpanzee. In *Behavior of Nonhuman Primates,* Vol. 4., A. Schrier and F. Stollnitz, eds. New York: Academic Press, pp. 117–184.

Ghirelli, Antonio 1992. *Storia di Napoli.* Turin: Einaudi.

Givens, David 1977. Shoulder shrugging: a densely communicative expressive behavior. *Semiotica*, 19:13–28.

Goffman, Erving 1961. Fun in Games. In Erving Goffman, *Encounters: Two Studies in the Sociology of Interaction.* Indianapolis: Bobbs-Merrill.

Goffman, Erving 1963. *Behavior in Public Places*. New York: The Free Press.

Goffman, Erving 1974. *Frame Analysis*. Cambridge, MA: Harvard University Press.

Goffman, Erving 1981. Replies and responses. In *Forms of Talk* by Erving Goffman. Philadelphia: University of Pennsylvania Press, pp. 5–77.

Goldin-Meadow, Susan 1979. Structure in a manual communication system developed without a conventional language model: language without a helping hand. In *Studies in Neurolinguistics*, Volume 4, H. Whitaker and H. A. Whitaker, eds. New York: Academic Press, pp. 125–209.

Goldin-Meadow, Susan 1982. The resilience of recursion: a study of a communication system developed without a conventional language model. In *Language Acquisition: The State of the Art*, Eric Wanner and Lila Gleitman, eds. Cambridge: Cambridge University Press, pp. 51–77.

Goldin-Meadow, Susan 1993. When does gesture become a language? A study of gesture used as a primary communication system by deaf children of hearing parents. In *Tools, Language and Cognition in Human Evolution*, Kathleen R. Gibson and Tim Ingold, eds. Cambridge: Cambridge University Press, pp. 63–85.

Goldin-Meadow, Susan 2003a. *The Resilience of Language*. New York: Psychology Press.

Goldin-Meadow, Susan 2003b. *Hearing Gesture: How Our Hands Help Us Think*. Cambridge, MA: The Bellknap Press of Harvard University Press.

Goldin-Meadow, Susan and Carolyn Mylander 1984. *Gestural Communication in Deaf Children: the Effects and Noneffects of Parental Input on Early Language Development*. Monographs of the Society for Research in Child Development, 49, Nos. 3-4.

Goldin-Meadow, Susan and Carolyn Mylander 1990a. The role of parental input in the development of a morphological system. *Journal of Child Language*, 17: 527–563.

Goldin-Meadow, Susan, David McNeill, and Jenny Singleton 1996. Silence is liberating: removing the handcuffs on grammatical expression in the manual modality. *Psychological Review* 103:34–55.

Goodwin, Charles 1981. *Conversational Organization*. New York: Academic Press.

Goodwin, Marjorie H. 1980. Processes of mutual monitoring implicated in the production of description sequences. *Sociological Inquiry*, 50:303-317.

Graf, Fritz 1992. Gestures and conventions: the gestures of Roman actors and orators. In *A Cultural History of Gesture*, Jan Bremmer and Herman Roodenburg, eds. Ithaca, New York: Cornell University Press, pp. 36–58.

Graziano, Maria 2003. Open hands across cultures. Tesi di Laurea in Linguistica Inglese, Facoltà di Lingue e Letterature Straniere, Università di Napoli "Orientale".

Groce, Norah 1985. *Everyone Here Spoke Sign Language: Hereditary deafness on Martha's Vineyard*. Cambridge, MA: Harvard University Press.

Gullberg, Marianne 1998. *Gesture as a Communication Strategy in Second Language Discourse: A Study of Learners of French and Swedish*. Lund: Lund University Press.

Hadar, Uri and Brian Butterworth 1997. Iconic gestures, imagery and word-retrieval in speech. *Semiotica*, 115:147–172.

Haddon, Alfred C., ed. 1907. *Reports of the Cambridge Anthropological Expedition to the Torres Straits. Volume III Linguistics*, S. H. Ray, ed. Cambridge: Cambridge University Press.

Hall, Edward T. 1959. *The Silent Language*. Garden City, NY: Doubleday and Co.

Hall, E. T. 1966. *The Hidden Dimension*. Garden City, NY: Doubleday.

Hall, Edward T. and Trager, George L. 1953. *The Analysis of Culture*. Washington, D.C.: American Council of Learned Societies.

Hanna, Barbara E. 1996. Defining the emblem. *Semiotica*. 112:289–358.

Harris, Roy 1987. *The Language Machine*. Ithaca, NY: Cornell University Press.

Harris, Zellig 1951. *Methods in Structural Linguistics*. Chicago: Chicago University Press.

Haskell, Francis 1993. *History and its Images*. New Haven, Connecticut: Yale University Press.

Haviland, John B. 1993. Anchoring, iconicity and orientation in Guugu Yimithirr pointing gestures. *Journal of Linguistic Anthropology*, 3:3–45.

Haviland, John B. 2000. Pointing, gesture spaces and mental maps. In *Language and Gesture*, David McNeill, ed. Cambridge: Cambridge University Press, pp. 13–46.

Heider, Fritz, and Marian Simmel 1944. An experimental study of apparent behavior. *American Journal of Psychology*, 57:243–259.

Heims, S. P. 1975. Encounter of behavioral sciences with new machine–organism analogies in the 1940s. *Journal of the History of the Behavioral Sciences*, 11:368–373.

Heims, S. P. 1977. Gregory Bateson and the mathematicians: from interdisciplinary interaction to societal functions. *Journal of the History of the Behavioral Sciences*, 13:141–159.

Hewes, G. W. 1973. Primate communication and the gestural origin of language. *Current Anthropology*, 14:5-24.

Hewes, G. W. 1974. Gesture language in culture contact. *Sign Language Studies*, 4:1–34.

Hewes, G. W. 1978. The phylogeny of sign language. In *Sign Language of the Deaf: Psychological, Linguistic and Sociological Perspectives*, I. M. Schlesinger and Lila Namir, eds. New York: Academic Press, pp. 11–56.

Hibbitts, Bernard 1992. "Coming to our senses." Communication and legal expression in performance cultures. *Emory Law Journal*, 41:873–960.

Hockett, Charles F., and Robert Ascher 1964. The human revolution. *Current Anthropology*, 5:135–168.

Holler, Judith and Geoffrey Beattie 2002. A micro-analytic investigation of how iconic gestures and speech represent core semantic features in talk. *Semiotica*, 142:31–69.

Holler, Judith and Geoffrey Beattie 2003. How iconic gestures and speech interact in the representation of meaning: are both aspects really integral to the process? *Semiotica*, 146:181–216.

Howitt, A. W. 1890. Notes on the use of gesture language in Australian tribes. *Australian Association for the Advancement of Science*, 2:637-646.

Howitt, A. W. 1904. *The Native Tribes of South East Australia*. London: Macmillan.

Hymes, Dell 1974. *Foundations in Sociolinguistics. An Ethnographic Approach*. Philadelphia: University of Pennsylvania Press.

Iandolo, Antonio, 2001. *Parlare e scrivere in dialetto napoletano*. Napoli: Cuzzolin.

Iverson, Jana M. 1998. Gesture when there is no visual model. In *The Nature and Functions of Gesture in Children's Communication*, Jana M. Iverson and Susan Goldin-Meadow, eds. New Directions for Child Development, No. 79. San Francisco: Jossey-Bass Publishers, pp. 89-116.

Jakobsen, Roman 1972. Motor signs for 'Yes' and 'No'. *Language in Society*, 1:91–96.

Jancovic, Merry Ann, Shannon Devoe, and Morton Wiener, 1975. Age-related changes in hand and arm movements as nonverbal communication: Some conceptualizations and an empirical exploration. *Child Development*, 46:922–928.

Johansson, G. 1973. Visual perception of biological motion and a model for its analysis. *Perception and Psychophysics*, 14:201–211.

Johnson, Mark 1987. *The Body in the Mind. The Bodily Basis of Meaning, Imagination and Reason*. Chicago: Chicago University Press.

Johnson, R. E. 1991. Sign language, culture and community in a traditional Yucatec Maya village. *Sign Language Studies*, 73:461–474.

Jordan, I. King and Robin Battison 1976. A referential communication experiment with foreign sign languages. *Sign Language Studies*, 10:69–80.

Kaulfers, W. V. 1931. Curiosities of colloquial gesture. *Hispania*, 14:249–264.

Kegl, Judy, Ann Senghas and Marie Coppola 1999. Creation through contact: sign language emergence and sign language change in Nicaragua. In *Language Creation and Language Change. Creolization, Diachrony and Development*, Michael DeGraff, ed. Cambridge, MA: MIT Press, pp. 179–237.

Kendon, Adam 1972. Some relationships between body motion and speech. An analysis of an example. In *Studies in Dyadic Communication*, Aaron Siegman and Benjamin Pope, eds. Elmsford, New York: Pergamon Press, pp. 177–210.

Kendon, Adam 1973. The role of visible behaviour in the organization of social interaction. In *Social Communication and Movement: Studies of Interaction and Expression in Man and Chimpanzee*, Mario Von Cranach and Ian Vine, eds. London: Academic Press, pp. 29–74.

Kendon, Adam 1978. Differential perception and attentional frame: two problems for investigation. *Semiotica*, 24: 305–315.

Kendon, Adam 1980a. Gesticulation and speech: two aspects of the process of utterance. In *The Relationship of Verbal and Nonverbal Communication*, Mary Ritchie Key, ed. The Hague: Mouton and Co., pp. 207–227.

Kendon, Adam 1980b. A description of a deaf-mute sign language from the Enga Province of Papua New Guinea with some comparative discussion. Part I: The formational properties of Enga signs. *Semiotica*, 32:1–32. Part II: The semiotic functioning of Enga signs. *Semiotica*, 32:81–117. Part III: Aspects of utterance construction. *Semiotica*, 32:245–313.

Kendon, Adam 1981. Geography of gesture. *Semiotica*, 37:129–163.

Kendon, Adam 1982. The study of gesture: Some observations on its history. *Recherches Sémiotiques/Semiotic Inquiry*, 2:45–62.

Kendon, Adam 1983. Gesture and speech: how they interact. In *Nonverbal Interaction*, John M. Wieman and Randall P. Harrison, eds. Beverly Hills: Sage Publications, pp. 13-45.

Kendon, Adam 1984. Knowledge of sign language in an Australian Aboriginal community. *Journal of Anthropological Research*, 40:556-576.

Kendon, Adam 1988a. How gestures can become like words. In *Cross-Cultural Perspectives in Nonverbal Communication*, Fernando Poyatos, ed. Lewiston, New York: C. J. Hogrefe, pp. 131–141.

Kendon, Adam 1988b. *Sign Languages of Aboriginal Australia: Cultural, Semiotic and Communicative Perspectives*. Cambridge: Cambridge University Press.

Kendon, Adam 1990a. *Conducting Interaction: Patterns of Behavior in Focused Encounters*. Cambridge: Cambridge University Press.

Kendon, Adam 1990b. Signs in the cloister and elsewhere. *Semiotica*, 79:307–329.

Kendon, Adam 1992. Some recent work from Italy on Quotable Gestures (Emblems). *Journal of Linguistic Anthropology*, 2:77–93.

Kendon, Adam 1993. Human gesture. In *Tools, Language and Cognition in Human Evolution*, Kathleen R. Gibson, and Tim Ingold, eds. Cambridge: Cambridge University Press, pp. 43–62.

Kendon, Adam 1994. Do gestures communicate? A review. *Research on Language and Social Interaction*, 27 (3):175–200.

Kendon, Adam 1995a. Andrea De Jorio - the first ethnographer of gesture? *Visual Anthropology*, 7:375–394.

Kendon, Adam 1995b. Gestures as illocutionary and discourse structure markers in southern Italian conversation. *Journal of Pragmatics*, 23:247–279.

Kendon, Adam 2002. Some uses of the head shake. *Gesture*, 2:147–183.

Kendon, Adam 2004. Some contrasts in gesticulation in Neapolitan speakers and speakers in Northamptonshire. In *Semantics and Pragmatics of Everyday Gestures*, Roland Posner and Cornelia Müller, eds. Berlin: Weidler Buchverlag, pp. 173–193

Kendon, Adam and Stuart J. Sigman 1996. Ray L. Birdwhistell (1918-1994). *Semiotica*, 112:231–261.

Kendon, Adam and Laura Versante 2003. Pointing by hand in 'Neapolitan'. In *Pointing: Where Language, Culture and Cognition Meet*. Sotaro Kita, ed. Hillsdale, N.J.: Lawrence Erlbaum, pp. 109–137.

Key, Mary Ritchie 1977. *Nonverbal Communication. A Research Guide and Bibliography*. Metuchen, New Jersey: Scarecrow Press.

Kita, Sotaro 1993. Language and thought interface: a study of spontaneous gestures and Japanese mimetics. Doctoral Dissertation, Department of Psychology and Department of Linguistics, University of Chicago, Chicago, Illinois.

Kita, Sotaro 2000. How representational gestures help speaking. In *Language and Gesture*, David McNeill, ed. Cambridge: Cambridge University Press, pp. 162-185.

Kita, Sotaro and Asli Özyürek 2003. What does cross-linguistic variation in semantic coordination of speech and gesture reveal? Evidence for and interface representation of spatial thinking and speaking. *Journal of Memory and Language*, 48:16–32.

Klima, Edward S., and Ursula Bellugi 1979. *The Signs of Language*, Cambridge, Massachusetts: Harvard University Press.

Knowlson, James R. 1965. The idea of gesture as a universal language in the 17th and 18th centuries. *Journal of the History of Ideas*, 26:495–508.

Knox, Dilwyn 1990. Late medieval and renaissance ideas on gesture. In *Die Sprache der Zeichen und Bilder. Rhetorik und nonverbale Kommunikation in der frühen Neuzeit*, Volker Kapp, ed. Marburg: Hitzeroth, pp. 11–39.

Knox, Dilwyn 1996. Giovanni Bonifacio's *L'arte de' cenni* and Renaissance ideas of gesture. In *Italia ed Europa nella Linguistica del Rinascimento. Confronti e Relazioni*, Atti del Convegno internazionale, Ferrara, 20–24 marzo 1991, ed. Mirko Tavoni and others, Vol. 2. Ferrara: Franco Cosimo Panini, pp. 379–400.

Krauss, Robert M. and Uri Hadar 1999. The role of speech-related arm/hand gestures in word retrieval. In *Gesture, Speech and Sign*, Lynn Messing and Ruth Campbell, eds. Oxford: Oxford University Press, pp. 93–116.

Krauss, Robert M., Palmer Morrel-Samuels and Christina Colasante 1991. Do conversational gestures communicate? *Journal of Personality and Social Psychology*, 61:743–754.

Krauss, Robert M., Yihsiu Chen and P. Chawla 1996. Nonverbal behavior and nonverbal communication: what do conversational hand gestures tell us? In *Advances in Experimental Social Psychology*, M. Zanna, ed., Volume 28. New York: Academic Press, pp. 389–450.

Krauss, Robert M., Yihsiu Chen and Rebecca F. Gottesman 2000. Lexical gestures and lexical access: a process model. In *Language and Gesture*, David McNeill, ed. Cambridge: Cambridge University Press, pp. 261–283.

Krout, Maurice H. 1935. Autistic gestures: an experimental study in symbolic movement. *Psychological Monographs*, Whole Number 208, 46:1–126.

Kuschel, Rolf 1973. The silent inventor: the creation of a sign language by the only deaf-mute on a Polynesian island. *Sign Language Studies*, 3:1–27.

Kuschel, Rolf 1974. *A Lexicon of Signs from a Polynesian Outlier Island. A Description of 217 Signs as Developed and Used by Kagobai, the Only Deaf-Mute of Rennell Island*. Copenhagen: Psykologisk Laboratorium, Copenhagen University.

Kyle, J. G. and Bencie Woll 1985. *Sign Language. The Study of Deaf People and their Language*. Cambridge: Cambridge University Press.

La Barre, Weston 1947. The cultural basis of emotions and gestures. *Journal of Personality*, 16:49–68.

Laban, Rudolf and F. C. Lawrence 1947. *Effort*. London: Macdonald and Evans.

Lairesse, Gerard de 1738. *The Art of Painting in all its Branches, etc.* John Fredericke Fritsch, trans. London: Printed for the author and sold by J. Brotherton.

Lakoff, George 1987. *Women, Fire and Dangerous Things. What Categories Reveal About the Mind*. Chicago: Chicago University Press.

Lamedica, Nico 1984. *Oratori, Filosofi, Maestri di Sordomuti*. Cosenza: Pellegrini Editore.

Lamedica, Nico 1987. Gesto e linguaggio nel discorso in pubblico. In *Comunicazione e Gestualità*, Pio E. Ricci Bitti, ed. Milan: Franco Agneli Libri, pp. 159-170.

Lane, Harlan 1980. A chronology of the oppression of sign language in France and the United States. In *Recent Perspectives on American Sign Language*, Harlan Lane and François Grosjean, eds. Hillsdale, New Jersey: Lawrence Erlbaum Associates, pp. 119-161.

LeBaron, Curtis and Jürgen Streeck 2000. Gestures, knowledge and the world. In *Language and Gesture*, David McNeill, ed. Cambridge: Cambridge University Press, pp. 118-138.

Lebrun, Charles 1980 [1734]. *A Method to Learn to Design the Passions Proposed in a Conference on their General and Particular Expression, etc.* Translated by John Williams. Los Angeles, California: Augustan Reprint Society, Publication Numbers 200-201.

Leeds-Hurwitz, Wendy 1987. The social history of 'A Natural History of an Interview': A multidisciplinary investigation of social communication. *Research on Language and Social Interaction*, 20:1–51.

Lethbridge, Timothy, and Colin Ware 1990. Animation using behavior functions. In *Visual Languages and Applications*, Tadao Ichikawa, Erland Junger and Robert Korfhage, eds. New York: Plenum Press, pp. 237–252.

Levelt, W. J. M. 1989. *Speaking*. Cambridge, MA: MIT Press.

Li, C. N. and Thompson, Sandra A. 1976. Subject and topic: a new typology of language. In *Subject and Topic*, C. N. Li, ed. New York: Academic Press, pp. 447-489.

Liddell, Scott K. 1980. *American Sign Language Syntax*. The Hague: Mouton Publishers.

Liddell, Scott K. 2000. Blended spaces and deixis in sign language discourse. In *Language and Gesture*, David McNeill, ed. Cambridge: Cambridge University Press, pp. 331-357.

Liddell, Scott K. 2003. *Grammar, Gesture and Meaning in American Sign Language*. Cambridge: Cambridge University Press.

Lock, Andrew, ed. 1978. *Action, Gesture and Symbol*. London and New York: Academic Press.

Lock, Andrew 1980. *The Guided Reinvention of Language*. London and New York: Academic Press.

Lombardi, Mariano, ed. 1847. *Napoli in miniatura*. Napoli: Cannvacciuoli.

Macleod, C. 1973. A deaf man's sign language - its nature and position relative to spoken languages. *Linguistics*, 101:72–87.

McClave, Evelyn 2000. Linguistic functions of head movements in the context of speech. *Journal of Pragmatics*, 32:855–878.

McLuhan, Marshall 1962. *The Gutenberg Galaxy*. Toronto: Toronto University Press.

McNeill, David 1979. *The Conceptual Basis of Language*. Hillsdale, N.J.: Erlbaum.

McNeill, David 1985. So you think gestures are nonverbal? *Psychological Review*, 92: 350–371.

McNeill, David 1987. *Psycholinguistics: A New Approach*. New York: Harper and Row.

McNeill, David 1992. *Hand and Mind*. Chicago: University of Chicago Press.

McNeill, David 1999. Triangulating the growth-point – Arriving at consciousness. In *Gesture, Speech and Sign*, Lynn Messing and Ruth Campbell, eds. Oxford: Oxford University Press, pp. 77–92.

McNeill, David (ed.) 2000a. *Language and Gesture*. Cambridge: Cambridge University Press.

McNeill, David 2000b. Introduction. In *Language and Gesture*, David McNeill, ed. Cambridge: Cambridge University Press, pp. 1–10.

McNeill, David, Justine Cassell and Elena Levy 1993. Abstract deixis. *Semiotica*, 95:5-19.

McNeill, David and Susan Duncan 2000. Growth points in thinking-for-speaking. In *Language and Gesture*, David McNeill, ed. Cambridge: Cambridge University Press, pp. 141–161.

McNeill, David, Francis Quek, Karl-Erik McCullough, Susan Duncan, Nobuhiro Furuyama, Robert Bryll, Xing-Feng Ma and Rashid Ansari 2001. Catchments, prosody and discourse. *Gesture*, 1:9–33.

McQuown, Norman. 1957. Linguistic transcription and specification of psychiatric interview material. *Psychiatry*, 20:79-86.

McQuown, Norman A., ed. 1971. *The Natural History of an Interview*. Microfilm Collection of Manuscripts on Cultural Anthropology, 15th Series. University of Chicago, Joseph Regenstein Library, Department of Photoduplication, Chicago, Illinois.

Magli, Patrizia 1979. The system of the passions in eighteenth century dramatic mime. *Versus. Quaderni di studi semiotici*, No. 22:32–47.

Magli, Patrizia 1986. De Iorio, Andrea (1769-1851). In *Encyclopediac Dictionary of Semiotics*, Volume I, T. A. Sebeok, ed. The Hague: Mouton and Co., pp. 177–179.

Magli, Patrizia 1995. *Il volto e l'anima. Fisiognomica e passioni*. Milan: Bompiani.

Maher, Jane 1996. *Seeing Language in Sign: The Work of William C. Stokoe*. Washington, DC: Gallaudet University Press.

Mahl, George F. 1968. Gestures and body movements in interviews. *Research in Psychotherapy* (American Psychological Association), 3:295–346.

Maier-Eichorn, Ursula 1989. *Die Gestikulation in Quintilianus Rhetorik*. (Europäische Hochsculschriften, Klassiche Sprachen und Literaturen, Ser. 15, Vol. 41). Frankfurt-am-Maim: Peter Lang.

Mallery, G. 1972 [1881]. *Sign Language among North American Indians Compared with that among Other Peoples and Deaf-Mutes*. Photomechanic reprint of the 1881 Smithsonian Report ed. The Hague: Mouton.

Mandel, Mark 1977. Iconic devices in American Sign Language. In *On the Other Hand*, Lynn Friedman, ed. London and New York: Academic Press, pp. 57-107.

Mayer, Carl A. 1948. *Vita popolare a Napoli nell'età romantica*. Traduzione dal Tedesco di Lidia Croce. [Italian translation of selections from *Neapel und die Neapolitaner oder Briefe aus Neapel in die Heimat*. Oldenburg: 1840]. Bari: Giuseppe Laterza et Figli.

Meggitt, Mervyn 1954. Sign language among the Walbiri of Central Australia. *Oceania*, 25:2–16.

Mehrabian, Albert 1969. Significance of posture and position in the communication of attitude and status relationships. *Psychological Bulletin*, 71:359-372.

Meissner, M. and S. B. Philpott 1975. The sign language of sawmill workers in British Columbia. *Sign Language Studies*, 9:291–347.

Melinger, Alissa and Pim Levelt 2002. Gesture and the communicative intention of the speaker. Nijmegen: Max Planck Institute for Psycholinguistics, unpublished manuscript. [To appear in *Gesture*, 4.2 in 2004]

Michotte, Albert 1950. The emotions regarded as functional connections. In *Feelings and Emotions*, Martin L. Reymart, ed. New York: McGraw Hill, pp. 114–126.

Michotte, Albert 1962. *The Perception of Causality*. New York: Basic Books.

Monaghan, Leila 2002. Review of Lynn Messing and Ruth Campbell, eds. *Gesture, Speech and Sign*. Oxford University Press, 1999. *Language in Society*, 31: 125-128.

Monahan, Barbara 1983. *A Dictionary of Russian Gestures*. Tenafly, NJ: Hermitage.

Morford, Jill P. and Judy A. Kegl 2000. Gestural precursors to linguistic constructs: how input shapes the form of language. In *Language and Gesture*. David McNeill, ed. Cambridge: Cambridge University Press, pp. 358–387.

Morford, Jill, Jenny Singleton and Susan Goldin-Meadow 1995. The genesis of language: how much time is needed to generate arbitrary symbols in a sign system? In *Language, Gesture and Space*, Karen Emmorey and Judy Reilly, eds. Hillsdale, New Jersey: Lawrence Erlbaum, pp. 313–332.

Morris, Desmond 1977. *Manwatching. A Field Guide to Human Behaviour*. London: Jonathan Cape; New York: Harry Abrams.

Morris, Desmond, Peter Collett, Peter Marsh, and Marie O'Shaughnessy 1979. *Gestures: Their Origins and Distribution*. London: Jonathan Cape.

Mosher, J. A. 1916. *Essentials of Effective Gesture*. New York: Macmillan.

Müller, Cornelia 1998. *Redebegleitende Gesten: Kulturgeschichte, Theorie, Sprachvergleich*. Berlin: Arno Spitz.

Müller, Cornelia 2004. Forms and uses of the Palm Up Open Hand. A case of a Gesture Family? In *The Semantics and Pragmatics of Everyday Gestures,* Roland Posner and Cornelia Müller, eds. Berlin: Weidler Buchverlag, pp. 234–256.

Munari, Bruno 1963. *Supplemento al dizionario italiano*. Milan: Muggiani.

Nobe, Shuichi 2000. Where do *most* spontaneous representational gestures actually occur with respect to speech? In *Language and Gesture*, David McNeill, ed. Cambridge: Cambridge University Press, pp.186–198.

Ott, E. A. 1902. *How to Gesture*. Revised Edition. New York: Hinds and Noble.

Paura, B., and M. Sorge 1998. *Comme te l'aggia dicere? Ovvero l'arte gestuale a Napoli*. Napoli: Intra Moenia.

Payrató, Lluís 1993. A pragmatic view on autonomous gestures: a first repertoire of Catalan emblems. *Journal of Pragmatics*, 20:193–216.

Pike, Kenneth 1967. *Language in Relation to a Unified Theory of the Structure of Human Behavior*. The Hague: Mouton.

Pittinger, Robert E., Charles F. Hockett and John J. Danehy 1960. *The First Five Minutes. A Sample of Microscopic Interview Analysis*. Ithaca, New York: Paul Martineau.

Poggi, Isabella 1983. La mano a borsa: analisi semantica di un gesto emblematico olofrastico. In *Comunicare senza Parole*, G. Attili and P. E. Ricci-Bitti, eds. Rome: Bulzoni, pp. 219–238.

Poggi, Isabella 2002. Symbolic gestures: the case of the Italian gestionary. *Gesture*, 2: 71–98.

Poggi, Isabella and Emanuela Caldognetto, 1998. *Mani che parlano*. Padova: Unipress.

Poizner, Howard, Edward S. Klima, and Ursula Bellugi 1987. *What the Hands Reveal about the Brain*. MIT Press Series on Issues in the Biology of Language and Cognition, John C. Marshall, general ed. Cambridge, MA: MIT Press.

Posner, Roland, and Cornelia Mueller, eds. 2004. *The Semantics and Pragmatics of Everyday Gestures*. Berlin: Weidler Buchverlag.

Pucci, Giuseppe 1993. *Il Passato Prossimo. La scienza dell'antichità alle origini della cultura moderna*. Roma: La Nuova Italia Scientifica.

Quintilianus, Marcus Fabius 1922. *The Institutio Oratoria of Quintilian* with an English translation by H. E. Butler. The Loeb Classical Library. New York: G. P. Putnam and Sons. [For the sections where gesture is discussed, see Volume IV, Book XI, III: 1–2; lines 14–15; 61–149]

Radutzky, Elena, ed. 1992. *Dizionario bilingue elementare della lingua italiana dei segni*. Rome: Edizioni Kappa.

Rector, Monica, Isabella Poggi and Nadine Trigo, eds. 2003. *Gestures: Meaning and Use*. Proceedings of the Porto Conference on Gesture. Porto: Fernando Pessoa University Press.

Rémi Valade, Yves-Leonard 1854. *Études sur la lexicologie et la grammaire du langage naturel des signes*. Paris: Librarie Philosophique de Ladrange.

Rijnberk, G. Van 1954. *Le langage par signes chez le moines*. Amsterdam: North Holland Publishing Company.

Rimé, Bernard and Schiaratura, Laura 1991. Gesture and Speech. In *Fundamentals of Nonverbal Behavior*, Robert S. Feldman and Bernard Rimé, eds. Cambridge: Cambridge University Press, pp. 239–281.

Rizzolatti, G. and M. A. Arbib, 1998. Language within our grasp. *Trends in Neuroscience*, 21:188–194.

Robins, R. H. 1967. *A Short History of Linguistics*. London: Longmans and Co.

Rogerson, Brewster 1953. The art of painting the passions. *Journal of the History of Ideas*, 14:68–94.

Rohlfs, G. 1959/1960. Influence des élements autochtones sur les langues romanes (Problèmes de géographie linguistique). *Actes du Colloque International de Civilisations, Littérateurs et Langues Romanes*, Bucarest, pp. 240–247.

Roth, G. 1990. *Maps to Ecstasy*. London: Harper-Collins.

Roth, H. Ling 1889. On salutations. *Journal of the Royal Anthropological Institute*, 19: 164–181.

Roth, W. E. 1897. *Ethnological Studies among the North-West-Central Queensland Aborigines*. London: Queensland Agent-General's Office.

Ruesch, Jurgen 1953. Synopsis of the theory of human communication. *Psychiatry*, 16: 215–243.

Ruesch, Jurgen 1955. Nonverbal language and therapy. *Psychiatry*, 18:323–330.

Ruesch, Jurgen and Gregory Bateson 1951. *Communication: The Social Matrix of Psychiatry*. New York: W. W. Norton and Co.

Ruesch, Jurgen, and Weldon Kees 1956. *Nonverbal Communication: Notes on the Visual Perception of Human Relations*. Berkeley, California: University of California Press.

Sacks, Harvey and Emanuel Schegloff 2002. Home position. *Gesture*, 2:133–146.

Saitz, Robert L. and Edward J. Cervenka 1972. *Handbook of Gestures: Columbia and the United States*. The Hague: Mouton and Co.

Sampson, Geoffrey 1980. *Schools of Linguistics*. Stanford: Stanford University Press.

Santi, Serge, Isabelle Guaïtella, Christian Cavé, and Gabrielle Konopczynski (eds.) 1998. *Oralité et gestualité: communication multimodale, interaction*. Paris: L'Harmattan.

Sapir, Edward 1951 [1927]. The unconscious patterning of behavior in society. In *Selected Writings of Edward Sapir in Language, Culture and Personality*, David G. Madelbaum, ed. Berkeley and Los Angeles: University of California Press, pp. 544–559.

Schaffner, B., ed. 1956. *Group Processes: Transactions of the Second Conference*. New York: Josiah Macy Jr. Foundation.

Scheflen, Albert E. 1965. The significance of posture in communication systems. *Psychiatry*, 27:316–331.

Schegloff, Emanuel A. 1984. On some gestures' relation to talk. In *Structures of Social Action: Studies in Conversation Analysis*, J. Max Atkinson and John Heritage, eds. Cambridge: Cambridge University Press, pp. 266–296.

Schembri, Adam 2003. Rethinking 'classifiers' in signed languages. In *Perspectives on Classifier Constructions in Sign Languages*. Karen Emmorey, ed. Mahwah, New Jersey: Lawrence Erlbaum, pp. 3–34.

Schmitt, Jean-Claude 1990. *Il gesto nel medioevo* (Italian translation of *La raison des gestes dans l'Occident médiéval*. 1990. Paris: Gaillmard). Rome : Laterza.

Schnapp, Alain 1994. *La conquista del passato. Alle origini dell'archaeologia*. Milan: Arnaldo Mondadori.

Schnapp, Alain 2000. Antiquarian studies in Naples at the end of the eighteenth century: from comparative archaeology to comparative religion. In *Naples in the Eighteenth Century: The Birth and Death of a Nation State*, Girolamo Imbruglia, ed. Cambridge: Cambridge University Press, pp. 154–166.

Schuler, E. A. 1944. V for victory: a study in symbolic social control. *Journal of Social Psychology*, 19:283–299.

Scroggs, Carolyn L. 1981. The use of gesturing and pantomiming: the language of a nine year old deaf boy. *Sign Language Studies*, 30:61–77.

Seton, Ernest Thompson 1918. *Sign Talk. A Universal Signal Code Without Apparatus for Use in Army, Navy, Camping, Hunting and Daily Life*. New York: Doubleday, Page and Co.

Seyfeddinipur, Mandana and Sotaro Kita 2001. Gestures and disfluencies in speech. In *Oralité et gestualité. Interactions et comportements multimodaux dans la communication*, C. Cavé, I. Guaïtella and S. Santi, eds. Actes du colloque ORAGE 2001, Aix-en-Provence, 18-22 June 2001. Paris: l'Harmattan: 266–270.

Sherzer, Joel 1972. Verbal and nonverbal deixis: the pointed lip gesture among the San Blas Cuna. *Language in Society*, 2:117–131.

Sherzer, Joel 1991. The Brazilian thumbs-up gesture. *Journal of Linguistic Anthropology*, 1:189–197.

Siddons, Henry 1807. *Practical Illustrations of Rhetorical Gesture and Action, Adapted to the English Drama. From a Work on the Same Subject by M. Engel. Embellished with Numerous Engravings, Expressive of the Various Passions, and Representing the Modern Costume of the London Theatres*. London: Printed for Richard Phillips.

Siegel, J. P. 1969. The Enlightenment and the evolution of a language of signs in France and England. *Journal for the History of Ideas*, 30:96–115.

Siple, Patricia, ed. 1978. *Understanding Language through Sign Language Research.* New York: Academic Press.

Singleton, Jenny L., Susan Goldin-Meadow and David McNeill 1995. The cataclysmic break between gesticulation and sign: evidence against a unified continuum of gestural communication. In *Language, Gesture and Space*, K. Emmorey and J. Reilly, eds. Hillsdale, N. J.: Lawrence Erlbaum and Associates, pp. 287–311.

Slama-Cazacu, Tatania 1976. Nonverbal components in message sequence. Mixed syntax. In *Language and Man: Anthropological Issues*, W. C. McCormack and Stephen A. Wurm, eds. The Hague: Mouton and Co., pp. 217–227.

Slobin, Daniel 1987. Thinking for speaking. In *Proceedings of the 13th Annual Meeting of the Berkeley Linguistics Society*, Jon Aske, Natasha Beery, Laura Michaeliss and Hana Filip, eds. Berkeley, California: Berkeley Linguistics Society, pp. 434–445.

Smart, Alastair 1965. Dramatic gesture and expression in the age of Hogarth and Reynolds. *Apollo*, 82:90–97.

Sparhawk, Carol M. 1978. Contrastive-identificational features of Persian gesture. *Semiotica*, 24:49–86.

Spencer, Baldwin and Gillen, Francis J. 1899. *The Native Tribes of Central Australia.* London: Macmillan and Co.

Spencer, Baldwin and Gillen, Francis J. 1904. *The Northern Tribes of Central Australia.* London: Macmillan and Co.

Spitz, Rene 1966. *No and Yes: On the Genesis of Human Communication.* New York: International Universities Press.

Stam, James H. 1976. *Inquiries into the Origin of Language: The Fate of a Question.* New York and London: Harper and Row.

Stocking, George W. 1982. *Race, Culture and Evolution: Essays in the History of Anthropology.* Phoenix Edition, with a New Preface. Chicago: Chicago University Press.

Stocking, George W. 1987. *Victorian Anthropology.* New York: The Free Press.

Stokoe, William C. 1960. Sign Language Structure: An Outline of the Visual Communication Systems of the American Deaf. *Studies in Linguistics Occasional Papers* No. 8. Buffalo, New York: Department of Anthropology and Linguistics, University of Buffalo.

Streeck, Jurgen 1993. Gesture as communication I: Its coordination with gaze and speech. *Communication Monographs*, 60:275–299.

Streeck, Jurgen 2002. A body and its gestures. *Gesture*, 2:19–44.

Streeck, Jurgen and Ulrike Hartege 1992. Previews: gestures at the transition place. In *The Contextualization of Language,* Peter Auer and Aldo di Luzio, eds. Amsterdam: John Benjamins Publishing Co.

Strehlow, Carl 1978 [1915]. The sign language of the Aranda. English translation by C. Chewings of *Die Zeichensprache der Aranda*. From *Die Aranda- und Loritja-Stämme in Zentrale-Australien*, Teil 4, Abteilung 2, pp. 54-78. Reprinted in *Aboriginal Sign Languages of the Americas and Australia. Vol. II. The Americas and Australia*, Donna-Jean Umiker-Sebeok and T. A. Sebeok, eds. New York and London: Plenum Press, pp. 349-370.

Supalla, Ted 1982. Structure and acquisition of verbs of motion in American Sign Language. Doctoral dissertation, University of California, San Diego, California.

Supalla, Ted and Elissa Newport 1978. How many seats in a chair? The derivation of nouns and verbs in American Sign Language. In *Understanding Language Through Sign Language Research*, Patricia L. Siple, ed. New York: Academic Press, pp. 91–132.

Supalla, Ted, and Rebecca Webb 1995. The grammar of International Sign: a new look at pidgin sign languages. In *Language, Gesture and Space*. Karen Emmorey, and Judy Reilly, eds. Hillsdale, New Jersey: Lawrence Erlbaum Associates, pp. 333–352.

Talmy, Leonard 1985. Lexicalization patterns: semantic structure in lexical forms. In *Language Typology and Syntactic Description, Volume III: Grammatical Categories and the Lexicon*, Tim Shopen, ed. Cambridge: Cambridge University Press. pp. 57–149.

Talmy, Leonard 1991. Path to realization: a typology of event conflation. In *Proceedings of the 17th Annual Berkeley Linguistics Society*, L. A. Sutton, C. Johnson and R. Shields, eds. Berkeley, CA: Berkeley Linguistics Society, pp. 480-520.

Taylor, A. R. 1978. Nonverbal communication in Aboriginal North America: the Plains Indian Sign Language. In *Aboriginal Sign Languages of the Americas and Australia. Volume II: The Americas and Australia*, Donna-Jean Umiker-Sebeok and Thomas A. Sebeok, eds. New York: Plenum Press, pp. 223–224.

Tervoort, Bernard T. 1961. Esoteric symbolism in the communication behavior of young deaf children. *American Annals of the Deaf*, 106:436–480.

Tolman, Edward C. 1948. Cognitive maps in rats and men. *The Psychological Review*, 55:189–208.

Tomkins, William 1969 [1931]. *Indian Sign Language*. New York: Dover Publications.

Trager, George L. 1958. Paralanguage: a first approximation. *Studies in Linguistics*, 13:1–12.

Trevarthen, Colwyn 1977. Descriptive analyses of infant communicative behaviour. In *Studies in Mother–Infant Interaction*, H. R. Schaffer, ed. London: Academic Press, pp. 227–270.

Tuite, Kevin 1993. The production of gesture. *Semiotica*, 93:83–105.

Tylor, Edward B. 1865. *Researches into the Early History of Mankind and the Development of Civilization*. London: John Murray.

Tylor, Edward B. 1964. *Researches into the Early History of Mankind and the Development of Civilization* by Edward B. Tylor. Edited and abridged with an introduction by Paul Bohannan. Chicago: University of Chicago Press.

Umiker-Sebeok, Donna-Jean and T. A. Sebeok, eds. 1978. *Sign Languages of the Americas and Australia*. Two volumes. London: Plenum Press.

Umiker-Sebeok, Donna-Jean and T. A. Sebeok, eds. 1987. *Monastic Sign Languages*. Berlin: Mouton de Gruyter.

Versante, Laura (1998). Osservazioni comparative sulla deissi verbale e gestuale in alcune zone della Campania e dell'Inghilterra centrale. Tesi di Laurea, Anno Accademico 1996-1997. Facoltà di Lingue e Letterature Straniere, Istituto Universitario Orientale, Napoli.

Vico, Giambattista. 1984. *The New Science of Giambattista Vico.* Unabridged Translation of the Third Edition (1744) with the addition of the 'Practic of the New Science.' Thomas Goddard Bergin and Max Harold Fisch, translators. Ithaca, New York: Cornell University Press.

Voloshinov, V. N. 1976. *Freudianism: A Marxist Critique.* I. R. Titunik and Neal H. Bruss, trans. New York: Academic Press, 1976.

Volterra, Virginia, ed. 1987. *La Lingua Italiana dei Segni: la comunicazione visivo-gestuale dei sordi.* Bologna: Il Mulino.

Volterra, Virginia and Carol J. Erting, eds. 1990. *From Gesture to Language in Hearing and Deaf Children.* Berlin: Springer-Verlag.

von Foerster, H., Margaret Mead and H. L. Teuber, eds. 1949–1953. *Cybernetics: Circular, Causal and Feedback Mechanisms in Biological and Social Systems.* Transactions of Conferences, 5 volumes. New York: Josiah Macy Jr. Foundation.

Washabaugh, William 1986. *Five Fingers for Survival.* Ann Arbor: Karoma.

Wells, G. A. 1987. *The Origin of Language: Aspects of the Discussion from Condillac to Wundt.* La Salle, Illinois: Open Court.

Werner, Heinz and Kaplan, Bernard 1967. *Symbol Formation. An Organismic-Developmental Approach to Language and the Expression of Thought.* New York: John Wiley.

West, La Mont 1960. The Sign Language. Volume I: An Analysis. Volume II: Dialects. Ph.D. Dissertation, Indiana University, Bloomington, Indiana.

Wiener, Morton, Shannon Devoe, Stuart Rubinow and Jesse Geller 1972. Nonverbal behavior and nonverbal communication. *Psychological Review,* 79:185–214.

Wilkins, David 2003. Why pointing with the index finger is not a universal (in sociocultural and semiotic terms). In *Pointing: Where Language, Culture and Cognition Meet,* Sotaro Kita, ed. Hillsdale, New Jersey: Lawrence Erlbaum, pp. 171–215.

Wiseman, Nicholas Patrick Stephen 1853. Italian gesticulation. In *Essays on Various Subjects by His Eminence Cardinal Wiseman,* vol. 3. London: Dolman, pp. 531–555.

Wolff, Charlotte 1945. *A Psychology of Gesture.* London: Methuen and Co. Ltd.

Wollock, Jeffrey 1996. John Bulwer's (1606-1656) place in the history of the deaf. *Historiagraphica Linguistica,* 23:1-46.

Wollock, Jeffrey 2002. John Bulwer (1606-1656) and the significance of gesture in 17th-century theories of language and cognition. *Gesture,* 2:233-264

Wundt, Wilhelm 1973. *The Language of Gestures.* Translated by J. S. Thayer, C. M. Greenleaf and M. D. Silberman from *Völkerpsychologie, etc.,* First Volume, Fourth Edition, First Part Chapter 2. Stuttgart: Alfred Kröner, Verlag, 1921. The Hague: Mouton.

Wylie, L. 1977. *Beaux Gestes: A Guide to French Body Talk.* Cambridge, MA: The Undergraduate Press.

Yau, Shun-chiu 1985. Sociological and cognitive factors in the creation of a sign language by an isolated member of a hearing community. In SLR '83: Sign Language Research. W. Stokoe and V. Volterra, eds. Silver Spring, Maryland: Linstok Press, pp. 299–396.

Yau, Shun-chiu 1992. *Creations gestuelle et debuts du langage: creation de langues gestuelles chez des sourds isoles.* Paris: Editions Langages Croisés.

Young, Katharine 2002. The dream body in somatic psychology: the kinaesthetics of gesture. *Gesture,* 2:45–70.

Index